'GILDED PROSTITUTION'

Status, money, and transatlantic marriages,
1870–1914

'GILDED PROSTITUTION'

Status, money, and transatlantic marriages, 1870–1914

MAUREEN E. MONTGOMERY

University of Canterbury, New Zealand

R

ROUTLEDGE

London and New York

First published 1989
by Routledge
11 New Fetter Lane, London EC4P 4EE
29 West 35th Street, New York NY 10001

© 1989 Maureen Montgomery

Printed in Great Britain by
T. J. Press (Padstow) Ltd
Padstow, Cornwall

British Library Cataloguing in Publication Data
Montgomery, Maureen
'Gilded prostitution': states, money and
transatlantic marriages, 1870–1914.
1. Great Britain, Aristocracy. American
wives, 1870–1914
I. Title
305.5′2′0941

ISBN 0-415-00626-0

Library of Congress Cataloging in Publication Data
Montgomery, M.
'Gilded prostitution': status, money, and transatlantic
marriages, 1870–1914 by M. Montgomery.
p.   cm.
Bibliography: p.
Includes index.
1. Intercountry marriage. 2. Marriage—Great Britain—
History—19th century. 3. Upper classes—Great Britain—
History—19th century. 4. Upper classes—United States—
History—19th century. I. Title.
HQ1032.M65 1989   88–23948
306.8′45—dc19   CIP

For

RODNEY FOSTER

Contents

CONTENTS

Acknowledgements

I am grateful to the 17th Earl of Pembroke and the Honourable Mrs Gascoigne for their kind permission to quote from family papers. In addition, I thank the Houghton Library of Harvard University for permission to quote from the Oliver Wendell Holmes Papers and the Charles Sumner Papers; the Bodleian Library (Department of Western Manuscripts) for permission to consult the Harcourt Papers; and the Library of Congress (Manuscript Division) for permission to consult the Joseph P. Choate Papers, the Whitelaw Reid Papers and the William Howard Taft Papers. Lyrics from Noel Coward's 'The Stately Homes of England' have been reproduced with the permission of Methuen, London.

Publishers Note:
The phrase 'Gilded Prostitution' was first used by the journalist W.T. Stead writing about the tendency of transatlantic marriages. It has never been used other than as a figure of speech, and neither suggests that a transatlantic marriage was an act of physical prostitution, nor imputes than any of the transatlantic marriage partners was a prostitute. Its use in this book is as a relevant contemporary reference only.

Introduction

The entry of American women into the royal court and high society of Britain after the American Civil War has been referred to by contemporaries and biographers alike as an 'invasion'. Certainly the number of women travelling across the Atlantic was unprecedented. The hazards and discomforts of long-distance travel, let alone ocean crossings, had hitherto discouraged women of the middle and upper classes from embarking on long journeys. But the term 'invasion' referred to more than the sudden arrival of large numbers of American women; it signified a sense of intrusion and disruption. The influx of wealthy Americans of allegedly plutocratic backgrounds threatened to raise the standard of expenditure within smart society and to intensify competition in the aristocratic marriage market. It is possible to identify two reactions evoked by the introduction of American women into the elite circles of the British capital: admiration for their adventurous and inquisitive spirit, and fear for the consequences of their social success.

The focus of this study is on American women who married British peers or the younger sons of peers. Many American women married into the nobility of France, Italy, and other countries in western Europe, and a number of aspects raised in connection with Anglo-American marriages are applicable to the broader phenomenon of international marriages. Concentration upon the British peerage, however, offers a number of advantages. Above all, it allows an exploration of these marriages in terms of the cultural relations between Britain and the United States. Social contact between the British and the Americans inspired countless articles in the newspapers and serious journals of the times as well as writers of fiction. In such writings, frequent reference is made to transatlantic marriages, so that they appear to have been regarded as a barometer for the state of Anglo-American relations. It should perhaps be remembered that this was a time of closer diplomatic ties between the two countries, when the British government was making overtures of friendship towards the United States. Indeed, both contemporaries and historians have suggested that transatlantic marriages within the social elite promoted a sense of kinship between the two countries.[1] In light of this 'special relationship', there is much to be said for limiting the inquiry to Britain.

The terminal dates for this study of Anglo-American marriages are usually associated in the minds of European historians with the Franco-Prussian War of 1870 and the First World War. And, although the period 1870 to 1914 is familiar enough in British history, it might have been more appropriate to define the period as 1874 to 1910, beginning with the marriage of the Randolph Churchills and ending with the death of Edward VII, in whose social circle titled Americans became so prominent. It can be argued, however, that wars play a part in transatlantic marriages, most notably in the GI-bride phenomenon of the 1940s. Wars, for example, limit civilian inter-continental travel, and it is no coincidence that the first major period of inter-elite marriages involving American women coincided with an upturn in transatlantic travel after 1865. The Gilded Age witnessed significant improvements in steamships, which, together with the expansion of the American leisure class, contributed to this upturn.

Eighteen-seventy was an auspicious year for the future of Anglo-American marital alliances. Paris had been the most popular city amongst American tourists and expatriates in the first generation of travellers after the Civil War. But hostilities with Prussia diverted some of this leisure-class traffic away from France to London, where the Marlborough House Set around the Prince of Wales was beginning to acquire a reputation for conspicuous consumption. Its openness to wealthy businessmen and attractive American women made it an appropriate successor to the court of Louis Napoleon and Empress Eugénie. Edward VII's reign coincided with the peak years of transatlantic marriages, and the King became so closely identified with these marriages that his death appeared to herald the end of the social sway of American women at the British court. However, Anglo-American alliances continued after 1920, so it would be misleading to associate them too closely with Edward VII.

The First World War is an appropriate marking-off point, because the socio-economic upheaval connected with the war substantially altered the situation of the British peerage. Moreover, titled marriages were far less striking after the war unless they involved a monarch or a movie star or both. Even the popular fiction of the day noted the change:

> My dear child, any title under that of a Royal Prince or a Duke is dead as last year's hats. It's the fashion on this side to be sick of Europe and Europe's worn out idols. I don't know how long the fashion will live. But it's very much alive and kicking at present: sure to last a couple of seasons at least.[2]

The character, Lord Blacktowne, is registering here American xenophobia of the 1920s and the fickleness of the social elite. Before the war, as the story goes, he had made a fortune arranging introductions between rich Americans and titled Europeans. He tells a couple of young Irish aristocrats, who have come to New York to try their luck, 'Once, I was New York's British–American supermatrimonial agent. Now I've sunk to being a common or garden labor exchange.'[3] This work of popular fiction, published in 1923, gives the impression that the great age of transatlantic marriages was over by 1920, but actual figures suggest otherwise. After a temporary lull because of the war and subsequent reduction in transatlantic crossings by passenger ships, the number of Anglo-American marriages reached their pre-war levels and, by the eve of the next world war, surpassed all previous records (see Appendix F). But even though there is nothing to suggest that titled marriages were declining in frequency, it would still be fair to say that they had lost some of their novelty and publicity value. The initial years of extensive social contact are, therefore, more interesting for a study of cultural attitudes. A much deeper ambivalence existed then on both sides about the desirability of closer relations. We are much more likely to find strong statements of disapproval or endorsement at the time when Americans were beginning to make their presence felt in Britain – in terms of financial and commercial interests, tourism, and cultural influence.

The rise of plutocracy in Britain and the United States during the last third of the nineteenth century provides a further reason for identifying 1870 to 1914 as a distinct period in the history of transatlantic marriages. With regard to British society, millionaires

INTRODUCTION

from South Africa, Australia, the United States, and Europe congregated in the banking capital of the world and participated in London's high society. The entry of Americans into aristocratic society occurred simultaneously with the relaxation of social barriers against businessmen, including financiers of Hebraic extraction, and in some quarters the success of American women was even attributed to the financial support of Jewish bankers. As a result of the broadening of the social elite and the opening up of the peerage to industrialists and commercial men, much prejudice was expressed against the moneyed classes by the old guard in the landed aristocracy. It is within this particular context that the hostility shown towards American women marrying into the British peerage should be seen, especially since a number of them were businessmen's daughters.

On the other side of the Atlantic the emergence of a powerful moneyed elite had a significant impact on the social order in the larger cities, particularly New York. That great metropolis was a magnet for *nouveaux riches* families. It became the centre for fashionable society during the course of the nineteenth century as Boston and Philadelphia declined in social influence. The upper echelons there were perhaps less entrenched than the more conservative and tighter-knit circles of Boston Brahmins and Old Philadelphians. As will be seen, titled marriages were an integral part of the fierce competition in New York amongst wealthy families for social recognition.

During this period sixty American women married the holders of, or heirs to, a hereditary title. This figure represented approximately one-tenth of all peerage marriages and, according to David Thomas, one-half of the foreign alliances made by peers.[4] As marriage is one means of elite recruitment, a study of these American marriages can offer insights into the changes taking place within the peerage at this time. Younger sons of peers also contracted marriages with American women, and, although these marriages did not offer as much in terms of social prestige, they still brought Americans into the orbit of aristocratic society. The career prospects of a few younger sons were even enhanced by their marriage to an American. For example, Sir Michael Herbert's marriage to Belle Wilson was a point in his favour when a replacement for Lord Pauncefote, Britain's Ambassador in Washington, DC, had to be found in 1902. Had Herbert not died whilst serving

4

as Ambassador to the United States, it is likely that he would have received a peerage in his own right.

My approach to the subject of transatlantic marriages has been governed by an interest in the way that these marriages were perceived by contemporaries and especially in the image of the American girl in London society as conveyed by both literary and historical sources. There is a persistent cliché that transatlantic marriages were merely exchanges of titles for dollars. This view certainly predominated at the turn of the century and seems to have originated in the newspapers and popular novels written at this time. The notion of peers selling their titles was certainly not new or unique to this particular period, but it was closely identified with their marriages to American women. Like all clichés, the description of transatlantic marriages as mercenary exchanges has the inevitable effect of oversimplifying the circumstances surrounding inter-elite marriages, and this needs to be corrected. Clichés usually function in such a way as to discourage cognitive reflection,[5] and this perhaps explains why the idea of title for money is still current today. This is easily demonstrated by the portrayal of titled Anglo-American marriages in recent publications for popular consumption and British television dramatic productions. It is not surprising, then, that transatlantic marriages have hitherto been the province of writers for the popular market, such as Elizabeth Eliot (*Heiresses and Coronets*, 1959), Hesketh Pearson (*The Pilgrim Daughters*, 1961), and Ruth Brandon (*The Dollar Princesses*, 1980).[6]

Not only has our understanding of transatlantic marriages been obscured by the prevalence of clichéd descriptions, but our perception of the men and women participating in the marriages has been distorted by their representation as impoverished, grasping peers and ambitious, frivolous women. In other words, we have been handed down two negative stereotypes. Whilst I explore the evidence for the impoverishment amongst peers who married Americans, in order to determine whether there is any justification for the label, I am particularly interested in what I call the 'American heiress stereotype'. This is because of the interest shown in 'the American Girl' by writers of both serious and popular fiction. An examination of the fiction of the day contributes to our understanding of the functioning of the American heiress stereotype. Literary texts, however, are not the only source of stereotypes. Memoirs of contemporaries, newspapers, and journals provide ample evidence that many members of aristocratic society subscribed to a pejorative view of American women. The reasons for this, to anticipate the argument a little, are related to pressures upon the social, financial, and political status of the British aristocracy in the late nineteenth century.

In focussing upon the stereotyping of American women who married into the British peerage, I have taken note of some of the theories advanced by psychologists on the nature of stereotypes. The term 'stereotype' originally referred to a plate in the printing process which could be used repeatedly (the word 'cliché' has a similar etymology), and when first taken up by psychologists the conceptualization of stereotype was of a fixed image or belief. More recently, however, psychologists have argued that stereotypes are not necessarily fixed and that they can change from one socio-economic group to another. Some psychologists have distinguished between social and personal stereotypes, the former being based upon a consensus view and the latter held by an individual.[7] The American heiress stereotype, I have found, involved a large degree of consensus, but the specific details varied between writers, between cultures, and over time. In particular, I have used Gustav Ichheiser's study of the misinterpretation of personality in his book *Appearances and Realities* (1970) in analysing the content of the American heiress stereotype, especially as his approach has been useful for explaining the stereotype within a historical context.

American women were not solely categorized as American heiresses who were seeking to further their career in society by a fortuitous marriage to a peer. There is also what might be called the Isabel Archer type – the American girl 'affronting her destiny'. This was a much more positive response and usually made reference to the wit, intelligence, liveliness, and beauty of American women. Such a stereotype was likely to be held by those who welcomed the entry of Americans into London society and may possibly have been more common in the late Victorian rather than Edwardian era when the increase in the numbers of American visitors aroused hostility and resentment. Even the King, who had been renowned for his fondness for Americans, was alleged to have said that too many Americans were 'pushing into Society' and refused 'to be introduced to any newcomers'.[8]

In trying to formulate the content of the heiress stereotype I have examined, as aforementioned, newspapers, letters, memoirs, and literary journals and novels written around the turn of the century. To what extent the written evidence which has survived truly reflects attitudes towards titled American women is, of course, impossible to tell. The generalizations are more apparent in the memoirs of someone like Lady Dorothy Nevill or in the social commentary of the writer Marie Corelli or the journalist George Smalley, none of whom refers to specific individuals. On the other hand, newspaper articles on particular women were based on incomplete knowledge of these women, and the main focus, therefore, was placed on their external or public characteristics – i.e. their dress and appearance, the size of their father's fortune, and so on. From these details conclusions were drawn about their personality. The heiress stereotype still conjures up an image of empty-headed, pretty, spoilt, young women, and it is perhaps because of this that the subject of transatlantic marriages has rarely received the attention of historians.

One approach to the marriages of peers has been to quantify them in terms of the information they yield with regard to the degree of social exclusivity of the peerage. The studies of T. H. Hollingsworth, David Thomas, and Patricia Otto on marriage patterns in the British peerage have concentrated almost exclusively on the collection and interpretation of data, with the aim of establishing trends in the frequency of marriage and the choice of marriage partners.[9] Transatlantic marriages constitute a small but significant part of marriages made by peers and younger sons, and a chief concern of this study is to establish if and why they represent a major deviation from the overall pattern as determined by Hollingsworth, Otto, and Thomas.

In order to place transatlantic marriages in the context of peerage marriage patterns, I have selected two control groups of peers who married between 1880 and 1889, and between 1900 and 1909, along with two control groups of younger sons who also married in these two decades. I have used marriage cohorts instead of the more usual birth cohorts because they provide a more useful comparison with the case groups. The information sought is the social origins of women who married peers or younger sons, the number of offspring from their marriages, and the age of the man at marriage. It is, therefore, important to collect such data for a specific period rather than take a birth cohort in which the date of marriage can vary by as much as twenty years. The information for the control groups thus ties into the period more closely, and the changes between the two decades can be seen more closely. One might expect, for example, the earlier cohort to show a more conservative tendency to marry within the traditional aristocratic circle than the later cohort, but unless one takes a cohort based upon the date of marriage this kind of change cannot be shown with such precision. The control groups have been compiled from information in *Whitaker's Peerage* (1914), with additional details taken from *Burke's Peerage* and Cockayne's *Complete Peerage*. The control groups thus consist of almost all the peers, or younger sons of peers, who married either between 1880 and 1889 or between 1900 and 1909. Certain men were excluded from the control groups either because they, or their father, were raised to the peerage after the date of their marriage, or because they, or their father, married American women. No titled family appears in both the control group and the transatlantic group. Information about landholdings has been taken from Bateman's *Great Landowners*, and details of the gross estate left by peers, younger sons, and their wives have been compiled from the Probate Calendars in Somerset House. A comparison of the data for the control groups with that for the transatlantic groups makes it possible to determine whether the men who married Americans differed in any respect from the rest of the peerage as represented by the control groups. The case groups of peers and younger sons have also been compiled from *Whitaker's* and various editions of *Burke's Peerage*. They, too, include only men, or the sons of men, who were members of the peerage at the time of their marriage to American women.

Reference will be made, where the context merits, to other transatlantic alliances outside the case groups. These may include men who became peers after their marriage, baronets, and knights, as well as their American wives.[10] Lady Arthur Paget, née Minnie Stevens, was, for example, a well-known figure in the Marlborough House Set in the late nineteenth century. She married Arthur Paget, grandson of the first Marquess of Anglesey who was knighted for his service in the army. The Astors also merit inclusion in the discussion about Americans in British society although they have been excluded from the case group because the title was not created until 1916, ten years after William Waldorf Astor married Nancy Langhorne.

It would be fair to say that in the past twenty years, during which

time there has been a considerable amount of research in the history
of American women, the upper class has been somewhat neglected.
The focus of nineteenth-century historians has been the middle-
class woman in relation to such topics as the cult of domesticity,
the growth of women's education, access to the professions, reform
movements, and suffrage. Working-class women have also received
considerable attention, particularly within the framework of labour
history. Women's history, as a whole, has not reflected the biases
of traditional history in its concentration on the rich and powerful.
The group of women I have studied were, for the most part, the
daughters and/or wives of rich and powerful men, they were a
privileged group in society with regard to the material advantages
they enjoyed, and they attracted much publicity in the press. They
were not invisible women as such, but they do merit our attention
not so much because of what we ought to know of the lives of upper-
class women but because much of what we do know, in the form
of assumptions or from popular literature, is erroneous. Part of the
purpose of this study is to set the historical record straight but in
so doing to question the reasons for the under- and misrepresen-
tation of these titled Americans. Feminist historians are working to
compensate for the under-representation of women in the writing
of history; here, we have a case of where the women have appeared
on the page of the history book but have been dismissed as unimportant to the main narrative or treated in a very superficial way.

In contrast to historical studies of Anglo-American contact, the
figure of the American woman or girl has loomed large in American
fiction, and this has, in turn, been taken up by literary critics.[11]
The expatriate American heroine had a distinctive role in the fiction
of Henry James for exploring the nature of the American character.
The archetype American male, the businessman, was of far less
interest to him than the female beneficiary of wealth accumulated
from industrial enterprise, because the responsibility of providing
evidence of refinement and genteel manners lay with women.
'Woman', as Paul Eakin explains in his study of the New England
girl in the fiction of James and others, 'functioned as an all-purpose
symbol of the ideals of the culture, the official repository of its
acknowledged moral code.'[12] James's use of the young American
woman in a European setting sharply contrasts the American
'cultural ideal' with that of the Old World, and the latter is often
found to be wanting. James offered a more sympathetic portrait of

the American woman in Europe than any that can be found amongst British social commentaries or literary efforts. He was, moreover, aware of the commercial forces which financed her travel in Europe but which also imposed upon her a clearly defined role within the American family which was at variance with the major activities and interests of the male. The insights offered by James into the predicament of the American woman of the leisure class are invaluable – as are Edith Wharton's – and these will be explored in the chapters dealing with the American socio-historical context for transatlantic marriages.

In one sense what I am attempting to do is to appropriate a literary theme and examine it in its socio-historical context. In the following chapters I shall be looking at American women travelling in Europe, their success in entering London society, how they were regarded by members of that society, their possible motives for marrying into the peerage, what contributions they made to the social, political, and cultural life of the British capital, and the nature of their lives as spouses of titled British gentlemen. I wish to restore to these women an importance they once had, that of symbolizing a major transformation in the structure of both the British and American upper classes, the broadening of social and political elites, and the closer diplomatic and cultural relationship between Britain and the USA.

The term 'gilded prostitution' comes from a book written by the famous crusading journalist William T. Stead, who made his name in exposing the white-slave traffic between Britain and the Continent. In his chapter on 'Marriage and Society', in which he pointed to transatlantic marriages as one way by which American influence was being extended throughout the world, Stead wrote:

> It was rather a degradation of the idea of American womanhood to regard the American girl as a means of replenishing the exhausted exchequer, a kind of financial resource, like the Income Tax. Indeed, it is not too much to say that when there is no love in the matter, it is only gilded prostitution, infinitely more culpable from the moral point of view than the ordinary vice into which women are often driven by sheer lack of break.[13]

Who was the prostitute? The peer or the American girl? The parallel drawn here between transatlantic marriages and prostitution might have the reader wondering if Stead had intended to imply that it

was the titled American who was on a par with a common prostitute. After all, it is more common to place women than men in a
such a role. It could be implied that the American woman was
selling herself by entering into a monetary arrangement by which
she offered herself in return for a coronet. Prostitution involves the
sexual gratification of one party and the payment of the other; but
according to the popular representation of transatlantic marriages,
it was the man who was paid. And indeed, judging from the rest
of the chapter, Stead was, for the most part, defending American
women who married into the European nobility and criticizing the
way they were being exploited:

> It is only the more conspicuous heiresses who attract general
> attention, and in some cases the marriages have been anything
> but ideal. It has been a case of the bartering of dollars against a
> title, with a woman thrown in as a kind of arle penny to clinch
> the bargain.[14]

While Stead was prepared to distinguish between the more blatant
attempts by titled Europeans to secure a wife with a large dowry
and those matches which were 'accompanied by affection' even
when money was involved, there were others in British society who
would have regarded the American peeress as both prostitute and
client because she was regarded as the party who received the most
gratification as well as being the one who paid the money. The
alleged absence of a love relationship and the presence, instead, of
crude social ambition meant that the more extreme critics of Americans would have regarded them as 'gilded prostitutes'. It seems,
at times, that the peers who entered upon these marriages were
better able to retain their reputation. Possibly it was because they
were seen to be sacrificing their personal interests for the sake of
salvaging their estates. A double standard, it seems, existed in the
minds of the Victorians.

Above all, my interest is in the perspective of the women who
married into the British peerage. It should not go unremarked that
it is only the women who have left us any personal record of
transatlantic marriages. It was not customary for British aristocratic
men to write in any detail about their wife or marriage.[15] For
most of the American women, marriage into the peerage was an
adventurous step to take. Disregarding for a moment the glamour
that life as a titled woman might promise, since that is the view

11

INTRODUCTION

that predominates in the popular literature, marrying a member of the peerage involved a very major change in an American woman's life. In addition to the process of adaptation that women undergo in any marriage, these women, as immigrants, would also have experienced a period of transition during which they would have made adjustments to the culture of their new country. Just because Americans and the British share the same language it does not necessarily follow that American women did not undergo what today we call culture shock. In one sense they had some kind of preparation for the change of environment because their decision to marry a foreigner and live abroad would probably have entailed some level of rejection of their own culture – if only in the sense of rejecting the possibility of marrying an American and remaining in the USA. It is necessary to look beyond the common assumption that they only wanted a title and to see what other motives were involved in their decision to marry into the British nobility.

While titled Americans take centre stage in this study, my research has led me into areas where questions have been raised about the financial aspects of transatlantic marriages. I have chosen to deal with this in the context of the negative reaction to the marriages. I have been unable to prove one way or the other whether American women were married for their money. Not all of them came from wealthy families, of course. There are, however, some grounds for regarding Americans as a whole as better endowed with material resources than British peeresses, although not enough to warrant the wild speculation of American newspapers nor the contempt implied by the title-for-money cliché. What particularly stands out in the British social commentary during this period is a strong anti-American tendency to disregard anyone or anything from the USA. It appears to have been quite fashionable to express contempt for Americans, in particular for their materialism, at the turn of the century. Titled Americans bore the brunt of some of this criticism, but some may well have found it hypocritical in a nation where the wealthier classes far from denied themselves material pleasures or aspirations. Nevertheless, I think it is important to consider the reaction in Britain to American women marrying into the peerage as part of a much broader phenomenon of anti-American attitudes which have often coexisted (and still do) with a fascination for the United States and its culture.

Transatlantic marriages belong to the history of social and economic changes transforming both the British and American elite, of the expansion in world communications creating an international high society, and of the closer diplomatic and cultural relationship between Britain and the USA at this time. Any history dealing with relations between two countries has to take account of conflicting images that one country has of the other and its own self-image. Henry James made Anglo-American social relations the back-drop for his numerous stories and articles. Many of his fictional European characters are shown to be myopic in their perception of Americans. In this study, which touches on one of James's favourite themes, I have tried to suggest a revision of our views of titled Americans and transatlantic marriages, to get beneath the layers of anti-American feeling so as to understand why British society had such difficulty in coming to terms with titled Americans.

Part One

THE EXPATRIATE TRADITION

1

Transatlantic travellers: 'discoverers of a kind of hymeneal North-West Passage'

I think of the American who started on his *Wanderjahre* after the Civil War quite as one of the moderns divided by a chasm from his progenitors and elder brothers, carried on the way as they were not, and all supplied with introductions, photographs, travellers' tales and other aids to knowingness.

(Henry James, *William Wetmore Storey and his Friends*, 1903)

In late October 1875 the *Bothnia*, a Cunard steamship *en route* to Liverpool, ploughed into the heavy seas of the North Atlantic, battered by 'boisterous gales'. On board, Henry James, on his way to start a new life in Paris as a writer, sat on deck, wrapping himself up with blankets and swearing that the sea would not 'catch' him again for another twenty years. Clearly, James intended to stay in Europe for an extended period on this occasion. Anthony Trollope, meanwhile, sat below in his cabin penning a prescribed number of pages to his latest novel, as was his wont. It was also part of his routine, when travelling by sea, to request the ship's carpenter to construct a writing-table for him. James recounted the incident in his first letter home. His comment then on the British novelist was: 'he is the dullest Briton of them all. Nothing happened, but I loathed and despised the sea more than ever.' The details of this encounter with Trollope remained in James's memory and were vividly recalled when he came to write a short portrait of Trollope several years later in 1888. He declared them to be an illustration of how writing had become a mechanical process for Trollope and how they indicated the Englishman's unresponsiveness to 'mood or place'.[1]

Mood and place were very important to James, and, of course, consideration of both played a large part in his decision to live in Europe. He had made two adult trips prior to 1875, and it was as a result of them that his urge to live and work in Europe was first formulated. A letter to his parents during the second excursion in 1872 reveals that he had considered his intellectual and literary salvation to be dependent upon his establishing himself in Europe, while to his brother he had admitted an enjoyment of 'being in a denser civilization'.[2] These journeys and his earlier trips abroad with his parents had contributed to the profound unease that James had experienced living in Boston and Cambridge. He had complained, particularly after his independent excursion in 1860, of his boredom with the static societies of those communities and, as a way of escape, he would reminisce about his European travels.[3] Written whilst he was still in America, his earliest works of fiction also bear witness to his fascination for the European continent. His subject-matter in these and later stories was American travellers in Europe. Whether by chance, or because of a predisposition which had evolved during his own *Wanderjahre*, James had discovered a theme which not only had endless variations, but also highlighted one of the most sensitive areas of American thought: the cultural relationship between the Old World and the New.

Henry James was only one of many American artists and writers who moved to Europe after the Civil War. Some sought to keep abreast of avant-garde developments in art and literature in western Europe, particularly in France, others to escape 'the vast industrial beehive'[4] and write about a more established, richly textured society. James, Edith Wharton, and Ford Madox Ford among others found a more congenial atmosphere for their work in Europe away from the business-oriented society of their native land. Both James and Wharton had spent considerable time in Europe as children, which may account in part for their fascination for the Old World. Upon returning to the USA in 1872 after an extended trip of six years to Europe, Edith Wharton recalled a feeling of revulsion as the steamer docked in New York: 'the shameless squalor of the purlieus of the New York docks in the 'seventies dismayed my childish eyes, stored with the glories of Rome and the architectural majesty of Paris'.[5] As for American artists, the fashionable preference of American *nouveaux riches* for Botticellis, Raphaels, or Titians – paintings more in tune with the aristocratic pretensions of these nineteenth-century Medicis in their Renaissance-style palaces – contributed to the departure of young, up-and-coming artists, such as Frank Duveneck and William Merritt Chase, for the Ecole des Beaux Arts in Paris or the popular Munich schools.[6]

While older, patrician families like that of Edith Wharton had a genuine love of European culture and had travelled extensively on the Continent in the mid-nineteenth century, albeit as a way of reaffirming their refinement and good taste, they were soon to be joined by a new generation of wealthy Americans whose expensive tastes in European art were to some extent responsible for the expatriation of American artists. As the latest beneficiaries of capital accumulation in industrial America, these new transatlantic travellers had come to Europe to relieve themselves of their burdensome wealth in a manner guaranteed to attract attention, arouse envy, and violate the canons of good taste. Playing the traditional game of the *nouveaux riches*, they conspicuously spent and conspicuously consumed. Excluded, in some cases, from entering patriciate circles in established urban centres like New York and Philadelphia, these newcomers bypassed the authority of their own social elites and appealed to a higher authority – that of the royalty and aristocracy of western Europe – to arbitrate on their social position.

In the days before Grand Tours became fashionable amongst the new moneyed elite, Edith Wharton recalled that 'the self-respecting American on his travels frequented only the little "colonies" of his compatriots already settled in European capitals, and only their most irreproachable members!'[7] During that 'unadministered age', as James called it, entry into aristocratic circles of the European capitals had been achieved slowly and with difficulty. There was as yet no widely established network of personal contacts, letters of introduction, and colonies of American expatriates to fall back on. Few people, moreover, had previously travelled for pleasure; women in particular were unlikely to risk such a lengthy voyage to Europe. Frances Hodgson Burnett, in her novel *The Shuttle*, captured the mood of the early travellers before sea voyages became commonplace:

'A crossing' in those days was an event. It was planned seriously, long thought of, discussed and re-discussed, with and among the various members of the family to which the voyage belonged. A certain coldness, bordering on recklessness, was almost to be presupposed in the individual who, turning his back upon New York, Philadelphia, Boston, and like cities, turned his face towards

19

'Europe'. In those days when the Shuttle wove at leisure, a man did not lightly run over to London, or Paris, or Berlin, he gravely went to Europe.[8]

After the Civil War, however, travel for pleasure became yet another form of expenditure to be exploited by the *nouveaux riches*. Improvements in ocean travel themselves had greatly advanced the popularity of inter-continental travel, and after the end of the Civil War transatlantic steamship companies competed for the growing number of cabin-class passengers. On the European side, however, it was the rapid upswing in steerage traffic which contributed to the intensification of rivalry between the shipping companies. Marine technology was pushed forward in a bid to design faster ships with greater capacity. Fares, too, were affected. By 1883 steerage fares had fallen to four guineas, half the price they had been in 1860, whilst cabin rates had also come down. The immigrant traffic from Europe fluctuated dramatically, but the steady stream of cabin-class passengers provided a constant, if proportionately smaller, income. Companies competed for the cabin-class market in the provision of luxurious accommodation and service.[9] On the outward journey from Liverpool, first class might contain a few aristocrats, going west as young men were advised to do by Horace Greeley in 1851, on a Grand Tour or else to introduce British breeds of cattle to the western plains. On the return journey, and especially in summer, it would be booked to capacity by wealthy Americans visiting the old country perhaps to see where their families had come from or to test the exclusiveness of fashionable society in Europe. As Atlantic crossings became less hazardous, quicker, and more frequent and comfortable, there was a corresponding growth in tourist travel. This had a major impact on the mobility of women in the leisure class. Most capital cities and resorts in Europe had resident Americans or long-term visitors in the late nineteenth century. Paris, in particular, found favour with Americans, and it was here that many were able to establish their first foothold in European high society.

During the period of the Second Empire, Paris was the fashionable centre of social and cultural life in western Europe. The court of Queen Victoria contrasted unfavourably with its French counterpart where Empress Eugénie and Princess Metternich sported the latest Jean Worth creations. In some ways the Napoleonic regime foreshadowed both New York in the 1890s and the Edwardian court. Eugene Haussmann's construction of boulevards in the centre of Paris, the improvement of the Parisian railway network, the building of ornate mansions to house the *nouveaux riches*, and, above all, the opening of the new Opera House bring to mind James's response to the restless activity of New Yorkers in their period of frenetic urban growth: there was gold-dust in the Parisian air, too.[10] Conspicuous expenditure was in evidence in both public and private sectors. The Emperor's encouragement of technological and industrial development and the enormous outlay of public money on urban growth attracted speculators from all over France. The beneficiaries of this rapid expansion – bankers, contractors, stockbrokers, and the like – provided the backcloth to a brilliant display of wealth and talent at the imperial court.[11] Like Edward VII after him, Louis Napoleon had an entourage of successful businessmen, and he too had a penchant for the company of American women.[12]

In 1867 the Jerome family, Mrs Jerome and her three daughters Clara, Jennie, and Leonie, moved from their stylish house in Madison Square Garden (modelled, incidentally, on the new mansions of the Second Empire) to a fashionable *quartier* in Paris.[13] They are just one example of an American *nouveau-riche* family which chose to take up residence in Paris and fared better in European society than at home in New York. Recalling the time her family spent in Paris, prior to the Empire's collapse, Jennie Jerome wrote:

> Never had the Empire seemed more assured, the Court more brilliant, the fetes more gorgeous. The light-hearted Parisians revelled in the daily sights of royal processions and cavalcades. The Bois de Boulogne and Champs Elysées, where we were living at that time, were crowded with splendid equipages. I remember often seeing the Empress Eugenie, then the handsomest woman in Europe, driving in her daumont, the green and gold liveries of the postilions and outriders making a brave show.[14]

Clara, the eldest daughter, made her debut at the imperial court, but in 1870, before Jennie could follow in her sister's footsteps, the Jeromes had to flee across the Channel, like other American residents, to escape the invading Prussian army. Britain's proximity to the French coast and the comfort of landing upon a more politically stable shore were doubtlessly reassuring to these wandering expatriates. They were accompanied by French aristocratic refugees who helped them to gain easy access to the noble households of London's high society. The Jeromes owed their success to the Duc de Persigny.[15]

The diversion of Americans from Paris to London in 1870 proved to be long-lasting. France did, however, recover its popularity amongst the American social elite by the 1890s and it would always be the centre for *haute couture*. During the Third Republic, Worth's most important customers were the wealthy Americans who patronized his rooms in the rue de la Paix. But whereas, in the 1860s, women like Mrs Lillie Moulton of Massachusetts had gone to him for their gowns to wear at the Tuileries, Americans now bought their Worth gowns to wear at royal levées in London.[16]

More important, though, was the timing of the American diversion to England. For it was just at this time that the Prince of Wales had begun to establish an alternative social milieu to Victoria's court amongst the smart set. He turned the annual Cowes Regatta into a fashionable event on the social calendar, and it was by no means a minor coincidence that it was at the 1873 Regatta that Jennie Jerome met and became engaged to Lord Randolph Churchill. Their marriage is usually taken to be the first of the great transatlantic marriages. The French imperial court of Louis Napoleon had, so to speak, bequeathed to the British crown its leading role in western Europe as a focus for *haute couture*, conspicuous consumption, and plutocratic ambition.

Once a few American women had established themselves in London, it was easier for others to follow. Lady Arthur Paget was among the most prominent of the American hostesses who catered for the growing demands of her countrywomen wishing to enter London society. James may well have had Minnie Paget in mind when he was writing *The Golden Bowl*.[17] His portrayal of Fannie Assingham as pioneering a trail in the London marriage market calls to mind the role of Minnie Paget. One is also reminded of her by the following extract from a book on London society published anonymously in 1885:

> The fair Yankee has no sooner made a conquest and led an English aristocrat to the altar than she commences immediately to consider what she can do for her compatriots with the leverage in her hands. . . . Altogether she is an acquisition to society, though her independence, her impatience of restraints, and

especially her incessant efforts to advance by matrimonial alliances or otherwise the interest of her countrywomen, may sometimes prove fertile in mischief.[18]

Minnie and her mother, Mrs Paran Stevens, had travelled round Europe in the 1870s after the death of her father, a New York hotel proprietor. Mrs Stevens had managed to overcome the snobbery of the New York elite with her popular dinners and Sunday entertainments and had established the family socially using her skills as a hostess and her husband's wealth. Her daughter's marriage was crucial in solidifying the family's social status, and it was apparently to this end that mother and daughter mixed in European aristocratic circles. The Stevens women found London society especially hospitable and secured entry into the Marlborough House Set. Minnie was approaching her twenty-fifth birthday when she married Paget in 1878. As a married woman in London society and a member of royal circles, Minnie was in a good position to introduce friends of hers into high society. It is alleged in the popular literature that she did so for money.[19] Her best known protégée was Consuelo Vanderbilt (later Duchess of Marlborough), who described in her memoirs the scrutiny she underwent 'by a pair of hard green eyes' when introduced to Minnie, who was being asked to bring her out: 'Tulle must give way to satin, the baby décolletage to a more generous display of neck and arms, naïveté to sophistication. Lady Paget was adamant.'[20] What she lacked in looks, Consuelo was expected to make up for in her dress. Certainly the impression given of Lady Arthur Paget was of a calculating professional in the art of introducing newcomers to society.

The assistance of a compatriot or friend was doubtlessly invaluable for Americans unfamiliar with court protocol or the rules of precedent. Much of the etiquette and formality of relations in American high society had been imported from Europe, but the additional complications of the aristocratic social systems presented a formidable barrier. A reference to these kinds of problems can be found amongst the letters which the young Belle Wilson wrote to her parents whilst visiting Europe with her sister and brother-in-law. She described the ceremony, for example, involved in entertaining royalty and, in particular, the custom to provide a finger bowl for the Prince of Wales only when dining. Amused by this 'remnant of an old feudal custom', she recounted to her mother:

Mr Poker remembered this just in time and told us and it was very fortunate as neither Ogden nor any of the rest of us knew of this habit. It would have been a most shocking piece of ignorance to see us all at the table comfortably dipping our fingers into our bowls.[21]

Belle Wilson had a fortuitous entry into royal circles: the yacht of her millionaire brother-in-law, Ogden Goelet, caught the eye of the Prince of Wales during the 1886 Regatta, and he invited himself aboard *The Norseman* for tea. Belle commented on the incident in her letter home:

> the Prince's kindness to us *made* our visit to Cowes. Without it for so short a time as a week of course we would have had no foothold and would have had no time to make one for ourselves – and, of course, his kindness to us was greatly owing to his last 'mash' (excuse vulgarity), Mr Poker, and also his desire to see new things and in consequence curiosity about the 'Norseman'. The 'Norseman' has made her everlasting reputation[,] everyone at Cowes was talking about her beauty and the perfect taste and luxury of her decoration.[22]

Access to high society in Britain was largely supervised by its female members with the help of a formal system of etiquette and rituals, such as a court levée or even entertainments in private homes of prominent individuals, which established who was acceptable.[23] The increase in the number of American women with access to the Prince of Wales undoubtedly widened the opportunities for other Americans to participate in aristocratic functions. What this tells us is that women had an important function in the high society of both Britain and the USA; not only did they determine its exclusiveness but they also played a substantial part in the formation of marital alliances. Mothers of titled Americans appeared to have had more than a helping hand in the courtship of their daughters.[24] They would have, in any case, supervised the social contacts of their offspring but, by taking their daughters to Europe for a Season or two soon after coming out in Society, they would have increased the possibility for relations to be formed between their daughters and European aristocrats. What motivated American families to encourage such relations in the first place has to be examined against the background of American high society after the Civil War. A key question for this study is whether titled marriages played a role in the shifting nature of that society and the increasing competitiveness of the new moneyed elite in its bid for high social status. Part of the explanation for the increase in transatlantic marriages after 1870 could well lie with the changes taking place at the upper levels of American society.

THE AMERICAN LEISURE CLASS

Introduction to Part Two

One overriding theme, a sense of change, marks the writings of native New Yorkers of the late nineteenth century. Change meant different things to different people. To Henry James what stood out most, on his return to the city of his birth after a twenty-year absence, was the display of wealth: 'There was gold-dust in the air, no doubt, – which would have been again an element of glamour if it had not rather lighted the scene with too crude a confidence.'[1] The city he had left in 1883 was just beginning then to experience the effects of rapid economic expansion and to receive at Ellis Island boat-loads of eastern Europeans. By 1904 evidence of both showed clearly in the different character of the New York which James rediscovered.

Henry Adams, a fellow expatriate, but a Bostonian by birth and temperament, also stepped off the boat in New York in 1904. Commenting on his arrival in New York forty years earlier, after eight years at the Court of St James's, Adams had referred to the changes taking place as a result of the 'revolution' of 'the great mechanical energies'. Now, in 1904, he feared that change had gone out of control:

> The outline of the city became frantic in its efforts to explain something that defied meaning. Power seemed to have outgrown its servitude and to have asserted its freedom. The cylinder had exploded, and thrown great masses of stone and steam against the sky. The city had the air and movement of hysteria, and the citizens were crying, in every accent of anger and alarm, that the new forces must at any cost be brought under control.[2]

Images of chaos accumulate with each successive phrase. Adams, in true New England fashion, found the liberation of new, unfamiliar forces in disharmony with his concern for order. New York had changed beyond recognition. James's observation about the conspicuousness of wealth and Adams's about the uncontrolled nature of power point to the magnitude of the change. Just one measure of this change is the number of millionaires resident in the United States: it had increased a hundredfold. Individual fortunes had also reached phenomenal proportions. Whereas John Jacob Astor's 20 million dollars had been considered a landmark in 1848, John D. Rockefeller had accumulated a personal fortune of more than one billion dollars by 1913.[3]

The increase in the size and number of multi-million fortunes after the Civil War had far-reaching consequences for the upper levels of the social structure in the United States. In provincial capitals like Boston, Philadelphia, and New York the social authority of the patriciate was undermined by the emergence of the new moneyed classes with their superior financial resources. The social prominence of the older elite had rested upon sometimes dubious claims to prestigious family lineage or some form of landed wealth combined with long-term residence in one locality. But in so young a country, attempts to form a hereditary upper class proved premature, for the post-Civil War *nouveaux riches* had vast supplies of money with which to press home their claims to status. The displacement of the urban patriciate in these older cities was not, however, total. Some of its members joined forces with the new vintage of millionaires and war profiteers and attempted to re-establish a closed caste supported by a more extensive network of power and wealth, capable of discriminating against even newer wealth.

Transatlantic marriages with titled Europeans were an integral part of this attempt to draw clear lines of demarcation around the wealthiest families in American society. Some families looked to European coronets as a means of establishing themselves as members of the social elite, but titled marriages soon became the centre of controversy in the American press. They were seen as blatant attempts to 'aristocratize' the American upper class, which went against the grain of democratic beliefs. Moreover, they were most closely associated in the public mind with the *nouveaux riches* of the post-Civil War era, families like the Goulds, the Fields, and the Vanderbilts. It would have been a bitter irony that such families sought social connections with aristocracies of birth rather than talent because these were people who had succeeded within the American system. They had reached the pinnacles of wealth and power and, instead of upholding the national belief in equality of opportunity, they were allying themselves with a social system of hereditary privilege. Certainly, by the turn of the century, marrying a foreign nobleman was denounced as unpatriotic.

There are two levels of analysis which need to be considered here. First, there are the factors operating within a competitive social elite, such as New York's Four Hundred, which placed a certain value on international marriages with members of the European nobility; and, second, there is the possible range of more personal motives which prompted individuals to contract such alliances. Chapter 2 will deal with the public side of high society life and place transatlantic marriages with British peers in a context which will relate to the concerns of families vying for high social status, while Chapter 3 will focus on the predicament of the American woman in the leisure class, drawing more heavily from the fictional representation of such women in both popular and serious works of literature.

2

'Pecuniary competition' and the search for status: New York's high society

By the 1870s New York could lay claim to being the social capital of the nation, attracting wealthy families from elsewhere in the United States. Native New Yorkers spoke in terms of an invasion and declining standards, not unlike London society's response to the American invasion.[1] Indeed, it appears as though the wave of *nouveaux riches* which flooded New York was the same one which washed through the drawing rooms of Mayfair. In this regard alone, New York merits special attention in understanding the increase in transatlantic marriages from the 1870s onwards. Another reason for focussing on New York is that it was the alliances between peers and the daughters of New York businessmen which particularly attracted a great deal of publicity and gave rise to the stereotype of the American heiress. Even so, it should be remembered that a significant proportion of titled Americans neither came from New York nor were especially wealthy. Among these women, one could include Frances Butler, daughter of the British actress Fanny Kemble and a Southern plantation owner, Pierce Butler. She married a young clergyman, the Honourable James Leigh, in 1871, and they spent the early years of their marriage rebuilding the Butler estate in Georgia which Frances had managed since her father's death in 1867.[2] Alys Pearsall Smith, another American woman of modest fortune, married the young Bertrand Russell in 1894. Her family had lived in England since 1887. Their move from Philadelphia had come about as a result of long-standing connections with evangelicals in Britain and the marriage of their elder daughter to an Irish barrister.[3] Neither of these marriages could be regarded as a stereotypical Anglo-American alliance and they are not amongst the best-known examples.

By focussing on the more publicized matches between New York women and the British nobility, the evidence will inevitably reinforce the argument that a major part of the motivation behind transatlantic marriages was social ambition. Whilst I do not dispute this, I think it is important to qualify this generalization by emphasizing that not all transatlantic marriages necessarily improved the social status of the American women involved – for example, Boston Brahmins like Martha Cameron and Mary Sturgis, or Proper Philadelphians like Frances Butler and Elizabeth Wadsworth. And in other cases, social ambition had a very small part to play compared with love, compatibility, and other reasons of a non-mercenary nature. Nevertheless, it is important to examine the association of New York's social elite with titled marriages, since it was these marriages in particular which aroused so much criticism and gave rise to the heiress stereotype. Three aspects of New York society will, therefore, provide the focus of this chapter: (1) the rise of great fortunes after the Civil War, (2) the attempt to establish a ritualized society of privilege, and (3) the search for a model of elitist life-style.

Interest in the great captains of industry has scarcely flagged since the great upsurge in individual and corporate wealth after the Civil War. Major New York newspapers have filled their columns with news of the spectacular stock-market successes and corporation coups as well as with eulogizing obituaries on the pioneers of modern capitalism. Left-wing organs have inevitably approached these landmarks in economic history from a very different perspective – in the 1880s and 1890s, for example, the muck-raker press printed diatribes by Henry Demarest Lloyd and others about the less than scrupulous methods employed in business transactions. But the more positive interest of the press in pioneers of industrial capitalism may be attributed, in part, to the view that the existence of highly successful businessmen was proof of the American Dream, or 'universal opportunity', as David Potter called it. Rags-to-riches stories, albeit exaggerated, made good reading.

Sigmund Diamond in his study of *The Reputation of the American Businessman* has argued from the premise that a primary function of the press was to associate certain selected 'heroes' with 'attitudes considered essential for the preservation of society'.[4] In the case of the great industrial moguls, he has shown how the press has

presented such men as Commodore Vanderbilt and J. P. Morgan
as embodiments of highly prized values in American culture –
industry, determination, opportunism – and as men who took full
advantage of the abundant resources and opportunities in the
economy. Indeed, Senator Chauncy Depew is quoted as having said
of the Commodore that he was 'a conspicuous example of the
products and possibilities of our free and elastic conditions'.[5] The
emphasis shifted, according to Diamond, from praise of the entre-
preneur's personal characteristics to an appraisal of the capitalist
system itself. This shift, however, neither corresponded with the
incorporation of the American economy nor took account of the
decreasing opportunities for men outside the business elite to rise
to executive level in the great corporations. By the early twentieth
century, apologies for big businessmen appeared to be a desperate
revival of earlier dreams for the universality of opportunity despite
growing evidence of exclusiveness amongst the men who owned and
controlled the great corporations. The gap between appearances
and realities continued, nevertheless, to be glossed over in the press
with varying degrees of success.

The myth about social equality and unfettered opportunity was
sustained, then, in the American consciousness by nationalistic rhetoric found in the press and in public speeches. In the early years
of the new republic the stress was placed on the need to demonstrate
to the Old World the advantages to be gained by the abolition of
social restraints and inherited privileges. But the development of
an entrepreneurial elite, its manipulation of the economy, and its
entrenchment in the higher reaches of the social structure (in the
sense that high social status was passed down to succeeding generations along with the financial means with which to support it)
threatened these time-honoured values.

At the time, however, it was not altogether apparent that the first
great founders of multi-million fortunes were establishing powerful
dynasties which would survive for generations. Business elites, like
the overseas merchants and bankers of the Jacksonian era, had, in
their time, attempted to lay the foundations of a more permanent
upper class only to be displaced by the wealthier business magnates
of the Gilded Age.[6] The process by which families intermarried and
attempted to establish themselves as a more closed socio-economic
elite took several decades. But, in the 1930s, it sufficiently interested
Frederick Lundberg for him to disclose just how extensive the inter-

locking of the post-Civil War commercial dynasties had become within seventy years. According to his assessment, the 60 richest families in the United States were buttressed by a further 90 families of 'lesser wealth' and, together with 350 families with incomes of at least $100,000, constituted a 'modern industrial oligarchy' which controlled the country.[7]

Despite Lundberg's profession of objectivity in his treatment of the subject, it is immediately apparent that he judged this 'oligarchy' to be a subversion of American political and social ideals. Two statements demonstrate this: 'The uprush of the American fortunes, led by the monolithic Rockefeller accumulation, emphasizes that although the United States was once a great political democracy it has not remained one.'[8] He went on to say that not only did the great American corporations like Standard Oil display feudal characteristics similar to those of the crown properties of old European dynasties (such as the Romanovs and Hapsburgs), but they also dwarfed the latter. The second statement was made with reference to titled marriages: 'It is one of the many ironies of the situation that the United States should be pumping forth dividends and rents to support persons in stations so alien to the American concept of social status.'[9] Given prevailing aristocratic pretensions in the United States, which took the form of ornate châteaux, social registers, and mock heraldry, this situation was perhaps not quite so ironic. There was an inevitable tendency, however, for Lundberg and other critics to focus on the more blatant expressions of anti-democratic tendencies, i.e. the corporation and titled marriages. Lundberg can be seen as voicing the fears of those Americans who felt that the early beneficiaries of industrialization were shutting the doors behind them, deliberately closing off the channels of mobility and enterprise and practising nepotism within the businesses they owned. The discovery that social status and wealth were becoming increasingly hereditary and that the social elite consisted of members who had not 'earned' their privileged position was cause for concern in a republic which had placed such high value on labour and the principles of *laissez-faire*. It is in this light, then, that we can see the periodic attacks from Populist and Progressive groups as keeping alive the doctrine of social equality and preventing the wealthy from developing a completely conscience-free enjoyment of their wealth.[10]

Corporations had their counterparts in the social world. The drive to consolidate improvements in social status was no less strong than the drive to protect advances made in business. The sudden acquisition of vast wealth, in conjunction with the multiplication of large fortunes, destabilized the upper-class structure in American cities, particularly in the older communities of the Atlantic seaboard. The overwhelming of the old urban patriciate by the first generation of post-Civil War rich threatened to make social distinction readily available to anyone with the requisite financial resources, notwithstanding the fact that many of those families which had come to dominate high society in the late nineteenth century had taken at least one generation to launder their newly acquired wealth. John Jacob Astor, August Belmont, and Commodore Vanderbilt had stood on the fringes of New York's upper circles before the Civil War. Because he was a banker with influential connections in European society, Belmont's assimilation had been more successful. Astor and Vanderbilt, on the other hand, had to be content with laying the foundations of their respective dynasties. Both shifted the sources of their original fortune into property of a more respectable nature: Astor reinvested his millions from fur-trading in New York real estate, while the Commodore transferred his fortune from wartime shipping contracts to the New York Central Railroad. The two women who married the grandsons of these family-founders, Caroline Schermerhorn and Alva Smith, displayed comparable tenacity in their efforts to secure their respective family's position within the social elite. At a time of increased social mobility and when their own rise to fame and fortune was still quite recent, they had a vested interest in raising social barriers around the upper circles.

C. Wright Mills, however, has interpreted the changes in the structure of the New York upper class as a breaking down of the aristocratic exclusiveness of the 'fine old families of metropolitan society'.[11] In his analysis of the formation of a 'nationally recognized upper social class' in the period 1865 to 1914, he largely followed the version of events given by Mrs May King Van Rensselaer. A descendant of the Dutch patroons whose fortunes had originally been made in trade, Mrs Van Rensselaer looked upon events of the 1880s and 1890s as signalling the disintegration of the genteel and cultivated society of her youth.[12] For her, the old Dutch families, who had resided in New York City since before the Revolution, had constituted an aristocracy (though Mills rejected this term). Apart from setting great store by lineage, they formed a close-knit group reinforced by intermarriages and small, exclusive entertainments.[13] But, according to Mrs Van Rensselaer:

> In the decade following the Civil War, there came a great change. Until those years society had remained static, unthreatened by invasion. All at once it was assailed from every side by persons who sought to climb boldly over the walls of social exclusiveness.[14]

The deluge had begun. The golden age of aristocracy has passed. The quiet, cultured, and dignified life-style of former days had been replaced by one which was brash, extravagant, and highly publicized. Mrs Van Rensselaer and other New Yorkers of her generation, such as Edith Wharton, thus represented the transformation of New York's elite and their own individual displacement.

Mills accepted Mrs Van Rensselaer's notion that the old (bourgeois) elite and its particular attempt to establish a 'pedigreed society' had been swept aside by the *nouveaux riches* of the Gilded Age.[15] Other historians, including E. Digby Baltzell, have also used the idea of an exclusive elite giving way to a more open, upper-class structure based on wealth rather than lineage.[16] But Mills did not accept the aristocratic designation Mrs Van Rensselaer gave to the ante-bellum social elite of New York. He pointed to the virtually constant process of assimilation of new wealth into the established elite: 'no matter what its pretensions, the American upper class is merely an enriched bourgeoisie, and that, no matter how powerful its members may be, they cannot invent an aristocratic past where one did not exist'.[17] This assertion contains echoes of an earlier observation about the American upper class. Francis J. Grund, an Austrian-born immigrant, wrote in the 1830s: 'This aristocracy here is itself nothing but a wealthy overgrown *bourgeoisie*, composed of a few families who have been more successful in trade than the rest.'[18] Though it may be true that New York society had always comprised second- or third-generation new rich, neither Grund, a contemporary foreign visitor, nor Mills, a modern American sociologist, attributed significance to the fact that it took families like the Astors and the Vanderbilts at least two generations, if not three, to attain a firm social footing. The rate of assimilation before the Civil War was much slower than in the period after.

For Mrs Van Rensselaer the *arrivistes* of the 1870s were the antithesis of the Dutch aristocracy, and she was, predictably, contemptuous of the usurpers who had supplanted the small, exclusive society of her youth. Mills, on the other hand, played down the contrast between the two elites. Both, by the logic of their arguments, precluded a discussion of the post-war elite in aristocratic terms. In a more recent and detailed analysis of New York society, Frederic Cople Jaher has argued, in similar terms to Mills, that the ante-bellum patriciate was displaced by an unstable and fluid elite of wealthy families after the Civil War. As regards the old elite, however, Jaher has shown that its representation as 'an orderly, organic community with high standards of rectitude' was an indulgence in nostalgia on the part of the Knickerbocker establishment.[19] In fact, contrary to Knickerbocker accounts, he argues that the ante-bellum patriciate in New York was not as well developed as its counterparts in Boston and Philadelphia. What these interpretations of social change at the upper levels of American society demonstrate is that there were strong tendencies towards aristocratic pretensions both before and after the Civil War. It is immaterial, in one sense, whether or not we can pin a label to these elites; what is important is how members of the elite regarded themselves, for it was their self-perception which governed their actions to restrict access to their ranks or to reinforce their claims to elite status by marital alliances with American families of wealth or with the European nobility.

While the consensus appears to be that the American upper class became more broadly based after the 1870s, it would be wrong to think that members of the elite were more relaxed about admitting newcomers. The tendencies to assert claims to high social status were still present; what changed was the way in which those claims were established. Society became a much more public affair, and society pages in the daily newspapers were a useful way of publicizing the activities of fashionable society and the names of people who wished to be associated with it. Jaher suggests that the Four Hundred – that mythical number of the chosen few which was supposed to correspond to Mrs Astor's guest-list – was an aberration in the history of New York's upper strata. But it would be more appropriate to see the Four Hundred as a reassertion of exclusivity after a period of marked social transformation. The methods may have been unorthodox within upper-class traditions but they were in keeping with the new emphasis on publicity and with parallel developments in London society.

Caroline Schermerhorn Astor's name is synonymous with the Four Hundred. Her own marriage to William Astor in 1853 symbolized the merger of the new moneyed elite with the old patriciate, which took place on an ever-increasing scale from the 1850s onwards as the pace of industrialization quickened. The Four Hundred was itself an attempt to combine the resources of the new rich with the families of distinguished lineage. Ward McAllister, a retired Georgian lawyer with influential connections in New York, became Mrs Astor's 'Lord Chamberlain'. He quickly recognized in her the ability to discriminate amongst the increasing number of aspirants for inclusion in New York's inner circles and enlisted her help with the Patriarch's Committee.[20]

In 1872 McAllister gathered together twenty-five men for the purpose of arranging a series of winter balls. The formation of this group was a deliberate attempt to bring together men of wealth and men of distinguished lineage. It included, among others, two Astors, two Livingstons, a Van Rensselaer, a Schermerhorn, and Lewis Rutherfurd. The Patriarchs, as they called themselves, were responsible for the invitations to these balls, and it was hoped that the judicious selection of guests would ensure that these people would constitute the inner sanctum of New York society. As McAllister recollected:

> We knew then, as we know now, that the whole secret of the success of these Patriarch Balls lay in making them select, in making it extremely difficult to obtain an invitation to them, and to make such invitations of great value; to make them the stepping stone to the best New York society, that one might be sure that anyone repeatedly invited to them had a secure social position.[21]

The Patriarchs were one of the earliest manifestations of the post-bellum elite's desire to make high society exclusive. The establishment of clubs and societies, entertainments in private ballrooms, and the publication of the New York Social Register, which first appeared in 1888, were all part of the attempt to forge a group identity. It was the scale and style of these activities which offended members of the older elite, causing them to denounce the Four Hundred as vulgar. Publicity, however, was crucial to the efforts of

Ward McAllister and Mrs Astor in establishing an exclusive society which could command nationwide attention.[22]

The rapid expansion of the wealthier classes in New York had destroyed the family network which had hitherto sufficed as a basis for social life and group identity amongst the relatively small Knickerbocracy. Now, in the 1870s, people of wealth had greater difficulty in establishing who their social equals were. A more impersonal system was required to determine membership of high society – indeed, the system which did replace the kinship structure sometimes discriminated between members of the same family. In Britain this problem of expansion had been resolved by the emergence of a 'new formalized system of etiquette'.[23] McAllister and Mrs Astor resorted to similar tactics.

In the same way that the London season emerged in the early nineteenth century with a fixed calendar of social and sporting events, so too, in the late 1870s, did the New York Season begin to assume a definite form.[24] Certain balls inaugurated the season, debutantes were usually honoured with a supper and dance at Delmonico's, and the third Monday in January was reserved for the Astor ball. Throughout the winter months Mrs Astor held receptions in the afternoons – traditionally a ceremonial time of day – as well as weekly dinners for an even narrower circle of friends and acquaintances.[25] As in London, the ritual of introductions, leaving cards, calling, and dining conformed to a set pattern of protocol. The most famous occasion on which this protocol was publicly seen to be strictly observed was Mrs William Kissam Vanderbilt's fancy-dress ball in March 1883 when Mrs Astor had to call on the said Mrs Vanderbilt in order to receive an invitation to the ball – by so doing she 'recognized' Mrs Vanderbilt in Society.[26] In the summer months of July and August, Newport came into its own. Ward McAllister had turned the Newport Season into a rehearsal for New York's, and the same pressures were attendant upon aspirants to this artificially select circle.[27]

In 1892 McAllister gave the *New York Times* a much-publicized list of people adjudged by him to be 'in Society'. This list, an alleged roll-call of the Four Hundred, helps to indicate the nature of this circle – its careful blend of the new moneyed elite and the older New York families. In his article 'Style and Status', using McAllister's list, Jaher has analysed the social make-up of the Four Hundred. He has distinguished four sub-groups amongst the individuals and married couples listed. The largest of the four was the Knickerbockers, and this included the Livingstons, the Van Rensselaers, the Schuylers, and the Rhinelanders. These older families were reinforced by a second sub-group – members of Philadelphia's Main Line and the Boston Brahmins. Third, there was a substantial number of New York mercantile families, some of whom had intermarried with the older clans. And finally, there was the component of self-made men or *arrivistes*, including the Bradley Martins and the William Collins Whitneys, who constituted the second largest group.[28] The majority on McAllister's list, Jaher asserts, had either old or great wealth, came from New York, and appeared in the Social Register.

McAllister's list is reproduced in Dixon Wecter's *Saga of American Society*.[29] It includes 307 persons of whom 98 were wives or widows and 50 were single women. The list fell short of Four Hundred by 93, and Wecter speculated that some of the people omitted could have been abroad or may have retired from Society at the time of publication. Alternatively, the list may have been the Patriarch's guest-list with a few visitors to New York added. Wecter provided information about the occupation of the 160 male members on the list, and they can be classified as follows: 64 businessmen (including retired); 47 professional men; 35 men with invested or inherited income; 8 sportsmen and clubmen; 3 visitors; and 3 with no occupation listed. Lawyers dominated the professional group: there were 35 active or retired lawyers in the Four Hundred according to Wecter. About one-third of the businessmen were described as brokers, another third were bankers, and the remainder were manufacturers or merchants. Of those with inherited wealth or an income from investments, 18 received money from real-estate holdings. If Wecter's information is correct, the list indicates that the male members of the Four Hundred did not constitute a leisure class in the strict sense of the term.

Marriages with titled foreigners were symptomatic of the aristocratic pretensions of the post-Civil War elite in New York. As we noted earlier, Frederic Jaher's view of the Four Hundred was that it was an exceptional phase in the history of New York's upper strata. As for its association with titled marriages, he writes:

> trends started in the last days of the Four Hundred – divorces, marriages with titled Europeans, and lionizing of athletes, actors,

and actresses – made it a transitional order between New York's *haute monde* and the Café Society that flourished between the world wars in that city, London, and Paris.[30]

He appears from this to identify titled matches more with the twentieth-century 'international set' than with Mrs Astor's circle. While transatlantic marriages reached their first peak in the 1890s, and continued long after the demise of the Four Hundred, it should be noted that the trend was established in the 1870s and did not *start*, as Jaher argues, in the 1890s. Since the increase in transatlantic marriages coincided with the emergence of the Four Hundred, it seems likely that there was a connection between them.

With the help of Wecter's list of New York's Four Hundred, we can determine the extent to which the Four Hundred were associated with titled marriages involving to the British peerage. Four women on the list married into the British peerage: Mary Leiter (Lady Curzon), Adele Grant (Lady Essex), Margaret Crosby (Lady Huntingfield), and Edith Kip (the Honourable Mrs Coventry). Also on the list is a well-known American expatriate in London society, Mrs Cavendish-Bentinck (née Elizabeth Livingston), who married the great-grandson of the third Duke of Portland. Mary Leiter was a visitor to New York at the time the list was published. She originally came from Chicago, but in 1881 her family moved to Washington, DC. According to her biographer, Mary was taken up by Ward McAllister during her first season in New York in 1888, and was invited to one of the Patriarch Balls.[31] Altogether there were eighteen American women in the British peerage who were either daughters or close relatives of members of the Four Hundred:

Margaret Crosby	listed in her own right
May Goelet	daughter of Mr and Mrs Ogden Goelet
Adele Grant	listed in her own right
Augusta Jay	daughter of Col and Mrs William Jay
Mary Livingston King	related to the New York Livingstons
Edith Kip	listed in her own right
Mary Leiter	listed in her own right
Marguerite Leiter	sister of Mary Leiter
Katherine McVicar	related to Mr and Mrs H. W. McVicar
Cornelia Martin	daughter of Mr and Mrs Bradley Martin
Beatrice Mills	daughter of Mr and Mrs Ogden Mills

Helen Post	related to Mr and Mrs Charles A. Post
Adelaide Randolph	stepdaughter of William Collins Whitney
Jean Reid	niece of Mr and Mrs Ogden Mills
Mildred Sherman	daughter of Mr and Mrs William Watts Sherman
Consuelo Vanderbilt	great-niece of Mr and Mrs Cornelius Vanderbilt
Pauline Whitney	daughter of Mr and Mrs William Collins Whitney
Belle Wilson	sister of Grace and Orme Wilson and Mrs Goelet

Almost all of these women were members of the new rich. At least two women, Mary Livingston King and May Goelet, had Knickerbocker connections.

Of the 102 American women who married peers or the younger sons of peers between 1870 and 1914, 50 came from New York and 18 of them had connections with the Four Hundred. The origins of the remaining 52 women can be shown as follows:

New England	7
Eastern seaboard (excluding New York)	12
South	12
Midwest	7
Far West	7
Unknown	7

Working from Hartzell's list of titled Americans, Jaher found that almost half of the women came from New York,[32] as is borne out by the above list, which includes only British marriages. As relatively few women came from other established communities, he took this to indicate that the 'patricians in Philadelphia, Charleston and Boston were more secure in their inherited ascendancy than the newly risen rich'.[33] It should perhaps be pointed out, in qualification of this statement, that the women from these older cities did not necessarily come from the patriciate. As the information for Anglo-American marriages shows, very few of the women from Massachusetts and Pennsylvania came from older families. The smaller proportion of women from these other cities compared to New York,

43

therefore, does not prove that the patriciate was more secure but rather that New York had become the social and financial capital of the post-Civil War era and the home of many of the wealthiest banking and business families.

Given the predominance of New Yorkers amongst titled Americans in Britain and the special significance of New York for the *nouveaux riches* in the United States, it is possible that the attempt to create a more exclusive elite with a formalized structure in the late nineteenth century was an important catalyst for transatlantic marriages. In one way, it may have acted as a catalyst in that those families unable to secure entry to Mrs Astor's circle bypassed New York and attempted to establish a foothold in European society instead. In another way, the movement towards exclusiveness meant a greater intensity of competition amongst *nouveau riche* families jockeying for position in New York society, and one facet of this competition was titled marriages. Securing a European title was a means of asserting one's eligibility for the upper circles. According to C. Wright Mills, the exclusiveness of Mrs Astor's society began to wane in the 1890s, especially after McAllister published his list of the Four Hundred and his book, *Society As I Have Found It*. Mills felt that McAllister's departure from the scene symbolized the failure to create a pedigreed society of wealth and birth.[34] While this is probably true, the disappearance of the Four Hundred left in its wake an interlocking network of very rich families such as the Rockefellers, the Harknesses, the Fields, the Harrimans, the Mellons, the Fords, the Berwinds, the Vanderbilts, and the Astors. Some of the names dating from that period are today the recognized names of elite families. Perhaps McAllister's fall from grace meant that the upper classes no longer required his services – they had successfully managed to recreate a family system on which to base elite membership and so no longer needed the publicity McAllister had provided to advertise the fact. Indeed, as protests against the inequitable distribution of wealth became more strident there were very good reasons for retreating from the limelight. In a similar way, the impersonal nature of the large corporations guarded from public view the powerful individuals behind the scenes. Certainly, in the 1930s, social critics like Frederick Lundberg refused to believe professions of openness and accessibility.

The exclusiveness which McAllister and Mrs Astor attempted to impose on New York's upper circles may have been as arbitrary as it was artificial, but the Four Hundred marked a crucial, if transient, stage in the development of American society. Henry James once remarked that the rebuilding on Fifth Avenue – part of the social transformation – was 'part of the effort of "American Society" to find out, by experiment, what it would be at'.[35] As I have argued, this institutionalization of social ritual on European lines in the 1880s and 1890s was one of the most overt expressions of an aristocracy-in-the-making in nineteenth-century America. It was an aristocratic experiment which ultimately failed, but not without leaving in its place an upper class of great wealth and power with a hereditary core of families.

The dominant image of England amongst a fairly wide section of America's wealthier classes in the nineteenth century was derived from romanticized tales of aristocratic life and reinforced by the much-publicized successes of the American women in the Marlborough House Set. After 1870, with the disappearance of the French imperial court, the British nobility provided the most stable model of an elite for Americans to emulate. Confronted with the challenge of social climbers and wealthy newcomers, London society had learnt to deal with the pressures of a fluid socio-economic situation, and New Yorkers were keen to adopt similar strategies for vetting aspirants. An education at one of the top private schools and Ivy League colleges became one method of restricting entry into elite circles.[36] Membership of a gentleman's club was another. As a substitute for *noblesse oblige*, plutocrats gave generous donations to charities, educational institutions, and art foundations, but, at the same time, these often became outlets for surplus wealth, measured in the amount of personal interest to be accrued from philanthropic investment rather than a genuine expression of obligation towards the national community.

In the spring of 1900 scorn was heaped on John D. Rockefeller's intention to set up a charitable foundation. The announcement of the new foundation had opportunely followed four years of legal proceedings against Standard Oil. The English journal *Vanity Fair* was cutting in its cynicism: 'this sudden spasm of benevolence is merely a desperate move to create a wave of favourable public sentiment which shall have unofficial influence with the Supreme Court'.[37] Writing in the 1930s, Dixon Wecter criticized American

society's preoccupation with 'wealth and bluff indiscriminate philanthropy' and its neglect of the 'quieter obligations of an aristocracy'.[38] Expensive philanthropy was open to charges of 'conspicuous
consumption', in Veblen's terms, a demonstration of the ownership
of wealth.[39]

A more overt form of conspicuous consumption and one which
revealed the extent of the fascination of the leisure class for Europe
was the frantic competition on Fifth Avenue in New York and
Ocean Drive, Newport, to build European-style stately homes. Elizabeth Drexel Lehr, later Baroness Decies, saw, within the span of
her childhood, Fifth Avenue

> pass from the era of modest discreet-looking brick and brownstone
> houses, each with its high stoop striving to look as much like its
> neighbour as possible, to the splendours of the great gawdy
> palaces which proudly reared their Italian, Gothic or Oriental
> structures to house the new millionaires.[40]

Just as concrete multi-storey office blocks could be viewed as visual
symbols of the growth in power of the investment-banking houses
and corporations in the world of business, so too with European
châteaux in the world of high society. Moves towards social consoli-
dation and organization modelled on European aristocratic society
determined an architectural style as imposing as the more functional
office blocks of Wall Street. Upon revisiting New York, James had
sensed that, behind the impressiveness of the skyscrapers and the
technological feats and wealth they represented, there was a shal-
lowness to the new prosperity. He used such words as 'provisional',
'temporary', 'illusion', and 'insecurity'. Above all, the 'tall build-
ings' were 'crowned not only with no history, but no credible possibility of time for history, and consecrated by no uses save the
commercial at any cost, they are simply the most piercing notes in
that concert of the expensively provisional'.[41] The 'elegant domi-
ciliary' and 'exorbitant structures' of Fifth Avenue were equally
insincere and insecure in James's view.[42]

The most famous society-architect of this era, Richard Morris
Hunt, pandered to the desire for symbols of gracious living. He was
generously patronized by the William K. Vanderbilts, who gave
him the commissions for both their Fifth Avenue mansion and
Marble House, their summer home. Newport, Rhode Island, a
watering place of Narrangansett Bay, is still studded with Hunt's

architectural extravaganzas including The Breakers, Belcourt, Château-sur-Mer, and Ochre Court. They once belonged, respectively, to Cornelius Vanderbilt II, August Belmont, William S. Wetmore, and Ogden Goelet. An even greater number of houses in Newport were built by the firm of McKim, Mead and White. Between 1876 and 1889 this firm had at least one construction in progress every year. Mrs Stuyvesant Fish's Crossways (1898) and Mrs Herman Oelrich's Rosecliff (1902) are two of its most famous Newport creations. Hunt's training in Europe was very much in evidence in his designs: he imported rare marbles and alabasters from Italy and North Africa and Caen stone from France for his Vanderbilt clients. Among the many extravagances in The Breakers is the plumbing in the tiled bathrooms – the choice of not just hot-and-cold rain water but salt water, too.

A curious insight into the personality of Willie Vanderbilt is available to visitors to Marble House. One of his eccentricities was a fascination for Louis XIV: Marble House was Newport's Versailles with its gold ballroom, portraits of the Sun King and Louis-Quatorze bronze furniture in the dining-room, a copy of Bernini's bust of Louis XIV on the first-floor landing, and a portrait of Versailles' architect hung juxtaposed with one of the obliging Mr Hunt. Mrs Vanderbilt had her own fantasies. The ceiling of her bedroom features the goddess Athene, renowned for her wisdom and power, but not for motherhood. This mansion and others offer fascinating glimpses of their millionaire proprietors. There was more than a hint of megalomania about the William Kissam Vanderbilts.

These monuments to wealth, however, stood empty for ten months of the year. Marble House was unoccupied for twelve years after the Duke of Marlborough had proposed to Consuelo Vanderbilt. Out of the forty years it was in Alva Vanderbilt's possession, Marble House was used for a mere eighteen summer seasons. Such ostentatious waste did not escape public censure, although today both Hunt and his patrons are lauded as great contributors to the American architectural renaissance. This waste was ridiculed with biting wit in the fiction of Edith Wharton:

the possession of a ball-room that was used for no other purpose, and left for three-hundred-and-sixty-four days of the year to shuttered darkness, with its gilt chairs stacked in a corner and its chandelier in a bag – this undoubted superiority was felt to compensate for whatever was regrettable in the Beaufort past.[43]

A number of these white elephants now have tourists' cars motoring up their drives as they stand as testimony to the unbridled opulence of the Gilded Age.

European-style mansions provided an appropriate setting for the activities of New York's charmed circles. As a young girl, Consuelo Vanderbilt used to peep through the balustrade of the orchestra's gallery and gaze at the spectacle of her mother's parties below:

> The long dinner-table covered with a damask cloth, a gold service and red roses, the lovely crystal and china, the grown ups in their fine clothes. The dining-room was enormous and . . . on one side a huge stained-glass window, depicting the Field of the Cloth of Gold on which the Kings of England and France were surrounded with their knights, all not more magnificently arrayed than the ladies a-glitter with jewels seated on high back tapestry chairs behind which stood footmen in knee-breeches.[44]

It is quite clear that people like the Vanderbilts thought of themselves as a nobility no less splendid than any European one. They tried to convince themselves and the rest of the world of this with their imitation of the public display, ritual, and protocol of European court life.

Marble House exemplifies the wealth, exclusiveness, and Anglophilia of the social elite in New York in this period. It stands as testimony of a particular era in social, economic, and cultural history when events and circumstances combined to bring the elites in the United States and Britain into closer union. Appropriately, it was in the Gothic Room of this European-style mansion that the Duke of Marlborough proposed to the young Consuelo Vanderbilt in 1895.

Publicity, as we have noted, was an essential factor in this self-glorification and competition for social acclaim, but it could also prove very harmful. In the season of 1897–8, a harsh winter of high unemployment, Mrs Bradley Martin, with an economic theory akin to Lady Warwick's,[45] staged a fancy-dress party to 'stimulate' the economy. Thousands of dollars were spent on costumes as guests vied with each other in their glittering garb; and whilst the host, Bradley Martin, dressed up as Louis XV, August Belmont wore armour of gold and steel. As in England, following Daisy Warwick's costume party in February 1895, the press fulminated against this meaningless squandering of money. Robert Blatchford had taken it upon himself to explain the realities of labour and production to Daisy Warwick, but no such socialist editor in New York came forward to enlighten Mrs Martin. Instead, the Martins fled to London and lavished their hospitality and surplus wealth on real kings and queens.

The democratic political system was not accompanied by a democratic social system in the United States, and this became particularly apparent after the Civil War when the accumulation of large fortunes undermined the principle behind divided inheritance. Wealth remained within families, resulting in the formation of a self-perpetuating oligarchy. Unequal distribution of wealth became more obvious as the century wore on, and with it came increasing caste consciousness. The social structure still allowed for mobility and flexibility, but at the top of pyramid there were signs of a closed caste developing. Fears of an entrenched oligarchy were expressed in Anglophobic denunciations and in attacks on aristocratic pretensions, of which the condemnation of transatlantic marriages was very much a part. Eventually, these emotions subsided, but the reasons for this had less to do with transatlantic marriages than with the social, economic, and political upheavals of the early twentieth century.

The rise in transatlantic marriages belongs to the period when the amassing of great fortunes was creating a fast-expanding class of *nouveau riches*. The latter used their wealth to support their claims to social distinction by spending it on impressive palaces, lavish entertainments, Parisian gowns, and luxurious steam yachts. The creation of the Four Hundred was an attempt to control the effects of the rapid expansion of the moneyed classes. Since that elite fashioned itself after European court society, elements of the *nouveaux riches* excluded from Mrs Astor's circle went direct to the fountain of social authority to legitimize their claim to membership of high society. They found England, in particular, remarkably receptive to wealth, and its aristocracy willing to marry their daughters. These new families then returned to America to reap the benefits of their social success in Europe. This state of affairs lasted, however, only as long as Americans continued to look to Europe

for cultural and social leadership and while the national elite was
working out its own formula for membership.

3

'For them he slaves':
American women of the leisure class

'Isn't marriage your vocation? Isn't it what you're all brought up for?' Lawrence Selden, a young New York lawyer, asked of Lily Bart, in *The House of Mirth* (1905).[1] The heroine had to admit it was true. 'What else is there?' she replied. The alternatives for a young woman of the leisure class were few. Changes taking place in the educational and employment opportunities for middle-class women scarcely altered the attitudes of the elite towards women's role in life. While feminists of the late nineteenth century were agitating for women to be given access to higher education and the professions or arguing, as Charlotte Perkins Gilman did, that housework was merely a means by which women 'paid' for their security,[2] the leisure class was at pains to stress its financial ability to make paid work and most domestic work unnecessary for its women. Consequently, the education of daughters was ornamental and centred around accomplishments which would win a husband, such as music, dancing, and foreign languages, and these were usually acquired with the aid of governesses or at one of the few fashionable schools for young ladies. Nancy Astor, for example, was sent to Miss Brown's Academy in New York to round off her education and prepare her for her debut.[3] Consuelo Vanderbilt, another American who married into the British peerage, had both a French and a German governess as a young child and later 'two so-called finishing governesses in residence'.[4] In the nineteenth century the wealthier classes did not take seriously the education of daughters: governesses and finishing schools were more a proof of parental income and pretensions to gentility than an attempt to give daughters a thorough academic training. The flourishing of women's colleges from the 1850s onwards, e.g. Vassar, Wellesley, Smith, and

Bryn Mawr,[5] did little, in their early years at least, to alter the obdurate habits of a plutocratic class which viewed its daughters in terms of collateral.[6]

Since so few young women of the leisure class enjoyed even a rudimentary grounding in academic subjects, it follows that few of them pursued professional careers or undertook paid work. Only a small number of professions were open, in any case, to women in the late nineteenth century. The profession which accepted the largest number of women was, of course, teaching; law and medicine were more circumspect in their admission of the female sex.[7] One of the few professions compatible with genteel status was writing, though even that was considered bohemian and outlandish in certain quarters. Any other occupation meant a decline in social standing, so Lily Bart's plaintive reply was not without justification. Failing marriage, living on an allowance in the ignominious position of an 'old maid' (as it was negatively characterized at the time) would probably have been preferable to a young woman of the upper class,[8] and, up until the First World War, outlets for her energies would have been restricted to entertaining, philanthropy, and the arts. But in a society where people competed fiercely for social distinction, the position of a spinster could be a precarious one, so that the pressures to marry must have been considerable.

We have already pointed to one source of pressure upon daughters of the leisured elite to marry well: the increasing competitiveness amongst aspirants to, and members of, fashionable society. Marriage to a man whose high social status was affirmed could advance, or consolidate at least, a family's social career. If suitable spouses could not be found at home, then the European marriage market provided an alternative supply of eligible husbands with more visible social credentials. Hereditary titles were deemed to carry weight, even in a republican society which had renounced them, and thus marriage with a European noble was invested with the power to secure entry into any exclusive social circle. But apart from family ambitions, young American women had to contend with the pressures of their own predicament as ornamental appendages in a leisure class which provided no substitute for useful employment and instead expected women to take responsibility for establishing or maintaining claims to genteel status. Marriage was supposed to be woman's true vocation, and yet married life in the American leisure class (to the late twentieth-century mind) did not exactly hold out great prospects for self-fulfilment unless a woman was socially ambitious, enjoyed entertaining, and could find sufficiently rewarding the limited demands of motherhood in a house of nannies, governesses, and servants. Marriage, moreover, determined the life-style of a woman in the more patriarchal society of late nineteenth-century America. Her husband's way of life became hers, and there was a certain amount of predictability about the demands that would be made upon her. But marriage to a foreign nobleman, regardless of the attractions of medieval castles, court ritual, and coronets, was not a decision to be taken lightly. The adventure of living abroad could soon be subdued by homesickness and culture shock or, as Edith Wharton expressed it, being 'isolated in her new world, no longer able to reach back to her past, and not having yet learned how to communicate with her present'.[9] Depending upon the openness of her newly adopted social family, an American woman's marriage into the European nobility meant adapting to new customs, learning new codes of behaviour, and tolerating comments about American habits or peculiarities of speech intended to make the newcomer feel like an outsider.

Social ambition is the motive most frequently alluded to in expla-nations for so many American women marrying titled husbands around the turn of the century. But to accept this as the most important factor in transatlantic marriages is to accept the cliché of title for money and to dismiss these women as 'gilded prostitutes' who sold themselves for a coronet. We need to go beyond the widely accepted image of titled Americans in order to understand what appealed to them in a marriage with a member of the British peerage. Seeking the answers to this involves turning the problem on its head and asking, what were the alternatives to an international marriage? This, then, focusses the inquiry on the predicament of American women in the leisure class: their position as wives and daughters, their education, and their realm of activities. Many of the issues discussed here form part of a much larger debate within the United States about the role and position of women in society. They touch on a multitude of questions about women's lives: woman's suffrage, higher education facilities for women, women's rights before the law, divorce, birth control, and many others. Throughout the nineteenth century the question of what constituted woman's sphere, particularly that of middle-class and upper-class women, troubled many Americans. Clergymen, doctors, academics, writers, and journalists participated in a general debate in publications of various kinds on how women should behave and what occupations, pecuniary or non-pecuniary, were appropriate to the female sex. As the century wore on, more and more women were making a bolder bid for independence, an independence of both mind and pocket. The term 'New Woman' is often used to characterize the type of woman who was seeking to expand the range of activities open to her and to have more control over her life. Admittedly, the class of women we are concerned with here constituted a tiny percentage of the American female population and was not proportionately represented amongst the ranks of feminists, but as women they were bound to be affected by changes in the political, economic, and legal status of women, and some of the ideas in circulation about the proper sphere for women were pertinent to their specific situation.

Many of these ideas were topics in fiction written by and for women at the turn of the century. The status quo tended, on the whole, to be upheld in the more popular novels of the day, but writers like Louisa May Alcott, Sarah Orne Jewett, and Charlotte Perkins Gilman were, in their fiction, challenging the conventional roles of women in marriage and the workforce.[10] Edith Wharton, an American writer who has enjoyed more enduring fame as a novelist over the years than Jewett or Gilman and whose work is currently seeing something of a revival, provided critiques of the position of women in the American upper class and is therefore of especial interest in this study. Her last novel, The Buccaneers (1938), has particular relevance because its deals directly with titled marriages, but The House of Mirth (1905) and The Custom of the Country (1913), too, provide an excellent literary representation of New York society at the turn of the century and a damning indictment of both the marriage market and marriage in a patriarchal culture which subordinated women to a position of ornamental idleness. Edith Wharton herself, as a member of New York's upper crust, is an interesting figure. Her own experiences of courtship and marriage reveal some of the problems confronting a young woman expected to marry someone of appropriate social standing and to conduct the rest of her life as a dutiful mother and society hostess.

Soon after her debut in New York society in 1879 – a private affair in Mrs Levi Morton's ballroom – Edith met Harry Stevens, son of the hotel proprietor Paran Stevens and brother of Lady

Arthur Paget.[11] The Stevens family had only recently 'arrived' in
New York society after the tireless efforts of Mrs Stevens and her
exhausting campaign in London society to marry her daughter,
Minnie, into the British peerage. Things were alleged to have
proceeded between Edith and Stevens to the point of betrothal, but
his mother brought pressure to bear, and the engagement was called
off. One explanation proffered by Edith's biographer, R. W. B.
Lewis, is that Mrs Stevens sought revenge for an earlier snub by
Edith's family; another is that Mrs Stevens wanted to delay her
son's marriage until his 25th birthday when he would assume sole
control over his inheritance.[12] A few years later Edith, then aged
23, married Edward Wharton of Boston, a gentleman of leisure.
Though his social credentials were more than adequate, Teddy
Wharton was not the obvious choice for a woman with literary
interests. Edith Wharton's biographer claims that Walter Berry,
then a young lawyer and one of Edith's admirers before her
marriage, was frightened off by her 'persistent intellectuality'.[13] Why
Edith married Wharton remains a mystery. Lewis suggests that she
may have been becoming 'less marriageable', but it seems questionable that at 23 Edith Jones was destined for the proverbial shelf.[14]
Rumours, like those concerning her broken engagement to Stevens,
may well have been damaging. Perhaps maternal pressure was
brought to bear on the misfit daughter who preferred books to
dancing. At any rate, the occasion of her wedding received scant
attention in Edith's memoirs: 'At the end of my second winter I
was married.'[15]

During her early married life Mrs Wharton threw herself into
domestic activities. She and her husband lived in a small house in
Newport on a modest, inherited income substantially augmented in
1888 by the death of a relative. Edith wrote of these years: 'I
continued to live my old life, for my husband was as fond of society
as ever, and I knew of no other existence, except in our annual
escapes to Italy. I had as yet no real personality of my own.'[16]
Although Edith Wharton had conformed and married in accordance
with the rules of her parents' social set, her marriage eventually
proved an empty vessel for the values of that class. She did not
identify with her husband's interests, which were limited to the
social and sporting life, and such were their sexual relations that
motherhood was out of the question. In the end, the stress of leading
a desultory existence of restless socializing and touring round

Europe without the compensations of a fulfilled married life, combined with the longing to commit herself to writing, brought on a nervous breakdown. By the time she had recovered from this emotional crisis, she had set her mind on becoming a writer:

> The publishing of 'The Greater Inclination' broke the chains which had held me so long in a kind of torpor. For nearly twelve years I had tried to adjust myself to the life I had led since my marriage; but now I was overmastered by the longing to meet people who shared my interests.[17]

For ten years or so, Mrs Wharton had conformed to the conventional role of a wife in the leisure class.

The pressures on women to conform were reinforced by what has been called the cult of domesticity – the veneration of the home and woman's role in it. The separation of the home from the workplace, brought about by the development of factories and improvements in public transport in the towns as part of the Industrial Revolution, confined married women to the home. The home, as conventionally portrayed by the marriage-guidance books and publications for women, became the place of refuge from the world of money-making and a haven for Christian and moral values. It was also known as the private sphere, as opposed to the more public world of the male, and 'privacy' became an end in itself, denying women participation in activities outside the home lest they conflict with her primary role as child-bearer and home-maker. Indeed, the virtues associated with the 'Angel in the House' stemmed from woman's function as a child-bearer; the basis of male subjugation of women was, after all, this fundamental biological difference. Passivity, piety, gentleness, and patience, the virtues of true womanhood, have to do with the bearing and rearing of children; and although the nature of women's lives in the upper classes precluded a more constant exercise of these virtues in the activity of child-rearing, women in this social stratum were, nevertheless, expected to conform to the submissive, nurturing role outlined by the ideology of mainly middle-class writers.[18] What is clear from the ideas associated with the cult of domesticity is that it was assumed that most, if not all, women got married. It was in the role of wife and mother that they were portrayed as exercising their special influence over moral and spiritual matters. Figures for the proportion of married women in the leisure class are not available, but we do know from the Census returns that of all women born between 1855 and 1889 at least 88.9 per cent married during the period covered by this study.[19] Women in all social strata, therefore, were expected to marry: it was truly their 'vocation'.

The idea of the 'Angel in the House' was carried to a further extreme with the development of the American leisure class. Woman's exclusion from remunerative labour was exacerbated by the employment of servants which made even her roles as house-keeper and mother virtually redundant.[20] Instead, her responsi-bilities lay chiefly with upholding standards of genteel behaviour, providing evidence through the observance of social rituals, e.g. calling and leaving cards, of the family's rightful claim to elite status. Above all, her efforts were focussed on successfully directing the social intercourse of her offspring to ensure desirable marital connections. Women's influence over kinship alliances is perhaps best demonstrated by a newspaper article on the Wilson family entitled 'The Science of Marrying Well – a Study of Three Sisters and a Mother', which appeared in a New York paper in 1902.[21] The story concerned the successful marriages of the Wilson children to members of wealthy and prominent New York families in the late nineteenth century, but the accolade is especially reserved for the mother, Mrs Richard T. Wilson. For example:

In the exclusive set of New York, there cannot be found any woman who has guided the destinies of her children with such unerring aim to success. . . . When the children of a family are remarkably fortunate in matrimonial ventures, it is conceded that this fact is due to the guiding hand of the mother in question.

This so-called 'fact' remained uncorroborated in the rest of the article. Nevertheless, the concentration on Mrs Wilson's alleged matchmaking skills serves to make the point that it was both proper and laudatory that mothers make such efforts to further the social ranking of their family.

In addition to her duty to display refined manners and cultivate social contact with families of similar standing, the leisure-class woman played an even more important role as a consumer. The significance of consumption for the leisure class is well known because of Thorstein Veblen's work. Possibly influenced by Veblen, a writer for *The Nation* discussed the position of women in American society in terms of the businessman's wife performing an essential economic function in her expenditure of money and display of the social graces.[22] Her conspicuous use of money and leisure attested, so the article says, to her husband's 'economic prowess' and did not, as was commonly assumed, signify that American women were petted, indulged, and allowed more autonomy in the home and in society. The correspondent manages to turn the stereotypes of submissive husbands and spoilt wives on their heads to reveal the oppression of the upper-class woman in a culture which, as Veblen expressed it, required her 'to consume largely and conspicuously – vicariously for her husband' and to refrain from 'vulgarly useful employment'.[23] 'These offices', Veblen went on, 'are the conventional marks of the un-free, at the same time that they are incompatible with the human impulse to purposeful activity.'

The insistence that women had to carry the responsibility for putting 'opulence in evidence'[24] meant that there was a considerable disparity in the functions of the male and the female in the leisure class. Henry James noted a conversation he once had with Edward Godkin, editor of *The Nation*, about the 'growing divorce' in America between the woman of leisure and her mate, the American businessman, who was absorbed in 'sordid interests', antipathetic to hers.[25] James saw dramatic potential in what he called the 'abyss of inequality', the tension between two opposing forces, the one aristocratic, the other democratic.[26] Much earlier in the century the gulf between the sexes had been a topic deemed worthy of notice in the writings of foreign visitors. Captain Basil Hall and Mrs Trollope both remarked on the 'strong line of demarcation between the sexes'.[27] Captain Hall had lamented the absence of female influence on American communities but did not believe that American men had deliberately kept women in subjugation. Mrs Trollope, on the other hand, had been concerned about the stultifying effect it had, not only on the quality of social life but also on women's lives. In her provocative commentary on American society, published in 1832, she had noted: 'all the enjoyments of the men are found in the absence of women. They dine, they play cards, they have musical meetings, they have suppers, all in large parties, but all without women'.[28]

By the end of the century, however, this social segregation was described in very different terms. Whereas Mrs Trollope had implied that society in the 1830s served only men's pleasures, commentators in the late nineteenth century were saying that society was dominated by women. Elizabeth Drexel Lehr, for example, observed in her memoirs how Wall Street millionaires made poor dinner companions, looking awkward in their stiff white shirts and dinner jackets: 'They either talked of business or sat silent and apathetic through course after course, too nerve-racked by the strain of building a fortune to be able to relax.'[29] By the time of Mrs Astor's social leadership, then, Society would seem to have become a predominantly female affair. Price Collier, who wrote a book in the 1900s about English society from an American perspective, thought English society compared more favourably with America's where the women reigned supreme. In disconsolate tones he wrote: 'it never seems quite as though the social adjustment of things is right when woman becomes conspicuous'.[30] What we can conclude from these various commentaries dating from the 1830s is that in the earlier period the emphasis appears to have been on the adverse effects of social segregation upon women, while later commentators seem to suggest that segregation was to women's advantage in so far as they had more control over events but that this in itself was unnatural.

Elizabeth Lehr's description of an upper-class dinner party can hardly be said, however, to be the ideal state of affairs for either sex. The gulf between the leisure interests of men and women seems to have been a reflection of a deep-rooted problem in the roles of the sexes in the upper class. Her description hints at one of the most persistent stereotypes of the genteel couple in American society: that of the overworked husband flogging himself to death to keep his wife and family in fineries and elegant surroundings. An early proponent of this stereotype was the English writer Harriet Martineau, who wrote of wealthy New York merchants snatching their breakfast in a hurry to get to the office and returning home in the evening exhausted, while their wives frittered the day away watering flowers, reading the latest European novel, and paying a visit to the milliners.[31] Though critical of the merchants' wives leading useless lives, as indeed was Harriet Beecher Stowe,[32] Martineau's criticism nevertheless fitted in with the conventional idea that women were lucky to be spared the toils and worries of money-making. Fifty years later, Lady Randolph Churchill testified to the continuation of this state of relations in the prosperous classes by implicitly condoning the subordinate position of women as retainers and dependants:

The hard-working businessman of Wall Street, steeped all day in the making of dollars, wants when he comes home to find his women folk beautifully dressed and their surrounding in keeping: for them he slaves – that is the object of his life and work.[33]

The source of Lady Randolph's dowry was her father's profits from speculation on the stock market and the rent from the Jerome house in Madison Square, New York. In her youth she had been accustomed to a luxurious life-style. In this statement she does not criticize the extravagance of American women but rather colludes in this state of affairs whereby women of the leisure class are, effectively, pensioned dependants.

Edith Wharton, however, found the underlying principle of subordination distressing and produced a critical analysis of high society in her fiction. The sterility of the position and role of women in the leisure class is never far below the surface of her novels. Fighting against the pertinacity of the ideal of the lady of leisure, both in her own life and in her writing, Wharton sought to dispel the myths and expose the frustration, oppression, and misery behind the genteel façade. *The Custom of the Country*, written intermittently between 1908 and 1913, reveals some interesting stereotypes of people in New York society. Undine Spragg, the protagonist, is the daughter of a self-made millionaire with little understanding of the mysteries of money-making. Pampered and spoilt, she assumed 'that there were ample funds to draw upon, and that Mr Spragg's occasional resistances were merely due to an imperfect understanding of what constitutes the necessities of life'.[34] Undine's reckless expenditure throughout her life can be seen, I would suggest, as an unconscious act of revenge on the limitations of her freedom.

In much of her fiction Wharton portrays marriage as a trap, and in *The Custom of the Country* she hits out forcefully at the subservient role assigned to women of the upper classes. In her own sphere of Society and marriage, Undine Spragg is the female counterpart of the Wall Street stockbroker. Aggressive and ruthless, she changes husbands as dispassionately as a businessman buys and sells stock. Lacking alternative channels for her energy, she exploits, in turn, her three husbands and the millionaire Peter Van Degen in pursuit of some undefined sense of self-fulfilment. The major theme of the novel is the failure of marriage at the upper levels of American society, and Mrs Wharton places the blame squarely on the shoulders of the husband:

> To slave for women is part of the old American tradition . . . in this country the passion for making money has preceded the knowing how to spend it, and the American man lavishes his fortunes on his wife because he does not know what else to do with it.[35]

Though Veblen would probably have disagreed with this, Mrs Wharton pointed to the consequences of conspicuous consumption. In her view, women were spoilt and, like children, locked up in an artificial world protected from the economic struggle and led to believe that the existence of money is guaranteed.

Mrs Wharton argues, through her mouthpiece in the novel, Charles Bowen, that it is against the custom of the country to involve wives in the challenges and anxieties of earning a living.[36] Ralph Marvell, Undine's second husband, is a member of the old New York elite (hardly the average man), who is forced to give up his profession as a lawyer for a more lucrative career in real estate to pay for Undine's extravagances. He, too, is trapped by a system geared towards achievement and evidence of financial resources, which is alien to his own preference for a quiet, genteel life-style. Mrs Wharton's concept of society, as revealed in her memoirs and fiction, appears to be of a male-created diversion for women, serving no serious purpose. Wharton/Bowen suggests that men's attitudes towards women have to change or else the institution of marriage will completely break down.

There were already signs of trouble before the First World War. The rising divorce rate and the fall in the birth rate gave rise to serious alarm about the sanctity of marriage. The efforts of mainly middle-class women to extend their sphere of influence outside the home, and particularly their demands for access to higher education and professional careers, provoked fierce condemnation.[37] Doctors warned that excessive academic work would have a harmful effect upon the reproductive system and thereby called into question women's attitudes towards motherhood.[38] The fact that many of the first generation of women college graduates did not marry at all or married later in life did not help matters and confirmed men's worst fears about the efficacy of women's education.[39]

While women of the middle classes were challenging restrictions on their legal and political rights, on their choice of careers, and on their freedom of movement, young women of the elite were far more confined in their options. The ideal woman held up to them as a role model can be seen in the drawings of Charles Dana Gibson. His women were elegant and chaste, destined to be married 'well'. The only expression of liberty for the 'Gibson Girl', as she was known, was through taking advantage of the new sports or the latest technology in the form of the motor car. Women of the leisured elite did not have much to do with the woman's movement, apart from one notable exception, Mrs Alva Belmont (see Chapter 10). They were not particularly notable in their challenge to the separation of spheres, and this was probably because of the material advantages they enjoyed. Their sense of purpose in life rested chiefly upon the demands of running an extensive household in more than one location with domestic staff to supervise and of maintaining the family's social status through entertainments and socializing in the right circles.

Women of the leisure class no doubt felt varying levels of self-fulfilment in performing their expected roles and reaping the rewards of being able to run an efficient household and compete successfully for high social status.[40] But marriage to a diplomat or statesman would probably have offered more of a challenge than being the wife of a capitalist: there was the opportunity to make a real contribution to the promotion of a husband's career. It is possible that women in this class may have placed a certain value on the opportunities available to them in a marriage for playing a more useful role or for pursuing interests of their own. Examples of women in the social elite taking their own initiative, however, in promoting the arts or education, or in performing philanthropic acts, were very few and far between. Gertrude Vanderbilt Whitney is perhaps one of the best known members of the Four Hundred in her generation who patronized contemporary artists. Grace Dodge, the copper heiress, was a rare example of a woman who exchanged high society for social work. She set up the first Working Girls' Club in New York.[41]

The British aristocracy, on the other hand, had a much stronger tradition of involvement in public and philanthropic activities. In many cases, marriage to a British aristocrat offered American women greater potential for extending their sphere of influence into areas of real power and usefulness. The *New York Times* obituary notice quoted Lady Decies, an American, as having said in 1920:

> It is difficult to say whether for the American woman an American necessarily makes a better husband than an Englishman. But there is little doubt that responsibilities which an American woman must accept if she marries an English country gentleman are good for her. They usually give her a fuller and more useful life than she would spend as the wife of a man of equal position in her own country.[42]

This view is not taken, however, by writers of popular fiction who dealt with the question of the role of women in marriage, and it is interesting to note here the contrasts that were made between 'domestic' and transatlantic marriages.

Anglo-Americans, a novel written by Adelina Kingscote, alias Lucas Cleeve, around the turn of the century, compares the attitudes of British and American husbands towards their wives. The plot is fairly typical: a rich American heiress makes a disastrous match with a foreign noble and returns home appreciating the virtues of the American male with his intense 'reverence' for women and his 'humility'.[43] Courted by a young American, the heroine, Sadie Perkins, asks herself, before leaving for Europe, why she cannot take the simple step of accepting her wealthy and adoring suitor:

> Why was she not satisfied . . . to marry Herbert and settle down, as everyone had done before her? Was it, could it be, that the ring of truth, of unvarnished sentiment, of reality, was too crude for her, that greed openly expressed was ugly, that the refuge of culture must of necessity be hypocrisy, or at least a graceful evasion of bald certainties? . . . As she looked upon a woman's life to-night, it seemed to her that it was at once patched and jerky, made up of little nothings which men play the farce of thinking much of.[44]

Restless and spoilt, she rejects her parents' pretensions to culture, with their portraits by Sargent and European furniture, and sails to Europe in pursuit of the real thing. Impressed by aristocratic philanthropy and the well-mannered behaviour of British aristocrats, she marries a young viscount. Under her influence he takes up issues of reform in Parliament – labour, corporations, wages – and she finds more scope for her genuine interest in social reform.

But instead of culture she finds hypocrisy and instead of freedom to express her own individuality she finds repression:

> The Englishman marries as he buys a horse, a picture; the woman is part of his domesticity, but the note of domesticity in himself is wanting. His wife must always be there to wait on his moods, not he on hers.[45]

The moral of the tale, neatly packaged for an American female audience, was, of course, that they should realize the worth of their own men, who made better husbands despite their faults and lack of culture. Of course, the nature of the narrative requires that there be no loose ends: Sadie divorces her husband and takes up philanthropic work with Herbert, whom she marries, while the Viscount marries his mistress. Cleeve slips in a political statement that Anglo-American marriages will grow rarer: 'Young America no longer wishes to merge itself into another nation. . . . Art, refinement, comfort, luxury, emotion – these are creeping to America; no need to go abroad for them.'[46]

This theme is echoed in other popular novels, such as Frances Hodgson Burnett's *The Shuttle* (1907) and Gertrude Atherton's *American Wives and English Husbands* (1898). In the latter, the American wife of an English peer learns that 'to live comfortably with an Englishman you've got to become his habit, and to be happy with him you've got to become his second self'.[47]

Motivation is a tricky matter to deal with. We are forced into speculating about the possible reasons why a particular group of women opted for foreign husbands. Without any specific evidence – autobiographical information is few and far between as well as problematic (as we shall see in Chapter 8) – we are left with interpreting the more public side of life rather than the private and the personal. As far as we can tell, American women of the leisure class were brought up to regard marriage as their vocation, and, within a fiercely competitive elite structure, marriage was an important means of establishing a family's social ranking. To some daughters of the American plutocracy, transatlantic marriages may have represented an escape from these pressures, or perhaps offered even something more in the way of useful occupation, adventure, and romance. Some women may have seen such a marriage as an opportunity to broaden their horizons in a social milieu which was more closely commensurate with political society – in this case, the world of Parliament and British imperial government. In support of these conjectures, we can turn to the evidence regarding the careers of transatlantic brides in Britain, but before doing so we need to consider the other side of the coin: the pressures operating within the British peerage which encouraged British men to depart from traditional marriage patterns.

AMERICANS IN LONDON SOCIETY

Introduction to Part Three

Within my twelve years' experience of it, it is marvelously meta-morphosed and I think one can trace the march of democracy in many more ways than in the presence of John Bright in the Cabinet. Still the aristocratic element holds its own by its immense powers of absorption and by its prodigious concentration of wealth.[1]

This was the opinion of the American historian and diplomat John Lothrop Motley,[2] expressed in a letter written in May 1870 to his friend and patron Charles Sumner, who had helped to secure for him the appointment at the Court of St James's. In the same month, the son of a predecessor of Motley's at the Legation drove up St James's Street pondering on the changes since his arrival in the British capital nine years earlier. 'Never had the sun of progress shone so fair,' pronounced Henry Adams.[3] He too noted Bright's inclusion in Mr Gladstone's Cabinet. The Liberal Ministry seemed to herald a new age of reform with its assault on aristocratic patronage in the army and the Civil Service, the two great sources of employment for younger sons of the aristocracy. Adams, however, was sceptical about the planned Liberal reforms. Nor was he able to identify with the preoccupations of the ascendant generation in Society and therefore refused to make 'his court to Marlborough House, in partnership with the American woman and the Jew banker'.[4] Adams's sympathies were too radical for him to take heart in the moderate legislative attempts to curb the aristocracy's power, and too republican to adopt the latest American fashion of eulogizing the Prince of Wales. Nevertheless, both Bostonians testified to the new forces of change at work in British society in 1870 even though they also expressed scepticism about their effect on the power of the aristocracy.

Within a generation, however, significant changes had taken place within Britain's social and political elite. These have been widely debated by historians such as Walter Arnstein, William Guttsman, Arno Mayer, and Michael Thompson. Walter Arnstein, for example, has argued that the aristocracy survived challenges both to its domination of national and local government and to its claims to social prestige at least until 1902 if not the First World War.[5] Indeed, much of the discussion centres around the aristocracy's acceptance of 'new wealth' and the creation of new peers.[6] At the start of our period, in 1870, the peerage was closely identified with the great landowning class. John Bateman's summary table of landholdings shows 400 peers amongst the great landowners of England and Wales, representing approximately four-fifths of the peerage in the late nineteenth century.[7] In fact, until 1885, the overwhelming majority of new peers used to come from the landed classes, which ensured the continued identification of the ruling class with the landed aristocracy. In his study of new peerage titles in the Victorian and Edwardian years, Ralph Pumphrey identified only 25 men 'associated' with commerce and industry amongst the 241 new peerage titles granted between 1837 and 1885 (i.e. 10.37 per cent), and as few as seven of these industrialists and commercial men were of non-aristocratic background.[8] After 1886, however, men associated with commerce and industry represented a much higher proportion of recipients of new titles: 31.98 per cent in the years 1885 to 1911. Of these, two-thirds were from a non-aristocratic background. The introduction of 48 new families over a period of twenty-six years when the peerage consisted of over 600 families in 1885 was hardly likely to have much immediate impact on the nobility, as Pumphrey points out; but the marked increase of new peers without aristocratic connections does indicate, at least, that the social composition of the peerage was beginning to change during our period.

It was just at this juncture, then, when leading lights of industry and trade were beginning to take their seats in the House of Lords in more significant numbers than ever before, that Americans were looking to the British aristocracy as a model of elite formation. Some of these American Anglophiles were industrialists and capitalists themselves, and found London society both accessible and friendly

towards men of business. Landed aristocrats and wealthy businessmen began to mix much more freely in high society than they
had ever done before. Nevertheless, social contact was still regulated
by the rituals of Society and their effectiveness in 'screening' potential members. In the late nineteenth century the multiplication of
large non-landed fortunes imposed considerable pressures on the
formalized code of etiquette and system of introductions, which had
developed during the Victorian era. Leonore Davidoff has noted
that the 'introduction of foreign-made fortunes' resulted in 'a certain
amount of anti-Semitic and anti-Yankee feeling' but states that 'it
should be kept in perspective' because the 'whole basis of Society
was growing wider'.[9] There was a marked tendency to associate the
influx of Americans into London society with a growing commercial-
ization of high society, which indicates the unease felt by the older
elite as the cost of providing the 'theatrical show', to use Walter
Bagehot's words, spiralled.[10] If wealth became the most important
factor in determining elite membership, then many members of the
landed aristocracy were going to find it increasingly difficult to
maintain their claims to high social status with the competition of
the new millionaires.[11] The British response to Americans entering
London society and marrying into the aristocracy needs to be
considered within the wider framework of the social transformation
of the peerage after 1870 in order to understand the depth of feeling
aroused by their presence. Chapter 5 will deal with the more intimate form of the aristocratic embrace, i.e. in terms of marriage, but
first the role of Americans will be examined in the more general
context of the merger of the landed and commercial elites.

4

American invasion or aristocratic embrace? The entry of Americans into London's high society after 1870

I was lunching with a man at the Bachelor's only yesterday who swore he knew a fellow who had met a man whose cousin worked.
(P. G. Wodehouse, 'The Goalkeeper and the Plutocrat', 1911)[1]

Up until the late nineteenth century the ruling elite was synonymous with the great landed aristocracy, and membership was to a large extent hereditary. It was not a closed elite – newcomers were admitted – but access was regulated and followed certain guidelines in relation to landownership, behaviour, and life-style. The gradual erosion of political power[2] and the decline of landed income[3] from about the 1880s onwards weakened the landed elite's dominance of society and politics; but, as Michael Thompson has suggested, the 'drive to acquire status' by the upwardly mobile, combined with the 'flexibility of the social arrangements operated by the aristocracy', enabled the great landed families to survive as social arbiters.[4] These 'social arrangements' involved receptions, balls and dinners in private homes, levées, Drawing Rooms, and garden parties in royal households, and the more public events patronized by royalty and the aristocracy, such as Ascot Week, the Henley Regatta, and Cowes Week.[5] The London Season, which ran from May to July, when wealthy landed families came up to town, attracted hundreds of social climbers and foreign plutocrats. This was the time of the year when aristocratic matrons and the Prince of Wales vetted newcomers and accorded social recognition, since the rest of the year was spent either in the country or on the Continent. In 1886 a correspondent for *Harper's* claimed that the rich entered Society by securing 'the patronage of some lady within the charmed circle of the *grande monde*' who issued, on their behalf, invitations to a ball.[6] If the ball was a success and they were able to follow it up the following year, then they were regarded as being 'in Society'. The use of sponsors was a recognized part of the process by which newcomers were taken up by the social elite. Introductions, leaving cards, and calling also constituted part of the elaborate procedures for determining social acceptance. The leaving of cards, for example, was heavily invested with symbolism in a highly ritualized society which could be exceedingly intolerant of outsiders. If a person 'in Society' failed to leave a card within seven to ten days of receiving a card from a newcomer, that omission signified to the newcomer that the acquaintance would not be pursued.[7]

By the end of the Victorian period, Society had expanded enormously.[8] Although the code of conduct was maintained by and large, there was an emotive response to the widening of Society and decline in standards. Lady Dorothy Nevill described the changes thus:

> The forties and fifties were aristocratic days, when the future conquerors of Society were still 'without the gate.' The vast increase of railways, however, ended all this exclusiveness, and very soon the old social privileges of birth and breeding were swept aside by the mob of plebeian wealth which surged into the drawing rooms.[9]

Lady Dorothy Nevill is referring here to the British-based *nouveaux riches*, some of whom had acquired titles by the turn of the century. Despite her somewhat scornful attitude towards 'plebeian wealth', she acknowledged the public-spiritedness and generosity of 'this new plutocratic class' but added, pointedly, that they 'owe their present position' to the 'excellent tradesmen' from whom they are descended. In spite of old prejudices against retailers, stockbrokers, and the like, wealthy businessmen (especially financiers) found their passage into the upper social strata smoothed by the willingness of the aristocracy to align itself with the new sources of power and influence in late Victorian and Edwardian society. In fact, it was this openness of the old landed elite which, as Michael Thompson argues, helped it to survive the challenge of new wealth before First World War.[10]

Whereas in the past newcomers had been assimilated into the landed elite, by the late Victorian period the prerequisites for social recognition had changed. It was no longer essential, for a wealthy financier at least, to retire from commercial activity, purchase a landed estate, and adopt the life-style of a country gentleman.[11] This was particularly evident amongst the Prince of Wales's circle of friends which included such men as Sir Ernest Cassel, Sir Thomas Lipton, and members of the famous Rothschild family, who maintained an active interest in their business affairs. The social recognition of businessmen by high society in conjunction with the increase in the number of industrialists and commercial men raised to the peerage after 1886 were manifestations of significant shifts in the structure of Britain's ruling elite. Businessmen were increasingly accepted on their own terms; and the merger of the landed elite with commercial magnates was, in fact, a two-way process, as T. H. S. Escott put it: 'Our territorial nobles, our squires, our rural landlords great and small, have become commercial potentates; our merchant-princes have become country gentlemen.'[12] This has been confirmed by the fact that younger sons were picking up lucrative positions in the City, that peers were adding their names to the boards of directors of City firms, while corporate financiers, merchants, newspaper proprietors, and distinguished professional men were entering the country-house world, being appointed high sheriff in the counties, and sitting in the House of Lords. Such developments were not always seen in a positive light, in spite of the fact that a number of peerage families could trace their social rise back to a fortune made in trade or banking or, indeed, that some peers had profited handsomely from industrialization and urbanization by selling or renting land to railroad and construction companies or by developing the mineral resources of their land. William and Catherine Whetham, two British eugenicists, were especially concerned about the implications of this intermingling of the aristocracy with the more materialistic elements in the middle classes and took a conservative line in their approach to this change. They saw the aristocracy in terms of an honourable, self-sacrificing elite which, in performing non-remunerative public services, set 'before the nation a higher ideal than that of the market or the country house' and 'a good example . . . to the "idle rich", who fail to appreciate their moral obligation to repay in voluntary service to the community the means with which they are endowed as a trust'.[13] This romanticization of the role of the aristocracy was symptomatic of the attempt to polarize aristocratic and plutocratic ideals. Part of this may have stemmed from a resistance to social and economic change associated with urban forces, and this would explain the rhetorical overtures made to a distant and mythical past in which aristocrats were viewed as the benevolent patriarchs of a rural society. The main concern seems to have been that the aristocracy was being displaced from its pre-eminent position of power and influence by a plutocracy of wealth which was responsible for new habits of speculation amongst the old elite and for making wealth 'the ultimate end of existence'.[14]

The ennoblement of businessmen, the social recognition accorded prominent financiers by the Prince of Wales, and younger sons seeking employment in the City provide the back-drop to the entry of Americans into London society. Yet it must be said that the merger of the landed elite with commercial wealth has so far been dealt with in terms of male activities. This largely reflects the historiography of elite transformation in Britain around the turn of the century. In his study of the 'aristocratic embrace', F. M. L. Thompson has stressed the honours system, the absorption of new men into the expanding public service, and the social acceptance of new men as being the major channels of absorption.[15] Likewise, W. D. Rubinstein has concentrated on the social mobility of men in his work on 'the very wealthy'.[16] If we are to understand how Americans, and particularly American women, fit into the pattern of social change, then our concept of such change needs to replace women in the organization of elite society. Above all, we have to consider whether the aristocratic embrace, which Thompson deals with in terms of new men being taken up by the landed elite, can include women and the institution of marriage. For him 'the aristocratic embrace was more important in winning friends and followers than in leading to the marriage bed'.[17] Americans, of course, do not fit into the same category as wealthy British commoners: confining the discussion briefly to men again, American visitors did not pose the same danger to the aristocracy's influence over politics or the public service. Americans participated in the London Season to secure social recognition from an elite which had a much longer tradition of holding power and status than any which existed in the United States. It is in that respect that there is some common ground between Americans and other men of wealth in London society, and it allows for a discussion of the influence of Americans on the aristocracy's attitude towards businessmen. It is quite clear from the American point of view that the process of securing social acceptance included the marrying of daughters to members of the British elite. A marriage alliance conveniently cemented the attainment of high social status on a more permanent basis, otherwise claims to such status might have to be renewed annually, which was an expensive business. One can look upon this in two ways: either it was in the age-old tradition of social aspirants using their daughters and wealth to get a foot in the door, or it was the natural consequence of inter-elite contact in an age when transatlantic travel became much more commonplace.

There are two points, then, which need to be raised. First, did the influx of American visitors between 1870 and 1914 play any role in the transformation of Britain's landed elite into 'an upper class of varied origins'? And second, can transatlantic marriages be considered a part of this change?

The London Season, as we have noted, provided the opportunity for Americans to enter aristocratic households and be presented at court. By the time Americans began coming in large numbers to the British capital for the Season, social events were, as Leonore Davidoff has argued, mostly regulated by women, and it was the marriage market which had become Society's 'surviving claim to serious attention'.[18] A small number of British peeresses were still recognized as leaders of Society. An anonymous contributor to *Ladies' Realm* in 1896 listed the Duchesses of Buccleugh and Devonshire and Ladies Londonderry, Cadogan, Ilchester, and Ellesmere as the 'true representatives and leaders of Society', as opposed to 'the wives of the *nouveaux riches*' or 'Anglicized Americans who are always advertising themselves and their parties in the newspapers'.[19] No matter, it seems, to what extent titled Americans made their presence felt in London society with frequent and well-publicized entertainments, they did not lose their 'outsider status'. In fact, the competition of American hostesses with their British counterparts aroused considerable resentment.

Americans were highly conspicuous in their conspicuousness, especially those in the Marlborough House Set, and they quickly became associated with the hedonism and extravagances of that social clique. Sensational publicity often accompanied their activities in British society. In 1906, for example, an American newspaper gave an extensive list of 'American Capital Being Spent to Amuse His Majesty'. It included the following names:

HOW AMERICAN INCOMES ARE BEING SPENT IN ENGLAND[20]

J. Pierpont Morgan $200m
(stock tips and works of art)

A. J. Drexel $100m
(yachting parties)

Mrs Ogden Goelet $5m
(yachting parties)

Bradley Martin $15m
(deer shooting)

W. W. Astor $300m
(river fetes)

Duchess of Manchester $8m
(feeding the peasantry)

Duchess of Roxburgh $20m
(country house parties)

Duchess of Marlborough $15m
(charities, public bazaars)

Hon. Mrs Ward $5m
(pheasant shooting)

Countess of Granard $6m
(dinners and parties of all kinds)

Countess of Craven $15m
(shooting parties)

Lady Paget $6m
(small dinner parties)

Mrs A. H. Paget $10m

Lady Willoughby d'Eresby $1m

Mrs David Beatty $8m

Lady Alistair Innes-Kerr $1m

Lady Cheylesmore $3m

Viscountess Deerhurst $3m

Lady Herbert $3m

Lady Donoughmore $5m

Hon. Mrs H. Coventry $2m

Hon. Mrs F. Guest $5m

Hon. Mrs A. Johnstone $2m

Marchioness of Dufferin $2m

The intention behind the article was to expose the folly of spending American dollars for the amusement of the British monarch and in the pursuit of 'social distinction', but at the same time the article exhibits a tone of self-congratulation which suggests that Americans were able to keep up with the pace of entertaining the King. Three years earlier, the *New York World* had carried a story alleging a foreign plutocratic conspiracy involving Consuelo, Dowager Duchess of Manchester. According to the report, her houses in Grosvenor Square, Richmond, Ascot, and Biarritz were at the disposal of the King for his entertainments, and it was calculated that Consuelo must have been spending more than $25,000 a week. As her income was allegedly nowhere near that sum, the paper proferred the following speculation:

> The explanation of the mystery of her resources which is offered in court circles is that she represents a secret syndicate of million-aires, which includes Sir Ernest Cassel, Sir Thomas Lipton, Secretary Pokiewski of the Russian Embassy, some members of the Rothschild family, A. J. Drexel and several other Americans. These gentlemen jointly foot the bills, it is asserted, each contribu-ting an agreed-upon sum.[21]

The list is an impressive roll-call of the characters in the demonology of the die-hard aristocrats in British society: Jewish financiers, Russian diplomats, tradesmen, and American millionaires. It is significant that Americans are linked here with some of the more traditional victims of race and class prejudice. This was not uncommon, however, at that time: one London newspaper went so far as to compare Hebraic finesse in the money market with that of American women in the London marriage market.[22] As early as the 1870s, just when American women were beginning to figure prominently in court circles, a more forthright allegation was made about the behaviour of American women around the Prince of Wales. A group of prominent ladies of title, including the Duchesses of Leeds and Bedford, requested that Archbishop Benson organize a 'moral mission' and 'devotional meetings' for women of their class with a view to influencing aristocratic society and checking the recent decline in moral standards.[23] They attributed to Americans in the Marlborough House Set the so-called 'moral rot' that was ruining London. This kind of prejudice against Americans was much more widely expressed at the turn of the century when Americans participated in London society in much more significant numbers. Nevertheless it is interesting to note that the concern about the American 'influence' on the Prince of Wales was articulated right at the beginning of the period.

In one sense this evidence, which highlights the anxieties and fears of the aristocrats, points to a prominent role played by American women in the perception of Society's barriers being lowered. Jews and Americans were frequent targets for the critics of the growing hedonism and materialism of smart society. The focus on the 'foreign' elements in London society, together with the concentration on Edward VII, who is seen as having played an instrumental part in the social entry of plutocrats and American women,[24] tended to draw attention away from the landed aristocracy and its attempts to adapt to the shifts in economic power. It should be said, however, that transatlantic marriages were not merely fashionable because of the King's penchant for beautiful American women; rather, they were symptomatic of the social amalgamation that was going on within British society from the middle of the nineteenth century onwards.

When Americans began to flood London society from the 1870s on, the social transformation of Britain's elite was already well under way. Despite this, however, it is usual to find this change associated with the influx of Americans in memoirs of the late Victorian period. Probably the best known reference to this is Lady Dorothy Nevill's observation:

> It was in the 'seventies that two new and powerful forces began to make their influence felt in Society, for about that time Americans . . . began to come to London in considerable numbers, and then began those Anglo-American marriages which are now quite common. About this time also the Stock Exchange began to make itself felt as a social power outside the City.[25]

To Susan Tweedsmuir, a granddaughter of Lord Ebury, the entrance of the moneyed classes into London society meant prudent marriages with American heiresses and a rise in the cost of living:

> When I grew up, society was expanding and becoming more moneyed, and a less rural standard was creeping in. . . . Some eldest sons of peers married Americans and other heiresses, which buttressed the family fortunes at the cost of bringing in much higher standards of smartness in clothes and equipages.[26]

The writer Marie Corelli was more outspoken in attributing to Americans in London the new habits of conspicuous expenditure: 'America's . . . influence on the social world teaches that "dollars are the only wear". English Society has been sadly vulgarized by this American taint.'[27] Although, in retrospect, the American influence on British society and culture in the late Victorian and Edwardian years was both powerful and highly publicized, there is no evidence to suggest that Americans were the sole, or even a major, cause of the transformation of aristocratic society. Their appearance in London coincided with, rather than preceded, the entry of financiers like Baron Hirsch and Sir Ernest Cassel into the highest social circles. Americans entered London society, moreover, for virtually the same reasons as plutocrats from other countries, namely, to affirm their social status and to identify themselves with a well-established elite long used to deference and respect. In much the same way as the British themselves and other foreign millionaires, Americans bought or rented country mansions, competed for presentation at court, and provided expensive entertainments for the Prince of Wales.

The transformation of the British peerage, then, had begun long before the introduction of American brides. Throughout the nineteenth century peers used many different resources to combat the encroachment of capitalist and democratic forces upon their preserves of power. The challenge of new wealth was not new in itself. What was different after 1870 was the fact that the aristocracy could not muster the financial resources and overawe it with an even greater display of extravagance. This meant, therefore, that the barriers against commercial and industrial wealth were lowered, and the power and prestige of elite status were shared with the new captains of industry and finance. 'Entrance qualifications' were not so demanding as they had been in the past. Businessmen no longer had to spend at least two generations on the land before seeking entry into Society, and less searching questions were made of people's backgrounds, provided that they possessed the necessary supply of beauty, wit, or money to deflect close scrutiny.

The British peerage, as we have seen, was undergoing a major social transformation in the late nineteenth century, and this involved a departure from the traditions and customs of landed society. The publicity and disapproval which transatlantic marriages met with seem to suggest that they represented a significant break in the usual marriage patterns of peers and their sons and were symptomatic of the more widespread restructuring of the British elite. Michael Thompson, however, has contended that marriages with 'American heiresses' were not especially innovatory:

> The novelty and glamour of these moves to call in young and vigorous dollar stock to refresh the old and sometimes decaying English aristocracy naturally attracted attention, but they were in fact no more than a striking new version of the old established practice of marrying new wealth.[28]

At this point in his argument about the transformation of the nobility, Thompson is placing transatlantic marriages within the context of the aristocracy's 'new respect for money' and increasin tendency to marry new wealth. He has maintained the view, too, that the aristocracy held its position until the First World War.[29] But what began as the traditional operation of the aristocratic embrace in the 1870s could no longer regulate the rate at which aristocrats were marrying brides from overseas rather than daughters of large landowners in Britain. Just taking the numbers for peeresses alone (and only those whose husbands were peers or the heir at the time of marriage between 1870 and 1914), there were at least four American peeresses in 1880 and over fifty by 1914. In addition to this there were the American wives of younger sons, baronets and knights who swelled the ranks of the titled British elite. Even if there had not been a world war to deplete the ranks of the landed aristocracy and cripple it with death duties, their displacement would still have occurred: the signs were there in the years after 1870. However, there is a further point to be made about Thompson's interpretation of transatlantic marriages. American heiresses did not comprise all the American brides in the British peerage. Many of the women were wealthy by British standards, but very few were heiresses in the conventional sense of the term. Only two women left over half a million pounds at death; one was a peeress and the other the wife of a younger son. Moreover, not all American marriages signified a response to a fall in income. As we shall see in a later chapter, it was not necessarily those peers worst hit by the agricultural depression who married Americans. Transatlantic marriages were, therefore, neither by their conception nor by their effect, a mere repetition of old solutions to financial problems. In fact, a surprising number of titled Americans left very little money at death.

In his study of peerage marriage patterns, T. H. Hollingsworth has asserted that marriages by peers to commoners (i.e. exogamous marriages) reflected major social transformation during two periods when there was a marked change in the proportion of commoner spouses to nobles. The first period was in the reign of George II, from around 1710 to 1735, and the second in the late nineteenth century, between 1870 and 1895. The causes of the first 'revolution' are not clear, though Hollingsworth has suggested that the social rise of the City merchant may have been a factor. The reasons for the second, however, are more apparent:

> This is more familiar as a time of social transformation, and the peerage was then beginning to be affected by manufacturers and by American millionaires. It marks a second stage in the process by which the peerage has gradually ceased to be identical with the ruling class. Instead of turning in upon itself, the nobility has sought to keep some of its prestige by marrying with money or distinction.[30]

Thompson has queried Hollingsworth's use of the term 'commoner' in his analysis, because it includes daughters of the landed gentry who were a traditional source of brides for peers.[31] He nevertheless endorses Hollingsworth's general conclusion about the late nineteenth-century period. A further point that might be raised with regard to Hollingsworth's use of terminology is whether, in fact, the peerage did become less synonymous with the ruling class. It was not the peerage which, at this point in time, ceased to be identical with the ruling class but the landed elite, because, as we have noted earlier, the peerage was broadening its social base and strengthening its links with the new sources of economic and political power. Apart from these questionable interpretations of the data, the main point, however, still holds good, i.e. that towards the end of the nineteenth century there was an upswing in exogamous marriages. If gentry alliances were a more or less constant factor in the nineteenth century, then the increase in marriages to commoners can probably be accounted for by alliances with the daughters of businessmen and industrialists, Americans included.

It should also be noted that some of the peers and younger sons with American wives were businessmen themselves. They include:

4th Earl of Camperdown	associate of a London engineering firm
Viscount Deerhurst	mining interests in Australia; member of the London Stock Exchange
8th Earl of Egmont	proprietor of a cement business
3rd Baron Fermoy	rancher and miner in the United States
Baron Lawrence (younger son)	director of railroad and other companies
3rd Baron Revelstoke	director of Baring Brothers Ltd
9th Earl of Sandwich	company director
14th Earl of Winchilsea	member of the London Stock Exchange

Four of these men left over £100,000 in personalty at death, and two of them had married wealthy women. Baron Queensborough is an interesting case, although he has been excluded from the case group because he was the grandson of the first Marquis of Anglesey and raised to the peerage after his first marriage to an American. His alliance through marriage with a prominent New York business family proved advantageous. In the 1870s he had sailed to America with five pounds in his pocket to seek his fortune. After working on a ranch in the West, he had invested his money in Minnesota real estate, which had given him an excellent rate of return.[32] After his marriage he became involved in the management of several companies, including the Chihuahua and Pacific Railroad, Siemen Brothers & Co. Ltd, Caxton Electric Developments, and the Third Canadian Development Trust. This marriage would appear to signify a departure from more traditional, aristocratic patterns of career and marriage. There is no definite trend of peers or younger sons breaking away from the more usual career patterns having married outside the aristocracy, but the fact that some business peers married Americans, or that some peers or younger sons became involved in commercial enterprises after their marriage, seems to suggest that transatlantic marriages were part of the general move within the peerage away from established patterns of career and marriage.

In conclusion, it is apparent that Americans were an integral part of the transformation. Their arrival in London coincided with the period when social barriers were relaxed, and many were able to take full advantage of this in their pursuit of social recognition by the most prestigious hereditary elite in western Europe. The more socially ambitious Americans rented or bought mansions owned by aristocrats, entertained lavishly in London society, patronized the same institutions as British aristocrats, and married into the peerage. Even if their contemporaries did no more than record the extravagant new habits Americans introduced into London society and their financial contributions to the survival of some landed families, the social acceptance of American plutocrats nevertheless entailed more than their paying generously for their pleasures. In fact, their social success contributed to the acceptance of a business ethic which was reflected in the flight of young aristocrats to the City and their growing fascination with the stock market. Some British aristocrats, like Moreton Frewen, brother-in-law of Lady Randolph Churchill, were genuinely inspired by the successes of self-made American businessmen, if not allured by the possibilities of quick fortunes to be made by investing in American mineral resources, cattle ranches, or railroads.

Transatlantic marriages were indicative of a general trend among the landed peers to break with ancient tradition and pursue careers not previously invested with gentlemanly status, to find alternative sources of income more remunerative than land, and to marry outside conventional circles. These marriages may well have been regarded as a short cut to wealth, a less painful form of adaptation to the new social arrangements, and certainly less drastic than selling land or going into business; but it must be noted that, once taboos against commerce were lifted, it became much easier and more natural for peers *without* pressing financial reasons to associate themselves with new wealth.

The humorous reference in P. G. Wodehouse's short story, quoted at the beginning of the chapter, to the difficulty aristocrats had in comprehending paid work points to what was, in fact, for them a serious problem. Both the economic climate of the period and the shift in attitude towards commerce and industry as a source of employment and wealth, if not wives, were encouraging more and more members of the landed classes to abandon time-honoured ways and to widen their circle of acquaintance. 'The Goalkeeper and the Plutocrat' ends appropriately with the Earl's son marrying the plutocrat's daughter and joining his father-in-law in cornering the wheat market, whilst the plutocrat declares that he will ring the Prime Minister and buy a title.

5

The London marriage market

The lowering of social barriers to aristocratic society in the late nineteenth century had important repercussions on the London marriage market. With high birth no longer an essential determinant of elite membership, it was easier for resourceful young women of beauty and personality outside aristocratic circles to gain access to men of higher social standing than themselves. This, in turn, exacerbated a demographic imbalance within the marriage market and caused much concern within aristocratic families trying to find suitable marriage partners for their daughters. The crisis was all the more acute for landed families suffering from a fall in income as a result of the agricultural depression, since their daughters now had to compete against women with superior financial resources from the wealthy business classes, foreign and British. There had always been marital alliances with the daughters of bankers or successful businessmen, but the growing acceptance of alliances outside traditional aristocratic circles, together with the influx of foreign plutocratic families, seemed to threaten the entire fabric of aristocratic social arrangements at the turn of the century.

Much of the resentment felt towards Americans in London society stemmed from pressures within the marriage market and contributed to the stereotyping of American women as 'forward hussies' and adventuresses. At the same time, it was commonly assumed that American women were married because their dowries were generous, producing another stereotype, that of the impoverished peer. The question of money is central to the perception of transatlantic marriages, but before looking into this aspect, we need to understand the overall pattern of marriages and the aristocratic strategy governing the formation of alliances. As this was a time of considerable social change, particularly with regard to the status of women, we have to take account of the factors governing choice of spouse and the way in which these affected the operation of the aristocratic marriage market. Second, there is the financial side to aristocratic marriages, i.e. marriage settlements, which needs to be discussed in relation to the growing concern about the materialistic nature of personal relationships.

Marriage performed two basic functions within aristocratic society. First, it was a means of regulating membership of the landed elite. Demographic studies of the British peerage have shown that endogamy, i.e. marriages within the peerage, was an important principle governing aristocratic marriages and that, even though most members of the peerage married outside the peerage, their spouses were usually chosen from the wider gentlemanly class.[1] Marriages of both the daughters and sons of peers were a reflection of the social standing both of individual families and of the peerage as a whole, which was matter of pride for peers.[2] They provided important opportunities for peerage families to reaffirm or improve their social status, to increase their influence in political spheres, and to improve their financial standing. Individual families could personally vet newcomers and, in the light of certain advantages to be gained by an alliance, could assess their suitability in terms of behaviour, respectability, and financial status. In the case of a prospective bridegroom from outside the peerage, his credentials would be considered with regard to his conformity to the gentlemanly code of conduct, his social background and career, and his capacity to maintain an aristocrat's daughter in the style to which she was accustomed. In the case of a prospective bride, the subject of such scrutiny was more likely to be her father, because women generally took their status from men. Seen from the point of view of the peerage as a whole, marriage provided an opportunity not only to maintain the prestige of the nobility, but also to assimilate rival groups or upwardly mobile individuals.[3] A very fine balance had to be struck between accommodating new socio-economic groups and successful members of the upper-middle class, and protecting the social calibre of the peerage.

Second, marriage was essential for the continuation of the male line and the transmission of property. In a world governed by the principle of primogeniture, the marriage of the heir was particularly crucial to the survival of the main branch of the family and the preservation of the estate. This is not to say that the marriages of siblings were unimportant or less bound by strategic decisions concerning a family's advancement, for they, too, involved the transfer of property. Dowries for daughters and annuities for younger sons, for example, had to come from the same patrimony, and it was therefore important to arrange these outgoings in accordance with the size of the estate. The marriages of heirs, however, were more strictly governed by social convention since their choice was largely determined by the need to maintain the family's prestige and financial standing.

If caste-consciousness was so important in the contracting of aristocratic marriages, what implications did this have for transatlantic marriages and the peerage? In her study of marriages made by the daughters of Scottish peers, Patricia Otto has argued that the strong sense of caste within the aristocracy severely prescribed the circle from which a peer's daughter could draw her lifetime partner. While her brother could marry a wealthy businessman's daughter and have the alliance sanctioned by the family, she could not, by the same token, marry a businessman without adversely affecting her social position and risking ostracism.[4] If women in the peerage were reluctant to marry into the classes below, or even prevented by family pressures or social conventions from doing so, then their position in the marriage market was a particularly difficult one. Apart from the competition with women of non-aristocratic background, they also had to contend with a shrinking supply of eligible marriage partners, as the younger sons of peers were either delaying marriage or not marrying at all.[5] The difference in attitude towards daughters' marriages, then, exacerbated the problem of sexual imbalance in the marriage market, but it was the increasing competition from American women for aristocratic husbands that was usually seen as the main cause of the shortage of suitable male spouses.

David Thomas also deals with the question of caste or, rather, with what he refers to as 'exclusivity' in his study of the social origins of marriage partners in the British peerage. He asserts that the decline in the proportion of endogamous marriages towards the end of the nineteenth century was related to an increase in marriages with the daughters of foreigners rather than with the daughters of commoners.[6] This, he then argues, 'has important consequences for an evaluation of the social exclusivity of the peerage' in that less emphasis can be placed on the marriages to the daughters of businessmen or manufacturers. Moreover, foreign alliances, even if 'motivated by material gains', represented less of a threat to the exclusiveness of the peerage than marriages to British commoners. However, this raises a problem. Thomas did not break down his category of foreigners by occupation and include them in his category of commoner marriages. There seems to be little justification in distinguishing between foreigners and commoners when the aim is to analyse the social origins of spouses. By treating foreign marriages in a separate category without further comment on the social origins of foreign women marrying peers and younger sons, Thomas has underestimated the number of alliances with daughters of businessmen and industrialists. Second, with regard to the claim that foreign marriages posed less of a threat to the exclusivity of the peerage, Anglo-American marriages, which formed a substantial proportion of all foreign marriages, were, I would suggest, symptomatic of a move away from landed wealth.

We can verify these counter-arguments by using information about the social origins of spouses in both the case and control groups. The control groups comprise almost all the marriages of British peers in the decades 1880–9 and 1900–9, with the major exception of those involving American women as these constitute parts of the case group. If we add the transatlantic marriages which occurred in the 1880s and 1900s to the appropriate control group, we then have more or less complete figures for peerage marriages in these years, bearing in mind the method of selecting both case and control groups. Table 5.1 breaks down the information available about the fathers of women who married peers in the two specified decades in terms of whether they were nobles or commoners and in terms of the occupation of untitled commoners. Foreigners who were not members of the nobility have been kept as a separate category. The figures in Table 5.1 more or less confirm Thomas's findings that the proportion of in-marriages, i.e. those marriages of peers (or heirs) with the daughters of peers (or heirs), was declining after 1870. His figures show that slightly less than one in two heirs (approximately 42 per cent of all marriages by heirs) married within the nobility up to c. 1870, with the proportion falling to one in three (approximately 30 per cent) thereafter.

Because Thomas's figures are based on birth cohorts, it is not possible to give precise dates for the decline of in-marriages.[7]

Table 5.1 Numbers and proportions of marriages made by peers to the daughters of nobles and commoners, broken down by rank or occupation, in the decades 1880–9 and 1900–9, with Americans listed as foreigners and not by occupation

Rank or occupation of wife's father	Peers who married 1880–9		Peers who married 1900–9	
	No.	%	No.	%
Nobility:				
Peer	47		39	
Royalty	1	32.07	0	19.90
Foreign noble	3		2	
Other titles:				
Baronet	13	8.18	12	8.25
Knight	0		5	
Commoners:				
Relative of peer or baronet	26	16.35	39	18.93
Landed gentry	12	7.55	30	14.56
Public service	1		1	
Military officer	4		8	
MP	5		2	
Clergyman	4	8.81	3	8.74
Professional	0		3	
Actor	0		1	
Foreigners	14	8.81	26	12.62
Unlisted	29	18.24	35	16.99
	159	100.01	206	99.99

Table 5.1 shows that the decline in endogamous marriages from 32.07 per cent in the 1880s to 19.81 per cent in the 1900s is almost compensated for by the twofold increase in marriages with the daughters of landed gentry, whereas Thomas has found a decline in the proportion of marriages with the gentry in the late nineteenth century.[8] The proportion of marriages within the traditional aristocratic circle thus remained virtually constant over the two decades. As *Burke's Peerage* tends not to supply information about the occupation of the wife's father, unless he is a member of the landed or

titled elite, a large number of men are shown as foreigners or unlisted.

Using our information about transatlantic marriages, it is possible to break down the occupations of American fathers-in-law and list them according to the categories of commoners used in Table 5.1. American alliances accounted for 71.43 per cent and 67.86 per cent of the foreign marriages listed in Table 5.1 (that is, 6.29 per cent and 9.22 per cent of all marriages in the 1880s and 1900s, respectively), and so information concerning the social origins of American brides will make an important contribution to the overall picture of marriage patterns in the British peerage. Of the 29 American peeresses included in Table 5.1, we have details of the occupation of 22 of their fathers. Some men had more than one profession during their life time, and so the first occupation has been taken. The highest proportion of American women, approximately one-third, came from families in the business classes, but it is interesting to note that slightly more than a quarter of them also came from families in the traditional gentlemanly class in the British sense, i.e. lawyers and military officers.

Men previously listed as foreigners in Table 5.1 have been reclassified in Table 5.2. They have either been listed according to their occupation or included with other commoners whose occupation is unknown. As we have noted, Thomas contended that the decline of in-marriages could not be explained by an increase in marriages to the daughters of businessmen or manufacturers alone. It is apparent from Table 5.2, however, that there was a very small increase in the alliances with businessmen's daughters which were previously included in the foreigner category.[9]

Until more is known about the marriages of peers with commoners, Thomas's assertion must remain unsubstantiated. The difference in the proportions of endogamous and exogamous marriages between the two decades seems to indicate that commoners were becoming increasingly important as a source of brides for peers. Some commoners were traditionally linked with the nobility, such as the gentry, the military, the church, and the legal profession, and together they formed the outer perimeters of aristocratic society. The increase in alliances with the business and, to a much lesser extent, acting professions, however, seems to indicate that towards the end of Victoria's reign Society was beginning to recognize wealth, beauty, and talent more openly. The ability to

Table 5.2 Numbers and proportions of marriages made by peers to the daughters of nobles and commoners, broken down by rank or occupation, in the decades 1880–9 and 1900–9, with Americans listed according to their occupation

Rank of occupation of wife's father	Peers who married 1880–9		Peers who married 1900–9	
	No.	%	No.	%
Nobility	51	32.08	41	19.90
Other title or relative	39	24.53	56	27.18
Landed gentry	12	7.55	30	14.56
Public service	1		1	
Military officer	6		10	
Politician	5		2	
Clergyman	4	12.58	3	14.56
Professional	1		4	
Actor	0		1	
Businessman	3		9	
Unlisted	37	23.27	49	23.79
	159	100.01	206	99.99

entertain or be entertaining was quickly becoming a passport to smart society, and the fact that peers were marrying actresses and businessmen's daughters is a clearer indication of the improving social status of such women than their entry into elite circles would suggest.

Matrimonial negotiations assumed an air of urgency in the late Victorian era when families in the landed elite attempted to pursue a course that would prolong their domination of government and society. Yet, during this period when daughters of the aristocracy were facing stiffer competition in the marriage market, the whole process of courtship and marriage was being questioned by the generation entering the market around 1870. Children were beginning to exert greater autonomy over the decision as to when and whom to marry.

In the sixteenth century, arranged marriages constituted the norm within the titled aristocracy, but since then there has been a gradual shift away from the parental control of mate-selection, first towards a situation where the child vetoed the parents' choice of spouse, and then to one where the parents had a veto on their children's choice. These changes in the patterns of courtship and parental supervision have been well documented by Lawrence Stone.[10] By about 1870 the system of courtship in aristocratic circles had entered its present phase whereby children were able to make their own choice of partner without necessarily having to defer to the parental veto. In practice, however, parents were still able to exercise considerable control over the selection of a spouse. Financial restrictions could be placed on a younger son's allowance or a daughter's dowry. More important, however, was the exercise or parental influence through social conventions concerning etiquette and gentility and through the operations of Society in general.[11] The formal nature of Society and the restrictions on access, even though these were becoming more relaxed towards the end of the nineteenth century, enabled aristocratic parents to control indirectly whom their progeny met outside the home. The Countess of Malmesbury, in a contribution to a book about the modern marriage market, justified the existence of the London Season as an opportunity for young people of the same class to meet and for parents to supervise the arrangements. In her opinion, too many marriages were taking place between people of different classes and nationalities and they were turning out badly. According to Lady Malmesbury, upper-class girls with little notion of the value of money and incapable of judging the merits of a prospective husband required careful guidance.[12]

Although children were claiming an increasing share of the initiative in selecting their marital partners, a number of factors severely limited their freedom of choice. Towards the end of the nineteenth century the daughters of aristocrats faced a crisis in the marriage market: spinsterhood was on the increase. Patricia Otto gives the figure for British peers' daughters who remained single as one in three.[13] Spinsterhood became a much-discussed phenomenon in Victorian England. In ladies' magazines of the day, articles about 'old maids' and employment for gentlewomen multiplied.[14] The Census Report for England and Wales confirmed that unmarried women in the age group 15 to 45 years outnumbered unmarried men by 11 to 10, but the growing proportion of spinsters between 1851 and 1911 was related to a sexual imbalance in the population rather than a growing tendency of women choosing to remain single.[15]

To what extent the rising incidence of spinsterhood amongst

daughters of the aristocracy was seen as a crisis is hard to determine. We can nevertheless speculate that the prospect of having unmarried daughters on their hands was not one which was cherished by aristocratic matrons. Victorians tended to regard spinsters as abnormal. Medical opinion supported this view because of the overriding concern with woman's reproductive ability and belief that a woman who did not marry and have children was at risk to uterine disorders and, of course, hysteria.[16] So strong was the belief that women should marry and fulfil their natural duty that most mothers would have regarded it as their responsibility to ensure that their daughters took their 'rightful' place in Society. In fact, seven anxious Belgravian mothers wrote to *The Times* in 1861 complaining that an openly recognized anti-matrimonial element pervaded Society.[17] Spinsterhood was, quite simply, blamed on men being unwilling to marry. The reluctance of some men to marry may be attributed to the fortunes of younger sons, which were an important variable in the London marriage market.[18] Changes in their financial circumstances had repercussions on the supply of eligible aristocratic men. With the opening up of the traditional gentlemanly professions to men of middle-class backgrounds and the retrenchment of some aristocratic families, some younger sons of landed aristocrats were being edged out of positions formerly within the scope of aristocratic patronage. Colonial or military service abroad became more attractive to younger sons wishing to maintain their aristocratic life-style, because the cost of living tended to be lower than in Britain. Whilst serving with the 4th Hussars in India, Winston Churchill found that he could afford a higher standard of living and maintained a rented bungalow with two acres, stables for thirty horses, and three butlers.[19] The paucity of Englishwomen of gentle birth in colonial society also provided for a more informal, male-dominated society with fewer demands on limited resources. The attractions of life abroad, then, took younger sons out of the marriage market, either temporarily or even permanently.

Growing material expectations inhibited opportunities for marriage. Men of the middle and upper classes usually delayed marrying until they could afford to set up their own establishment in a style to which they were accustomed. However, with the rise in the cost of living in London society in the late nineteenth century, the delay may have been even more prolonged. Amongst the control groups the age at which peers made their first marriage was higher in the 1900s than in the 1880s; there was an increase of approximately 8 per cent of men aged 30 or more who married for the first time. Younger sons in the control groups tended to marry at a later age than their elder or eldest brother, and the corresponding increase for them in the over-30 age group was 11 per cent. This tendency to marry at a later age is reflected in the transatlantic groups of peers and younger sons but with a markedly higher proportion of men marrying at the age of 35 or more than in the control groups. Most of the men with American brides, nevertheless, married between the ages of 25 and 29.

Reasons for men marrying later in life and the continued trend of younger sons to marry later than their elder brothers in the late nineteenth and early twentieth centuries were probably much the same as in the period covered by Lawrence Stone in *The Family, Sex and Marriage*. That is to say, the continuing increase in the autonomy of children over mate selection and, as far as younger sons were concerned, the need for an aristocrat to establish himself in a career and accumulate sufficient capital to enable him to marry within the elite were prime factors in the trend towards later marriages.[20] Improvements in health standards and child care, which reduced infant mortality rates significantly in the nineteenth century, may provide another possible explanation for men delaying marriage, particularly eldest sons, who had the additional pressure of producing an heir. Bachelorhood was also on the increase towards the end of the Victorian period. Thomas's figures show that the highest incidence of bachelorhood occurred in the cohort of peers' sons born between 1870 and 1879.[21] One in three males in the cohort never married, and of these the majority were younger sons. To what extent this was a matter of personal preference, rather than something enforced by financial circumstances, is again difficult to judge, but the increase in unmarried men and the tendency, within the peerage, to delay marriages undoubtedly contributed to a shortage of eligible male spouses in the marriage market which had to be filled from groups outside the nobility.

In her analysis of peerage marriages, Patricia Otto has suggested that spinsterhood was not necessarily caused by a shortage of marriage partners – daughters of peers did, after all, present an opportunity for social mobility for men from the wider aristocracy – but reflected, rather, a growing preference of women for spinsterhood.[22] The idea of women choosing to remain single was, of course, a threat to the 'cult of domesticity' and to the idea of marriage as woman's vocation; and it is not surprising, therefore, that contemporaries should have blamed men, as the Belgravian mothers writing to *The Times* did, for anti-matrimonialism and should have accused them of not fulfilling their duties. Because of the few opportunities they had for the attainment of financial independence, spinsterhood was less attractive to women of the middle classes, but for daughters of peers with a personal allowance, on the other hand, spinsterhood may have been a preferable alternative to marriage *per se* or to marriage with a commoner. No doubt the Belgravian mothers were of a generation which had experienced a higher probability of marriage and felt that their daughters ought to marry. Blaming men for remaining single was bound to strike a sensitive chord in a society which placed such a high value on marriage. Later, however, the blame was shifted to American women and to the alleged tendency of men to marry for money.[23] Money was, after all, at the heart of the matter, and the apparent increased emphasis given to the material benefits of marriage threatened to discredit the holy institution.

Otto's work shows that the way in which the situation in the marriage market was perceived by aristocratic matrons bore little relation to the actual reasons for the increase in the number of unmarried women, and it is this gap between illusion and reality which is particularly pertinent to this study of the American heiress stereotype. It is less important to know, in some ways, whether aristocratic daughters were choosing to remain single than to know that certain elements in high society regarded this development as deplorable and blamed anyone or any group of people who encouraged it.[24]

The growth of child autonomy over mate selection may provide some explanation for the increase in exogamous marriages. It is possible that the increase in such marriages reflected the trend towards companionate marriage and the relaxation of elite social barriers, but the most popular explanation provided by the newspapers and contemporary social commentators was the desire for financial gain. This concentration on the financial details of prospective marriages and the frequent criticisms of aristocratic mothers for selling their daughters may actually stem from a conflict of ideas about the nature of marriage as well as from a growing feminist consciousness about the limitations placed on women's lives. The notion of companionate marriage had wide currency amongst the middle classes, and their condemnation of aristocrats marrying for money may be an explicit criticism of elite social arrangements. Changing attitudes towards (1) marriage settlements and (2) heiresses illustrate this divergence in views.

Marriage settlements had long been a traditional feature of matrimonial alliances within the landed classes. The business side of marriage arrangements was shrouded under a sacred cloth of tradition and accepted formality, and solicitors were usually left to deal with the legal intricacies. Contributions towards a couple's maintenance and provisions for offspring of the marriage came from the two families involved. The contribution from the wife's family was known as the dowry, or portion, and this was settled on the couple, though the husband usually held control of it, and the wife was allowed a small sum known as pin money. The husband's sole right to dispose of his wife's property, which came to him on marriage, was curtailed by the Married Women's Property Acts of 1870 and 1882.[25] One of the first Americans to be initiated into the English custom of marriage settlements was Leonard Jerome.[26] He proposed to settle an annual income of £2,000, on his daughter Jennie alone and a third of his fortune upon his death.[27] The Duke's lawyer informed Lord Randolph that the proposed trust deed was not in accordance with English custom, that is to say that the bulk of the dowry should have been settled on Lord Randolph for life with a small amount of pin money settled on Jennie for her personal use. Jerome was persuaded to modify his settlement despite his reservations about making his daughter 'so entirely dependent' upon her husband. It was not, he assured the Duke, anything to do with his lack of trust in Lord Randolph but a question of American customs.[28] Worn down by the bitter haggling over the negotiations, Jerome could not resist a passing shot at the nature of English marriage settlements: 'My daughter although not a Russian Princess is an American and ranks precisely the same and you have doubtless seen that the Russian settlement recently published claimed *everything* for the bride'.[29] Perhaps Jerome felt that the negotiations had been designed to imply his inferior social position by forcing him to make repeated concessions.

Negotiations over marriage settlements were sometimes a major stumbling-block in Anglo-American marriages and could cause acute embarrassment. The Duke of Roxburghe, who eventually married the Goelet heiress, allegedly broke off discussions with William Astor over the marriage settlement for his daughter Pauline. The *New York Evening Journal* reported that the Duke had objected 'to the stringency of the marriage settlement as arranged by Mr Astor. He considers this stringency offensive to his personal dignity and social position.'[30] The undisclosed reason for this stringency may well have been similar to what Leonard Jerome had had in mind, namely, that the dowry should be for the sole use of his daughter.

Another common feature of aristocratic marriages was the value placed on heiresses in the marriage market. They were considered prize catches, especially if a marriage involved a transfer of landed property to the husband's family. Christopher Clay had shown, however, that this was not always the case.[31] He argues that brides with large dowries were more effective than heiresses in rescuing or enhancing a family's fortune. In the nineteenth century popular interest nevertheless concentrated on the heiress as a figure indicating the priority of material motives in marriage. Anthony Trollope, for example, presented the clichéd view of heiresses in his novel *The Way We Live Now* (1875) in the following manner:

In such families as his [Lord Nidderdale's], when such results have been achieved, it is generally understood that matters shall be put right by an heiress. It has become an institution, like primogeniture, and is almost as serviceable for maintaining the proper order of things. Rank squanders money; trade makes it; – and then trade purchases rank by re-gilding its splendour.[32]

A further example is afforded by the *Sixpenny Magazine*. In 1861 it published an article on 'Heiress Hunters', condemning those aristocrats who, empty of pocket, preferred to acquire wealth through the labour of others, i.e. in the form of dowries, rather than soil their hands with the ink of commerce'.[33] These two examples seem to indicate that the notion of heiresses was associated with exploitation by potential suitors and husbands; but, with regard to American heiresses, as we shall see, the idea of men exploiting wealthy women was completely reversed.

By far the most outspoken critic of the aristocratic marriage market was Marie Corelli. She bitterly attacked the sale of women:

It is an absolute grim fact that in England, women – those of the upper classes, at any rate – are not today married, but bought for a price. The high and noble intention of marriage is entirely lost sight of in the scheming, the bargaining and the pricing.[34]

She denounced the London Season in no uncertain terms, calling it a cattle show, where young women were paraded in public and sold to the highest bidder.[35] The writer George Moore depicted the predicament of young women in the marriage market in his novel *A Drama in Muslin* (1886). Through the eyes of the protagonist, Alice Barton, Moore renders the degradation and humiliation experienced by young women brought out in Dublin society at a time when the Irish landed gentry was experiencing acute financial difficulty. The moment of self-revelation occurs for Alice when she is sitting on the high benches with the chaperons at the state ball, having had only one waltz with an 'old man of sixty' while her beautiful younger sister is in constant demand:

> she thought of the resultless life, the life of white idleness that awaited nearly all of them. What were they but snow-flakes born to shine for a moment and then to fade, to die, to disappear, to become part of the black, the foul-smelling slough of mud below? . . . And by what delicate degrees is the soul befouled in this drama of muslin, and how little is there left for any use of life when, after torture and disgrace, the soul, that was once so young, appears on the stage for the fourth act.[36]

Moore's stated intention was to write a critique of the position of women in the Irish landholding class, and he claimed to be 'the passionless observer, who, unbiased by political creed, comments impartially on the matter submitted to him for analysis'.[37] Despite his claims to objectivity, Moore's motivation for writing on such a topic must be seen in the light of his own social position – he owned over 12,000 acres in Mayo – his personal experience of the Dublin marriage market, and his choice of a topical subject with which his middle-class readership was already familiar. Likewise, Corelli, twelve years later, was addressing a female readership aware of the tawdrier aspects of the marriage market. The manner in which both Moore and Corelli treat the subject in their respective genres is full of moral outrage, and their ultimate intention appears to have been to attack the social elite and its cultural hegemony. The aristocracy was, after all, supposed to be socially superior and was therefore expected to be exemplary in matters of morality, honour, and behaviour. There is no doubt whatsoever that Corelli blamed the aristocracy for the moral and social blight, as she called it, of modern society. She accused the British aristocracy of a laxity in morals and an indifference towards marriage vows.[38] It is significant that, in replying to Corelli's attack, two titled ladies argued that the extravagance and worldliness of the present generation were exceptional neither to their class nor to modern times. Both Lady Jeune and the Countess of Malmesbury adopted moral tones, and Lady Jeune, in particular, maintained that girls enjoyed society, the gaiety, and 'the *wholesome* excitement which a season gives them'.[39]

Neither Moore nor Corelli referred specifically to American women in their attack on the London marriage market. Both were, in fact, sympathetic to Americans and welcomed their entry into London society.[40] Their criticism of aristocratic marital arrangements was confined to a discussion of the way in which prices were placed on daughters' heads and their mothers manoeuvred within the market to secure the best deal for the family. The system whereby the marriage of a daughter involved the transmission of wealth was, after all, a feature of life in the British landed classes, and if wealthy Americans were successful in adapting to it, then this was less a reflection of their rapacity than of the vulnerability of the marital system to fluctuations in the size of dowries being offered. But this, needless to say, was not the point of view taken by those aristocrats unable to compete with the new plutocrats. Indeed, the reaction to Americans marrying peers, as recorded in the British press, exposed the worst features of aristocratic social conventions in a way that made Moore's and Corelli's comments almost redundant. An example of this act of unconscious self-incrimination can be found amongst George Smalley's observations on English life. Smalley, an American correspondent, noted the British reaction to the marriage of Mrs Hammersley to the Duke of Marlborough in 1888, which, according to him, revived interest in transatlantic marriages. He quoted the comment of a British lady on 'the American invasion', reported by a prominent Conservative journal: she had called American girls 'sad poachers'.[41] Smalley also observed that the 'English Mother' tended to regard the 'American Girl' as 'the most formidable of competitors' – a term he found particularly coarse.[42]

The description of American women as 'poachers' or 'invaders' not only betrays the anxiety felt about the diminishing opportunities of British aristocratic girls in the marriage market, but also exposes the whole conceptualization of marriage as a desperate measure to assure, at best, a family's social position or to avoid, at worst, the humiliation of having unmarried daughters. As we have already noted, a daughter's marriage was a reflection of her family's social and financial standing. Leaving aside personal factors, if she married 'well', this would seem to indicate a sizeable dowry or the importance of the family in society or both. Appearances were all important: whatever the real reasons were for an individual marriage, the status of the husband invested the union with a particular meaning in terms of aristocratic social conventions.[43] Conversely, if a daughter married 'poorly', this would be interpreted as a set-back to her family's financial position and social progress. A letter written by Mary Harcourt to her stepmother-in-law (both women were American) gives some indication of contemporary attitudes towards daughters in London society:

> Poor Mildred Chelsea isn't it *cruel* luck. 5 Girls!!! What an inflic-tion she will now say 'not only have I got 5 girls (instead of 4) but I have got to find 5 fools to marry them' which was her speech when she was blessed with 4 daughters.[44]

Clearly, a large number of daughters are viewed here as a distinct disadvantage. First, they increased the financial burden on the patrimony, because dowries or allowances had to be provided for each daughter. Second, it was unlikely, unless the family was wealthy and prestigious, that all the daughters would marry, and if the dowries had to be small on account of there being five daugh-ters then the opportunities for making important alliances and promoting the family's position were reduced. Leaving aside these implications, however, Lady Chelsea's statement underlines the acceptance of the deep-seated assumption that girls should marry and discloses, or hints at, the difficulty of finding husbands.[45] The use of the words 'infliction' and 'fools' also makes plain the degra-dation of aristocratic women.

George Smalley attempted to explain the desirability of American girls in London society, albeit in clichéd terms, by pointing to the isolation and subordination of young English girls in the aristocracy. On coming out, he wrote in 1889, the English girl is still in the nursery . . . still the nonentity, still the shy, silent, unformed creature she was. She is not sure of herself, or of anybody else. She has no conversation. . . . She has been taught to be timid. Opinions, ideas, initiative of her own, the meeting on equal terms with youngsters in black coats and white ties, any kind of frank friendly intercourse, any knowledge of the world or of life – all these things are to her forbidden.[46]

Biographical evidence confirms Smalley's impression of the restrictions placed on the freedom and enjoyment of young Englishwomen. Lady Randolph Churchill, for example, recalled: 'To go by oneself in a hansom was thought very "fast" – not to speak of walking, which could be permitted only in quiet squares or streets.'[47] She was writing here of the rules of behaviour for young married women. Englishwomen also found the rules overwhelming:

No longer a fledgling, I was allowed more liberty and choice after the first year. I was still forbidden to be alone with a man except by chance in the country. A married woman must bring me home from a ball. For walking and shopping and even driving in a taxi, a sister or a girl was enough protection.[48]

This illustrates Smalley's point that 'The relations between the sexes in youth are ten times more natural, genuine, and right in America than in England' and explains why the lack of inhibition displayed by an American woman was mistaken in Britain for forwardness and lack of breeding.[49] Apart from defending the American girl against the charge of forwardness, Smalley also defended her against the accusation that it was the size of her dowry which ensured her success. He felt Englishwomen could have been as well endowed as Americans in terms of both education and money had it not been for primogeniture: 'If English fathers persist in sacrificing their daughters to their sons,' he asked, 'what else can be expected?'[50] These sentiments are echoed by Consuelo Vanderbilt Balsan's comments on English life:

I pitied the limited outlook given by so restricted an education, and wondered what chance a girl so brought up had against a boy with a public school and college background. Later on I was to find that English girls suffered many handicaps, and I came to realize it was considered fitting that their interests would be sacrificed to the more important prospects of the heir.[51]

On the more positive side, Smalley accounted for the success of the American girl in the London marriage market by referring to her personality and manners. Although he asked that each marriage be judged on its own merits, he was not averse to offering a few generalizations about the American girl's attractions. Neither forward, as British matrons claimed, nor timid like English girls, the American girl succeeded in London society because of 'her sense of equality'.[52] Smalley was not alone in pointing to this characteristic. The following appeared in a New York newspaper as a quotation from an American lady explaining to a titled foreigner the attraction of American girls: 'From early childhood they are trained to habits of self-reliance and independence. I think . . . they are taught to be "not afraid" of people, and that alone indicates a sense of graceful ease in manners and conversation'.[53] This sense of equality is illustrated by the attitude of Hannah Whitall Smith (mother of Alys Pearsall Smith) towards moving in aristocratic circles in London: 'My independent spirit would revolt, I fear, at the idea of anyone lording or ladying it over me.'[54] Much to her relief, Hannah did not find British peers any more elegant than her American acquaintances. Nevertheless, her attitude shows an independence of mind and a lack of preoccupation with the finely graded hierarchy within the British upper classes. All in all then, Smalley's comments seem to have been in tune with the predominant view in the United States of the success of American woman in Europe, namely, that it was her 'intelligence, quickness, freshness, animation, fulness of character, often her brilliancy, always her individuality' – characteristics symptomatic, above all, of her democratic and republican upbringing – which attracted the European male.[55]

Smalley's treatment of the subject of the American girl in the London marriage market inevitably involved a conflict of cultural suppositions. As an American, he rose to the defence of the American girl against the charges that she was successful only because of her wealth and her forwardness. In return, he supplied, along with some interesting and valid points about relations between the young in America, a string of clichés about the character of the all-American girl – clichés which would have been acceptable to, and expected by, an American readership because the British accusations hit a tender nerve about the manners and materialism of Americans. At the same time, these clichés were also intended for an implied British readership. The *London Letters* can be read both as a defence of American values and an attack on British aristocratic marital arrangements.

It was this conflict of cultural values, of manners, and of language which provided Henry James with a wealth of material for his short stories and novels. In one particular story, James made use of the stereotyped reactions of British matrons to American women. In 'An International Episode' (1878), the image of the American woman as an adventuress is the pivot of an intricate narrative which highlights cultural misunderstandings between Americans and the English. Percy Beaumont, 'the clever man', declares he cannot understand Americans, but in spite of this admission it is he who is responsible for applying the stereotype to a young American woman, of whom his cousin becomes enamoured, and for bringing down upon the woman the full weight of aristocratic censorship in the personage of the Duchess of Bayswater.

Even before he has met Bessie Alden, Beaumont is alerted to the danger of a young single woman having access to his charge, Lord Lambeth, an eligible ducal heir with the prospect of £100,000 a year. Beaumont warns his cousin not to get 'entangled' with any American women:

> 'I fancy they are always up to some game of that sort,' Beaumont continued.
>
> 'They can't be worse than they are in England,' said Lord Lambeth judicially.
>
> 'Ah, but in England,' replied Beaumont, 'you have got your natural protectors. You have got your mother and sisters.'[56]

Bessie Alden is spending the summer in Newport with her sister, Mrs Westgate, to whose house the two men have been invited. Beaumont's uneasiness at the Westgates' home is obvious to Mrs Westgate, who is conscious of the implicit insult in his behaviour, i.e. he does not think her sister is good enough for his cousin. Attuned to the innuendoes of Beaumont's conversation with her because of her previous experience and knowledge of British aristocrats, Mrs Westgate assures Beaumont emphatically: 'She is not in the least a flirt, that isn't at all in her line; she doesn't know the alphabet of that sort of thing. She is very simple, very serious.'[57] When in London the following summer, Mrs Westgate is convinced that Beaumont's infrequent visits and the Duchess's tardy call indicate their fear and suspicion of Bessie's motives. While Mrs Westgate tries to protect her younger sister from being labelled as an adventuress, she would also like to frighten the Duchess and Beaumont by making Bessie out to be the adventuress they think she is, and then having her reject Lambeth's offer of marriage. This would compensate Mrs Westgate for all the past insults and snubs she has received from British aristocrats, but she cannot proceed unless Bessie's affections are disengaged, and this she cannot count upon. Indeed, throughout the story the state of Bessie's feelings for Lord Lambeth are ambiguous. Things are brought to a head when Lord Lambeth invites Mrs Westgate and Bessie to his country home, since this obliges his mother to call on the two Americans. Mrs Westgate, however, believes the call to be more than a mere formality: 'They meant to overawe us by their fine manners and their grandeur. . . . They meant to snub us, so that we shouldn't dare to go to Branches.'[58] Mrs Westgate is anxious not to let the Duchess win at this game of social politics, but her sister declines Lambeth's invitation to Branches and brings to an end relations between them – the implication is that she has rejected Lambeth's offer of marriage. Once again, Mrs Westgate suffers the ignominy of a British aristocrat getting the better of her. As she and Bessie quit England for the Continent it looks, to all intents and purposes, as though the Duchess has frightened them off.

This reading of 'An International Episode' suggests that relationships between appearances and realities are the essential interest of the narrative. Conversations take place within a shared linguistic code which preserves the appearance of utmost civility. The formalities of introduction, leaving cards, and calling are strictly followed and determine the state of social relations between people, but James contrasts the American and English exercise of these formalities. The snub occurs because British visitors to Mrs Westgate's home in Newport do not show the same openness to strangers or social inferiors when they are in the role of host, and thus make plain the social standing of Mrs Westgate in relation to themselves when she visits them in London.[59] These forms of etiquette remove the necessity of direct confrontation; each action encodes a meaning for the social context. Hence the Duchess does not have to tell the Americans to decline her son's invitation, she can imply it by suggesting that she herself may not be able to go to Branches.

James also plays on the notion that people never seem to be what they really are, which was part of the Victorian social convention which prevented people from saying what they thought. Bessie's undisguised interest in Lambeth's title and position is interpreted by Beaumont as an implicit desire to marry him. She does not yet share the same code, unlike her sister who is 'nice to everyone', including Beaumont, even though she does not 'care two straws' for him. Bessie soon discovers the existence of a different code of behaviour, however, when her sister tries to warn her of the interpretation that might be placed on her interest in Lambeth. Unable to understand her sister's circumlocution, Bessie remarks: 'I have never heard in the course of five minutes . . . so many hints and innuendoes. I wish you would tell me in plain English what you mean.'[60] The reader is also taught a lesson in the unreliability of appearances. At the beginning of the story, when Beaumont and Lord Lambeth are sitting down to their first dinner in New York City, we are told:

> They were extremely good natured young men, they were more observant than they appeared; in a sort of inarticulate acciden- tally dissimulative fashion, they were highly appreciative. This was, perhaps, especially the case with the elder, who was also, as I have said, the man of talent.[61]

The narrator deliberately miscues the reader as to the character of Beaumont. Beaumont does not, as it turns out, justify any of these descriptions: we are given no evidence of his good nature or powers of observation, and he is appreciative in a *deliberately* rather than an *accidentally* dissimulative fashion. Dissimulation is, in fact, the art of social politics – the ability to disguise true feelings – and this is brought home to us in the final sentence: 'But Bessie Alden seemed to regret nothing.'[62] The American woman has finally been taught to disguise her true feelings, and the reader cannot tell whether she refused Lambeth because she genuinely did not want to marry him, or whether she did so because she felt she could not marry him.

James's story is an interesting illustration, albeit in fictional form, of the way stereotypes can be blithely applied without proper refer- ence to the individual(s) concerned. Nowhere in the tale does the narrator attempt to explain the motives of Beaumont or the Duchess for wanting to end the relationship between Lambeth and Bessie Alden, and, since the narrator is unreliable, we cannot know for certain that the portrayal of Beaumont and the Duchess is not stereotyped. Almost inevitably, one English reviewer, Mrs F. H. Hill, took exception to the portrayal of the English nobility in 'An International Episode'. James replied to her criticism: 'One may make figures and figures without intending generalizations – generalizations of which I have a horror.'[63] Mrs Hill had obviously missed the point of the story.

The demography of the London marriage market provides a vital clue to the hostile response American women came up against in the late nineteenth and early twentieth centuries. The perception that there were too few eligible men and that Americans were 'muscling in' and raising the stakes contributed to a siege mentality. American women were seen as a threat to the landed elite's dominance of the marriage market and of Society. Clearly, however, this view was not shared by all aristocrats. For those families who did 'embrace' American daughters-in-law, they were women of charm, beauty, and talent who were more than capable of playing the role of Society hostess and promoting family interests. Americans played the game according to British aristocratic rules: they participated in the marriage market and negotiated settlements in much the same way as other members of the social elite. The fact that they could be identified as a distinct group by their nationality and that their marital arrangements attracted considerable attention in the press – even when marriages were arranged in haste as in the case of the ninth Duke of Manchester and Helena Zimmerman[64] – meant that there was a greater awareness of their increasing frequency. Since American women, particularly those connected with the commercial and financial elites, were not a traditional source of commoner brides, it is hardly surprising that British aristocrats and others of an anti-American persuasion would have regarded transatlantic marriages as contributing to the lowering of social barriers. But, as we have seen in the previous chapter, the arrival of Americans coincided with, rather than instigated, the opening up of Britain's upper classes. We have to distinguish, then, between the ongoing changes affecting the British peerage and the impact which Americans had on the social exclusiveness of Britain's highest-ranking families. Contemporaries associated the two closely, but I would argue that the reason for this had to do with a need for a scapegoat. Martin Wiener's conclusion about the British response to industrialism in this period can be applied to the response to the social challenge of the plutocracy.[65] That is to say, that the anxieties of the landed elite were 'projected' on to Americans, and it was American women who could be more easily disparaged than the daughters of British businessmen. Floor-cloth manufacturers from Britain might be knighted and their daughters married because of the need to contain the home-based challenge to the landed elite's pre-eminence; American women only had to be tolerated as the wives of British peers, not their families. Americans represented a foreign challenge and could be dealt with in nationalistic terms. The anti-American element to the response to Americans was, therefore, largely a displaced anxiety about the real threat of the non-landed elites to the traditional aristocracy.

'GILDED PROSTITUTION': MONEY AND MARRIAGE

Introduction to Part Four

So far, we have dealt with the reasons for the growing numbers of Americans coming to London after 1870, the possible motives of Americans in marrying into the British peerage, and the hostility of their reception in Britain, which has been related to the opening up of the British upper class and the pressures within the marriage market on the supply of eligible aristocratic husbands. In this part of the book, which is central to the approach adopted in this study of transatlantic marriages, we will focus on the nature of the response to Americans marrying into the British peerage. The cliché of title for money and the stereotypes of the impoverished peer and the American heiress clearly point to an anxiety about the financial aspects of these marriages. Even in the United States, the most publicized feature of Anglo-American alliances was the dowry and later the money spent on entertainments in British society. But the type of derogatory allegation made about titled Americans was not exclusively connected with money, although the concern about commercialism was often at the root of other criticisms. The alleged sterility of upper-class American women, for example, was tied into the debate about the obsession of Americans with conspicuous consumption. What is perhaps the most fascinating feature of dealing with the reactions to transatlantic marriages is the way in which they feed into the various aspects of life causing anxiety amongst the British social elite, i.e. the lowering of social barriers, the growing commercialism of the Season, the shortage of aristocratic males in the marriage market, the displacement of the landed elite from its position of social prominence by those with superior financial resources, and the effect of allegedly barren women on the future of the peerage. The reactions indicate an elite which was highly defensive about the erosion of its social, economic, and political power, and all of these combined into what was at times a fiercely nationalistic sentiment.

Americans were easily seen as the real threat to the British aristocracy: they were the citizens of a democratic republic which did not have a nobility of birth and which was a growing influence on political and economic relations in the western world. Americans were seen as responsible for new habits, customs, and forms of behaviour. Nor was it just the aristocracy which felt threatened by the American phenomenon. The sense of decline pervaded British society as its military power and its leadership in industry and commerce were being overtaken by the United States. Anti-American sentiment crossed class boundaries.

6

Title for money:
the persistence of a cliché

The Stately Homes of England
How beautiful they stand,
To prove the upper classes
Have still the upper hand;
Tho' the fact that they have to be rebuilt
And frequently mortgaged to the hilt
Is inclined to take the gilt off the gingerbread,
And certainly damps the fun
Of the eldest son –
But still we won't be beaten,
We'll scrimp and screw and save,
The playing fields of Eton
Have made us frightfully brave –
And tho' if the Van Dycks have to go
And we pawn the Bechstein Grand,
We'll stand by the Stately Homes of England.
(Noel Coward, 'The Stately Homes of England,
1938)[1]

Marrying for money, as is well known, was not considered unusual within the British aristocracy. There was a long tradition of peers seeking brides with handsome dowries. In 1861 the *Sixpenny Magazine* ran an article entitled 'Heiress Hunters' in which it described the tactics of men with 'an old name and a young face' who could 'ferret out dowries, scent a mile off a wealthy father-in-law, and fall at a dead set before the rich heiress'. These 'poverty-stricken patricians' sought out 'wealthy retired merchant(s) or shop-keeper(s)', it alleged, married their daughters, and settled down to a comfortable life, taking on unpaid sinecures and building up a reputation for performing public service.[2] This was written shortly before the heyday of transatlantic marriages and is an example of the title-for-money cliché applied to the marriages of aristocrats to businessmen's daughters. So predominant was the cliché that virtu-

113.

ally any marriage to a person outside the landed elite was categorized as an exchange of the prestige and social status of a title for
a large dowry. When American women began to marry into the
British elite in significant numbers after 1870, their marriages
quickly fell into this category. In the year of the Marlborough–Vanderbilt wedding, Henry Labouchere's *Truth* commented that the
dream of the daughters of New York 'dollar-magnates' was 'to
marry English noblemen', and 'where one side has to offer a title
and the other side money, the dream is easily realized'.[3] Marie
Corelli put it more colourfully:

> there is always a British title going a-begging, – always some
> decayed or degenerative or semi-drunken peer, whose fortunes
> are on the verge of black ruin, ready and willing to devour,
> monster-like, the holocaust of an American virgin, provided bags
> of bullion are flung, with her, into his capacious maw.[4]

The crucial question is: did members of the British nobility marry
American women for their money? This may be an obvious question
to ask but it is not an easy one to answer. As with determining
social ambition on the part of the American bride and her family,
the evidence upon which a judgement has to be made is of a public
nature. First of all, we can turn for information about landed income
to the fourth edition of John Bateman's *The Great Landowners of Great
Britain and Ireland* (1883).[5] This can give us some idea about the
gross income available to landed peers but, even then, it does not
provide a complete picture of income derived from land because of
Bateman's exclusion of property in London. Since we do not have
information about the non-landed income of individual peers, the
second source of information, the probate returns, is a better, more
reliable indicator of wealth. Even with this, however, there are
problems, because some persons may have avoided death duties by
disposing of part of their wealth prior to death.[6] Bateman and the
probate calendars are nevertheless the best available guides to the
financial standing of peers and younger sons. It should be stated at
the outset, however, that a narrow economic explanation cannot
provide the total answer to a phenomenon which, in itself, cannot
be defined as purely economic. Just because a peer left under £5,000
at death does not signify that he married for money. The financial
data, therefore, are crude and open to interpretation. They have to
be placed alongside biographical information where this is available

and the evidence examined in the previous chapter which demonstrated that marriages to the daughters of American businessmen (or any businessmen for that matter) deviated from the normal marriage pattern of peers.

A further word of caution should be sounded in relation to the two indicators of financial status which will be analysed here, i.e. gross annual rental from land and gross evaluation of property left at death. Both sources of information have serious drawbacks, as they provide only gross figures, and thus the statistics gleaned from the probate calendars and Bateman's *Great Landowners* must be treated with extreme caution, especially because the period of study is one in which landed income was declining and debts rising. Even though W. D. Rubinstein, who has spent much time in analysing the information available in the probate calendars at Somerset House, regards the gross value of realty and personalty as 'a better guide than the net to ascertaining the standard of living enjoyed by the testator, since his debts did not normally have to be repaid in a lump sum during his lifetime', this cannot detract from the stringent circumstances that many landowners experienced at that time.[7] Rubinstein himself deals with the wealthier landowners in his larger study of wealth in Britain, but quickly passes over the effects of the agricultural depression on landed income with the general comment that 'it was the super-rich, particularly those with lucrative non-landed sources of wealth, who could best weather the storms'.[8] If this is indeed the case, and the cliché holds good, then one might reasonably expect that very few peers with substantial landholdings and larger personal fortunes married rich American women. Still, even these two conditions do not sufficiently substantiate or invalidate the cliché without more detailed information about the outgoings of peers. After all, peers with larger incomes tended to have larger commitments with regard to dowries for daughters, pensions, political expenses, charities, and the upkeep and improvement of their real estate and farms. As a general rule, the larger the income was, the greater the expenditure.

One possible explanation for the upturn in transatlantic marriages after 1870 is that peerage families were beginning to experience a fall in landed income as a result of the great agricultural depression. We can formulate a hypothesis, then, that peers with very large landholdings would be the least likely to deviate from traditional marriage patterns, because they would be in a better position, as Rubinstein has suggested, to withstand a fall in income and would not be pressed to unusual measures to counterbalance the effects of the agricultural depression. It might also be claimed that within the London marriage market the peers with long rent-rolls would have commanded a better bargaining position with the prestige that was attached to landownership and the capital that it represented. Using Bateman's domesday survey of the great landowners, we can compare the annual rentals of transatlantic peers with those of peers in the control groups, and thereby determine whether transatlantic peers predominated in either the small or large landowner category.[9] The figures given for rent-rolls and acreage are, of course, pertinent to the year in which the fourth edition appeared, i.e. 1883. We can take this hypothesis a step further by combining the information about landed income with that for gross effects at death and see not only whether peers who left small fortunes were more likely to marry Americans but also whether there is any correlation between the size of landed income and wealth (as determined by the value of property at death). In Table 6.1 peers have been divided into three groups for both sets of data to facilitate the comparison. Taking landed income first, by comparing the figures in the total column we find that the majority of peers in both groups owned land which generated an income of between £10,000 and £50,000 per annum. With regard to the more substantial landholders, approximately 7 per cent of peers with American brides had rent-rolls in excess of £50,000 per annum compared to 12 per cent of the control-group peers. At the bottom end of the scale, almost twice as many control-group peers had rent-rolls under £10,000 per annum. A relatively small landed income does not necessarily indicate, of course, that a peer was in financial difficulty. In fact, among the seven transatlantic peers with a landed income under £5,000 are three men whose families had been raised to the peerage since 1850, i.e. Lords Cheylesmore, Revelstoke, and Russell.[10] The other three men were Lord Ellenborough, the sixth and seventh Viscounts Exmouth, and Lord Falkland, who sold his Yorkshire estate in 1900. Of the seven only the sixth Viscount Exmouth left less than £45,000 at death, while Lord Revelstoke, director of the banking firm Baring Brothers & Co. Ltd, was the richest wealth-holder in the case group. At the other end of the scale, peers with rentals of £50,000 or more did not necessarily leave large fortunes, although there is more of an overlap with regard to this in the control groups, so that there is no clear evidence of a correlation between the size of landed income and wealth.

Table 6.1 Comparison of peers in the control and transatlantic groups showing gross annual rental and gross effects left at death expressed as percentages of the total number of landed peers

Gross Annual Rental	Un-listed	Under £10,000	Between £10,000 and £50,000	Over £50,000	Total
			Gross valuation figure from probate calendar		
Transatlantic peers:					
Over £50,000	1.75	0.00	3.51	1.75	7.02
Between £10,000 and £50,000	17.54	14.04	10.53	26.32	68.43
Under £10,000	8.77	3.51	5.26	7.02	24.56
	28.06%	17.55%	19.30%	35.09%	100.01%
Control-group peers:					
Over £50,000	4.38	0.00	2.02	5.39	11.79
Between £10,000 and £50,000	21.89	2.36	7.74	21.55	53.54
Under £10,000	13.80	4.04	9.77	7.07	35.68
	40.07%	6.40%	19.53%	34.01%	100.01%

Whereas most peers in both groups had a landed income of between £10,000 and £50,000 per annum, the probate figures show that most peers left over £50,000 at death. However, there is a wider variation in proportion for those men leaving less than £10,000, with almost three times as many peers in the case group falling into this category compared to the control groups. Table 6.1 enables us to pinpoint this clearly, and it is the peers with an annual landed income of between £10,000 and £50,000 who particularly stand out. The ten peers in the transatlantic group were the Dukes of Manchester, the Duke of Newcastle, and Lords Bagot, Cork, Fermoy, Gosford, Hertford, Portsmouth, and Somers. Five of them were divorced by their American wives, at least three of whom were heiresses, and one of the divorcés was declared bankrupt in 1910. Judging from the newspaper evidence, financial considerations figured prominently in the marriages of at least four of these peers.

If the fall in landed income was a major factor in encouraging peers to break away from traditional marriage patterns, then we might expect the transatlantic peers to own estates primarily in the hardest-hit regions of England and Wales, i.e. the corn-growing districts. This would substantiate the claim that during the years of the great agricultural depression peers with shrinking incomes sought respite from their enforced entrenchment with expedient marriage alliances. Using P. J. Perry's map of agricultural failure in England and Wales for 1881–3, the peak years of the depression, Table 6.2 indicates the proportion of estates owned by peers in both control and transatlantic groups in the counties divided into classes corresponding to the rate of bankruptcy determined by Perry.[11] All estates of 1,000 acres and above have been included. Table 6.2 shows that very few estates owned by peers in either group were in the worst-affected counties, although the proportion is slightly higher in the transatlantic groups for classes V, VI, and VII. The proportions for all classes do not differ by more than 5.50 per cent, which means that the geographical location of the estates of transatlantic peers is roughly the same as that for the peerage as a whole. This may suggest, in turn, that transatlantic peers were not more likely than other peers to have suffered a fall in agricultural rentals, though it is obviously difficult to determine the precise nature of their financial situation without more detailed information about individual estates. Some estates, such as Lord Rosslyn's in Fife, contained rich coal-fields. Others were located within large cities, such as Lord Calthorpe's Warwickshire lands which were part of the Edgbaston area of Birmingham and were developed for suburban housing.

Table 6.2 Agricultural failures, 1881–3: a comparison of the location of estates owned by peers in the control groups and peers in the transatlantic groups

Class 12	Control groups No. of estates	%	Transatlantic groups No. of estates	%
I	37	10.76	4	5.26
II	102	29.65	23	30.26
III	56	16.28	9	11.84
IV	127	36.92	31	40.79
V	11	3.20 ⎫	1	1.32 ⎫
VI	9	2.62 ⎬ 6.40	5	6.58 ⎬ 11.85
VII	2	0.58 ⎭	3	3.95 ⎭

Note: Agricultural failure (assignments and bankruptcies, annual average by counties), 1881–83 as a percentage of the farming population in 1881; (I) less than 0.1 per cent; (II) 0.1 per cent to less 0.2 per cent; (III) 0.2 per cent to less than 0.3 per cent; (IV) 0.3 per cent to less than 0.4 per cent; (V) 0.4 per cent to less than 0.5 per cent; (VI) 0.5 per cent to less than 0.6 per cent; (VII) more than 0.6 per cent.[13]

Another important factor in the geographical location of estates which should perhaps be included is the number of estates of 1,000 acres and upwards in Ireland. On top of difficulties caused by the crisis in the agricultural world, political troubles in Ireland affected landed income. The spread of the Irish lands correlated with the actual amount received. In the control groups a total of 194 estates in Ireland were owned by 98 peers (i.e. 32.00 per cent of landed peers); in the transatlantic groups 28 estates were owned by 14 peers (i.e. 25.00 per cent). Given the financial difficulties that many peers experienced with their Irish estates, one might have expected a larger proportion of Irish peers in the transatlantic groups; but, in fact, a substantially smaller proportion of peers who married Americans owned land in Ireland.

In summary, the hypothesis is to some extent proven. Large landholders were not conspicuous in the case group, bearing in mind, of course, that they were a small minority in any case. Only four peers with a landed income in excess of £50,000 married Americans: Lords Calthorpe, Ancaster, and Anglesey and the Duke of Roxburghe. There are no obvious indicators as to why any of them might have married Americans. Roxburghe and Calthorpe had commissions in the army, both serving in the First World War; Ancaster had political ambitions and was a Member of Parliament for sixteen years before succeeding to the earldom in 1910; Anglesey's marriage to Mary Livingston King was his third and her second, their previous spouses having died. The Duchess of Roxburghe and Lady Ancaster were wealthy New Yorkers, and Lady Anglesey's father was a railroad director and cotton manufacturer, so that wealth could have been a factor in their marriages; Lady Calthorpe was from Newport, Rhode Island, and at her death left less than any other American peeress. Where the two groups differ significantly is in the middling ranks of landowning peers. It is possible that those with moderate incomes from land were more at risk to the vicissitudes of the economy and rising costs of maintaining social leadership, especially if their income was less diversified than that of peers owning less land. But by interpreting the data in this way, we are still assuming that peers married Americans for money, and this has yet to be substantiated.

The second factor indicative of financial status, gross amount left at death, is perhaps more useful in testing the notion that it was the particularly impoverished peers, regardless of landed income, who sought American wealth to solve their financial difficulties. Table 6.3 is a more detailed summary of data obtained from the probate calendars at Somerset House than Table 6.1. It compares the gross estate left by transatlantic peers with that left by peers in the control groups. This enables us to assess the financial status of peers with American wives against the rest of the peerage as represented by the control groups.[14] The figures reveal a close similarity in proportion between the two groups except in two highly significant categories: those peers leaving less that £1,000 and those leaving more £500,000. One in six transatlantic peers left under £1,000 compared to one in fifty in the control groups, while no transatlantic peer left over £500,000,[15] compared to eighteen peers in the control groups, of whom ten were millionaires.

Table 6.3 Comparison of gross estates of peers in the transatlantic groups and peers in the control groups

Probate calendar valuations	Total	%
Transatlantic groups I and II:		
Over £500,000	0	0.00
Between £100,000 and £500,000	14	33.33
£50,000 and £100,000	6	14.29
£10,000 and £50,000	11	26.19
£1,000 and £10,000	4	9.52
Under £1,000	7	16.67
	42	100.00
Control Groups I and II:		
Over £500,000	18	9.28
Between £100,000 and £500,000	67	34.54
£50,000 and £100,000	27	13.92
£10,000 and £50,000	62	31.96
£1,000 and £10,000	16	8.25
Under £1,000	4	2.06
	194	100.01

Of the seven transatlantic peers who left very small personal fortunes, four had been married to, and were divorced by, wealthy American women. They were Baron Fermoy (who married Frances Work, daughter of Commodore Vanderbilt's business associate), the ninth Duke of Manchester (whose first wife, Helena Zimmerman, was the daughter of a railroad director from Cincinnati), and the Marquess of Hertford (who married Alice Thaw of Pittsburgh). The fourth member of this coterie, the fifth Earl of Gosford, was also divorced by his wife. He was once married to the daughter of an American diplomat, Jack Ridgely Carter. The Carters were not a poor family by high society's standards, but, judging from newspaper reports, Mildred Carter did not have quite the same reputation as an heiress as either Frances Work, Helena Zimmerman, or Alice Thaw.[16] Frank Work was said to have disapproved of his daughter's marriage to James Burke Roche (later Baron Fermoy) and in his will threatened to disinherit the two sons of the marriage if either or both should succeed to the barony. The grandsons received 3 million dollars from Frank Work when he died, but the elder of the two chose to go against his grandfather's wishes and returned to England to become the fourth Baron Fermoy in 1920.[17] Fermoy's career was described as 'picturesque' and said to have included cattle ranching and gold mining in the USA, exploration in Patagonia and blockade-running during the Russo-Japanese War.[18] This coincidence of divorce, wealthy wives, and peers in straitened financial circumstances seems to lend some credence to the cliché of title for money, and we will return to this later. In general, then, the figures give a strong indication that the poorer rather than the richer peers made transatlantic marriages.

If we compare the figures for the gross estate left by American peeresses with those for peeresses in the control groups, the cliché is to some extent reinforced.[19] As Table 6.4 shows, only four American peeresses left less than £10,000 (i.e. Ladies Calthorpe, Falkland, Huntingfield, and Orford). A much larger proportion of peeresses in the control groups feature at the bottom of the table: nearly half of those who married in the 1880s and a third in the 1900s. At the other end of the scale, however, American peeresses are not more conspicuous than those in the control groups. They represent a similar proportion of those leaving in excess of £100,000 to the women who married peers in the 1900s. As most of the control-group peeresses were members of the traditional aristocratic circle, it is not so surprising to see that the control groups show a 6 per cent decline in the number of women leaving more than £100,000.

Transatlantic marriages increased significantly in the late 1890s and 1900s, which may reflect a possible decline in the amount of money available for dowries within the landed elite. American peeresses predominate in the £10,000 to £100,000 bracket, so that a

Table 6.4 Comparison of gross estates of peeresses in the case and control groups

Probate calendar valuations	Case group		Control group I		Control group II	
	No.	*%*	*No.*	*%*	*No.*	*%*
Over £500,000	1	3.57	2	3.57	0	0.00
Between £100,000 and 500,000	4	14.29	10	17.86	10	15.63
£50,000 and £100,000	7	25.00	5	8.93	7	10.94
£10,000 and 50,000	12	42.86	13	23.21	27	42.17
£1,000 and 10,000	2	7.14	23	41.07	16	25.00
Under £1,000	2	7.14	3	5.36	4	6.25
	28	100.00	56	100.00	64	99.99

significant majority of them (85.71 per cent) left more than £10,000 compared to 53.57 per cent and 68.74 per cent in the two control groups. If we take an average of the amount of money left by peeresses, Americans are by no means overwhelmingly wealthier at death. The average size of an American's personal fortune was approximately £87,000 compared to £88,000 for the first control group and £48,000 for the second. The median size of fortune is, however, a better guide for comparing the case and control groups, and more clearly demonstrates the superior wealth of the American peeresses. The figures are:

Case group	£34,709
Control group I	£12,032
Control group II	£21,789

There is no definite correlation between the rank of the husband and the personal fortune of the wife in either the case or control groups, nor is there a correlation between the personal fortunes of husbands and wives, except for the fact that a higher proportion of American peeresses did leave a larger personal fortune than their husbands, with the difference ranging from £15,000 to £500,000 (i.e. 34.62 per cent compared to 25.00 per cent and 26.56 per cent). The data still do not address the question of whether financial motivation was a factor in the choice of spouse. It would only have been possible to infer this if American peeresses had been very obviously wealthier than women in the control groups.[20] On the other hand, there may well have been some grounds for the general perception of titled Americans as better off, but not for thinking that they were preferred to British women. Given the publicity surrounding

American dowries, it is surprising not to have had more convincing results as to their financial standing.

There is no such doubt, however, when we take the average and, more importantly, the median of the amount of personalty left at death by peers. There is a very marked difference between the case and control groups, as the following figures show:

	Average	Median
Case group	£102,360	£46,129
Control group I	£263,838	£65,213
Control group II	£276,114	£79,288

This is the one clear indicator that peers with American wives were less well off than most peers. We still may not be able to infer financial motives, but this does help us to understand why contemporaries were so obsessed with the financial aspects of these marriages.

Peers who were heavily in debt and seeking to marry elicited much attention from the press on both sides of the Atlantic. A certain notoriety was affixed to those who had been spending beyond their means rather than to the landowner experiencing a decline in his standard of living as a result of the general contraction of agricultural returns. Extravagance or recklessness was frowned upon within the peerage, especially since the mid-Victorian peerage had managed to rid itself of the ill repute that its forebears had fallen into at the end of the eighteenth century. Honouring debts had become such an integral part of the concept of a gentleman that excessive personal debts jeopardized an individual's reputation. Rumours of financial insolvency often caused acute embarrassment and attracted the attention of gossip columnists. For example, speculation about the financial problems of Lord and Lady Essex resulted in newspaper reports that Lady Essex, née Adele Grant of New York, had set up a laundry business while her husband was seeking a buyer for their Hertfordshire estate.[21] The *New York Evening Journal* carried the story of how Lady Essex had allegedly offended her husband's patroness, Lady Meux, and caused an allowance of $15,000 to be withdrawn.[22] It predicted that the couple would have to 'take up their habitation in some cheap city on the Continent'. It was Adele's brother who eventually bought the Cassiobury estate in 1908. In spite of their alleged financial difficulties, the couple left over £200,000 gross in personalty.[23] The tone of these remarks which appeared in American newspapers is clearly a mocking one. Much political currency was to be made in the United States from pointing to the British aristocracy and showing 'how are the mighty fallen', but the same is probably true in a British context in so far as certain sectors in society had much to gain from the disintegration of the old landed elite. The paranoia of an aristocracy with its back to the wall is very much in evidence in the attitude of Society towards its errant members. The forced sale of land, marriage to a business-man's daughter, or a position with a firm in the City kept aristo-cratic doors open to the growing number of suppliants eager to exploit the misfortunes of the ruling class, or at least this was how some aristocrats viewed the rising new men of wealth. Comprom-ising with the plutocracy may in some eyes have been regarded as a betrayal of class values, and the denunciation of mercenary motives hid a variety of reactions to the displacement of the ruling class.

The number of Anglo-American alliances made purely for finan-cial gain was probably very small, but the disproportionate amount of publicity they attracted was an important factor in the formation of the clichéd view of these marriages. The notoriety attached to transatlantic marriages took a number of forms, such as sensationalist newspaper-reporting of the movements of a reputed fortune-hunter, the gambling proclivities of a titled American's husband, or a contentious divorce case or bankruptcy.

Lord Acheson, later the fifth Earl of Gosford and a nephew of the Earl of Derby, was a reputed fortune-hunter. He had his name linked in the American press to at least three American women. In 1905 the Minneapolis *Tribune* reported his intended visit to Newport:

> It is said the youthful Viscount is devoted to Miss Gladys Mills, and is endeavouring to win her heart and hand.
>
> He has hovered about her in London all summer, and is said to be hopeful of victory. . . .
>
> The earldom, which is an Irish one, is not rich, and the Mills' fortune would be very useful in burnishing up aristocratic bear-ings that have been tarnished for lack of gold.[24]

Gosford is the bee 'hovering' around the honey-pot; he is also the knight in armour fighting for 'victory', but his armour is 'tarnished', and the 'polish' metaphors ('burnishing' and 'tarnished') suggest he is an inferior courtier paying homage not to his bride-to-be but to her father's 'gold'. The implication is that it is a one-way exchange. A year later the Whitelaw Reids denied Acheson's interest in their daughter, Jean.[25] Finally, in February 1910, the papers were able to announce Gosford's genuine engagement to an American: Mildred Carter. His reputation as a fortune-hunter was conveniently glossed over by the *New York World*, which described him as an 'admirer' of American women.[26]

The fifth Earl of Rosslyn attracted a great deal of notoriety throughout his life. In 1890, soon after he had married Violet Vyner against his parents' wishes, his father died leaving a healthy estate at Dysart and collieries in Fife which provided an income of £17,000. Rosslyn quickly ran through his inheritance as his gambling debts mounted and took out a mortgage of £107,000 on Dysart to pay back the money-lenders. In 1896 Dysart was sold to Sir Michael Nairn, a floor-cloth manufacturer, and the following year Rosslyn declared himself bankrupt. Rosslyn remained in the limelight after this ebb in his fortunes; his first wife divorced him, and he took up acting. During this venture into the Thespian world he had a whirlwind romance with an American actress, Anna Robinson, who became his second wife. He denied allegations that he had married her for her money, but within two years he was back in the divorce courts. Rosslyn then became an *habitué* of Monte Carlo, gambling heavily.[27] Rosslyn's life history unusually combines all the prime sources of notoriety in aristocratic society: divorce, gambling, bankruptcy, and marriage not only to an American but an actress as well. Such a spectacular run of misfortune and scandal was bound to have an impact on the image of transatlantic marriages.

The upkeep of a large estate without the advantages of rents from urban or railroad property or mines required efficient and enlightened management at a time of falling prices for agricultural products. Extravagance on the part of the life-tenant could quickly turn a healthy estate into an encumbered one. The Dukes of Manchester were hard pressed in the late nineteenth century to maintain their level of income. The eighth Duke, who had made one of the earliest matches with an American woman in 1876, had attempted to relieve his large estates in Huntingdonshire and Armagh from their crippling debts. Notwithstanding the family's plight, the ninth Duke maintained his spendthrift habits. He blamed other people's expectations of prominent peers of the realm: 'the standard of living demanded of dukes is higher than that demanded of men without titles, quite irrespective of whether the latter class may happen to be wealthier than the former.'[28] The rivalry of millionaire-businessmen for conspicuous display in high society had already begun to tell on aristocratic income. After inheriting a fortune from her brother subsequent to her husband's death, Consuelo Manchester herself participated in the lavish expenditure in court circles. Her son, Kim, also joined forces with the new men in Society with the help of a Cincinnati heiress, Helena Zimmerman. In 1900 they had eloped to London from the United States and had married in a Marylebone parish church.

Very occasionally the marriages of British peers to American women attracted the kind of adverse publicity more commonly associated with their continental counterparts. Annulments were rare: three out of a total of fourteen transatlantic marriages brought to an end were annulled. The first was the marriage of the Hon. Edmund Fitzmaurice to Caroline Fitzgerald in 1894 after five years of marriage; the second was that of the Earl of Yarmouth (heir to the Marquess of Hertford) to Alice Thaw (daughter of a Pittsburgh millionaire) after only three years; and the third was the annulment of the Duke of Marlborough's marriage to Consuelo Vanderbilt, five years after a divorce had been granted. The Yarmouth–Thaw wedding appeared to be doomed from the start. It was divulged at the court proceedings that the wedding ceremony had been delayed when the Earl requested payment of the dowry in advance.[29] At the time, the *New York Journal* had reported Yarmouth's receipt of a writ for the repayment of a loan for £317.[30] Interest concerning the financial arrangements of the annulment equalled the gossip about the dowry. There were reports that Lady Yarmouth was paying our vast sums of money to pay her husband's debts, and this prompted a legal representative of the Thaw family to issue the following statement:

> There appears to be some misapprehension in regard to the fortune of the Countess. It is all in her own control. The Earl of Yarmouth has not squandered her wealth. A large part of her fortune was placed in the hands of trustees by her father, under his will, and previous to the marriage of the Countess she placed the remaining portion in a private trust for her own use, and it is being held in this country and under her control. Money is sent to her from America as she wants it. The Countess set aside

an allowance for the Earl under the marriage settlement which he receives monthly.[31]

The following month, however, the *New York Times* reported that the Countess had agreed to continue paying the Earl an allowance of $40,000 per year.[32] Allegedly, this was in return for the Earl's agreement to the nullification of the marriage; he did not contest the decree, which was granted on the grounds of non-consummation. The statement given to the press about the financial arrangements of the estranged couple reveals a concern to show that not only was the trust fund held in America, but that expenditure was controlled by the Countess and not by her husband. Clearly, there was growing sensitivity about the money expended on titled marriages and allowances for husbands at this time, but it was also doubtlessly embarrassing to the Countess that she was obliged to continue providing an income for her ex-husband. The *New York Times* certainly tried to insinuate that the annulment had been bought. In the light of growing criticism about the motivation for titled marriages, the annulment of the Yarmouth–Thaw marriage would have reinforced the view that such marriages were not based on love and affection.

A double standard seems to have existed in the attitudes towards the men and women involved in transatlantic marriages. While there is evidence to support the stereotyping of peers as 'impoverished', relatively or literally speaking, there is surprising little evidence as to the wealth of titled Americans apart from newspaper reports. Yet it was the bride's wealth which tended to attract the most publicity rather than the financial standing of the husband. May Goelet, for example, was called 'America's Richest Heiress'; Margaretta Drexel was described as 'clever, vivacious, rich', and 'the star "catch" of London society' in 1908; while one article about Beatrice Mills's marriage to Lord Granard appeared beneath the heading 'Cupid, Croesus and the Coronet', and another alleged that she would be wealthier than either of the Duchesses of Marlborough or Roxburghe.[33] The focus on the bride's wealth would certainly have reinforced the cliché of title for money as regards the financial motivation of the peer, but American women did not marry only the most prestigious title-holders in British society. In fact, there is no correlation at all between the rank of the husband and the amount of personalty left by the wife. Two of the wealthiest women to marry into the British landed elite were Florence Breckinridge, who married a baronet who was subsequently raised to the peerage, and Mary Burns, who married the son of a leading statesmen who was also raised to the peerage after their marriage.[34] A significant number married younger sons of peers, baronets, knights, members of the landed gentry, and MPs.[35] Amongst the latter we may include Joseph Chamberlain, Sir Lyon Playfair, and Sir William Harcourt.

The questions of financial motivation and social ambition are perhaps more problematic when considering the marriages of younger sons. Without the prestige of the family's title and the possibility of inheriting a landed estate, one might well expect younger sons to figure well down the list of eligible bachelors in high society, especially if Americans really were aiming to claim high social status by marrying into the titled nobility. However, there were forty marriages to the younger sons of peers between 1870 and 1914, representing 40 per cent of all transatlantic alliances involving members of the peerage. It is important, then, to consider the status of younger sons in the marriage market, particularly as they provide a useful comparison to the marriages made by their elder brothers.

Younger sons certainly benefited from the American preference for British titles over continental ones. It seems that the stability of the British aristocrat's social and financial status was appealing to New York debutantes, according to an article on New York society which appeared in a British journal in 1893. Its author, Mayo Hazeltine, commented: 'the splendid magnates of Britain, whose youngest sons, indeed, and remotest kinsmen, shine with a reflected lustre quite strong enough to dazzle the republican eye'.[36] Unlike their European counterparts, British younger sons were distinguished from their elder brothers in the use of titles. Younger sons of earls, viscounts, and barons have the courtesy title of 'Honourable', while the sons of the two upper ranks of the British peerage enjoy the more prestigious courtesy title of 'Lord'. Since the prefix 'Lord' is also used in place of Marquess, Earl, Viscount, or Baron, younger sons of dukes and marquesses might be mistaken for peers. The difference between the two usages, however, is in the interposition of the first name in the case of the younger son, hence the Duke of Marlborough's second son was addressed as Lord Randolph Churchill and not as Lord Churchill who was an entirely different person. Nevertheless, amongst those less familiar with the subtle differentations between lords who were peers and lords who were younger sons, the ambiguity might be used to advantage.

Some Americans familiar with the rules of precedence within the British peerage made sharp distinctions between the various ranks. American newspapers conjectured that when Lord Acheson's proposal to his daughter was rejected, Whitelaw Reid, the United States Ambassador to Britain from 1905 to 1912, was aiming his sights on Prince Arthur of Connaught or Prince Frederick of Teck as a possible son-in-law. A New York paper alleged that Reid 'longed to annex an English title, the older the better'.[37] His daughter's final choice, the Honourable John Ward, younger son of the Earl of Dudley, may well have proved particularly appropriate to Reid. For, although he had openly expressed his desire for an American son-in-law to offset criticism in the United States of his ambassadorship, he may privately have desired a titled connection. A younger son was, after all, less conspicuous than a peer. A letter to his wife in response to her suggestion that they invite their niece, Beatrice Mills, and her future husband, Lord Granard, to Dorchester House after their wedding gives some insight into Reid's thoughts on the subject of title marriages:

> Carter also seemed dubious about it – his point being that these international marriages are intensely unpopular at home, and that this particular incident might give the critics who are always complaining of my being too English for an American Ambassador, anyway, a chance to sneer at my now establishing a secondary functionary of the Royal household in Dorchester House! I don't think there is much in this, and I should have a good deal of contempt for the opinions of people who were influenced by it. Still, we have seen in the past four years on what very trifling points they can raise a clamor in the newspapers.[38]

Marriage with a younger son of a noble household brought American women within the orbit of London's high society. It could provide all the advantages of marriage to a peer with regard to entry into the inner social circles, access to royalty, and perhaps recognized social status.[39] The experience of Minnie Stevens is a case in point. Her foothold in London society had been somewhat precariously secured after six years of unsuccessful courtships with French dukes and Irish lords by her marriage to the grandson of the Marquess of Anglesey. Suspicions about the limited extent of her fortune had put off several titled suitors, but with the aid of Lady Waldegrave, a famous London hostess, and her close friend, Consuelo, Lady Mandeville (later Duchess of Manchester), Minnie was able to marry into the nobility.[40] George Smalley, the London correspondent of the *New York Times*, may have had Lady Arthur Paget in mind when he denied the presence of the money motive in Anglo-American marriages:

> If she [the American woman] had those personal qualities which insure social success she was welcomed; if she had not, her millions would be of little use to her. The husband is but one step; it is what follows upon marriage, it is the influence of the American girl after marriage upon English society, that has to be explained.[41]

This was a clever way of trying to deflect attention away from the money which passed hands as a result of the marriage settlement on to the more positive contributions of American women to British society. However, the excitement on both sides of the Atlantic about the 'export of US dollars' or the rescue of an historic estate could not be abated. The finances of the elite remained a constant source of interest.

Younger sons were usually dependent upon pensions from the family estate, and any assessment of their income at the time of marriage would probably show that most of them had relatively low incomes, although a few would have had promising financial prospects if in business. Lord Randolph Churchill received an annual allowance of £1,100 from his father at the time of his marriage to Jennie Jerome and an allowance of £2,000 per annum from his father-in-law, inclusive of 'pin money' for Jennie.[42] Lord Randolph died in 1895 leaving £70,000 in personalty, but very little was left after his debts had been paid.[43] Throughout the twenty years of their marriage the Churchills experienced financial difficulties. Both fathers were hard pressed to maintain their family's standard of living. Hit by falling rents and the increasing cost of maintaining Blenheim, the seventh Duke of Marlborough had sold off family treasures and retrenched on his expenditure, while Leonard Jerome had been badly burned in the Panic of 1873 and had never fully recovered from this reversal. The 1870s were difficult years for British estate-owners and American capitalists alike.

It is interesting to recall in this connection that during the marriage negotiations there were difficulties about the amount to be settled on the couple by Leonard Jerome. The Duke had put up a great deal of opposition to the marriage and had intimated to his son that 'under any circumstances, an American connection is not one that we would like. . . . you must allow that it is slightly coming down in pride for us to contemplate the connection'.[44] In fact, he had made extensive inquiries into Jerome's social and financial standing in order to decide the suitability of the alliance. The Duke's informers were not able to confirm Jerome's social position but did say that his credit was good despite his set-back in 1873. Wealth accumulated from speculation in stocks and shares, however, did not have the same respectability and solidity of landed wealth amongst aristocratic circles in the 1870s.[45] Ironically, after his death, both the Duke's eldest son and grandson married wealthy American women. No doubt a larger dowry would have sweetened the pill for the seventh Duke, or at least Jerome seemed to think so, when he wrote to his daughter: 'You are no heiress and it must have taken heaps of love to overcome an Englishman's prejudice against "those horrid Americans".'[46]

Whilst it is apparent that Lord Randolph Churchill could not have aspired to improving his financial position greatly by his marriage to Jennie Jerome, what of other younger sons starting out on serious careers in law, diplomacy, or politics? Were they more likely to marry wealthy wives or, to put it another way, to attract women of wealth? A son-in-law who was not merely interested in securing a comfortable income for life through marriage might well have more appeal to both American fathers concerned about the ethics of providing an income for an aristocratic son-in-law and American women seeking a more fulfilling role as a wife beyond the demands of domesticity. Generally speaking, younger sons were still fairly traditional in their choice of occupation. The overwhelming majority took commissions in the army or navy, a few rose to the rank of general or admiral. Alternative choices were politics, the church, the diplomatic corps, the Civil Service, or the law. Younger sons with American wives did not deviate from this overall pattern. Perhaps the most noticeable factor in a comparison of occupations is that there was a higher proportion of diplomats or colonial civil servants in the transatlantic group. Five younger sons – Michael Herbert, Thomas Grosvenor, Alan Johnstone, Ronald Lindsay, and Francis Plunkett – married American women in the early stages of their diplomatic careers. Grosvenor died young (aged 44) from pneumonia while serving as Secretary of the British Embassy at St Petersburg in 1886. Johnstone, knighted for his diplomatic services, was an Envoy Extraordinary and Minister Plenipotentiary at The Hague when he retired from the service. Herbert, Lindsay, and Plunkett reached the rank of Ambassador. Johnstone, Plunkett, and Herbert were all in the running for the ambassadorship in Washington, DC, in 1902, to which Herbert was eventually appointed. None of them left large amounts of personalty (£4,622, £11,260, and £7,924 respectively), but their wives did leave substantially more (£33,484, £28,239, and £723,200 respectively). Belle Herbert was, in fact, the wealthiest of the American wives of the younger sons. It is impossible to draw conclusions about the monetary motives that may or may not have been present from only three marriages, besides which a fourth marriage, that of Sir Ronald Lindsay, reveals a different situation. He died in 1945 leaving £134,147, whilst his first American wife died in 1918 leaving £4,350.[47] Apart from the five diplomats in the younger-son group, there were five MPs (Sir William Carington, Edmund Fitzmaurice, Charles Ramsay, Lord Randolph Churchill, and Frederick Guest), a clergyman (James Leigh, Dean of Hereford), and two senior-ranking military officers (Sir Cecil Bingham and Sir Horace Hood). Of the rest, the majority had army commissions, and two were barristers. Five men were already well established in their careers at the time of their marriage to an American woman: Lord Sir William Beresford, Hon. Sir Cecil Edward Bingham, Hon. Sir Horace Hood, Hon. Rowland Leigh, and Edmund Fitzmaurice.[48] But a number of men married in the early stages of their career. Frederick Guest, for example, started his political career after his marriage to Amy Phipps, a Pittsburgh heiress, and no doubt benefited from his wife's income when conducting his electoral campaigns.

As to whether younger sons were able to attract wealthy wives, we can consult probate calendar information again. By combining the figures for probate and the occupations we can test another hypothesis: were younger sons with American wives more likely to have serious careers? Six men left over £40,000, and all had distinguished careers, but only two married women of reputed wealth (for which no information was found in the probate calendars): Frederick Guest and Lord William Beresford. Beresford

married towards the end of his career, having previously spent
twenty years in India first as an ADC and then as Military Secretary
of successive Viceroys. Although his wife had briefly been a duchess,
her social career in London society had been hampered by the fact
that the Duke of Marlborough had been a divorcé and was ostracized by the Marlborough House Set following the Aylesford
scandal. While her former marriage was regarded as an exchange
of title for money, her marriage to Beresford is usually seen in a
more sympathetic light. It was considered as a happy union, and
a son was born of the marriage.

Table 6.5 A list of younger sons of peers with Americans wives showing
full-time occupation (if any), amount of personalty at death, and wife's
personalty at death (arranged in order of husband's wealth)

Name	Full-time occupation	Personalty	
		Husband	Wife
Edmund Fitzmaurice[a]	MP	£181,275	—
Sir Ronald Lindsay	Diplomat	134,147	£4,350
Frederick Guest	MP	87,227	(heiress)
Lord Randolph Churchill	MP	75,971	38,097
Sir William Carington	MP	70,803	11,657
Lord William Beresford	Military Secretary to Viceroy of India	47,036	(heiress)
Henry Coventry		31,248	192,645
Lionel Guest		26,431	—
Sir John Ward		16,023	(heiress)
Hugh Northcote		11,448	—
Sir Francis Plunkett	Diplomat	11,260	28,239
Rev. James Leigh	Dean of Hereford	11,005	4,829
Sir Cecil Bingham	Major-General	10,006	—
Sir Michael Herbert	Diplomat	7,923	723,200
Sir Horace Hood	Rear-Admiral, RN	7,681	—
Hugh Howard		5,530	—
Sir Alan Johnstone	Diplomat	4,622	33,484
Harold Hawke		4,419	1,044
Lord George Cholmondeley		4,383	3,702
Rowland Leigh	Barrister	4,093	—
Murrough O'Brien		4,064	—
Charles Coventry		2,948	—
Amyas Northcote		2,316	6,789
Lord Alastair Innes-Kerr		1,085	—

[a] Received peerage in own right after marriage

Of the remaining eighteen men for whom we have information
from the probate calendars, only two married women from wealthy

American families: Sir Michael Herbert (Belle Wilson) and Sir John Ward (Jean Reid). As far as we know, the other sixteen women were not reputedly wealthy. Edith Kip was the granddaughter of Pierre Lorillard, a New York businessman, and the divorced wife of Richard McCreevy, a San Franciscan. Her ex-husband had married a divorcée, Lady Gray-Egerton, and there was considerable anxiety that Edith's marriage to Henry Coventry, who had two American sisters-in-law, would attract the attention of Father Black, who was renowned for his opposition to divorcés remarrying. In addition to the excitement this was causing, the newspapers mentioned that she had rented Stonor Park from Lord Camoys for seven years, was spending $50,000 on alterations, and had bought a house in a fashionable West End street. The American expatriate community turned out in force for her wedding at St James's, Piccadilly.[49] One of the wedding guests was Mrs Samuel Sloan Chauncey, née Alice Carr, who married General Sir Cecil Bingham three years later. Bingham was said to have 'been in love with Mrs Chauncey for a long time', although her name had been linked to other suitors, such as Lord Rosebery, Arnold Morley, and Prince Miguel Braganza.[50] Her sister had married Lord Newborough in 1900 and left property worth £13,064 at death. Lord George Cholmondeley married an actress, Loretta Mooney. Lord Alastair Innes-Kerr, brother of the eighth Duke of Roxburghe who married an American heiress, married Anne Breese of New York. In its report of Innes-Kerr's marriage, the *New York World* made every effort to stress the non-materialistic nature of this alliance: 'Lord Alastair is by no means wealthy and his is absolutely a love match.'[51] The Duchess of Roxburghe, née May Goelet of New York and a niece of Belle Herbert, was alleged to have encouraged Lord Alastair's courtship of a woman described in the newspapers as 'highly cultivated' and 'classically beautiful'. Ironically, May Goelet's wedding to Roxburghe four years earlier had attracted a great deal of attention and criticism from the American press. The *New York Times*, among others, gave full details of her father's income from real estate.[52] In summary, the transatlantic marriages of younger sons reveal a tendency – and it is no more than that – for the more ambitious or career-oriented younger sons to marry into the wealthy, and primarily business, elite. They appear to have been less influenced by tradition and to have allowed financial considerations to play an important part in their choice of *both* career and wife.

The fact that is was so often assumed that peers married Americans only for their money does not necessarily mean that financial considerations were paramount in all cases. As elite marriages, it would be reasonable to expect that both parties would own substantial property. If there were obvious disparities between the husband's and wife's wealth, this might well indicate that financial factors were present but it does not prove that they took precedence over others. The probate returns reveal only four cases where the wife's wealth was considerably superior, i.e. where the wife left at least more than £100,000 than her husband. They were Lady Craven, the Hon. Mrs Coventry, Lady Michael Herbert, and the Duchess of Manchester. There might well have been a few more to add to this list if some marriages had not ended in divorce. For all the newspaper reporting, though, about rich heiresses and millions of dollars being spent by Americans on dowries and maintaining establishments in London, few of the titled Americans were in the super-rich bracket. But then again, this should be placed in perspective, as most of the women would not have been rich in their own right but would have been the beneficiary of wealth accumulated by previous husbands, fathers, brothers, or other male relatives. It would be wrong to expect that most of the women would have had personal fortunes in excess of £500,000. Nevertheless, the average amount left by titled Americans does slightly exceed that of their husbands, so that there would have been some grounds for perceiving American women as richer than many members of the peerage, although some were clearly not. That American women were classified as heiresses *en bloc* would seem to suggest a certain degree of resentment or envy or even opportunism.

It is in the nature of clichés that they are used excessively and indiscriminately. The wife of a peer only had to be an American for the assumption to be made that he had married her for her money. And it is true in the case of transatlantic marriages that while some, and I would argue the minority, were to all intents and purposes a case of titled men marrying wealthy women to help them out of their straitened financial circumstances, not all marriages were so obviously materialistic. Upper-class marriages are more vulnerable to interpretations which laid emphasis upon their economic character, which is not to say that financial considerations are not present in all marriages but that keener interest is shown in the handing over of substantial property in the marriage settlement. The persistence both of the cliché and the stereotypes of the impoverished noble and the American heiress owe much to the notoriety of a few alliances which attracted much publicity. At a time when many noble families felt besieged by the pressures on them to try to maintain their leadership of society, negative publicity of this sort may well have been unwelcome. The exposure of the material side to marriage would have conflicted with the gentlemanly code of conduct, according to which money matters were not discussed in public. The revelations about a peer's misdemeanours would have undermined some of the mystique of the nobility, and, even in what was regarded as a hedonistic society, scandals were avidly avoided. We should not underestimate the pressures to conform. This was a time of social change when the aristocracy was keener than ever to retain its power. It would not have greatly assisted elite solidarity if men were breaking rank and seeking brides outside the traditional sources of aristocratic wives. Such marriages put pressures on the elite to reassert its leadership role and demonstrate its ability to assimilate newcomers. That is why the description of the arrival of Americans as an invasion is so significant: it indicates that the aristocracy was unable to contain the challenge and saw itself as being overwhelmed. Likewise, the weight of the negative characterization of Anglo-American marriages fell upon the American brides: it was their material motives which were questioned rather than those of their husbands. By attributing an unhealthy obsession with money to Americans, the British elite could blame Americans (and Jews) for the unwelcome changes taking place within the power structure of British society. Americans were held responsible for the watering down of aristocratic lineages, rising costs in London society, and lowering standards.[53] There was more, then, to the American heiress stereotype than just an acknowledgement of American wealth: there was, as we shall see, caught up in this a reservoir of resentment, envy, prejudice, and anxiety.

7

The American heiress:
the formation of a stereotype

Of all supposed factors in history, scandal about women was
commonest and least to be trusted.
(Henry Adams, *History of the United States* (1918), 1: 345)

In the 1870s there were few titled Americans in London society but
they made their mark and were popular members of the Marlborough House Set. In these early years of the 'hymeneal North-West
Passage' American women were, at times, victims of ignorance and
prejudice and treated as a joke. Lady Randolph Churchill recalled:

> In England, as on the Continent, the American woman was
> looked upon as a strange and abnormal creature, with habits and
> manners something between a Red Indian and a Gaiety Girl.
> Anything of an outlandish nature might be expected of her. . . .
>   As a rule, people looked upon her as a disagreeable and even
> dangerous person, to be viewed with suspicion, if not avoided
> altogether. Her dollars were her only recommendation, and each
> was credited with the possession of them, otherwise what was her
> *raison d'être*?[1]

Jennie's niece by marriage, Consuelo, Duchess of Marlborough, did
not fare much better more than twenty years later when Lady
Blandford made remarks to her 'revealing that she thought we all
lived on plantations with negro slaves and that there were Red
Indians ready to scalp us just round the corner'.[2] Belle Wilson
encountered similar misconceptions about life in the United States.
Whilst visiting Cowes during her 1886 European tour, a frosty
British matron told Belle that she thought America had to be 'a
dreadful place' as Americans did not have servants. When Belle
enlightened her, the British matron retorted that she had thought
Americans did not like to be servants, whereupon Belle replied:
'They don't. All our working class are English.'[3] British aristocrats
either had some strange notions about the barbarity of American

137

life or were professing belief in popular misconceptions in order to put down young American women. Either way, such exchanges point to a clear undercurrent of prejudice.

As the number of transatlantic marriages increased, American women became less of a victim of British aristocratic humour and more of a threat to the exclusiveness of aristocratic circles. In fact, it was the marriage of Mrs Lilian Hammersley to Lady Blandford's ex-husband (the eighth Duke of Marlborough) which had provoked the comment from one British mother that American women were 'poachers' in the London marriage market and behaved like 'forward hussies'.[4] The success of Americans in capturing titled husbands was viewed with resentment by mothers with daughters of marriageable age on their hands. By the early 1900s, however, the invective had switched from a contempt for uncouth, ill-bred ex-colonials and dismissal of Americans' ambitiousness and social climbing to a much more aggressive form of hostility. In 1904 H. B. Marriott-Watson described American women as cold of heart and cool of head in one of his articles for *The Nineteenth Century and After*.[5] For him, the American woman was allowing her personal ambitions to dictate sexual relations, and this spelt danger for the future of the race: women were not marrying for love and devoting themselves to motherhood. A year later, a more extreme view was expressed by an anonymous contributor to the *Contemporary Review*. The author took up this theme of American women shirking motherhood and alleged that American peeresses were having a devastating effect upon British families: the failure of some women to produce male heirs meant that some titles would become extinct.

We can characterize this shift of attitude in another way. Whereas in the 1870s and 1880s the general view was that Americans were married for their money, by the peak years of transatlantic marriages, 1895–1905, American women were being portrayed as the ones who were doing the exploiting, buying titles. Attitudes definitely hardened towards Americans around the turn of the century, and yet this was a time when Anglo-American societies were flourishing, such as the American Society of London (1895), the Anglo-American League (1898), the Society of American Women (1899), the Atlantic Union (1901), and the Pilgrims (1902).[6] Attitudes towards transatlantic marriages, it would appear, did not coincide with the activities of politically minded groups in London society trying to promote Anglo-American friendship. Even though the social contact between the British and Americans elites increased, there is no real evidence that the British aristocracy felt more at ease with the growing number of transatlantic marriages. There was a underlying anxiety about the implications, and this was related, above all, to the role of money. The almost indiscriminate use of the term 'heiress' would appear to confirm this.

In addition to the frequency with which titled Americans were described as heiresses, it is possible to identify a stereotypical image of these women presented in the newspapers, journals, contemporary fiction, and autobiographies of the period. Along with wealth went a set of characteristics which denoted the social origins of 'the American heiress' and accounted for her success in the London marriage market. The stereotype cut across both British and American culture, although there were different aspects depending upon the nationality and cosmopolitanism of the perceiver. Within British society the formation of this stereotype denoted a need amongst contemporaries to understand the changes taking place around them and it performed a specific function. But before looking at the way the American heiress stereotype operated in Britain, we need to establish its content, that is to say, the characteristics which were attributed to these women.[7]

Contemporary fiction is a rich source of American heiress stereotypes, From such novels as *The Shuttle, Transplanted Daughters, The Anglo-Americans*, and *His Fortunate Grace* – all written in the 1900s – we can construct a composite American heiress. The woman herself was usually the daughter of a rich businessman who had made his money since the Civil War. She often had the reputation of being a beauty and was considered an individual, that is to say, someone with character. In many stories, it was the mother who was anxious for the daughter to marry well and who saw advantages accruing to herself by allying her daughter to a noble household, even if the suitor was penniless and this was almost always the case. The family was usually based in New York and moved in fashionable circles. This fictional stereotype was not far removed from the way that titled Americans were described in newspapers or perceived in London society, with a few added embellishments to represent the American woman in a more negative light. Among the features most likely to provoke comment were the woman's appearance, her behaviour, and her social origins.

Newspaper reporters of Anglo-Americans weddings on both sides of the Atlantic were obsessed with the physical appearance of the bride. British papers, such as the *Daily Mail* or *Vanity Fair*, were particularly inclined to dwell on this, as the following examples illustrate:

> The bride . . . is a tall and beautiful blond.[8]

> She is of graceful figure, fond of athletics, of intensely artistic temperament.[9]

> The Duchess of Marlborough is becoming one of the most popular women in London. She is a very popular woman, generous, exceedingly amusing, and pleasant. She has considerable good looks as well.[10]

The New York newspapers were even more prone to giving glowing descriptions of Americans who married into the British peerage. The *New York World* contained descriptions of Mrs McCreevy (the Hon. Mrs Coventry), Eloise Breese (Lady Ancaster), and Anne Breese (Lady Innes-Kerr) as being, respectively, 'a lovely and vivacious woman', 'very handsome, with a brilliant complexion, dark curly hair and dark eyes', and 'classically beautiful'.[11] Anyone reading either British of American newspaper accounts would have been left with the distinct impression that most of the American women who married into the peerage were renowned beauties. More general comments on American peeresses reinforce this impression of beauty, as do descriptions of individual Americans contained in memoirs.[12] The sixth Duke of Portland, for example, remembered Consuelo Manchester for the way 'she took Society completely by storm by her beauty, wit and vivacity, and it was soon at her very pretty feet'.[13] Consuelo was described in one New York paper in 1898 as having been 'one of the loveliest girls in the United States'.[14] Consuelo Vanderbilt Balsan referred to her compatriot, Mary Curzon, as 'a dazzling beauty'.[15] There is no shortage of testimonies to the beauty of many of the titled American women in London society, and, while the emphasis placed on physical attractiveness varied from person to person, it is nevertheless apparent that beauty was an integral part of the heiress stereotype. It could even be suggested that beauty went hand in hand with the notion of wealth and reinforced the view that only exceptionally wealthy or beautiful women outside the aristocracy were successful in marrying into the class above.[16]

Another aspect of the physical appearance of American women frequently commented upon was the way they dressed. Frederick Martin, an American whose niece married the Earl of Craven, wrote of American peeresses: 'They believe in the value of advertisement, they like to see society paragraphs about their jewels and their gowns.'[17] The Society columns in both American and British papers were filled with the details of gowns and jewellery worn at weddings and balls. *Queen*, especially, concentrated on the dresses of the women in its column headed 'Fashionable Marriages'. Mary Leiter's wedding dress, for example, was described as

> a white satin trained gown, trimmed with old point lace, which had been worn by her mother and her grandmother at their weddings. Her only ornament was a diamond brooch, the gift of the bridegroom; and she carried a bouquet of the loveliest white orchids.[18]

Belle Herbert, writing to her parents about her first trip to Cowes, made frequent mention of the dresses she and her sister, May Goelet, wore:

> Monday night Mr Mackay gave a pretty dance and I wore a lovely grey tulle ball dress which I had all beautifully packed to send home. It was immensely admired . . . and it was so lucky that I had pretty dresses as everyone talked so much about our clothes. . . . Our Cowes week was most disastrous on our clothes everything that we wore there is nearly ruined so that I am afraid it will be rather hard on Papa's purse.[19]

Clothes are, of course, an essential part of stereotyping, since they give some indication of a person's wealth and social standing, and Belle Wilson's comments reveal the pressure in smart society to conform to its standards of conspicuous expenditure. The selection of an appropriate gown for a social function also indicated that the wearer was *au fait* with the latest fashions and customs in Society. Consuelo Vanderbilt Balsan recalled how on one occasion the Prince of Wales brought to her attention her neglect to wear 'the prescribed tiara' at a dinner in their honour: 'The Princess has taken the trouble to wear a tiara. Why have you not done so?'[20]

One man who benefited from the demand for fashionable gowns to wear in London was the Parisian couturier, Jean Worth. In fact, on the occasion of Worth's death, the *Illustrated London News* commented that

> Worth was fortunate enough to secure the patronage of the Empress Eugénie in the hey-day of the Empire, but he ruled that sovereign as he ruled the American heiresses who, in the degenerate days of the Third Republic, became his chief clients.[21]

In 1867, several years before transatlantic marriages had become frequent occurrences, an article appeared in *Harper's* severely criticizing American women's devotion to French fashion.[22] It denounced the 'ludicrous' way in which American women avidly followed Parisian fashions and adopted the latest styles without thought as to their suitability. It claimed that Parisian fashion leaders were physically unattractive and asked the question:

> Why should American women so strenuously endeavour to follow out the Paris fashions, which are invented by capricious women of rank and wealth, or by the dress-makers, who, with the intention of inciting their customers to inordinate expenditure, rack their imaginations for the purpose of producing 'something new'?

The article sets up an interesting opposition between the simple, practical, unostentatious daughters of the American Republic and the conniving, avaricious European dressmaker with his wasteful, vain, aristocratic clients. The criticism is hammered home with a final point about the 'baneful influence' these American slaves to Parisian fashion were having on American society: the inability of young men to afford to marry extravagant wives, the encouragement of flirtation, the rendering of domesticity as distasteful, and worst of all the incompatibility of such women with a home life. This critique of American women in the leisured elite prefigures the argument which developed later about the growing anti-domestic inclinations of young women.

American women may have been amongst the best-dressed women in London, but the extent of their wardrobe testified ultimately to the financial resources of their family. In Belle's letter to her parents, the account of her success at Cowes is to a large degree attributed to the expensive gowns she had just purchased in Paris, and the excuse for such an outlay was that it attracted the attention of royalty. The implication is that a comparatively small sum spent on clothes could reap large rewards. Moreover, Belle was implying that her success would be a reflection of her father's financial standing. This is, of course, similar to Thorstein Veblen's argument about dress as 'an expression of the pecuniary culture'. 'In the common run of cases', he wrote,

> the conscious motive of the wearer or purchaser of conspicuously wasteful apparel is the need of conforming to established usage, and of living up to the accredited standard of taste and reputability. It is not only that one must be guided by the code of proprieties in dress in order to avoid the mortification that comes of unfavourable notice and comment . . . but besides that, the requirement of expensiveness is so ingrained into our habits of thought in matters of dress that any other than expensive apparel is instinctively odious to us.[23]

Veblen went on to say that expensive clothes signified that the wearer both consumed 'a relatively large value' (an important fact to demonstrate to members of his/her own social group or the one s/he aspired to join) and consumed without producing (a demonstration for the benefit of social inferiors). In accordance with Veblen's theory of the leisure class, the expenditure of Americans on Parisian gowns – the annual visit to Worth's rooms to purchase his latest creations for the coming Season – was intended as a 'subtler sign of expenditure' to be interpreted by a knowing elite as proof of their social worth.

Moving on to behaviour, there are perhaps three main aspects of the behaviour of American women which received much comment: their speech, their character, and their expenditure of money. In her memoirs, Lady Randolph Churchill noted the tendency to reduce Americans to one type and the way in which American speech was ridiculed in *Punch* and elsewhere:

> The innumerable caricatures supposed to represent the typical American girl depicted her always of one type: beautiful and refined in appearance, but dressed in exaggerated style, and speaking – with a nasal twang – the most impossible language. The young lady who, in refusing anything to eat, says, 'I'm pretty crowded just now,' or in explaining why she is travelling alone, remarks that 'Poppa don't voyage, he's too fleshy,' was thought to be representative of the national type and manners.[24]

Henry James took Trollope to task for his treatment of American speech in fiction. The gross grammatical errors of Isabel Boncassen's speech in *The Duke's Children* were, according to James, more representative of the English misapprehension of American speech than of American speech itself. In his critique of Trollope, James seems to be implying that the English novelist's portrayal of the American girl was wholly misconceived, that if Trollope could not discover 'the mysteries of her conversation' then he could not possibly get the rest right.[25] The American accent and idioms or colloquialisms were one more characteristic which could be held up to ridicule, as they still are today, and which could be used to emphasize that Americans did not fit in. In Britain, of course, accent was (and still is, to some extent) used as an indicator of social class.

When examining the way contemporaries described the character of the American woman, it becomes evident that, in fact, two different positions were adopted. On the one hand, there were social commentators like Frederick Martin, Smalley, and Corelli who wrote of the independence, adaptability, charm, energy, and resourcefulness of 'the American woman', while, on the other, there was the image of the rich, overdressed social climber who fawned upon titled aristocrats.[26] Corelli actually made the distinction between the two types and called the latter the 'American Female Bounder'.[27] She characterized this type as follows:

> She is fond of 'frocks and frills' – and wears an enormous quantity of jewels, 'stones' as she calls them. She 'pushes' herself in every possible social direction, and wherever she sees she is not wanted, there, more particularly than elsewhere, she continues to force an entry.

It was this type, 'the Bounder', which was closest to the American heiress stereotype.

The notion of American women buying their way into the best society, as opposed to being naturally taken up by members of that society, implied that, apart from their wealth, these women had little to recommend them. This in turn, undermined the concept of Society as a collection of people 'chiefly distinguished for their good-breeding, culture and refinement'.[28] In 1905 *Vanity Fair* published an article about the way in which the new American ambassador and his wife (the Whitelaw Reids) were using their influence to discriminate amongst their compatriots. It went on to say: 'Within the last ten or fifteen years, mysterious strangers from across the Atlantic, better furnished with dollars than credentials, have turned up in our midst, and have been taken unquestioningly at their own valuation.'[29] This relaxation of social barriers was attributed to the expense of entertaining, and there is, in fact, ample journalistic evidence that Americans were providing some very lavish entertainments during the London Season. The *New York American* noted, in a self-congratulatory tone, that

> The dominance of Americans has been the most striking feature of the social season just closed, admitted on all sides to be the most successful and brilliant in a generation. This distinction has been achieved mainly by the lavish entertainments of Americans and the invigoration they have infused into almost all society functions during the last few months.[30]

Another American newspaper report was more ambiguous in its comments about the expenditure of Americans in London society. While it unequivocally stated that the motive behind such expenditure was social ambition, it also insinuated that London society was not as superior as it purported to be: 'Much as the English sneer at Americans, particularly rich Americans, dollars will more readily win position in London than anywhere else in the world.'[31] T. H. S. Escott, amongst others, blamed the rise in the cost of living within smart society on American millionaires competing with colonial plutocrats. This sort of attitude towards American expenditure on entertainments was behind much of the resentment about the social success of Americans in London.[32] This resentment, however, coexisted with a favourable response to those Americans who provided entertainments. *Vanity Fair*, for example, praised American hostesses in London as follows: 'they entertain with an originality, an entrain, and, above all, a splendid disregard for money, which our sadly handicapped aristocracy cannot afford to imitate.'[33] In a similar vein, a dinner and concert given by Mrs Bradley Martin, mother of Lady Craven, was praised in an article entitled 'America in London', published in *The King*.[34] Whether people resented or welcomed wealthy Americans into the inner circles of London society, they assumed that Americans were willing to pay handsomely to gain entry. And it was this willingness to spend money in order to establish or maintain their social position which was associated with American heiresses.

Appearance and behaviour are not the only factors which contribute to the perception of a person. Information relating to life-style and social origins will also affect the way that someone is 'placed' in our experience of different social types. A woman might be considered wealthy and competitive in Society, but if she is a British aristocrat different deductions will be made about her behaviour from those about a businessman's daughter. Knowledge of the social origins of an outsider to London's social elite, however incomplete, was crucial to the weighing up of a person's acceptability.

American women were closely associated with New York and the Four Hundred. The British tended not to make the finer distinctions between Americans from different parts of the country, as Jennie Churchill complained:

> The wife and daughters of the newly-enriched Californian miner, swathed in silks and satins, and blazing with diamonds on the smallest provocation; the cultured, refined, and retiring Bostonian; the aristocratic Virginian, as full of tradition and family as a Percy of Northumberland, or a La Rochefoucauld; the cosmopolitan and up-to-date New Yorker – all were grouped in the same category, all were considered tarred with the same brush.[35]

Nor did they make, so it was alleged, distinctions between Americans of reputable social standing and parvenues. Americans themselves were of course keenly aware of the origins and age of wealth and regarded it as an insult that British aristocrats failed to be discriminating. As *Vanity Fair* reported: 'It has happened that members of that exclusive body the "Four Hundred" have been dreadfully shocked to find some compatriot who is taboo on the other side of the water received with open arms in Belgravia and Mayfair.'[36] 'And as for the American women who had themselves presented at the English court', wrote Edith Wharton in her memoirs, 'well, one had only to see with whom they associated at home!'[37] With the appointment of Whitelaw Reid as Ambassador to Britain in 1905, it was hoped that he would exercise more control over presentations at court than his predecessor.[38] American expatriates in London, such as the Duchesses of Marlborough and

Roxburghe, Mary Curzon, and Jennie Cornwallis-West, were said to 'resent being classified with some other Americans who come over and try to push themselves into the inner circles'.[39]

Henry James's short story 'The Siege of London', published in 1883, deals with the predicament of three Americans already established in London society who are called upon to vouch for a compatriot, Mrs Headway. The narrative hinges upon Mrs Headway's past. All we are told is that she is a Westerner and, although a wealthy widow at the opening of the story, she has been married and divorced several times. We know as much about Mrs Headway's past as her suitor, Sir Arthur Demesne, and his mother. The Demesnes are curious about Mrs Headway, they do not quite know what to make of her. Sir Arthur, it is said, 'hardly knew by what standard to measure her . . . and yet it was impossible not to see that she had a standard of her own'.[40] In order to find out if she is a suitable person to marry, Sir Arthur and his mother approach three Americans who are acquainted with Mrs Headway. The first is a rich man of leisure, George Littlemore, whom Sir Arthur visits to ask if Littlemore knows anything against Mrs Headway. But Littlemore makes it quite clear that he does not wish the subject to be broached, as he later tells his friend, Rupert Waterville: 'He [Sir Arthur] has no right, at any rate, to ask me such a question.'[41] The scene between the two men highlights the delicacy of Sir Arthur's quest for information and Littlemore's response. Littlemore is not prepared to tell Sir Arthur what he has already told Waterville, namely that Mrs Headway is not respectable, and he cannot be evasive because this would indicate that Mrs Headway's standing was questionable, so he has to lie. But the situation does not arise. Sir Arthur hesitates for a minute as he takes his leave of Littlemore but finally realizes that he cannot ask him such questions. To have done so would have been presuming upon an intimacy between himself and Littlemore which does not exist. Littlemore, moreover, has been introduced to him by Mrs Headway as an old friend of hers, and by asking Littlemore for any personal information about Mrs Headway, Sir Arthur would have been asking Littlemore to break a confidence. Littlemore tells his friend Waterville that he would have been duty-bound in any case to lie to protect Mrs Headway's honour. In fact, he says it would be 'a joke to see her married to that superior being!'[42] Waterville, however, finds the situation uncomfortable, especially as he is a junior secretary at the US Legation and feels a certain amount of responsibility: 'he asked himself more than once how far it was permitted to him to countenance Mrs Headway's pretensions to being an American lady'.[43] When he is cornered by Lady Demesne, he follows Littlemore's line of defence by refusing to say anything against Mrs Headway.

Finally, Lady Demesne writes to Littlemore's sister, Mrs Dolphin, who has married a Hampshire squire and settled in England and who is 'usually not taken for an American'.[44] Mrs Dolphin discusses the letter with her brother, who admits that Mrs Headway has not 'behaved properly' but he still does not regard her as being 'much worse than many other women'.[45] Although inwardly 'irritated' by Mrs Headway's success in London, Littlemore still regards it as amusing. His sister, too, can appreciate that English society has only itself to blame for being so lax. She complains to her brother: 'English society has become scandalously easy. I never saw anything like the people that are taken up. . . . It's like the decadence of the Roman Empire. You can see to look at Mrs Headway that she's not a lady.'[46] Nevertheless, Mrs Dolphin does not like the way Mrs Headway has 'abused the facilities of things', that is, taken advantage of the ignorance of the British. And it is for this reason that she feels it is her 'duty', her 'responsibility', and her sense of 'decency' which require her to inform the Demesnes. She tells her brother:

> What I see is a fine old race – one of the oldest and most honourable in England, people with every tradition of good conduct and high principle – and a dreadful, disreputable, vulgar little woman, who hasn't an idea of what such things are, trying to force her way into it. I hate to see such things – I want to go to the rescue![47]

But the crux of the matter for Mrs Dolphin has less to do with her romantic notions of the British aristocracy and more to do with her own self-interest as someone who is 'a party to an international marriage', as we are told: 'Mrs Dolphin naturally wished that the class to which she belonged should close its ranks and carry its standard high.'[48]

As early as 1883, then, James had hit upon a tendency amongst American expatriates which became more pronounced over the next thirty years or so, i.e. for the Americans who had succeeded in establishing their social position in Europe to make it harder for those who came after them. Mrs Dolphin, we are told, 'borrowed distinction' from being one of a few American women in England. If international marriages became commonplace she would lose the interest of those who found her a novelty. At the same time, the opposition of titled Americans to newcomers, especially those with less reputable social origins than themselves, can be understood as a desire to retain the value of their achievement in gaining entry into European society. The opening up of the nobility to anyone of wealth would have severely detracted from the status which they had acquired. This response is exactly the same as the one of New Yorkers in the fluid social situation in the last third of the nineteenth century.

Edith Wharton, who had herself expressed contempt for social climbers in the Gilded Age, satirized the attempts of the newly rich to establish a foothold in fashionable society in her unfinished novel, *The Buccaneers*:

> When Colonel St George bought his house in Madison Avenue it seemed to him fit to satisfy the ambitions of any budding millionaire. That it had been built and decorated by one of the Tweed ring . . . was to Colonel St George convincing proof that it was a suitable setting for wealth and elegance. But social education is acquired rapidly in New York . . . and Mrs St George had already found that *no one lived in Madison Avenue*, that the front hall should have been painted Pompeian red with a stencilled frieze, and not with naked Cupids and humming birds on a sky-blue ground, and that basement dining-rooms were unknown to the fashionable [emphasis added].[49]

What Edith Wharton was pointing to here is the way that location of a residence, and even the way it was painted, was a means of determining whether a person, or family, was in Society or not. Only those within the inner sanctum were, after all, informed as to the latest fashion in décor. It is rather revealing about Wharton's social prejudices that the vestibule of her family's home on West Twenty-third Street, just off Fifth Avenue, was in fact painted 'Pompeian red'.[50] Fashion, whether it be in dress, furnishings, portrait painting, or types of entertainment, acted as a form of social arbitration; it was also a test of financial standing. In Veblen's terms, this is classified as 'pecuniary canons of taste', where a consumer conforms to 'a standard of expensiveness and wastefulness in his consumption of goods'.[51] But such indicators of a person's social status would not have been readily available to the British elite. In London Americans would have rented the homes of aristocrats or stayed in fashionable hotels which would have underscored the impression of their substantial financial resources without necessarily detracting from their claims to social recognition. The relative anonymity of Americans away from home and their detachment from certain signs of their social position such as place of residence made it difficult, as we have seen illustrated in 'The Siege of London', for the British to judge Americans. That is perhaps why there is a considerable degree of interrelationships amongst titled Americans in Britain: there were at least ten sets of sisters who married into the British elite and another five women who married into the peerage twice.[52]

British aristocrats were not totally at a loss in trying to place Americans socially. As we have already noted in an earlier chapter, the Duke of Marlborough made inquiries by letter about Leonard Jerome. The Duke's reaction to the reports he received was duly conveyed to his son:

> from what you tell me and what I have heard, this Mr J. seems to be a sporting, and I should think vulgar kind of man. I hear he drives about six and eight horses in New York (one may take this as a kind of indication of what the man is).[53]

The vulgarity of Jerome's sporting proclivities was compounded by the fact that he made his money by speculating on the stock market. The precariousness of such income and the daily business of calculating monetary gain would have been anathema to the Duke. The occupation of a prospective daughter-in-law's father was one way of judging a person's social standing – but according to British rather than American standards. Even so, although the main distinction for aristocrats would have been between landed and commercial wealth, there was an advantage to marrying the daughter of an American businessman as opposed to that of a British plutocrat – the source of American wealth would have been relatively anonymous. This double standard is illustrated rather well by the predicament of Mrs Gordon Selfridge, who, in 1909, wished to secure an invitation to a court levée in London. Presentation at court was, of course, the ultimate test of social acceptability in Britain. It was a keenly sought distinction, and Americans competed for the invitations to Drawing Rooms and levées at the disposal of the American Ambassador. Whitelaw Reid, conscious of some of the criticism that his predecessors had attracted by failing to filter out those Americans of dubious reputation, was at pains to scrutinize the social qualifications of the many applicants. In 1909 he was approached by Mrs Selfridge. As the wife of an American businessman, she was 'perfectly eligible', as Reid told Mrs Taft, but as 'the wife of a shop-keeper in London in sharp and aggressive daily competition with other shopkeepers', she could not qualify for presentation.[54] To break the rule against people in trade would have offended British retailers and put the court and the Embassy in an awkward position.

The basic characteristics of the American heiress, therefore, are that she was beautiful, dressed expensively, talked with an unpleasant accent, knew how to be charming and win men over, was 'pushy', and the daughter of a wealthy New York businessman. As time went on, certain characteristics were embellished to support a more negative view of American women which emphasized the detrimental effect they were having on the peerage. By the turn of the century conjecture and prejudice contributed to an image of the American woman as frivolous, vain, and calculating. Money appeared to be at the heart of it all, and this has already been amply demonstrated in the way that the appearance, behaviour, and social origins of Americans were described in newspapers, journals, social commentary, and memoirs. Transatlantic marriages exacerbated a conflict between the aristocratic code and the new values of the plutocratic class, and it is in this context that we can best understand how the heiress stereotype functioned. Despite the fact that big businessmen had been filtering into Society for over a generation and that some had received the additional kudos of hereditary peerages, protests against them became more strident around the turn of the century. As well as from within aristocratic circles, plutocrats attracted criticism from outside the upper classes. In right-wing political quarters the alliance of the aristocracy and plutocracy spelt corruption, while the eugenicists, William and Catherine Whetham, blamed the *nouveaux riches* for the demoralization of the upper classes.[55] There was a certain degree of distrust of both businessmen and their ethics, but there was no British counterpart to the American Progressive movement attacking corruption in the business world.

The particularly hostile view of American women which gained currency in the early 1900s must be seen against this background of distrust and suspicion of the business classes in general. Marriott-Watson placed a very sinister interpretation on transatlantic marriages. Writing for *The Nineteenth Century and After* in 1903, he warned British society of what was in store *if* Britain followed the United States into the commercial age.[56] He regarded the cold-bloodedness of American females, which he represented as the calculations of an imaginary Chicago pork-butcher's daughter buying an English coronet, as a sign of America's degeneracy. He fully accepted the popular notion of American men devoting their lives to money-making while leaving their wives to the pursuit of pleasure and 'abnormal activities', and argued that the worship of titles, money, and Society was harmful to women. He made it very clear that such preoccupations caused infertility; this was the result most to be feared, and his rhetoric was structured to make this point with the greatest effect: 'overworked men and nervous women tending to sterility, and living upon an artificial plane', he warned, 'do not promise a brave future for the nation'.[57]

An even more extreme stance was taken by an anonymous contributor to the *Contemporary Review* two years later. In an article comparing titled American women to titled colonials, the author slighted the American contribution to British society and alleged that the influence of American women in Society 'makes for cheapness'.[58] S/he claimed, furthermore, that transatlantic marriages were less productive than colonial alliances in terms of offspring. This type of polemical, racist literature found an audience amongst those primed by the ideas of the Radical Right and the eugenics movement in Britain. Some members of the aristocracy who embraced these views took their role as social leaders, 'weighted with the ultimate eugenic responsibility',[59] very seriously. Arguments put forward about the inability of American peeresses to bear children were intended to increase the fears of the British aristocracy about its inability to maintain its numbers.

The weight of these essentially racist arguments fell upon American women rather than upon the aristocrats who married them, or welcomed them into their social circles. It was Americans who were accredited with the taint of commercialism and moral weakness, not the peers who allegedly sold their titles, or the peeresses who sold introductions. The fear of the effects of materialism on social and political relations was displaced by attributing to Americans an even greater obsession with money. Whether this is true or not is less important than the fact that the aristocratic class, and the socio-economic groups which emulated it, failed to perceive how money had already become the basis of all relationships within its Society.[60] Americans, after all, were not responsible for marriage settlements, and some Americans objected strongly to the principle of financially supporting sons-in-law. Lady Dorothy Nevill, whose comments on the entry of American women into London society are widely quoted, no doubt struck a sympathetic chord amongst aristocratic families when she attributed to Americans the 'new conception of life', i.e. the idea that wealth was 'the ultimate end of existence'.[61] George Cornwallis-West, the second husband of Jennie Churchill and a relative of Lord de la Warr, was far less circumspect about the transformation of Society. As a beneficiary of plutocratic wealth and influence – Sir Ernest Cassel helped him to find lucrative employment with an electrical engineering firm – Cornwallis-West recalled the Edwardian years with much nostalgia: 'Those were wonderful days. Taxation and the cost of living were low; money was freely spent and wealth was everywhere in evidence. Moreover it was possessed by the nicest people, who entertained both in London and in the country.'[62] His emphasis on 'the nicest people' sounds like a rejoinder to all the criticism of plutocratic ostentation. Marie Corelli, in contrast, attacked both the aristocracy and plutocracy (Americans included) for their 'insane worship of wealth'. She regarded 'cash power' or 'money-dominance', i.e. the use of wealth to buy position and power, as an 'American taint' as far as its origin was concerned, but it was certainly not her intention to turn Americans into scapegoats by making them solely responsible for modern-day ostentation. Instead, she was at pains to show how the aristocracy had willingly abandoned older standards of 'simplicity, sincerity and hospitality' for vulgar ostentation, self-advertisement, and greed.[63] In fact, her harshest censure was reserved for the titled aristocrat who tried to use his title for financial gain. In her portrayal of American women in England, on the other hand, Corelli depicted the operation of the heiress stereotype with a slightly different emphasis: 'it often happens that the sight of a charmingly dressed, graceful, generally "smart" American girl attracts the stolid Britisher in the first place because he says to himself – "Money!" '64 Here, Corelli shows quite clearly that the material motives are exclusively confined to the British side. Her stereotypes, at least, were not drawn to uphold the status quo.

In the 1890s Elizabeth Banks, a young American journalist, exposed the vulnerability of the landed elite to financial pressures by inserting the following advertisement in a London newspaper: 'A young American Lady of means wishes to meet with a chaperon of Highest Social Position, who will introduce her into the Best English Society. Liberal terms. Address, "Heiress".'65 Within two days she had received eighty-seven replies, including some from titled personages. One Lady X proposed a visit to the South of France that winter, presumably as a rehearsal for the following London Season during which she promised to present 'Heiress' at a drawing-room. The terms Lady X proposed were £100 per month in France, in addition to travelling and accommodation expenses, and £200 per month in London. The most telling point of all, however, was that Lady X asked for bankers' references to attest to her client's financial soundness, but made no inquiries as to her social position. Elizabeth Banks followed up this offer and wrote to Lady X emphasizing that she came from a family of no social standing or refinement, couching her reply in terms which would evoke a change of mind in the least of snobs. In fact, Lady X remained undeterred. Among the other replies, a dowager claimed that she could supply 'Heiress' with both social position and a husband for a total of £5,000. According to the young journalist, who interviewed some of her prospective chaperons, the offers appeared to be genuine and were generally from people who found themselves in a position of financial embarrassment.[66]

If British society was as commercialized as that of the United States, as indeed the evidence of writers like Corelli, Escott, and Elizabeth Banks would very much seem to suggest, why then did Marriott-Watson and other social commentators on Americans concentrate so much more on the materialism of American life?

Part of the answer lies in the belief that Americans posed a greater threat to aristocratic values, since both the number and size of American fortunes far exceeded those of British-based fortunes. W. D. Rubinstein has estimated that in the period in question American multi-millionaires were roughly twenty times richer than their British counterparts.[67] He has also suggested that, out of deference to the ritual of aristocratic social life, British millionaires were less ostentatiously conspicuous than Americans.[68] The Duchess of Marlborough was allegedly made to feel that 'certain standards' had to be maintained, and her 'democratic ideals' had no place in Churchill family tradition.[69] Other American peeresses were also made to feel that the onus of assimilation lay upon them, rather than upon the British family into which they married. It is feasible that the British landed elite felt they had a greater measure of control over native-born plutocrats than over the more independent-minded republicans with their superior financial resources.

A more convincing explanation, however, is the fact that British aristocrats could disassociate themselves from the current obsession with money and profits by blaming foreign plutocrats for lowering the tone of Society.[70] It deflected accusations about growing materialism away from an aristocratic social structure which depended upon wealth and conspicuous display. The extent to which wealth and financial standing were an important element in aristocratic power had been disguised by the emphasis placed on public service, honour, birth, and tradition; it was these values which had contributed to the exclusiveness of the landed aristocracy. Once Society and the peerage were open to men from all walks of life, regardless of birth and occupation, the only way of asserting social leadership was through the power of the purse. By blaming Americans and Jews for the change in standards, the aristocracy could draw upon powerful national prejudices and thus avoid too close a scrutiny of the aristocratic system itself.

The stereotyping of Americans as materialistic, which has persisted to the present day, tells us a great deal about the way the British perceived themselves in the years when the United States was beginning to have a major economic impact upon Britain. In one of the earliest discussions of stereotypes, Walter Lippmann attempted to explain how they functioned:

> in the great blooming, buzzing confusion of the outer world, we pick out what our culture has already defined for us, and we tend to perceive that which we have picked out in the form stereotyped for us by our culture.

But, he went on to say, it was not simply a matter of imposing order on reality, but also 'the projection upon the world of our own sense of our own value, our own position and our own rights'.[71]

Articles written by visitors to the United States offering a British perspective on the development of the young republic appear to have been in vogue around the turn of the century. They invariably involved a measuring of American society against an undefined but recognizable British standard. Frederic Harrison, for example, noted the rapid accumulation of wealth, and the absence of *noblesse oblique* amongst the elite.[72] Although the article is entitled 'Impressions of America', Harrison's observations of American life are strictly comparative. Amyas Northcote, younger son of the statesman Lord Iddlesleigh, also wrote an article for *The Nineteenth Century* which was more open in its attempt to evaluate American society from an English point of view.[73] Northcote set out to revise his countrymen's traditional set of cultural assumptions about Americans, not so much with the intention of unsettling British opinion of Americans but to try to deride American pride in democracy:

> In the land where all men are said to be born free and equal, and the titular distinctions of the Old World are supposed to be held in contempt, there is this large class . . . to whom the sayings and doings of the least known British peer are of more importance than those of their own President.[74]

The article contains many misconceptions and broad, generalized statements about the American elite, and in spite of his intentions Northcote reinforced existing cultural assumptions about Americans, i.e. that they lacked family tradition, that they pursued social distinction with an ostentatious display of their spending power, and that most gentlemen were commercial men, reckless and poorly educated. He saved his more generous words, i.e. 'charming' and 'accomplished', for American women. Whilst this may have been inevitable since his wife was an American, it nevertheless contradicted his description of American society as vulgar and materialistic. Unlike Marriott-Watson, Northcote was not prepared to see American women as part of the competitive, money-conscious commercial world.

Most of the articles written about United States in the late nineteenth and early twentieth centuries emphasized the American attitude towards money, both in the earning and the spending of it.[75] For Northcote, this aspect of American culture constituted the 'salient difference' between the two countries. This emphasis owes much to the tradition of classifying the business classes in Britain as 'the moneyed classes' and attributing monetary motives to all aspects of their behaviour. Disparaging of the different values held by the urban middle classes, the aristocracy traditionally considered them to be not only socially inferior, but also morally defective. Much emphasis, for example, was placed on the ability of a man of independent means to be objective in the political arena; as Taine observed:

> the monied man and the man of business is inclined to selfishness; he has not the disinterestedness, the large and generous views which suit a chief of the country; he does not know how to sink self, and think of the public.[76]

But by the closing years of the nineteenth century the old, hard core of the aristocracy was fighting a losing battle against the various encroachments on its power and position, so that these expressions of contempt for American entrepreneurs and their life-style were no more than fading echoes of a past era.

Blaming foreigners for the decline in standards in Society enabled the old ruling class to condemn with more ferocity the changes that were occurring within its social structure – changes which owed much more to domestic developments within the British economy than to the entry of foreign plutocrats into high society. It was, at the same time, easier and safer to condemn foreigners than to attack the British entrepreneurial class, and yet the criticism of foreign plutocrats was made largely in the familiar terms used to denigrate upwardly mobile members of the urban middle classes.[77] The antagonism towards the speedy entry of plutocrats into elite society was, however, inevitable. In the past, it had been possible to measure the power of aristocratic social prestige (and wealth) in terms of the number of generations it took for a rising family to be assimilated into the elite. It was bound to be disconcerting now that it took less than one generation to gain access to the elite, hence the lament that it was no longer possible to determine who was, and who was not, a gentleman.[78]

The stereotype of the impoverished peer who sells his title to redeem his position in the leisured, gentlemanly class presupposes the existence of a rich woman prepared to buy herself a title and social distinction, and the result – a marriage of convenience – is seen as a perversion of the sacred vows of marriage, as a kind of prostitution. These negative images of the impoverished peer, the heiress, and their unholy contract imply, in turn, an accepted standard of behaviour according to which men and women do not act for monetary motives; and, for the middle and upper classes at least, this standard was compatible with the gentlemanly code and the cult of domesticity.[79] The two images of women which relate to the cult of domesticity and its antonym, i.e. the Angel in the House and the Seductress, are both products of a patriarchal culture in which women are regarded, alternately, either as pieces of property or as sex objects. In other words, women do not exist for themselves; they exist for men as types, either as alluring mistresses or as blindly devoted wives, mothers, and daughters.

The stereotype of the American heiress was an intensely derogatory image of the American women who married into the British peerage. By classifying them as daughters of plutocrats, the stereotype attributed vulgar, materialistic motives to these women. The image also promulgated the view that the heiress was a seductress who used her beauty and cunning to lure young men away from their duties and responsibilities as members of the ruling class (duties which included marrying within their own class). The concentration on the physical attractiveness and beautiful clothes in the descriptions of American women is evidence of this. Such details were not merely given to satisfy the interests of fashion-conscious peeresses, or, if so, it would be too naïve to assume they were received simply as details of current fashion. Rather, they contributed to an envy and distrust of these women with their superior financial resources. And this, in turn, points to the complicity of aristocratic women in the creation of the heiress stereotype.[80] After all, they had the most to lose by the opening up of the aristocratic marriage market to women from the moneyed classes because, by the same token, the market was not opened up to the male members of these classes. Aristocratic women lost (male-defined) caste by marrying out of their class. Within their (albeit subordinate) position in the aristocratic social structure, women had a certain amount of room for manoeuvre, influence, and power, but they believed this sphere to be threatened by the introduction of American women with greater financial independence. Unable to avoid their own entrapment in patriarchal society (except by

158

undergoing great personal sacrifice), they acquiesced in a male ideology which regarded women as appendages of men.

8

Speculation, sensation, and scandal: the American response to titled marriages

International marriages ceased to be a novelty. As Bettina Vanderpoel grew up, she grew up, so to speak, in the midst of them. She saw her country, its people, its newspapers, its literature, innocently rejoiced by the alliances its charming young women contracted with foreign rank. She saw it affectionately, gleefully, rubbing its hands over its duchesses, its countesses, its miladies.

(Frances Hodgson Burnett, *The Shuttle*, 1907)

American attitudes towards international marriages were almost an exact reversal of the British response. Whereas in the post-Civil War period, American newspapers reported exuberantly of the triumphs of American women in conquering the hearts of European noblemen, after the turn of the century a cynicism set in about the motives of titled foreigners which turned to resentment. International marriages had at first provided an opportunity, it appears, for Americans to take satisfaction from the acceptance of their social elite in the 'best' European society; but once the novelty wore off and the number of divorces increased, there was less to be proud of. Titled marriages did not ensure an American woman's happiness. In fact, it transpired that some women had been deceived by bogus noblemen and fortune-hunters and that Americans were having to pay large dowries for the 'honour' of having a titled son-in-law.

It is difficult to pinpoint when attitudes began to change. Judging from the newspaper reports it was the continental nobility which was to be treated with utmost suspicion up until the first decade of the twentieth century. In July 1895 Richard Harding Davis wrote an article about Americans in Paris for *Harper's* in which he described the suffering titled American who had been 'so much misrepresented in the press, and so misunderstood'. The problem for her, Davis wrote, was that although a title may seem 'a very pretty and desirable object' when in New York, 'the title has to be worn in Paris', and 'its importance lies in the way in which it is considered there'. His impression was that American women who had married French titles were very disappointed.[1] In October 1898 the *New York American* revealed that a New York woman had agreed to pay an Italian marquis $30,000 ('rather a low price') when he married her daughter but she had failed to honour the contract. The Marquis had therefore sued her. The newspaper commented: 'In European countries it is considered natural and proper for an impoverished nobleman to sell his name and title in marriage to a low-born woman. To American eyes such a transaction can only appear disgraceful and unnatural.'[2] Two months later the *New York Journal* published a list of bogus continental European titles and how much Americans had paid for them.[3] On the whole, it was said that British titles were preferred: 'The American girls who married continental titles have many of them lived to regret the day, but the Anglo-American marriages, however, have been wonderfully free from all the after-bitterness in any way.'[4] During Edward VII's reign, American newspapers reported in positive terms the activities of American peeresses in London society and how Americans were welcomed. The *McKeesport Times* noted enthusiastically that 'all London' was interested in 'the struggle for social supremacy' between the Duchesses of Manchester and Roxburghe following the removal of the Duchess of Marlborough from the social scene.[5] In 1905 the *New York World Sunday Magazine* asked if *Burke's Peerage* was 'becoming Americanized' with all the marriages that had taken place and proceeded to go into detail about the latest matches. In answering the question 'Why is Europe winning so many American brides?' the article's author wrote that 'pages could be written of their beauty, their brains, their wealth, their cleverness'.[6] Even so, despite the self-congratulatory nature of some reports, others with a more sceptical or perhaps a wryer tone began to appear. One of the more outrageous articles poking fun at the American mania for titles provided a list of eligible bachelors in the British aristocracy 'for the information of American heiresses'.[7] But it was the amount of money being spent on entertaining in London or dowries and weddings which constantly obsessed the American press, and from about 1906 onwards there was growing criticism of the wastefulness of this expenditure. This is not to say that there had not previously been negative commentary on this issue but rather to point to a more concerted effort to criticize the wealthy's 'craze for foreign titles', as one paper put it.

Anglo-American weddings were usually elaborate affairs, and the press was not entirely responsible for the effect of conspicuous display which came across in the newspaper reports. Publicity was an important factor in the celebration of an alliance between a member of New York's social elite and noble household in Europe. Wedding ceremonies gathered together an extensive peer group to witness the conjugal alliance of one of its members to a prestigious outsider. The presence of distinguished members of the American elite, including past or present Presidents, not only endorsed the union and but also testified to the social position, power, and economic resources of the bride's family. The marriage of May Goelet to the Duke of Roxburghe in 1903 was, for example, front-page news in the *Journal* with the headline: 'Magnificent Scene in St Thomas's Church as America's Richest Heiress Is Wedded to the English Nobleman'. According to the *Journal*, the occasion was the most important social event in New York since Consuelo Vanderbilt's wedding in 1895, and among the guests it listed members of the Goelet, Wilson, Astor, Whitney, Morgan, Mills, Gould, Livingston, Rockefeller, Fish, Rutherfurd, and Oelrich families together with a handful of titled Anglo-Americans.[8] The wedding party represented many of the wealthiest families in New York with a judicious sprinkling of families descended from the older Dutch elite. The immense outlay of capital on the wedding ceremony was the crowning of a successful, but costly, venture to 'capture' a spouse outside the immediate circle of relatives, friends, and acquaintances from which a husband would normally have been found at far less expense. Seeking spouses from a prestigious social group abroad involved establishing and maintaining contacts away from home, spending several Seasons in London or elsewhere in Europe, and participating actively in Society there. For the Goelet family this pattern of contacts had been established over twenty years. May's parents had visited Cowes and been received in royal circles, and her aunt had married into a distinguished family in the British peerage. Marriages with British dukes were, nevertheless, rare events, and this particular alliance bears witness to the Goelets' financial prowess (and generosity) when it is recalled that negotiations between Roxburghe and William Waldorf Astor had broken down over the size of Pauline Astor's dowry two years earlier.[9]

One of the major reasons for international marriages, particularly amongst the new moneyed elite, was the need to assert claims to high social status. With the proliferation of such marriages around the turn of the century, however, it was questionable whether the 'symbolic' returns, to use Bourdieu's term, on the extensive outlay of capital justified that expenditure. As titled marriages became more commonplace and involved women outside the major urban elites, their prestige declined accordingly. More significant, however, were the doubts raised about the fairness of the exchange and the ethics of the marriage settlement. Noticeable in the complaints about transatlantic marriages are three key issues: the loss of capital, the exploitation of American women, and the betrayal of democratic principles. The marriage of daughters to foreign nobles was no longer regarded as a compliment: the American social elite had come of age.

Such was the frequency of foreign marriages within the American elite in the 1890s and 1900s that it became especially newsworthy to report the marriage of an American heiress to a fellow American. The following comments appeared in the *New York World* beneath the headlines: 'And She Picked a Pittsburgher though She Might Have Had a Duke or Even a Prince':

> She is not marrying young Mr Phipps for the money that some day he will have. She has plenty already, and more to come than ever she can spend. And she certainly doesn't marry him for social position, because no Mills needs social position from anyone in New York. . . . It is just a love match, pure and simple. There is no exchange of wealth for title; no barter of millions for a coronet.[10]

The opposition set up here between domestic and foreign marriages is intended not only to celebrate the marriage of equals, and thus marriage for love, but to condemn the materialistic motivation involved in the marriage of non-equals. It was a simple point, not always true but effectively made and repeated over and over in articles about titled matches. Marriage settlements were a matter of course for the British aristocracy, although it was always a delicate procedure to decide on the appropriate size of the bride's portion if she was marrying a man of superior social status.[11] It was tacitly understood that the dowry for a woman outside the aristocracy should be considerably higher than that for an aristocrat's daughter, but, although this signified that the bride's family was honouring the husband's family, the alliance was usually conceived of as being advantageous to both sides. It was, in fact, important that the settlements achieve some kind of balance between the two parties to avoid any charge that the wife was being sold. However, European exploitation of the American marriage market, even to the extent of European men passing themselves off as titled gentlemen, destroyed any sense of balance and mutual advantage. The rapid rise in the number of international marriages around the turn of the century along with the increasing incidence of such marriages ending up in the divorce courts alarmed Americans about the amount of money flowing out of the country in the form of dowries and the number of women falling prey to the unrestrained greed and unscrupulousness of foreign aristocrats. The success of exogamous marriages depended upon both parties 'misrecognizing' the reality of the exchange,[12] i.e. that it was a swap of title for money, otherwise this could bring the system of marriage settlements into disrepute by acknowledging the material motivation behind a conjugal relationship. But the abuse of the marriage settlement procedure shattered the illusion that it had been possible to maintain despite the rise of the companionate marriage, and the American press in particular sought to expose the 'true' nature of these negotiations and condemn this form of conspicuous expenditure by the nation's elite.

From the 1900s onwards, the alienation of American capital through the marriage-settlement system dominated the headlines in the Society columns of American newspapers. The following headlines illustrate the kind of sensationalist treatment of titled marriages often found in the press:

Dukedoms for Ducats: Europe is $900,000,000 Ahead of America in Trading of Titles for Treasure.

Jean Reid Fears 'Dot' Hunters.

We Pay the Freight: Seven Titles Purchased at a Cost of Seventy-Five Millions.[13]

Various figures for the total sum of money involved were published from time to time. In his book on the history of the more notorious captains of industry, Gustavus Myers put the figure at 200 million dollars in 1911. This is the figure more usually quoted by biographers and historians rather than the fantastic sum of 900 million dollars estimated by a 'well known New York banker'. The figures for individual fortunes changing hands in these marital arrangements were often quoted and were the source of much wild speculation. The account of May Goelet's wedding, for example, was followed by an estimation of her fortune at over 10 million dollars. The *New York Times* was more conservative in its estimate: it reckoned her personal fortune to be 5 million dollars.[14] The publicity given to the financial aspects of titled marriages was deliberately provocative. In 1908 the London *Times* alleged that it was the marriages of Gladys Vanderbilt to Count Szechenyo and Theodora Shonts to the Duc de Chaulnes which 'brought to the front the long-smouldering proposal in some way to tax the dowry or settlement which is usually a consideration of these marriages'.[15] It might have been more accurate to have stated that it was the rumours in the American press about the size of these two women's dowries which had aroused public outrage at the amount of money leaving the country. One newspaper claimed that the price of Gladys Vanderbilt's dowry had been set at $12,500,000.[16] The same paper published a table of foreign marriages, entitled 'Heiresses Who Have Taken Themselves and Their Millions Out of America', with a column for the amount of dollars 'We Lost'.

The wealth that was being given away to European noblemen by American millionaires was not regarded as their own private capital to be disposed of in whatever fashion they chose, as this particular article suggests. Its author, P. Harvey Middleton, opened his diatribe with an appeal to national pride:

> By our little fracas of 1776 we cut loose from royalty and all its insignia and set to work as plain Americans to develop the vast natural resources of our country. In the last hundred years or so we have, by virtue of considerable toil and much ingenuity, won from the ground and from the mines below the ground many billions of dollars, and under a republican government we have thriven to such an extent that the United States is today the happy hunting ground of the millionaire instead of the redskin.

The world freely admits that we have proved ourselves a great
and mighty people, with great deeds behind us. And what do
you think is being done with these vast fortunes that have been
earned by such heart-aching and back-breaking toil?[17]

Myers took a similar line, pointing out the irony that although 'the
Vanderbilts could not afford to pay their workers a few cents more
in wages a day, they could afford to pay millions of dollars for
matrimonial alliances with foreign titles'.[18] The money being
pumped into the decaying stonework of English castles was,
according to this interpretation, being diverted away from American
workers and industry, and this, of course, was a sensitive issue when
the American economy was experiencing periodic slumps and was
dependent upon foreign investment.

The ensuing furore, created largely by the press, culminated in
a debate on Capitol Hill in the summer of 1911 when Mr Adolph
J. Sabath, a Representative from Illinois, introduced a resolution
which, as recorded, directed 'the Secretary of State to secure information concerning American ladies marrying titled foreigners, why
certain ones have not been permitted to take part in the Coronation
ceremonies in London, and for other purposes'.[19] Mr Sabath's somewhat curious speech was reported in the *New York World*, a copy of
which was retained by Whitelaw Reid in his extensive collection of
newspaper cuttings which mentioned his name or that of any
member of his family. It is not clear whether Reid had other reasons
for keeping a copy of Sabath's speech, or whether the speech was
directed at Reid and his distribution of tickets to the coronation
ceremony. Sabath's resolution requested two pieces of information:
(1) the reasons for the exclusion of certain American peeresses from
the ceremonies for George V's coronation, and (2) a list of all titled
American women, the amount of money spent on securing their
titles, the sources of the money so spent, and the number of women
divorced or separated from their husbands. He went on to ask

to what extent our country is being benefited by this trade and
whether or not our earnest, sober-minded and brave women are
not frequently subjected to ridicule and to cheap European
nobility wit by reasons of this craze on the part of these trust-
made rich, who are suffering from chronic titleitis.[20]

If his concern for the fate of American peeresses was genuine rather than ironic, then Sabath seems to have differentiated between the women and their families. Did he consider these women to have been sold by their families and therefore deserving the protection of the United States Congress? The ambiguity of this last part of Sabath's speech was neatly avoided in the congressional record by the use of the vague phrase 'for other purposes'. The resolution was passed on to the Committee on Foreign Affairs, but there is no further record of it. Interest in the destination of American dowries and the question of taxation died down with the coming of the First World War, and the subsequent turn-around in the balance of trade with Europe doubtless led to the issue being of less burning concern.

The conception of titled marriages as a drain on American capital in the pre-war years owes much to the publicity that surrounded Consuelo Vanderbilt's marriage to the Duke of Marlborough. Next to the Gould–Castellane match, which had been solemnized eight months earlier in New York, Consuelo Vanderbilt's marriage was regarded as the most notorious *cause célèbre* in the history of transatlantic marriages. At the time, it attracted much attention because of the interest of the press in the social career of Mrs William Kissam Vanderbilt (who later became Mrs Belmont) and because of the recent divorce of Consuelo's parents. The *New York Morning Journal*, among others, reported details of the marriage settlement:

> The Duke of Marlborough spent the greater part of yesterday with his solicitor, R. Harding Millward, in completing the final arrangements for the settlement of Miss Vanderbilt's dot and his own transfers. The papers are now ready to be signed by which the future Duchess will receive the income from $10,000,000 during her life.[21]

The capital put up, however, was $2,500,000 in the form of 50,000 shares in the Beech Creek Railroad Company, and from this an annual dividend of 4 per cent (i.e. $100,000) was payable to the Duke of Marlborough and Consuelo Vanderbilt during their joint lives. In addition, William Kissam Vanderbilt made arrangements with the trustees in charge of the Beech Creek Railroad stock to pay his daughter an annual sum of $100,000 in four instalments 'for her separate use' for life.[22] Consuelo's recollection of the negotiations in her memoirs was brief:

> The marriage settlement gave rise to considerable discussion. An

English solicitor who had crossed the seas with the declared intention of 'profiting the illustrious family' he had been engaged to serve devoted a natural talent to that end. Finally the settlements were apportioned in equal shares, at my request.[23]

Whether Consuelo, then 19, would have had much influence over the final outcome is unlikely, but her brief allusion to the matter shows that, in so far as she reflected upon it at all, she regarded the settlement as an act of financial exploitation on the Duke's part. Gustavus Myers totted up the bill for the marriage as follows:

The wedding ceremony was one of showy splendor; millions of dollars in gifts were lavished upon the couple. Other millions in cash, wrenched also from the labor force of the American working population, went to rehabilitate and maintain Blenheim House, with its prodigal cost of reconstruction, its retinue of two hundred servants, and its annual expense roll of $100,000. Millions more flowed out from the Vanderbilt exchequer in defraying the cost of yachts and of innumerable appurtenances and luxuries. Not less than $2,500,000 was spent in building Sutherland House in London. . . . The Marlborough title was an expensive one. . . . All told, the Marlborough dukedom had cost William K. Vanderbilt, it was said, fully, $10,000,000.[24]

Myers's work was published at the height of the reaction to titled marriages, and in this particular case he was able to point to the waste of American money on titles, because the marriage broke down within a few years, resulting first in a legal separation in 1906 and then in divorce and nullification.

While the newspapers and social commentators catalogued the number of failed marriages and the losses, reckoned in millions of dollars, on bogus or impecunious nobles, novelists also took up the theme of rapacious aristocrats seeking to repair their fortunes by an expedient marriage to a wealthy American girl. By and large, popular fiction of the day repeated and reinforced the stereotypes and clichés of international marriages with a view to imparting the patriotic pride and moral values of middle-class America. Usually written by women, these novels imaginatively filled in the details behind the sensational stories in the press. Aiming specifically at a female readership, these women writers sought to warn American girls of the pitfalls involved in marrying across both cultural and class lines. The typical heroine knows little of Europe, and her images of it come from romantic travel fiction; upon marrying, she is rudely awakened by the cultural gulf between herself and her husband and the real nature of their relationship. Popular women's fiction of the late Victorian period attempted to provide a 'realistic' alternative to the romantic travel fiction of the early nineteenth century, and its picture of Europe was peopled with corrupt, avaricious figures, morally inferior to Americans.

In the second of two novels by Gertrude Atherton, *American Wives and English Husbands* (1898) and *His Fortunate Grace* (1907), Anglo-American marriages become more exploitative. Whereas the earlier novel dealt with the assimilation of an American girl into British aristocratic society, the second centred on the exploits of the Duke of Bosworth in the New York marriage market. The Duke openly admits his need of money: 'I am perfectly willing to state brutally that I wouldn't – couldn't – marry unless I got a half million [pounds] with her and something of an income to boot.'[25] The Duke breaks off his engagement to Mabel Creighton when her father loses heavily in a panic on the stock exchange, and he proposes to her friend, Augusta Forbes, who has a *dot* of 5 million dollars. Disgusted with his daughter's fascination for titles and her intention of restoring a ruined castle, Mr Forbes says to her: 'It doesn't occur to you, I suppose, that American-made millions should be spent in America, and that we have poverty enough of our own.'[26] This appeal to her hitherto socialist conscience (she had earlier asked her father to give her fortune away) fails, and the father is blackmailed into agreeing to the match by his wife's threat to transfer her personal property to the Duke. The exploitation, to be sure, is shown to be mutual in this story, but the 'hackneyed transaction' is portrayed as a betrayal of the values of American society, as ridiculing the American upper class and diverting funds away from American philanthropic enterprises.

In Frances Hodgson Burnett's novel *The Shuttle*, the villain is Sir Nigel Anstruther, a baronet heavily in debt, who borrows money to sail to New York to find a suitable bride. His victim is a millionaire's daughter, Rosalie Vanderpoel, whom he keeps captive in his country home and whom he forces to pay all of his bills. She eventually signs all her money over to her husband, who promptly deserts her. The marriage is seen as having occurred in the days when Americans were still under the influence of romantic fiction about English life:

> the Republican mind had not yet adjusted itself to all that such alliances might imply. It was yet ingenuous, imaginative and confiding in such matters. A baronetcy and a manor house reigning over an old English village and over villagers in possible smock frocks, presented elements of picturesque dignity to people whose intimacy with such a allurements had been limited by the novels of Mrs Oliphant and other writers.[27]

By the time Rosalie's sister is of age, Americans are better informed about Europe. Betty is educated in France and Germany, where she discovers that

> The English and Continental papers did not give enthusiastic detailed descriptions of the marriages New York journals dwelt upon with such delight. They were passed over with a paragraph. . . . It seemed to her that the bridegrooms were, in conversation, treated by their equals with scant respect. It appeared that there had always been some extremely practical reason for the passion which had led them to the altar. One generally gathered that they or their estates were very much out at elbow, and frequently their characters were not considered admirable by their relatives and acquaintances.[28]

The novel ends on an optimistic note with Betty marrying a British earl. Neither she not her husband can be regarded as having entered upon a mercenary alliance, since both are critical of those marriages in which there has been a large degree of exploitation on either side. Their marriage is supposed to represent a clearer understanding on both sides, a new era in Anglo-American friendship. 'It was all rather a muddle at first,' explains Lord Dunholm in the novel. 'Things were not fairly done, and certain bad lots looked on it as a paying scheme on the one side, while it was a matter of silly, little ambitions on the other.'[29]

For Burnett, international marriages were part of the growing relationship between Britain and the United States. She uses the metaphor of a shuttle weaving between the two shores bringing the two peoples closer together with 'threads of commerce' and 'literature and art'.[30] One of the threads is marriage: 'It was in comparatively early days that the first thread . . . was woven into the web.

Many such have been woven since and have added greater strength than any others, twining the cord of sex and home-building and race-founding.'[31] Early on in the novel, then, Burnett locates herself in the contemporary discourse of Anglo-American societies and politicians promoting Anglo-Saxon brotherhood. Some titled Americans were a party to this and saw themselves as helping to forge links between the two nations. Lady Randolph Churchill established and edited a journal for a brief time entitled the *Anglo-Saxon Review*. Some historians have since suggested that transatlantic marriages promoted a sense of kinship between the United States and Britain.[32] *The Shuttle* is somewhat atypical in this respect in its fictional representation of titled marriages.

Henry James's treatment of the 'international theme' in his fiction was more sophisticated and complex, although the essential element of the corrupt European, or Europeanized American, was still present in many of his stories. Jan Dietrichson, who has analysed the role of money in the portrayal of international marriages by both James and William Dean Howells, has shown that both writers tended to present excessive financial considerations as immoral and as an insecure basis for conjugal relationships.[33] Unlike most of their contemporaries dealing with the mercenary motivation behind titled marriages, James and Howells took their criticism much further. Buying titles was only one manifestation of a deep-rooted *malaise* affecting Americans within an increasingly materialistic society. According to James's and Howells's interpretation, the pursuit of wealth for its own sake eroded the ethical values and spiritual life of the nation.[34]

Edith Wharton, another major exponent of the international theme and critic of the plutocracy in American society but surprisingly omitted from Dietrichson's study, wrote a number of novels and short stories in which women were represented as a 'liquid asset, capable of earning symbolic profits', to use the words of Pierre Bourdieu.[35] In the aptly entitled short story 'The Last Asset', published in 1908 at a time of intense criticism of transatlantic marriages, the estranged husband and daughter of an ambitious American woman are used as a means for the 'social rehabilitation' of Mrs Sam Newell:

Mrs Newell spoke as if her daughter were a piece of furniture acquired without due reflection, and for which no suitable place

171

could be found. She got, of course, what she could out of Hermione, who wrote her notes, ran her errands, saw tiresome people for her, and occupied an intermediate office between that of lady's maid and secretary; but such small returns on her investment were not what Mrs Newell had counted on. What was the use of producing and educating a handsome daughter if she did not, in some more positive way, contribute to her parents' advancement?[36]

In this tale of the marriage of Hermione Newell to the Comte Louis du Trayas, Wharton introduces a new twist to the exchange of title for money. Mrs Newell, who is barely managing to survive on the fringes of smart European society, joins forces with a Jewish money-lender of dubious reputation in order to facilitate her daughter's marriage to a French count. She also enlists the help of an American couple, newcomers to wealth and high society, who pay for her expensive accommodation at Ritz's in Paris and her daughter's wedding. The Jewish Baron provides the *dot* which is essential to the successful conclusion of the marriage negotiations and, through his purchase of a French title for Mrs Newell's daughter, he salvages both his and Mrs Newell's social career. Although the marriage is based on the love of the couple for each other, it is, to all intents and purposes, an exchange, and is described in terms of high finance, with Mrs Newell represented as the arch manipulator wheeling and dealing behind the scenes. In this short story Edith Wharton highlights the exploitation of the daughter by an over-ambitious mother, an aspect of transatlantic marriages which drew unfavourable criticism from time to time in real life. The following comment of Theodore Roosevelt to Ambassador Reid in 1906: 'I thoroly [sic] dislike . . . these international marriages . . . which are not . . . even matches of esteem and liking, but which are based upon the sale of the girl for her money and the purchase of the man for his title' clearly shows his endorsement of the popular view of these marriages and his strong disapproval of the presence of materialistic motives.[37]

How transatlantic marriages came to be categorized as mercenary exchanges of title for money probably owes as much to speculation in the press about the size of the bride's portion as to the subsequent scandals when these marriages ended in divorce. One New York newspaper virtually predicted the outcome of the marriage of Mildred Carter to Lord Acheson: 'International complications are piling thickly upon us. Let us hope that all foreign marriage paths lead not to the divorce court. The pathway would be overcrowded with the addition of this year's crop.'[38] The paper insinuated that Mrs Carter had been campaigning against another American mother, Mrs Drexel, for a titled son-in-law. It suggested that she had got the better deal, despite all the rumours that had been circulated in the press about Acheson's matrimonial exploits. Privately, the marriage was regarded as a love match.[39] In 1927, however, Mildred, Lady Gosford, gave evidence in a divorce court that her husband had neglected her 'from the beginning', and the marriage had never been a success.[40]

A much greater scandal accompanied the nullification of Consuelo Vanderbilt's marriage to the Duke of Marlborough, greater even than the notorious Yarmouth–Thaw annulment. This was because of the Duke's rank and the publicity which had surrounded the marriage in 1895. It also had to do with the attempt to keep the annulment proceedings from the newspapers. The couple separated in 1906 amidst much gossip and rumour and finally divorced in 1921. An annulment was sought and obtained in 1926 on the grounds that Consuelo had been forced to marry the Duke against her will. Many years later, in 1953, Consuelo published her memoirs, *The Glitter and the Gold*. The story of her disastrous marriage and domineering mother has been retold in numerous biographies and other books. The Vanderbilt–Marlborough marriage has, as a consequence, become known as one of the most notorious exchanges of title for money.[41] By 1953, of course, most of the people who had known Consuelo at the time of her marriage to Marlborough were either dead or very elderly. Consuelo herself was in her late seventies. In her autobiography, Madame Balsan presented her first marriage as a loveless match and dramatized her role as a silent, suffering victim to maternal domination and aristocratic exploitation, and 'an American girl who held democratic views [and who] found it difficult to accept the assumption that birth alone confers superiority'.[42] Two observations might be made here. First, that the bitterness over the breakdown of the marriage had not receded after thirty years since her divorce, which is perhaps an indication of the intensity of the conflict and of the humiliation that inevitably accompanied the glaring publicity.

Second, that one of the few ways in which she could restore her pride was to represent her experiences as those of a victim whose personal feelings and national loyalty (to the United States) were overridden by those who were not just domineering but who were in a position of power in relation to her. Even so, one cannot help wondering why she would have deliberately dragged up a past that must have been painful to remember. In her foreword she writes that friends had encouraged her to describe the world of her youth which was so different from that of the 1950s. Reading between the lines, however, it would seem that one possible motive was that Consuelo wanted to put an end to doubts about the reasons for the annulment because of the outcry which had occurred when news of it was leaked to the press three months after it was granted.

The newspapers first got hold of the story in November 1926 when Marlborough sough an audience with the Pope in Rome. The *New York Times* ran an article on its front page on 11 November with the headline: 'Marlborough Seeks the Aid of the Pope'. Two days later the paper reported that an annulment had already been granted back in July 1926. By 15 November questions were asked as to why the couple had delayed seeking an annulment and it was revealed that Mrs Belmont had admitted that she had coerced her daughter into marrying the Duke. The story went off the front page for a few days only to return with an adamant denial from Madame Balsan that 'she had been forced into a loveless marriage'.[43] It is possible that Madame Balsan panicked when the story broke and that she tried to limit the damage to her mother's reputation. After all, the implications were that Mrs Belmont had sold her daughter along with a sizeable dowry for a coronet and this would have confirmed the worst prejudices against titled marriages. Although many biographers and historians have accepted the coercion story, there was some scepticism expressed in the press. In fact, various experts were called upon to give their opinion on the legal and religious requirements of annulment proceedings partly because of suspicions of bribery and the disbelief that the Duchess would have waited over 30 years before seeking an annulment. At first it was alleged that the Duke had asked the Pope to annul his first marriage so that he could be received into the Roman Catholic Church, but a few days later it was claimed that Madame Balsan had initiated proceedings.[44] In her memoirs, Consuelo stated that it was she who approached the Rota because Marlborough wanted an annulment

174

and also because it would appease the Balsan family, who, as French Catholics, could not receive her as a divorcée.[45]

The autobiography concurs with the evidence that Mrs Belmont and others gave to the Roman Catholic Diocesan Court of Southwark. In fact, the portrayal of Mrs Belmont could have been drawn with a view to substantiating the coercion story. She is presented as having been a stern disciplinarian who was able to impose her own choice of a husband for her daughter: 'Brought up to obey, I surrendered more easily to my mother's dictates than others nurtured in a gentler discipline might have done.' The tale of how Mrs Belmont had feigned illness when Consuelo threatened to marry Winthrop Rutherfurd is told in melodramatic detail.[46] One can imagine Alva pouring scorn on Consuelo's choice of husband when she had gone to such lengths to secure the Duke's interest but to what extent Consuelo was unpersuaded by her mother's preferred candidate, one can only guess. The *New York Morning Journal* reported a month before the wedding that 'the future Duchess ... [had gone] about all summer in her usual timid, shrinking way, accepting attentions from would-be suitors with a simple, childish artlessness....'[47] Of all the descriptions of Consuelo, this one seems to capture the fact that she was, after all, only 19 and, by all accounts, an immature 19-year-old.

Likewise, Madame Balsan's references to her first husband were brief and mildly derogatory. Her frequent complaint was of his contempt for 'all things American', which contrasts with her patriotism. But the worst that is said of the Duke is attributed to Consuelo's brother:

> When I broke the news of our engagement to my brothers, Harold observed, 'He is only marrying you for your money', and with this last slap to my pride I burst into tears. It was obvious that they would have preferred me to marry a compatriot....[48]

Harold would have been 11 years old at the time. It is possible to interpret Madame Balsan's treatment of Marlborough in her memoirs as a gesture towards his family, as not wishing to re-open old sores. Indeed, the overall effect is to suggest that he did not play an important part in her life and that their relationship was exceedingly formal.

By the time the narrative reaches the annulment episode, the reader is fully prepared for the revelation of Mrs Belmont's evidence before the Catholic authorities. Of her other Consuelo writes:

> My mother, with her usual courage, remained undaunted, but I suffered to see her in so unfavourable a light, knowing that she had hoped to ensure my happiness with the marriage she had forced upon me. Religious controversies are apt to be bitter; but there was no truth in the accusation that the Rota had been bribed.[49]

The proceedings were supposed to have remained private, and given the import of the evidence, one can perfectly understand why privacy was desired. It is possible that Mrs Belmont would not have consented to give evidence if she had known that it would be plastered over the front page of the newspapers. It was the Rota Tribunal which made public its findings, partly, one suspects, because of allegations of bribery and possibly because of Consuelo's statement to the press. She apparently told a reporter:

> I say once and for all, that the suggestion of undue pressure is the foulest slander that could have been uttered against my father and mother, both of whom thought only of my happiness. I may have been a little romantic and consequently over-enthusiastic at the time. To what extent, perhaps, I was easily persuaded in my own heart when the glamour of a first love was on me, that it was for my happiness that I was taking the step; but I want you to be clear that the step was mine and that I alone was responsible for it.[50]

This amazing statement contradicted the evidence given before the Diocesan Court and is totally at odds with her memoirs. Adjectives like 'a little romantic' and 'over-enthusiastic' are credible as a description of a young 19-year-old about to marry an English duke amidst a blaze of publicity in New York. No doubt Alva impressed upon her only daughter the prestige and honour which was being conferred upon her, that the Duke was the 'catch' of the season and that the marriage would be seen as one of the biggest coups the Vanderbilts had ever pulled off. The marriage was important to Alva who had recently divorced Willie Vanderbilt: it would help to rehabilitate her socially in ways not too dissimilar to Mrs Newell's in 'The Last Asset'. But when all is said and done, there is no evidence of overt coercion as such. Mrs Belmont's reasons for declaring that she had forced Consuelo to marry had very probably more to do with the very limited grounds upon which an annulment could be granted and the expectation that the findings of the Rota would be kept private.

When the couple had separated in 1906 the rift had been a bitter one. The *New York World* reported that 'a divorce either on one side or the other' would be the likely outcome.[51] Whitelaw Reid, who had recently taken up his post at the Embassy, found himself in an awkward position, for, if he had ostracized the Duchess, he would have proclaimed her guilt by implication. He explained his position to the President's wife three years later:

> The Marlborough side . . . produced not a particle of proof against the Duchess, while of his misconduct there never was a doubt. Consequently, I took the ground that as the young lady was an American, was the daughter of a man whom I had known from his boyhood, . . . I was more than ordinarily bound not to repudiate an American lady in London who was being violently assailed without proof.

Clearly, there was a dispute as to whose conduct was responsible for the breakdown. Reid did the honourable thing as a family friend and left his card on the Duchess, a symbolic gesture signifying that he regarded her as the injured party. He followed this with an invitation to Dorchester House at which royalty was present, having first cleared this with the Palace. But the King let it be known that unless the Marlboroughs overcame their difficulties, at least to the point of living together, they could not be received at court or attend functions at which royalty was present. Edwardian society was hopelessly hypocritical. Extra-marital affairs could be tolerated as long as they were discreet. It must almost have seemed as though history was repeating itself as the eighth duke had been ostracized in the 1880s following the Aylesford scandal. Reid suggested to Mrs Taft that such events were 'nothing unusual at Blenheim.'[52]

Society divided into two camps. Consuelo had the support of her family and the US Embassy. The *New York World* reported that the Duchess seemed 'rather relieved that her domestic affairs had come to a crisis, because, as they stood, life was almost intolerable.'[53] For a while, she faced powerful opposition from the Marlborough camp but even the Duke's relatives began to break ranks and his mother, Lady Blandford, was said to have been 'unexpectedly kind'. In fact, Reid reported to his wife in February 1907 that there had been 'an almost universal revulsion of feeling in the little duchess's favour'.[54] The King found Marlborough's conduct objectionable, 'especially in continuing to live off the Duchess's money'.[55] And Theodore Roosevelt declared his feelings in no uncertain terms to the Ambassador:

> the lowest note of infamy is reached by such a creature as this Marlborough, who proposing to divorce the woman when *he* at least cannot afford to throw any stone at her, nevertheless proposes to keep and live on the money she brought him.[56]

Reconciliation appeared to be out of the question. According to Reid, the Duke became more interested in patching things up when he was excluded from dinners of the Knights of the Garter and his wife also showed interest in a reconciliation for the sake of the children, but that it was a revengeful Mrs Belmont – now a militant suffragist who stood in the way.[57] Instead of divorcing – Marlborough may have been considering his political career – a deed of separation was drawn up. This protected the Duke from Consuelo applying in the future for divorce even if there were proof of his adultery because it would have been virtually impossible with the deed to prove desertion or cruelty as well. It was many years before either party explored the option of divorce. The Duke was apparently considering it in 1916 but it was not until 1920 that the petition was entered by which time it suited both parties and they remarried within two weeks of each other.

The Marlborough–Vanderbilt marriage was not simply a marriage of convenience or an exchange of title for money. Social ambition and financial considerations may well have played a part in the marriage but these were in any case part and parcel of elite marriages. Family honour and prestige, the continuation of the male line and the ability of a wife to play an active, albeit supportive, role in furthering the career of her husband were, as we have seen, also important. The presence of financial motives would not have been at all unusual and, in fact, there were enough examples of failed marriages in society in which money had a high profile. But, of course, what usually happened was that couples agreed to put on a front for the outside world. The Duke might well have been governed by an overriding concern to restore Blenheim but it is also possible that he misjudged the situation and underestimated the extent to which a young woman of 19 would have to adapt to her new surroundings in a different country (he himself was only 23). He would have, in any case, married a woman of wealth, assuming that any potential consort for one of the highest-ranking nobles in the land would have to be wealthy. But it is the clichéd view which retained considerable force, and Madame Balsan must have realized this in writing her memoirs. The great interest shown in the size of her dowry and the public perception of international marriages enabled her to cover up a possible scandal behind the failure of her first marriage and to rescue her mother's reputation.

The conceptualization of titled marriages as a sale of women clearly fails to allow for any complex motivation involved in inter-elite marriages and misrepresented the presence of financial considerations in all upper-class marriages, domestic and foreign. Despite the criticism levelled at members of America's wealthy upper classes for marrying into the European nobility, transatlantic marriages continued to increase in number. Much pressure, however, was placed on those women who married in the decade or so before the First World War, pressure which had not been evident in earlier alliances and which has not been evident since. The yellow press, in particular, was quick to seize upon any evidence of social pretension, financial waste, or scandal in connection with these unions in the newspapers of the day. Although he did not have transatlantic marriages specifically in mind at the time of outlining the new policy for the *New York World*, Joseph Pulitzer, the paper's proprietor from 1883 to 1911, declared:

> There is room in this great and growing city for a journal . . . dedicated to the cause of the people rather than to that of the purse potentates – devoted more to the news of the New than the Old World – that will expose all fraud and sham, fight all public evils and abuse – that will battle for the people with earnest sincerity.[58]

This statement was directed more towards big business *per se*, but it also applied to reporting on the private lives of businessmen and their families – the line of division between public and private with regard to the elite was drawn very faintly. Marriages were treated as virtual business transactions by the yellow press, which saw as its duty the need to point out to the public the alleged waste of United States dollars and the unpatriotic strategy of leading families seeking to ally themselves with foreign nobility.

There was no room in this type of discourse for a discussion of the personal preferences of American women for European husbands or the role and position of women in the American elite. No doubt some of the women who chose to marry British peers, or their younger sons, had high expectations of a brilliant future in a country where high society was still more or less synonymous with the political elite. If so, there were the examples of Lady Randolph Churchill, Lady Curzon, and Lady Naylor-Leyland to follow. The role of titled Americans as political hostesses in London society received much comment in the Edwardian years. Adaptability may have been the most frequently cited attribute of successful American ladies, but this tends to overlook the difficulties involved in being assimilated into a different culture and into a class where the emphasis was on formality and tradition. Madame Balsan did not hide the fact that, for her, one of the most difficult acts of accommodation was complying with the rigid codes of conduct and etiquette:

> I found that being a duchess at nineteen would put me into a much older set and that a measure of decorum beyond my years would be expected of me. Indeed my first contact with society in England brought with it a realization that it was fundamentally a hierarchical society in which the differences in rank were outstandingly important.[59]

It is, of course, possible that social ambition constituted a principal motive in Madame Balsan's decision to marry the Duke of Marlborough but that, when faced with the onerous duties involved in filling her position, her views of the marriage changed. In other words, it was through its breakdown that the marriage became an exchange of title for money.

The interest of the press in the marriage of Ambassador Reid's daughter, Jean, highlights some of the pressures that American women of the upper classes were under in their decision to marry. It is a particularly extreme example, as the marriage was given a peculiar political significance because of Reid's position. The private life of an Ambassador was not immune from the demands made upon him as an official representative of his country.

The American press indulged in speculation about the future of Jean Reid from the outset of her father's appointment to the Court of St James's:

It is not at all unlikely that Miss Jean Reid will be captured by one of the nobility during her father's ambassadorship in England. . . . Miss Reid is a stately and beautiful girl, a fine whip, a finished conversationalist and a delightful dresser. She cannot but strike the English people as a most fitting duchess or countess and the chances of her American beaux are getting very slim.[60]

As we have already noted, her name was linked to several known fortune-hunters, Lord Brooke, son of Daisy, Countess of Warwick, and Lord Acheson, who married another American diplomat's daughter. In the summer of 1906 the newspapers decided that Acheson was the most likely candidate, and their anticipation prompted his proposal to Jean Reid. Her comment on this to her father was: 'I suppose he felt bound to make that story good!'[61] A more delicate situation had arisen, in the meantime, over Jean's decision to marry a young man without resources or a title. This caused her father much consternation. He explained to Jean that it would be 'a great grief' to be parted from her, as this marriage would undoubtedly mean that she would be permanently settled away from her family, but of more importance was the discrepancy between his daughter and the young man in terms of status and wealth:

he is employed in the office of his father who is a Director in the Opera Company, and in the management of the Ritz hotels. I pointed out that under those circumstances he would necessarily live here and try to make his way, unless he came to us, to be put forward and pushed in America by his wife's relatives, which I fancied she would find galling or humiliating, at the outset. . . . if she stayed here in a class that gave her a position equal to which she has now, or has at home, it would still be a sad thing to part with her. This seems to me much worse, but I may take too gloomy a view.[62]

In his letter the following day, he repeated his concern about the social and financial incompatibility of the pair and the loss of status the marriage would entail for his daughter: 'She couldn't keep the rank we gave her, but would have to take her husband's level.'[63] Reid himself had married a woman both of higher social status and greater wealth than himself. Henry Adams classed him with William Collins Whitney and John Hay as men who 'owed their free hand to marriage'.[64] Reid's concern about his daughter's status reflected his own ambition and efforts to rise socially, and now that he had reached the pinnacle of his career, he would have liked his daughter to take the opportunity to marry well, as he wrote to his wife: 'If the child hasn't a fair share of ambition I've wholly misconstrued her character; and I can't help thinking her love attack is a mild one.'[65] Reid clearly subscribed to the upper-class convention of the day that marriage had to be based upon more than mutual affection. But he did stress in both this instance and later, when Jean accepted the Hon. John Ward's proposal, that his daughter's happiness was paramount. This happiness, according to his way of thinking, had to do with a material equality between his daughter and her future husband, otherwise the marriage would be regarded as 'a case of fortune-hunting'. Jean had already been sought after by suitors with a keen eye on her dowry, and it was only natural that Reid should have wanted to protect his daughter from this kind of exploitation. The only way to ensure this was for her to choose a partner of corresponding social status, with either a substantial income or good career prospects.[66]

Reid's social ambition was much discussed in the American newspapers, especially as he had turned Dorchester House into one of the most socially prominent embassies in London. Carter, who was critical of the change in tone, wrote to his former chief: 'Dorchester House and its doings are certainly very regal and with the proclivities of this capital such hospitality has made it quite the centre and the envy of the other Embassies.'[67] The *New York Sun* estimated the rental of Dorchester House to have been twice Reid's ambassadorial salary.[68] Given this conspicuous expenditure of his private income on establishing his family's social position in London, it is not surprising that Reid had high hopes for his daughter's future.

Despite his public statements expressing his preference for an American son-in-law,[69] Reid showed no such patriotic scruples about his daughter's acceptance of a proposal of marriage from the Hon. John Ward. Writing to his wife, he described his reaction to Jean's 'very frank sweet charmingly written letter' informing him of her decision:

I told her the letter filled me with anxiety, not unpleasant; that the nearest thing to our hearts was her happiness; . . . I knew of

no objections to Mr Ward; what I did know of him, both personally and as to his record, had made a good impression; but that
the first essential was that they should have enough time to know
each other and to know their own minds.[70]

On this occasion the parental veto was not exercised. Ward fitted
Reid's idea of a suitable husband for his daughter. He was the
younger son of the Earl of Dudley, had seen service in South Africa
during the Boer War, and was an equerry to Edward VII. Perhaps
even more significantly, Ward could not be accused of fortune-
hunting, a fact noted with satisfaction by even the most critical of
American newspapers.

The American press used the occasion of Jean Reid's wedding to
reflect upon the change in the state of diplomatic relations between
the two countries. The *World* contrasted the coolness of the British
court towards Abigail Adams, wife of the first American representative in London, to the warmth of the reception of King Edward
and Queen Alexandra to Jean Reid, but cynically added that part
of the improvement had come about as a result of expediency and
snobbery.[71] Two years earlier, when it had been rumoured that
Jean was engaged to Acheson, the Boston *Globe* commented that a
generation ago the idea of an American Ambassador's daughter
marrying a peer would have evoked indignation and would have
embarrassed the government; but now, even the question of an
'abnegation of stern republicanism' was met with indifference.[72] In
an interview in 1900 Julia Ward Howe (1819–1910), a member of
the old guard in such matters, called the expatriation of Americans
to Europe an 'obliteration of American democracy and independence'; but, in reply to Mrs Howe's criticism of the Anglomania of
the rich, Mrs Frederick de Peysner claimed that Americans had
always copied English manners and that it took more than mere
wealth to enter good European society.[73] A complacency about
living abroad and marrying aristocrats was already well established
in the United States by the end of the nineteenth century. The
development of interpersonal relations between the American and
European elites withstood all the criticism. As William Dean
Howells pointed out in his review of Veblen's *Theory of the Leisure
Class*, the movement towards what he called the 'aristocratization
of society' in America was inexorable. He referred to the intermar-
riage of America's moneyed elite with the English aristocracy and

the residence of Americans abroad as 'the necessary logic of great wealth and leisure in a democracy', and called the fuss made by the press 'a foolish and futile clamor'.[74] Although the critics of titled marriages changed their emphasis, in the 1890s and 1900s, from the betrayal of democratic principles to the loss of American dollars, this did not dissuade the moneyed elite from continuing to strengthen its contacts with European high society. Acceptance into the European aristocracy still furnished a number of American *nouveaux riches* families with the means by which to claim high social status at home, and while this continued to be the case, patriotic appeals had little effect.

As we have seen, social ambition was only one of a possible range of motives for marriage, and the prospect of married life in British aristocratic society offered opportunities which were not readily available in American society. This aspect of marriage was not appreciated by an American press which, during a period of fierce competition between daily newspapers and the expansion of the newspaper industry in general, was more interested in creating news than reporting it. Sensationalism was the order of the day. Some contemporary novelists took their themes from this press coverage; others attempted a more serious treatment of the cultural conflict and the problems for American women attempting to adapt to a hierarchical society traditionally based on privilege and birth. The short stories of Henry James dealing with Americans in England tended to militate against the clichés and stereotypes of second-rate fiction by providing a wide variety of scenarios and characters. In Progressive America, however, attention was being drawn to waste and the concentration of wealth in the hands of the few, and transatlantic marriages seemed to provide examples of this – hence the wild speculation about dowries and demands for taxes on dowries.

Part Five

TITLED AMERICANS

9

Wives and mothers: the domestic roles of titled Americans

Anglo-American marriages became a controversial issue for aristocratic society in Edwardian Britain. Apart from the unease about so many alliances taking place between peers and businessmen's daughters, there was a growing alarm about the effect of American women upon the physical well-being of the peerage. Two views, which were diametrically opposed, were voiced at this time. For some, American brides were a source of much-needed new blood for an ingrown elite:

> one should look upon the frequent marriages of American heiresses with effete British nobles as the carrying out of a wise and timely dispensation of Providence. New blood – fresh sap, is sorely needed to invigorate the grand old tree of the British aristocracy, . . .[1]

But for others the influx of American peeresses did not bode well. Their failure to produce male heirs promised to bring about the extinction of some noble lines. The fertility of American women, particularly those identified as Anglo-Saxons, became a hotly debated issue on both sides of the Atlantic. Explanations were linked to social class, behaviour, and national origins and as such concurred with an already established judgement about American heiresses. The concern about titled Americans being genetically unsound originated in the debate about the declining birth rate. Attacks were also made on women who deliberately controlled their fertility and these were directly related to criticism about the behaviour of Americans as wives and mothers. Transatlantic marriages thus became part of an Edwardian obsession with eugenics and a conservative backlash against the emancipation of women which, in Britain, must also be seen within a tradition of anti-American sentiment.

In the United States the 1890 Census had revealed not only a fall in the birth rate but also a differential fertility rate amongst the various ethnic groups that constituted America's population.[2] Eugenicists, social scientists, and politicians became alarmed at the prospect of the older American stocks failing to maintain their predominance and blamed, among other things, the recent advances made by women beyond the domestic sphere. Women were demanding the vote, equal pay, equality before the law, greater access to higher education and professional associations, and greater sexual restraint on the part of their husbands. Changes in women's role and status in the family and society at large, in conjunction with the rapid increase in immigration from eastern and southern Europe, were perceived as a threat to the status quo of the white, male, Anglo-Saxon, Protestant establishment.[3]

An essential part of the ensuing debate over the birth rate, as Carroll Smith-Rosenberg and Charles Rosenberg have argued, was 'the explicit charge of female sexual failure'.[4] This charge is certainly clear from the speeches and writings of one of America's staunchest advocates of population growth at this time. President Theodore Roosevelt, in a letter to Hamlin Garland written during the peak years of the controversy over the question of national fertility rates, asserted that 'The woman who flinches from childbirth stands on a par with the soldier who drops his rifle and runs in battle.'[5] The President was unequivocal in his views on the proper sphere of women. In his Annual Message to Congress in 1906, a jeremiad to the nation on the diminishing birth rate, Roosevelt called the deceleration in population growth 'race suicide'. His address was the culmination of nearly fifteen years' study of the causes of the declining birth rate, and in it he called for a revision of the divorce laws.[6]

Thomas Dyer's study of Roosevelt's racial theories shows that, over the years, the President had corresponded with leading eugenicists and social scientists in the United States, including Edward A. Ross, the Wisconsin sociologist who invented the phrase 'race suicide'.[7] Roosevelt's answer to the problem was, quite simply, to encourage couples to have larger families, by appealing to their patriotic instinct, and praising domesticity as an appropriate virtue of womanhood. Dr J. J. Cronin, an American eugenicist who favoured selective breeding, disagreed with this stance. In an article for Albert Shaw's *American Monthly Review of Reviews*, he wrote: 'A very little study of sociology will convince the advocates of the "race suicide" idea that a few perfect children are far better for the nation and the family than a dozen unkempt degenerates.'[8] Roosevelt took exception to this article and replied in a letter addressed to the editor:

> Let him look up any serious statistics, or study any author worthy of reading on the subject at all, including Benjamin Franklin, and he will see that in the ordinary family of but one or two children there is apt to be lower vitality than in a family of four or five or more. All he has to do if he doubts this is to study the effects of the marriages with heiresses by the British nobility.[9]

It is not clear whether Roosevelt meant American heiresses or heiresses in general. He had probably read Francis Galton's study, *Hereditary Genius*, in which it was claimed that heiresses, i.e. sole surviving offspring of a marriage, were a 'notable agent' in the extinction of titled families.[10] But if Roosevelt himself did not explicitly make the link between *American* heiresses and the extinction of noble families in Britain, one supporter of his theories made it very clear indeed.

It was really only a matter of time before someone in Britain picked up on the concern about women in the well-to-do classes of American society and linked it to the disapproval of Americans marrying into the nobility. In 1905 the *Contemporary Review* published an anonymous article entitled 'Titled Colonials v. Titled Americans'. Drawing upon American medical literature, eugenicists' tracts, and the speeches of President Roosevelt, the author contended that marriage alliances with American women were having a detrimental effect upon the British aristocracy. S/he advocated that peers should marry instead women from the colonial elite, because they tended to be healthier and less materialistic as well as staunch upholders of traditional British ideals.[11] The article appeared at a time when British politicians had been voicing fears about the state of the population's health following revelations about the poor physical state of volunteers for the British army, and when eugenicists, doctors, and scientists were making public pronouncements about the demise of the 'higher orders' of the English-speaking people.[12] It was therefore of acute topical interest to a public made increasingly aware of the dangers of racial degeneration.

Not only does this article have to be read in the context of the eugenics debate about the birth rate in order to appreciate the significance of the issues it raises, but it must also be understood within the general context of anti-American sentiment, and the way that this is linked with hostility expressed towards plutocrats. There is also a third context for the criticisms made of American women with regard to their fertility and this has to do with the traditional conceptualization of woman's domestic role. The lack of fertility or interference with fertility, of which American peeresses were publicly accused, was seen to be a threat to family life and the future of the peerage.

The nature of the debate about the productivity of titled Americans moves the expression of anti-American feeling on to a new plane, even though some of the arguments were borrowed from American eugenicists. But, in the last analysis, all the furore over the issue amounted to 'sound and fury signifying nothing'. Transatlantic marriages continued unabated, and eventually the theories and opinions expressed during the controversy over the declining birth rate became unfashionable and untenable.

'Colonial' made two major allegations against titled Americans. First, s/he declared that American women were becoming increasingly sterile and that this was demonstrated by the high incidence of childless unions between titled Englishmen and Americans. Second, s/he asserted that American women were frivolous, superficial, restless, and showy and that they aimed 'at nothing higher than "having a good time".' The implication of the second allegation was that the excessive concern of American women with high society and the restlessness caused by the constant competition for social distinction contributed to their infertility. Such allegations had been heard before, but this particular writer added a new dimension to the conventional line of attack: s/he presented figures for the number of offspring from transatlantic marriages and compared them with figures for the colonial alliances of British peers. In view of the seriousness of these charges and the attempt to substantiate them with data, it is important to ascertain if there was any truth in the assertion that titled Americans were less fertile.

The so-called facts provided by 'Colonial' have been tabulated in Table 9.1. What they were intended to show is that titled Americans were far more likely to produce either no offspring at all or very few, and the conclusion drawn was:

> These figures are proof, if any were needed, of the growing sterility of American women, a fact which presents a serious problem to the United States as one of the Great Powers. In face of them the contention that by means of American brides fresh vigour may be imported into the British aristocracy is merely ridiculous.[13]

Table 9.1 Figures taken from 'Titled Colonials v. Titled Americans'

	American spouses	Colonial spouses
Number of marriages made by peers since 1840	30	23
Number of childless matches	19	4
Proportion of childless matches	63.3%	17.39%
Total number of offspring	39	63
Number of male offspring	18	29
Average size of family	1.3	2.7

Using information about the number of offspring from the transatlantic and control groups, we can establish the status of 'Colonial's' allegations concerning American women. We are not concerned here to prove whether marriages with titled colonials produced large numbers of offspring, but it is important to place transatlantic marriages within the context of all marriages made by peers. Taking first the claim that American peeresses were more likely to be infertile than their colonial counterparts, the number and proportion of childless matches between American women and peers were compared with the corresponding figures for the control groups (see Appendix J). Out of a total of 60 marriages between peers and American women, 17 (28.33 per cent) were childless compared to 18.12 per cent and 24.60 per cent in the two control groups. This suggests that transatlantic unions were indeed more likely to be childless, except that the mean proportion of childless marriages for those peers with American wives during the whole period, 1870 to 1914, is more than one in four, compared to one in five for the control groups combined. There is, then, a substantial difference between 'Colonial's' figures which showed that two in every three American marriages were childless and the figure of one

in four for the case group. The figures 'Colonial' gave seemed to
have been wildly exaggerated.

Although a higher incidence of childlessness amongst transatlantic couples can be confirmed, does this necessarily support
'Colonial's' claim that titled Americans were either sterile or reluctant to have children? After all, childlessness need not necessarily
be the result of the wife's infertility. In the first place, the woman
could have been past child-bearing age or the man impotent. As it
was customary not to supply the age of wives in *Burke's Peerage*, the
number of widows amongst titled Americans has been regarded as
roughly approximating to the number of women past child-bearing
age. Of the seventeen childless American peeresses, six were widows
at the time of marriage and all six married men aged 42 or more,
which is another possible indication that the women might have
been past child-bearing age, assuming that they were close to their
titled husband in age. However, one widow, Lily, Duchess of
Marlborough, married for the third time, after the premature death
of the Duke at the age of 48, and had a son by her third husband,
Lord William Beresford. Another widow, Mrs Colgate, was married
to Lord Strafford for only six months. Lord Ellenborough was 65
when he married Hermione Schenley, who was much younger than
him. In sum, age was a possible factor in six of the childless unions.
As for the other ten marriages, two ending in divorce involved
actresses, one was annulled, and, according to the biographical
information, the Russells chose not have children.

In the corresponding control groups, age was a possible factor in
16 of the 73 childless unions. That is to say, either the husband
was over 60 years or the wife was a widow, or both. Four widows
married men aged between 27 and 33 and have been excluded as
the women were probably still of child-bearing age. One marriage
was annulled within five years, and another ended after six years
because of the death of the wife. Age appears, therefore, to be less
significant as a factor in the control groups. With regard to younger
sons, the proportion of widows is lower in both the transatlantic
and control groups, as is the proportion of men over 60 years age,
and there is no obvious explanation for the higher incidence of
childlessness amongst the transatlantic groups.

Another erroneous assumption on 'Colonial's part is that it was
the American wife who was sterile rather than the titled husband
– a good example of the double standard. Moreover, it was assumed

that couples did not make a deliberate decision, as did Bertrand Russell and his wife, not to have children. 'Colonial' does not enter into any allegations about voluntary limitation of family size, preferring to impute simply from the figures on the number of offspring that American women were less productive than colonial women and that this did not recommend Americans as brides to an elite group concerned with passing property on to direct male heirs. In view of the contemporary debate about birth control, the omission is perhaps all the more noticeable, but then the subject was a delicate one, given Edwardian views on the use of contraceptives. On the other hand, the fact that 'Colonial' highlights the unfavourable comparison between colonials and Americans with regard to family size did implicitly raise the whole question of family limitation.

British and American eugenicists were disturbed that couples of proven fertility were limiting the number of their offspring to one or two children. Examining peerage families in the nineteenth century, two British eugenicists, William Cecil Dampier Whetham and his wife, Catherine, found a rapid fall in the number of births to fertile couples, from 7.1 in the 1830s to 3.13 in the 1880s.[14] They deduced from these figures that extinction was only a few generations off, thereby failing to take account of the recent improvements in obstetrics and postnatal care, resulting in a lower incidence of child mortality and higher life expectancy. These had reduced the need to produce large families to ensure the continuation of the male property line. In a slightly less overt manner than 'Colonial', they implicitly blamed Americans for the decline in the birth rate by claiming that the entrance of foreign plutocrats into the British elite had 'affected', if not 'demoralized', the behaviour of the established members of Britain's upper classes.[15] They reasoned that in order to improve the quality of the race, the 'best' classes should have a higher birth rate, and they made it their especial concern to exhort the British aristocracy and professional classes to have larger families.

The general consensus appears to have been that four children per marriage were necessary to maintain population growth[16] – hence President Roosevelt's strong words about women as traitors and cowards. Recent studies of birth control have shown that in both Britain and the United States the average number of offspring per family fell below four after 1900.[17] The Whethams and Sidney

Webb, among others, claimed that the decline was primarily amongst the prosperous classes, and this was later confirmed by the findings of the unofficial Birth Rate Commission established in 1913.[18] While imputations of sterility were made about childless Americans in the British peerage, those with small families were vulnerable to the diatribes of the 'race suicide' theorists or eugenicists who regarded deliberate limitation of family size by the 'intellectual and able classes' to be 'utterly wanton, selfish, and senseless'.[19] Dr John W. Taylor, a leading member of the British Gynaecological Society, lent his voice to the emotional outburst against birth control. In an article on the birth rate written in 1906, he called the use of contraceptives by married couples 'vicious and unnatural'.[20]

'Colonial's' figures for Anglo-American marriages in the British peerage showed that the total number of offspring from thirty unions was 39, i.e. an average of 1.3 children per marriage compared with 2.7 for colonial alliances. Once again, a comparison with information available from the transatlantic and control groups can help us to test the validity of 'Colonial's' figures. The mean number of offspring for peers with American wives is 2.02, with a slight increase for those marrying later in the period. This is lower than the figures for both control groups (2.91 and 2.58 respectively). Looking at the frequency distribution of children to determine family size, the difference between the transatlantic and control groups is more marked (see Appendix J). Anglo-American couples were far less likely to have large families: only two out of the sixty couples had more than four children compared to one-fifth of the control-group couples. Approximately one in every two transatlantic couples, moreover, were either childless or had one child only, compared to one in three couples in the control groups.

It is likely that the reason for the smaller family size in the transatlantic groups was the use of birth control (popularly known amongst English medical moralists in the 1880s as the 'American sin').[21] Certainly, by 1905, a large body of opinion in Britain, including doctors and intellectuals, was attributing the decline in the birth rate to voluntary limitation.[22] More recent studies have also shown that towards the end of the nineteenth century more and more couples, particularly among the well-to-do, resorted to birth control.[23] One of the few, though atypical, discussions of the problems of birth control and sexual relations emerges from the autobiography of Bertrand Russell and the biography of his first wife, Alys Pearsall Smith, which is contained in Barbara Strachey's group biography of her family.[24] The two accounts differ in their representation of the sexual relationship between Russell and his first wife, which is perhaps inevitable in such a private matter. Russell's account placed all the blame for the sexual problems of the relationship on Alys, although he did make some attempt to depersonalize them by generalizing about American women: 'She [Alys] had been brought up, *as American women always were in those days*, to think that sex was beastly, that all women hated it, and that men's brutal lusts were the chief obstacle to happiness in marriage' (emphasis added).[25] It is important to recognize the function of this generalization (marked in italics) within the context of Russell's difficulty in explaining the breakdown of his marriage: its purpose is to redirect some of the blame away from his wife.[26] But the use of the phrase 'she had been bought up', with the telling omission of the agent, i.e. by her mother, weakens the attempt to shift the blame away from himself. Russell's relationship with his mother-in-law had never been an easy one, and he came to recognize in Alys certain traits he disliked in her mother.[27] The implied reference to the influence of Alys's mother suggests that, in fact, Russell blamed his mother-in-law for his sexual problems with Alys.

Hannah Smith, as the extracts from her letters and journals in Strachey's biography show, was not opposed to marriage or having children, but she did seek to safeguard her daughters from what she regarded as the 'grievous oppression of men over their wives'. After making her first public speech on women's suffrage in 1882, she wrote to her elder daughter, Mary, that she would like to have her position as an equal to her future husband established in a legal document.[28] This emphasis on equality went further than the sharing of property and income; it extended to 'all the details of life, whether large or small'.[29] In the light of Hannah's views on pregnancy, these 'details of life' probably included sexual relations. When she first married Robert Pearsall Smith, Hannah had wished to delay having children:

> I am very unhappy now. That trial of my womanhood which to me is so very bitter has come upon me again. . . . It is all the more heavy a trial because my husband agreed with me in thinking that I am too young for such cares and such suffering and he promised

I should not again be so tried at least until I was twenty-five. . . .
Well, it is a woman's lot, and I must try to become resigned and
bear it in patience and silence.[30]

Silence, however, was not Hannah's way, and she discouraged her
daughters from marrying early. Hannah's ideas about the quality
of married partners and late marriage were connected. They were
also in tune with feminist and medical views, as recorded by Carl
Degler, about the over-indulgence of men in sexual activity. The
aim behind the movement to encourage restraint in marriage,
Degler tells us, was to protect the health of women and improve
their position in the family.[31] One of the Grimké sisters had argued
that women should have the right to choose when to become a
mother and how often – an idea that was taken up by members of
the Social Purity movement in the late nineteenth century.[32] The
matter was complicated by disapproval of artificial contraceptives
and belief that sexual intercourse should take place only for the
purpose of procreation. Hannah appears to have been in favour of
abstinence, and her daughter, Mary, also subscribed to this view
during her first marriage with Frank Costelloe. Strachey notes that
– following the birth of her first child – Mary, 'like Hannah before
her, determined to have no more children for a while, and a combination of squeamishness, the principles she then held, and Frank
Costelloe's Catholicism led to their relying on abstinence rather
than "checks".'[33] This is rather ambiguous: was Mary squeamish
about sex or about contraceptives? A letter to her mother recounting
her visit to Dr Elizabeth Garrett Anderson suggests that it was
artificial contraception to which she objected:

I do think it is *wicked* in physicians to give such advice to their
patients. It is a fortunate thing I have married a man who agreed
with my principles – I think it would almost have turned me to
hating my husband if he had wanted me to use any of Dr Garrett
Anderson's 'other ways'.[34]

Russell noted that Alys also assumed that intercourse should take
place only when children were desired.[35] Alys's views are recorded
in a letter she wrote to Russell in 1893:

I don't believe that it is a very wholesome relation between men
and women who love each other for spiritual and intellectual
reasons. I am afraid it might introduce an element that would

lower the others, always excepting, of course, when they mean to have children.[36]

As can be seen from this letter, Alys actually took up a more extreme position on the desirability of sexual relations than is evident in any of her mother's or sister's letters. When Lady Russell tried to obstruct the marriage by pointing to the danger of having children when there was a family history of insanity on both sides, Alys was prepared to forgo having children, which would have precluded the possibility of sexual relations altogether. Russell wrote that Alys had to 'modify her position on this point' after much persuasion. He attributed her reluctance to the 'notion that there was never any desire on the woman's part'.[37] She overcame her fears, and her mother was able to reassure Lady Russell that Alys and Bertrand lived as 'man and wife'.[38]

Sterility and controlled fertility are obviously quite different things. But even if transatlantic couples were practising some form of birth control,[39] any defence of American women against charges of sterility by alluding to the possibility that they were controlling their fertility would have provoked even more controversy. Such matters were not discussed openly, and it would have been impossible to prove without interviewing all the individuals concerned. One man did, however, attempt to defend American women. In an attack on the anonymous *Contemporary Review* article, he stated:

> Will President Roosevelt or the Bishop of London tell us that the failure of the eighteen American peeresses to have heirs was wilful, or deny them an eager desire to have the glory of presenting their husbands with an heir to his title.[40]

Barclay claimed that nearly all women wanted children – it was part of their natural instinct – and thus inferred that the reasons for childlessness had to do with physiological matters rather than a decision not to have children.[41] John Taylor, on the other hand, rejected Barclay's argument about American peeresses and maintained that birth control was the cause of the low fertility rate among the middle and upper classes (including American peeresses by implication).[42] The weakness of Barclay's case is shown precisely by this counter-attack coming from a fervent opponent of birth control. There was no way of rescuing the situation for titled Americans. Either way, 'Colonial' won his/her indictment against

American peeresses: readers of the debate faced the choice of either accepting the case for sterility or being appalled by the alternative explanation that they were wilfully limiting the number of children they had to bear.

The second part of 'Colonial's' criticism of titled Americans concentrated on their behaviour. S/he complained that they were superficial and restless, striving against each other 'in dress, inventiveness and display'. This fits in with the kinds of comments, noted earlier, which were frequently made at this time about American women. For example, C. de Thierry, in an article entitled 'American Women from a Colonial Point of View', considered American women as singularly lacking in individuality and 'intellectual weight' and given over to 'ostentation'. He asked: 'But what have they ever done, except to make society tawdrier and more unsatisfactory than it was before?'[43] The leading British journals of the day were thus full of condemnations of American women in high society. What is interesting for us, though, is the connection which was made during the controversy over the declining birth rate in both Britain and the USA between American women's absorption in social affairs and their alleged infertility.

Marriott-Watson, as found elsewhere, was especially vitriolic about the behaviour of American women. In this connection, he asserted that 'Overworked men and nervous women tending to sterility and living upon an artificial plane, do not promise a brave future for the nation.'[44] The article in which this appeared was called 'The Deleterious Effect of Americanization upon Women' and was published the year before 'Colonial's'. I would suggest that there are similarities in the way they both address the connection between fertility and behaviour in relation to American women.

James Barclay took issue with 'Colonial's' points about the restless pursuit of amusement and infertility of American women. He presented a counter-argument:

> The frivolities of a small section of wealthy society are not a cause of infertility, but a consequence. A wife without intellectual resources, disappointed in her maternal instincts, seeks distraction in society that she would gladly exchange for motherhood and home.[45]

Apart from the obvious insult, this was a poor argument against what was not only a spurious association between fertility and behaviour, but also an association which was widely believed to be true and which fitted in with certain contentions about the proper sphere of women, the influence of the plutocracy, and birth control.

To begin with, there was growing concern in the late nineteenth century that in the United States and Britain women were shunning their domestic duties. T. H. S. Escott, a British journalist, was disillusioned by the modern trends threatening the sanctity of family life. He wrote:

> The influences of the time are not favourable to domesticity, and in our progress towards cosmopolitanism the taste for the family life which was once supposed to be the special characteristic of England has to a great extent been lost.[46]

Escott charted the change, pointing to an 'increasing laxity' in conjugal relations and the way in which women aimed to achieve 'uxorial independence' through establishing new social customs, such as the 'five o'clock tea', picnics, and garden parties – occasions when women and their admirers could meet frequently and avoid unpleasant gossip.[47]

Thirty years later, the Whethams also pointed to the decline of domesticity and, in much the same vein as President Roosevelt, reminded women of their duties in the home: 'To bring forth, nourish, and educate children is, for the future of the race, more important work than any that falls to the lot of man.'[48] The Whethams linked the decline of domesticity with the influence of the plutocracy and the consequences upon women of the restlessness produced by increasing expenditure on luxuries.[49] Blaming the plutocracy for the upheaval in social life, for the new preoccupations of women outside the home, and for the 'perpetual motion' of daily life had, of course, a context of its own outside eugenics. The Whethams were borrowing conventional arguments about women's proper sphere and giving them a new emphasis by pointing to the consequences of the plutocracy's predominance in Society. In part, it was a recognition that the new wealthy industrial classes presented a serious and long-term problem for the landed classes, and certainly one that could not be ignored, because it demanded adjustments on the part of the aristocracy.[50] The anti-plutocratic argument conveniently incorporated American women, as many of them were members of the wealthy commercial and industrial elites and regarded as responsible for the extravagance and competitiveness in British social life. The ground had thus been well prepared: certain sections in British society were accustomed to the idea that the competitive social activities of American women were adversely affecting the financial position of the aristocracy. Persons who thus already had cause to feel aggrieved about the social success of titled American hostesses in London were now given additional reasons to sneer at, or rebuke, American women.

The argument that the excessive interest of American women in matters outside the home was incompatible with their maternal duties was a very powerful one. Moreover, it reinforced the stereotype of the American heiress and the traditional contempt of the aristocracy for the moneyed classes. But more than this, it was an essentially misogynistic argument. Just at the time when women's maternal functions were being extolled by certain people in America and British colonial societies who perceived a threat to the survival of the Anglo-Saxon race, women were more than ever challenging existing social arrangements. The very public campaign of women in the USA and Britain for suffrage, for example, entered into a more militant phase after 1900. Although women suffragists were at pains to disassociate themselves from 'free love' advocates and to argue that the vote would enable women to extend their benevolent and moral influence, the suffrage movement was still regarded as a threat to the family.[51] Many of the arguments against women's enfranchisement had been trotted out before in opposition to women's access to higher education and the professions. Feminists were constantly battling against entrenched ideas about women's subordinate position in relation to men and their role in the home. The Rosenbergs have shown how the medical establishment in the United States reinforced such ideas by insisting upon woman's physical frailty, by regarding her as 'the product and prisoner of her reproductive system', and by seeing her primary function as motherhood.[52] Each time, then, that women challenged the status quo, they were told what harm they threatened to bring to the welfare of the family and especially their children.

It would be interesting to know if American women were perceived in Britain as more successful in this challenge to the subordination of women. Certainly, they were regarded as exercising more independence, which was seen as both a negative and a positive characteristic. However, with regard to maternity, it is clear from the various articles appearing in the 1900s that upper-class American women were failing to fulfil their duties as wives and mothers. Criticism of family limitation by women needs to be seen in this context: if attempts to extend their sphere of activity outside the home were treated asneglecting maternal responsibilities, it is hardly surprising that attempts to reduce the frequency of births would also have been regarded as a subversion of the 'natural' function of women as child-bearers. Linda Gordon has interpreted this emphasis on women's maternal role as a means of regulating sexual relations and repressing female sexuality in these terms: 'the sexual standards became so rigid that all sexual activity outside motherhood became identified with (and often in fact led to) prostitution'.[53] Contraceptives were traditionally identified with extra-marital activity, and the use of them by married couples undermined the insistence upon the purpose of sexual intercourse as reproduction. Indeed, it undermined the fabric of family life in the eyes of many Victorians. Female contraceptives were even more alarming with the possibility that promiscuity might result from their use, inside and outside marriage. The idea of women controlling their own fertility ran counter to the powerful ideology of the male establishment and threatened to spill over into a general debate on women's rights with possible consequences for the nature of family life and male–female relationships.

The idea that a wife should determine whether or not to have children was incompatible with conventional views held in aristocratic circles. The emphasis in the landed elite on producing male children restricted women in their control of their own fertility. Consuelo Vanderbilt's experience as a young bride shows how important some families in the peerage regarded the production of a male heir as soon as possible after the wedding. At her first interview with the Dowager Duchess of Marlborough, she was apparently informed: 'Your first duty is to have a child and it must be a son, because it would be intolerable to have that little upstart Winston become Duke.'[54] The urgency with which American brides were encouraged to have children is reflected by the shortness of the interval between the date of the marriage and the birth of the first child: just under 75 per cent of American peeresses who produced offspring had a child within two years of marrying. Consuelo Vanderbilt had two sons within three years of marrying and thus ensured the continuation of the dukedom and estate in the main branch of the Churchill family. Peeresses were expected to produce at least two sons in case an accident befell the heir. This is confirmed by the data on offspring for the case and control groups. Around 50 per cent of all fertile couples had at least two sons. Given the aristocratic emphasis on sons, peerage families might also be expected to show a small proportion of couples with daughters only. In fact, the proportion for the two control groups is approximately one in twelve families compared to one in seven in the case group. If we combine the figures for childless marriages with those for families of daughters only, there is then a much higher proportion of transatlantic marriages which produced no male heirs compared to the control groups: 40.00 per cent compared to 25.50 per cent and 29.95 per cent.

The implication of 'Colonial's' criticism of the fertility of titled American women was that they were not fulfilling their proper duties as wives and mothers. Women who did not 'present their husbands with heirs' were accused of 'neglect'. Furthermore, 'Colonial' pointed out that there was 'not a single distinguished peer's son with an American mother' and attributed this to the 'purely social' influence of titled Americans on British society. S/he inferred from this that American women were more interested in high society and their own ambitions in that area of activity than in domestic cares and the future standing of the titled family into which they had married. T. H. S. Escott's opinion of the upper classes as a whole was particularly close to 'Colonial's' view of titled Americans. Escott charged the upper classes with neglecting their parental duties; he felt that women's growing preoccupation with Society was resulting in 'a mere superficial acquaintance' between parents and offspring.[55] He regarded the custom of wealthy parents discharging their duties to nannies and governesses, and the increasing cosmopolitanism of their life-style, as being in conflict with the need for parents to attend personally to the discipline and education of their children. He warned parents about the conse-quences of such neglect:

> If the father or mother does not invite and train the confidence of their son or daughter when the quality of truthfulness, which with children is an instinct, has not been abused or blunted, it will not be won in after life; and if son or daughter make shipwreck of their future, the parental grief may be deep and the disappoint-

ment severe, but a heavy responsibility will lie at the household door.[56]

Escott's views mirrored prevailing ideas of the prosperous middle classes concerning child-rearing. It was within this particular social class that the idea of childhood as a unique and special stage in life gained widest acceptance. It became increasingly accepted on both sides of the Atlantic that child-rearing required a more careful and studied approach from parents, and the market in handbooks on child care and education consequently flourished.[57] As these ideas took hold, aristocratic methods of child-rearing diverged increasingly from the alternative norm established by the middle classes.

In the nineteenth century, the American approach to child-rearing attracted a great deal of attention. European travellers in the United States found children unruly and parents indulgent.[58] The avoidance of corporal punishment and the display of tolerance and affection no doubt appeared to Europeans as a disastrous combination likely to produce self-indulgent adults. British parents, in contrast, were renowned for their reserve. George Curzon's mother placed duty before affection, while his father devoted his time to the Scarsdale estates. During Curzon's childhood, contact with his parents was restricted to morning prayers and holiday outings; the rest of the time the Curzon children were under the exclusive supervision of the governess, Miss Paraman.[59] One particular characteristic of American mothers attracted much attention in England: an indulgence which went against the maxim that children were to be seen but not heard. In her memoirs, Daisy Warwick recalled Jennie Churchill's handling of her sons:

> True to her American training, she did not check Winston when he asked questions or argued with her. I still chuckle when I remember how, as a schoolboy, he would comment to his face upon the views of such a politician as Lord Hartington, who afterwards became Duke of Devonshire. In those days people could not see any definite principle behind Jennie Churchill's upbringing of her sons, Winston and Jack. They did not realize that she was developing in them qualities which, in the ordinary course, take years to show themselves. She always found time to encourage her boys to express themselves.[60]

The same encouragement which European visitors to America had mistaken for indulgence was often a deliberate attempt to foster children's intellectual development and shape their character. Lady Randolph may have taken an active interest in the development of her two sons and shown them unreserved affection, but it is also true that they were left, like most children in aristocratic households, to the care of their nanny, Mrs Everest. In his memoirs of his early life, Winston Churchill sharply distinguished between the two women who were most important to him during that period: 'She [his mother] shone for me like the Evening Star. I loved her dearly – but at a distance. My nurse was my confidante. Mrs Everest it was who looked after me and tended all my wants.'[61] The relationship between Winston and his mother is, nevertheless, a notable one in the history of titled American women. Jennie fostered Winston's tastes for classical works, such as Gibbon's *Decline and Fall of the Roman Empire*. While he was stationed in India, she also sent him works (at his request) by Plato, Aristotle, Macaulay, Darwin, and Adam Smith, along with volumes of parliamentary history, in order to prepare him for the political career he had decided upon.[62] She fed him all the political gossip and accounts of debates in the House of Commons, which she had frequently attended during her husband's lifetime, and later, when Winston was embarking upon his parliamentary career, she entertained leading politicians for him. When he had been a pupil at Harrow, she had persuaded Edward Carson, the Conservative Member for Dublin University, to dine with Winston and discuss Liberal politics.[63]

Belle Herbert shared Jennie Churchill's approach to encouraging the inquisitiveness of a child's mind. She also had two sons, Sidney and Michael. At the age of 7, the younger of the two, Michael, was taken to the Grand Palais in Paris to see a cattle show, and Belle recorded his reaction in a letter to her father:

his brain has become ever since very vexed by subjects of Natural History, and he asks us the most indiscreet questions in the middle of luncheon! He was very anxious to know if all animals had their young in the Spring, and if we had a she-dog if we would now have puppies, also if cows and sheep laid eggs, or *how* they found their young – and if his canary lost its cock if it would still have eggs!! You see the conversation was a little embarrassing although I realize it is a good thing for his brain to be so active![64]

Belle's letters to her parents often mentioned the progress of the boys at school, or their health. Contacts between the grandparents and the boys were maintained with frequent visits to America. However, after the death of their father, Belle had to decide whether to spend another Christmas with her parents. She wrote to tell them that she had changed her mind about sailing to New York:

> I believe that the boys ought to spend their Christmas at Wilton this year. They have now spent three in America, and as this is to be their home they must not run away too much especially at these festival times. They must associate themselves as much as possible with England.[65]

There is evidence to suggest that pressure was brought to bear upon Belle to bring up Michael and Sidney in England. A letter from her brother-in-law, Sidney, Lord Pembroke, in December 1903, addressed to Belle in America, enclosed a clipping from the *Daily Mail* which reported that Sidney and Michael were to be brought up as United States citizens at the wishes of their mother. Sidney had received a letter from the King expressing concern that the report might be true. He told Belle that he was going to inform the King of her intention to carry out Sir Michael's wish that the boys should be brought up in England. However, he then wrote: 'We are so looking forward to having you back here again after the holidays, and hope that you have made up your mind to bring them back.'[66] Belle did return and took up residence at Carlton House Terrace.

A letter written many years later suggests that she had found it difficult to come to terms with the loss of her husband and had sought consolation in the love of her sons. Writing to the elder son just prior to his departure for France in 1916, Belle spoke of the 'real happiness' in her life being so close to her sons, and the lack of reticence between them. Towards the end of the letter she wrote: 'In the big things I feel an absolute confidence that you will yourself now choose the right from the wrong.'[67] Close ties of affection between mother and sons and between daughter and parents are very much in evidence in the Herbert–Wilson correspondence and offer a strong contrast to the relationships of George Curzon and Lord Randolph Churchill with their parents.

Michael Astor has recounted in his autobiography his very difficult relationship with his mother and his constant battle to escape from the 'tribalism' of the Langhornes. Following the traditional pattern of schooling, Michael Astor was sent to preparatory school in Sussex at the age of 8, followed by Eton and then Oxford. As far as he could see, this custom was not only designed to make children appreciate home more, but was also for the convenience of parents. While he was at Oxford the question of a career was broached, and his parents' expectations of academic distinction became keener. At this point, he began to rebel against the rigidity of the future in store for him as the younger son of a peer. His father impressed upon him the glories of public service as a subaltern in India and checked his unpunctuality, drinking, smoking, and language. Of his father, Michael wrote:

> Stern, benevolent, judicial in his view, he reigned, for the time being, like Jehovah, a figure to fear, respect and increasingly to resent. . . . driven too far by the man I needed as a friend, I volleyed my words with his, telling him I disagreed with most of his opinions.

While the struggle with his father centred on the choice of career, the problems of his relationship with Nancy were much deeper. Part of it had to do with her adherence to Christian Science, the principles of which she sought to impose upon her family. Human failure was put down to neglecting to read the Bible, as, for example, when his brother's rowing team were eliminated from a Henley competition and Nancy blamed her son for the defeat because he had not done his Bible lesson that day. Such judgements may have appeared harsh to the children at the time and contributed to the growing strain between mother and children. Part of it also had to do with Nancy's desire to dominate all those around her, not just in the way they behaved but also in what they believed. Michael thought his mother's 'urge to control the minds of her children made her wish to get too close'. Waldorf was too aloof to be friends with his son, while Nancy interfered so much that she failed to gain Michael's respect. He rebelled against what he called 'Langhorne possessiveness', the desire to maintain familial tentacles round each member of the household.[68]

Michael Astor grew up in a family where the emphasis was on moral and spiritual education, and even though his mother led a demanding life as a Member of Parliament she personally attended to the religious instruction of her children. Nancy Cunard, on the other hand, spent a solitary childhood on a Leicestershire estate in the company of nursemaids and governesses, where the only break in the monotonous routine was the dramatic arrival of her mother from London with a horde of guests for a 'country-house weekend'. Nancy Cunard was the only child of Sir Bache Cunard and his American wife, Maud Burke of California. Social ambitions precluded any maternal feelings on the part of Lady Cunard, and the difficulties of forming a relationship with her daughter were compounded by the irregular household arrangements. Maud Cunard lived apart from her husband and maintained a separate establishment in London. The example of Lady Cunard fits more closely than the previous ones referred to here to the stereotyped view of titled Americans as contained in the anonymous *Contemporary Review* article. Nancy remained with her father until, at the age of 14, her mother placed her in a fashionable London school. She studied abroad for two years and completed her education at a Parisian finishing school.[69] The bitter relations between mother and daughter were well known in London society in the 1920s, and biographers have attributed this to the lack of interest of Lady Cunard in her daughter as a young child.

In summary, the argument that American women were having a detrimental effect upon the British peerage by reason of their failure to produce children, especially male heirs, and their obsession with social life was one which took advantage of existing negative attitudes towards titled Americans. It played on the fears and anxieties of people about the survival of the Anglo-Saxon race and about the 'watering down' of the aristocracy through its alliances with women outside traditional circles. While it has been confirmed that American women in the British peerage tended to have smaller families and that there was a higher incidence of childlessness amongst Anglo-American couples, there is no absolute proof of sterility. 'Colonial's' allegations were based on a highly prejudiced interpretation of figures and were used to bolster the antagonistic view of plutocratic women and discourage further alliances between Britain's aristocracy and the American plutocracy. The contention that American women were inadequate as mothers was particularly antagonistic and without foundation. It seems that the criticism of American women as self-centred hedonists was designed to check any attempt by women in Britain to reject their prescribed roles as child-bearers, country-house chatelaines and family match-makers, roles which sustained the aristocratic, patriarchal family. American women's independence was seen as the real threat to the traditional family structure within the nobility, but if one looks at the marriages of their children, it will be seen that they contributed to the reinforcement of that structure: nearly two-thirds of the marriages of offspring from Anglo-American alliances were within traditional aristocratic circles. It is possible that 'Colonial's' motives, at least, stemmed from an anti-American prejudice and desire to promote stronger bonds between Britain and its colonial subjects. Regardless of a possible colonial context for such views, however, if we take the criticism of titled Americans from all these articles published in the Edwardian era, we have evidence of a much more hostile stance towards transatlantic marriages which belied the anxieties of an elite very much on the defensive.

10

Hostesses, political campaigners, and actresses: titled Americans and their public roles

Transatlantic marriages aroused such strong emotions that little attempt was made to discover the real titled American, hidden from view by racial and class prejudice. What little attention that has since been paid to American women in the peerage, moreover, has done nothing to contradict the heiress stereotype. American women married into the titled aristocracy of Europe for a variety reasons, and in this chapter on the public and social role of titled Americans we shall see how these women met the challenge of living in a traditional aristocratic society. Some of the autobiographical material used as evidence here will be familiar from other historical and biographical texts of the period, but the aim of the present study is to demonstrate the gap between the American heiress stereotype and reality, and the evidence will be presented within this very specific context.

CONSUELO VANDERBILT, DUCHESS OF MARLBOROUGH (1877–1964)

Consuelo Vanderbilt could have been the model for the American heiress stereotype. She was, after all, a rich New York woman, from a family which had recently asserted its claims to high social status, and her dowry came from three generations of capital accumulation in the railroad industry. Yet in spite of, or even because of, the notoriety of her alliance with the Duke of Marlborough, she managed to break out of the mould after her legal separation from the Duke.

Consuelo Vanderbilt spent fourteen years in London promoting women's education, supporting charitable foundations, and campaigning for the election of women to the London County Council. She used her title and her position to advance the causes of disadvantaged women and, in so doing, demanded to be considered as a person in her own right, rather than as a capitalist's heiress or a duke's consort. Her activities in these years clearly conflict with the typical image of a socially ambitious American peeress.

In 1909 Consuelo published an article in the *North American Review* on 'The Position of Woman' in which she urged women of the leisure class to take up political, artistic, or philanthropic work.[1] She used her intimate knowledge of aristocratic life in Britain to compare the roles of women in Britain and the United States, and to show how British women had taken up the political struggle for suffrage, and how seriously they viewed their duties as ladies of the manor, wives of politicians, or fund-raisers for charities. She asserted that, although such responsibilities bore the mark of feudal tradition, women in Britain were using them to extend their influence and control. Tracing the historical background of the position of women in society, she argued:

> Primitive women were . . . the guardians of their children, the transmitters of name, the custodians of wealth and in many cases, the electors and lawgivers. As organizers and householders, they reigned supreme, and with them rested the responsibility of providing food when the hunter was unsuccessful.[2]

Using this precedent, she contended that women should reassert their control over the matters which concerned them directly:

> Thus questions of sanitation affecting food-supplies, milk, water, drains and ventilation, questions concerning the education of children, their employment in factories, the regulations regarding the employment of women, the administration of relief to the poor, would be better and more effectively dealt with by women than by men.[3]

Ten years later these were the sort of questions which her compatriot, Nancy Astor, raised in the House of Commons.

The Duchess of Marlborough's article largely reflected her own position and activities in the period between her separation and divorce. Consuelo went to live in Sunderland House in 1906 after the highly publicized and contentious separation from the Duke.

Turning away from high society she sought personal consolation in philanthropic work. 'What had begun as an answer to a need for a new interest in my life', she wrote in her memoirs, 'became eventually my main way of life and gave it a meaning it had hitherto lacked.'[4] One of her earliest ventures was the organization of a home for the wives of first offenders where they could earn their keep by washing and sewing. She also opened the Mary Curzon Lodging House for Poor Women as a home for working girls.[5] In November 1913 she attracted the attention of the press again, but this time it was welcome publicity for the plight of women in sweated industries. There were several attempts around the turn of the century to draw attention to the conditions of women in such industries in both Britain and America. With two women trade union officials Consuelo arranged a conference at Sunderland House to which churchmen, politicians, and businessmen were invited to discuss the injustice and health hazards of sweated labour.[6]

Mrs Belmont, Consuelo's mother, had taken up the cause of women's suffrage in America, after the death of her second husband in 1908. In her own highly individualistic style, Alva Belmont cast aside the restraints of her class and of convention. She became a militant feminist, striding out at the head of a suffragists' parade along Fifth Avenue, establishing the Political Equality Association in New York State, arranging for Christabel Pankhurst to visit the United States, and representing, in an executive capacity, the Congressional Union and National Woman's Party.[7] Consuelo, herself, was involved in some of these activities and she was clearly influenced by the arguments of female suffragists. In the *North American Review* article, she endorsed militant tactics:

> Here [in Britain] women are at last uniting in one great deter-
> mined body to insist upon the completion of that long march
> towards the gates of freedom. . . . It is because womanly measures
> have failed to open the gates that they have resorted to more
> masculine ones. Not because they enjoy going to prison or making
> themselves objectionable, but because they know that no great
> reform has ever been brought about without public agitation of
> a more or less aggressive character on the part of those directly
> concerned.[8]

This might, at first, appear, to be an unusual stance for a duchess to take; the vast majority of women in the British aristocracy opposed

militancy on the suffrage question. Indeed, the anti-suffrage movement found much of its support amongst the female ranks of the
aristocracy.[9] In her memoirs, Consuelo Vanderbilt Balsan professed
more conservative views, expressing shock and distress over the
many cases of forced-feeding among hunger strikers and the suicidal
recklessness of suffragists.[10] Clearly, she did not approve of the more
extreme antics of the suffragists which resulted in physical injury
but, like many suffragists belonging to the non-militant National
Union of Woman's Suffrage Society, she did believe in agitating
and campaigning for suffrage and equality. During the First World
War, she set up the Women's Municipal Party to put up women
candidates in municipal elections, the aim being to get women on
to the local councils so that they could then fight for public health
measures to improve child welfare. In 1917, Consuelo herself
became a London County Councillor for North Southwark.[11] The
work which Consuelo Vanderbilt did at a municipal level in order
to improve the health and working conditions of women and children was, in some sense, paralleled by Nancy Astor's efforts at a
national level.

NANCY LANGHORNE, LADY ASTOR (1879–1964)

Lady Astor was one of the very few Virginians who became an
American peeress. The third daughter and eighth child of Chiswell
Dabney Langhorne and Nancy Witcher Keene, Nancy Langhorne
had been brought up in straitened circumstances during the years
of her father's struggle to build up the family fortune after losing
everything during the Civil War. By the 1890s, however, Langhorne
had his own railway contracting firm and had resumed the life of
a Southern country gentleman, and in 1896 Nancy was sent to a
New York finishing school.[12] After her brief marriage (1897–1903)
to Robert Gould Shaw, a member of a prominent Bostonian family,
Nancy twice visited England for the hunting season, mixing with
the titled elite amongst the sporting set in Leicestershire. She was
briefly courted by Lord Revelstoke, the senior partner in Baring
Brothers. On her third trip across the Atlantic, however, she met
Waldorf Astor (1879–1952). He was the son of William Waldorf
Astor who had left the United States after failing to secure a seat in
the United States Congress and who eventually settled in England,
becoming a naturalized British citizen in 1899. Although the

marriage of Nancy Langhorne and Waldorf Astor does not quite fit into the usual pattern of transatlantic marriages, as Waldorf was member of one of the most prominent New York elite families, Lady Astor was one of the most famous titled Americans in Britain.

Lady Astor was the first woman to take a seat in the House of Commons, and her parliamentary career spanned twenty-five years during which she espoused causes which had a direct bearing on the life of women and children. She spoke on a wide variety of issues, including pensions for blind persons, criminal and indecent assaults on children, cinema censorship and juvenile crime, the Education Act of 1918, the conditions of work for probationer nurses, the Juvenile Courts Bill, liquor traffic, the Temperance Bill, the representation of women in the Transport Advisory Committee, equal pay and opportunities for women in the Civil Service, and the Women, Young Persons and Children's Bill.[13] This selection comes from the index for the first Parliament in which Lady Astor sat in 1919–20, and for the next quarter of a century she was to maintain her interest in and concern for such issues.

Like the Duchess of Marlborough, Nancy Astor turned to social reform and politics in the hope of finding a greater sense of personal fulfilment. The great wealth and prominent social position in English society which she gained by her marriage to Waldorf Astor in 1906 had a debilitating effect upon her. In a way which is somewhat reminiscent of Edith Wharton's reaction to marriage and high society,[14] Nancy Astor became a semi-invalid for several years. As her son wrote: 'No prescription, no spa, nothing in the way of diet of change could help her. . . . and all that her doctors could tell her was that she was suffering from nervous exhaustion.'[15]

Her second marriage had given her the opportunity to make her mark as a Society hostess, and as the new mistress of Cliveden she set about turning it into a social centre on the banks of the Thames. Victor Cunard, a close family friend, wrote that at Cliveden

> everything seemed devised for gaiety and enjoyment and for a reasonable indulgence in such sensual pleasures as are provided by games, good food and bodily comfort. . . . with Nancy Astor at the end of the table, the most unpromising conversation could not become ponderous, and pomposity was unable to survive.[16]

Nancy had brought new life into the Berkshire mansion. 'The solemn feeling that went with punctuality, Victorian furniture and my grandfather', as her son Michael wrote, 'flew out of the windows.'[17] But these extraordinary bouts of energy and vitality alternated with periods of listlessness and lethargy. Boredom was her greatest enemy, and Nancy got bored very easily. Her son's perceptive comment that she was unable to 'flavour or indeed tolerate life in its quieter and gentler moods' vividly conveys the restlessness that she must have experienced when she exhausted herself with her own hyperactivity.[18]

Dogged by ill health and depression, she was unable to break out of a cycle of listlessness and vitality. The transformation from a popular divorcée pursued by suitors to the chatelaine of a country mansion with a subsequent loss of freedom was difficult to reconcile with her independent spirit. She sought solace in Christian Science, and this enabled her to overcome her physical debility. Her renewed vigour coincided with the additional responsibilities of Waldorf in Parliament. In 1916 Lloyd George appointed Waldorf his parliamentary private secretary, and after the war he became the parliamentary secretary of the Local Government Board and, later, the Ministry of Health.[19] There was a corresponding increase in Nancy's activities, with more meetings to attend, more dinners to arrange, and more charitable duties to fulfil. By the time Waldorf had moved to the House of Lords, a step he was loath to take, Nancy's confidence and health had returned, and she was ready to look beyond the purely social and supportive role of a politician's wife.[20]

Nancy continued her husband's work when she replaced him as Member for the Sutton division of Plymouth in 1919, but she also pursued her own interests in the welfare of women and children. In the 1920s she badgered the government about the inadequate number of women police officers in the Metropolitan Police Force, and about equal pay and opportunities for women in government service. During the depression years of the 1930s, she demanded action on women's unemployment, particularly within the cotton trade. In a lively debate on grants for employment schemes, she scorned the efforts of the Labour Party on the question of women's unemployment and insisted that she had always put women's questions 'above and beyond party'. Following her in the debate, a Mr Toole quickly discounted her complaints about the government's inaction. With contempt, thinly disguised by parliamentary rhetoric, he retorted: 'We always enjoy the Noble Lady's intervention in our debates because we succeed in securing a little diversity from her.'[21] Lady Astor tried in vain not to be a 'sex member' but, faced with such opposition, she was obliged to represent the 'woman's view' in such debates.

Her maiden speech in the Commons was on the drink law. Her own experience of being married to an alcoholic (i.e. Shaw) and her religious faith led her to take an uncompromising stand in the House on questions related to the sale of alcohol. A few months later she took a major part in the divorce debate, yet another issue which was pertinent to her own personal experience. Married at an early age to a wealthy Bostonian dilettante, Nancy had left Robert Shaw within three years and signed a deed of separation. She resisted her husband's plea for a divorce despite the fact that he had proved sufficient grounds for her to sue successfully against him: her stand in the matter had more to do with propriety and religious faith than her personal happiness. She was eventually forced, however, to sue for divorce in 1902 when her husband committed bigamy.[22] In spite of her own experience of marriage and divorce, she took a conservative line in the debate on the reform of the divorce laws.

Lady Astor was in a difficult position as a divorcée and as the sole woman Member in the House. Many people expected her to support the reform, but within the House and her own social milieu she was probably expected to take a more conservative stance. The King strongly disapproved of the public discussion of divorce and of the presence of two women on the Royal Commission. He maintained that divorce could not 'be discussed openly in all its aspects with any delicacy or even decency before ladies'.[23] Lady Astor resolved her difficulty by arguing that the time was propitious for a change in the laws – 'I would rather wait a little longer,' she declared, 'until the world is a little more settled and society is a little more settled'. She did not, therefore, argue against reform *per se*. Another argument she put forward to modify her own stance in opposition to the recommendations of the Royal Commission was to emphasize the effects upon women and children. A cross between a Pankhurst-style social purity campaigner and a Virginian vigilante, Lady Astor asserted that she wanted to suppress vice and immorality: 'I think the world is too loose altogether. What we need is tightening up. I want to tighten up the men as well as the women.'[24] Almost inevitably, she was accused of hypocrisy and faced the first major crisis in her new career. Horatio Bottomley exposed the details of Lady Astor's divorce from Robert Shaw in *John Bull* and revealed, furthermore, that she had listed herself as a widow in *Who's Who*. She received, however, full and continued support both from the Unionist Association in her constituency and from colleagues in the House of Commons, and the matter was dropped.[25]

In many ways, the issues Lady Astor took up in the House of Commons can be regarded as the kind of extension of women's sphere into the political arena for which the Duchess of Marlborough had called in 1909. Madame Balsan, who professed admiration for those women who demonstrated an independence of spirit, was a great fan of Lady Astor and paid tribute to her in her memoirs:

> During her parliamentary career she defended women's interests with a courage that compelled admiration even from those who opposed her views. She made a great many speeches on her feet and still more interjectory remarks from her seat; she could answer the Labour members in banter or in anger and be equally effective in either mood. She was adored by her constituents but disliked by the classic parliamentarians, who considered her repartees undignified. . . .
>
> Looking back on the little circle I knew of American women married to Englishmen, there are, I realize, very few who remained definitely Americans. Nancy Astor was one of these. Her high spirits, her sense of humour, her self-assurance, her courage, her independence are all of the American variety; and also her beauty.[26]

Amongst the titled Americans in Britain, Lady Astor was a major public figure. Her importance owes more, perhaps, to the fact that she was the first woman to take up a seat in the Commons than to her legislative achievements. Her election in 1919 must also have been a tremendous boost to the Anglo-American community in Britain, and certainly Consuelo Balsan's account betrays a fervent national pride in her countrywoman. Lady Astor managed to break away from the stereotypical image of the American heiress by going into public life and supporting causes which would improve the welfare of the working classes and of women and children in general.

JENNIE JEROME, LADY RANDOLPH CHURCHILL
(1854–1921)

Much important groundwork had to be done by women long before they were given the vote or allowed to stand for election to Parliament, and Jennie Churchill made a contribution to those efforts. In 1902 the journalist William Stead declared Lady Randolph to be 'one of the few American women who have counted for anything in English politics'.[27] Jennie was a pioneer in more than one sense: not only was she one of the first American women to marry into the upper echelons of the British aristocracy after the Civil War, but she was also the first titled American to play a significant role as a political hostess in the late Victorian era. Like other politicians' wives, she attended political meetings with her husband, listened to his speeches in the House, and canvassed for him at election time. But though she may have owed her prominent position in the world of British politics to her husband, and though that relationship was not always a happy one, Lady Randolph made the most of the opportunities her marriage gave her and opened up new avenues of activity for women in public life.

In a letter written to her younger sister, Leonie Leslie, during the general election of 1906, Jennie recounted: 'The election is most exciting – they say it will be a close thing. The female suffrage women are too odious. Every night they make a disturbance and shriek and rant. They damage their own cause hopelessly.'[28] Like many women of her class, Lady Randolph Churchill disagreed with the tactics of the militant suffragists. Her son, Winston, took an even more hostile stand and was one of the MPs most opposed to women members in the Commons. He told Nancy Astor: 'I find a woman's intrusion into the House of Commons as embarrassing as if she burst into my bathroom when I had nothing to defend myself with, not even a sponge.'[29] Lady Randolph herself signed the 'Appeal Against Female Suffrage' in 1889, but her own attempts to extend the limits of women's sphere suggest that she was not wholly out of tune with the improvement in the position and status of women in British society. In 1885 she conducted her first campaign for Lord Randolph's re-election to Parliament and made a speech to his supporters after the victory was announced. In her memoirs she recalled her feelings of exhilaration at that time:

I made a little speech to the crowd, and thanked them 'from the bottom of my heart' for returning my husband for the third time. I surpassed the fondest hopes of the suffragettes, and thought I was duly elected, and I certainly experienced all the pressure and gratification of being a successful candidate.[30]

Lord Randolph's third and last Woodstock campaign was the first which he left to his wife to organize. Her energy and ingenuity in soliciting votes from constituents and her temerity in knocking on doors and engaging in repartee with voters made her a valuable campaigner – a fact that her son was quick to recognize when he started out on his political career. At his first attempt to win a seat in the Commons, Winston contested Oldham in a by-election in 1899. The local Conservatives in Oldham set great store by Lady Randolph's presence, and the Oldham *Daily Standard* enthusiastically reported her attendance and speeches at various meetings and the warm reception she received.[31] Winston failed to secure the seat that year, but returned to Oldham the following summer to stand again as the Conservative candidate. His mother was in Scotland on her honeymoon with her second husband, George Cornwallis-West, but, notwithstanding this, Winston urged her to come down for the closing stages of his campaign; to secure the seat he needed her support and her contacts with leading politicians.[32]

Jennie's interest in politics was more latent than active during the early years of her marriage to Lord Randolph Churchill, who had won his first election three months prior to their wedding in 1874. Part of this had to do with the excitement of entering into the most exclusive circles of British society and keeping pace with the smart set around the Prince of Wales. Her first London Season left her with the impression that it had been 'a whirl of gaieties and excitement' in contrast to her relatively quiet life in Paris and, more especially, in contrast to the subsequent three years she spent in Dublin.[33] Part of it also had to do with the demands made on her in the domestic sphere: 'I had many new experiences in those early years, not the least trying being my attempt at housekeeping, which was very erratic, owing to the ignorance I often had cause to bemoan.'[34] These were also the years when Lady Randolph gave birth to two sons in November 1874 and February 1880.

A major reason for the delay in her involvement in politics, however, was the ostracization of Lord Randolph Churchill from high society following a serious rift between the Spencer-Churchills and the Prince of Wales over the Aylesford divorce scandal. Many of Society's doors were closed to the couple, and, in the circumstances, a tactful retreat to Ireland, to where the Duke of Marlborough had been posted as Viceroy, seemed the best solution. Lord Randolph acted as private secretary to his father for three years during this period but was often away attending his parliamentary duties at Westminster.[35] Jennie spent much of her time hunting or assisting the Duchess in her social and philanthropic duties. Although the withdrawal to Ireland had taken Jennie away from London and any possible involvement in her husband's parliamentary career, it was not, in fact, until a short time after the change of government in 1880 that Randolph himself started to take politics more seriously.[36] He had begun to realize his potential as a politician and to recognize how political success might compensate for an awkward position in Society, and with this change of heart he became more conscientious in attending debates in the House and more active in his opposition to the Liberals.

By the time the first Parliament of Gladstone's second Ministry opened, the Churchills had returned to the capital, taking up residence next door to Sir Stafford Northcote in St James's Place. Their home became the headquarters of the Fourth Party, a pressure group within the Conservative Party highly critical of the government and contemptuous of 'the ultra-Tories'. The group consisted of Sir Henry Drummond Wolff, Sir John Gorst, Arthur Balfour, and Lord Randolph. Jennie 'caught the fever' in these more hopeful years in her husband's career and witnessed the hatching of 'plots and plans' by the Fourth Party.[37] She began to establish herself as a political hostess in the 1880s, entertaining her husband's colleagues, accompanying him to political meetings, following political events closely, and attending debates at the House of Commons. She noted in her memoirs that in those days 'only a few ultra-political ladies' were present in the Ladies' Gallery, such as Mrs Gladstone, Miss Balfour, and fellow Americans Mrs Cavendish-Bentinck and Mrs Joseph Chamberlain. Later generations of Society women, she thought, were less interested in the debates and more concerned just to be seen at the House.[38]

In spite of financial limitations, Lady Randolph Churchill's dinner parties were nevertheless renowned in London's political circles. First of all, as Rosa Lewis, the famous Society cook, recalled: 'Lady Randolph Churchill only wanted a few things, but those

things she wanted the most perfect, and perfect things to eat. . . .
She always put all her money in a few things.'[39] Second, she entertained men of all political persuasions and sometimes men whose
ideological differences prevented them from talking to one another.
George Smalley recalled from these years an experiment initiated
by Jennie which she called 'the dinner of deadly enemies'. She
would invite to dinner, as Smalley explained, people who had not
spoken to each other in years and would rely on their breeding and
sense of obligation to her as their hostess to suppress their personal
animosities for the evening. He went on: 'The guests all knew each
other, and as they looked about the table they all saw that Lady
Randolph Churchill had attempted the impossible and had conqu-
ered. A social miracle had been performed.'[40]

Lady Randolph Churchill was one of the founder members of the
Primrose League which involved women in its organization from
the outset. The League was Sir Henry Drummond Wolff's brain-
child and constituted a network of Conservative associations
throughout the country. They were known as Habitations and were
used to marshal support at election time. One of the League's aims
was to 'embrace all classes and all creeds except atheists and
enemies of the British Empire',[41] and this reflected Lord Randolph's
own concern to break down the gulf which divided the classes
in Britain. Jennie became a Dame of the Primrose League at its
inauguration at Blenheim in 1883, and she travelled around Britain
establishing Habitations and giving public speeches.[42] In these years
she had more opportunity than most women to exercise some influence in the highest political circles and possibly felt little need for
the vote.

Jennie ran the election campaigns of her husband which took
place in the mid-1880s. Churchill was becoming a force to be
reckoned with at that time, attacking Gladstone and his Irish policy
at every opportunity, sniping at his own party's leadership for its
remoteness from the social problems of the new industrial centres,
as well as spreading a new creed which he called 'Tory democracy'.
In 1885, assisted by friends, relations, and other Members of Parliament, Jennie had secured Randolph's re-election for Woodstock. A
few months later she was again rallying voters but this time in
Birmingham, the stronghold of the Liberal prima donnas, John
Bright and Joseph Chamberlain. It was a formidable challenge,
and, though Churchill was not returned, the Radical minority was

much reduced. Lord Randolph was given a safe seat at South Paddington which he held at the next general election in July 1886, again with his wife managing the campaign. With so much of her time and energy invested in promoting Randolph's career, Jennie was understandably enraged when he miscalculated Lord Salisbury's response to his offer of resignation less than six months after being appointed Chancellor of the Exchequer. She wrote in her memoirs: 'When I looked back at the few preceding months, which seemed so triumphant and full of promise, the débâcle appeared all the greater. I had made sure that Randolph would enjoy the fruits of office for years to come.'[43] There was no doubt in her mind how much she had contributed to his success. With Randolph's career brought to an abrupt end, Jennie's own ambitions were dashed. Her dependence on her husband's political fortunes was never more clearly demonstrated. Not even her son's rapid progress in politics could restore to her the position and influence she had once had, even though she did much to further Winston's career. She carefully guided her son's political education, introducing him to politicians, arranging meetings for him, and giving him the benefit of her own experience. Born too early to enjoy the benefits of women's suffrage, Jennie's role was inevitably a supportive one in aiding both her husband and her son. Her understanding of political manoeuvring, her effectiveness at electioneering, and her nourishment of both Randolph's and Winston's ambitions reveal a remarkable talent for politics and an ability to overcome adversity.

There were numerous Americans amongst the ranks of political hostesses, including Lady Naylor-Leyland, Mrs Cavendish-Bentinck, Lady Willoughby d'Eresby (later Countess of Ancaster), Mrs Frederick Guest, Mrs Joseph Chamberlain, and Lady Elizabeth Harcourt. Whitelaw Reid, the American Ambassador, used to write letters to the President's wife, Mrs Taft, relating all the various events which involved these and other Americans. In the 1910 general election, a number of American women had campaigned for their husbands. In the ensuing turmoil over the right of the Upper House to veto legislation, some feared there would be another election within a few months. As Reid told Mrs Taft:

One of them was in here the other day, deploring the possibility of the Government's going out almost any day, and the probability that at any rate it seemed not likely to last beyond June. She was quite pathetic in describing the intense strain of the campaign and the amount of work that British constituencies expected from the wives of candidates; and almost tragic in throwing up her hands in despair at the thought of having to go through the same thing again within a few weeks or months.[44]

The Boston *Globe* made much of the presence of American heiresses in the ranks of the Liberal Party in Britain; it claimed that if it were not for these American ladies the Liberals would have no political hostesses![45] Among these hostesses it listed Mrs Guest, Lady Granard, and Mrs Lewis Harcourt. The Countess of Granard, née Beatrice Mills (a niece of Whitelaw Reid), was both a prominent member of the court set and active in support of the Liberal Party. Her strategies included dinners, receptions, opening bazaars, and supporting Liberal candidates in their constituencies.[46] It was alleged that, with the assistance of the Millses' money, she aspired to become a leading Liberal hostess. Another American newspaper claimed that Mrs Harcourt was the most active of the Liberal hostesses, outdoing even the Liberal leader's wife: 'she receives as many invitations to political gatherings as does Mrs Asquith. She is infinitely more energetic and she has twice that lady's enterprise.'[47] The same paper accredited Mrs Harcourt with the ambition of making her husband Prime Minister. It interpreted Mary Harcourt's presence at, and organization of, meetings, receptions, and bazaars, and her expenditure on political functions, as a publicity campaign for her husband and an opportunity to demonstrate the support he had outside Parliament. There is no reason to deny Mrs Harcourt's ambition, but the picture painted of Mary in the American press, with its insinuations of personal glorification aided by the Morgan fortune, must be placed alongside evidence taken from her correspondence with Lady Elizabeth Harcourt, her American stepmother-in-law.

MARY BURNS, LADY HARCOURT (187?–1961)

Mrs Harcourt was the daughter of a famous American banker, Walter H. Burns, and Mary Morgan, sister of John Pierpont

Morgan. The Burnses owned a Hertfordshire estate, North Mymms Park, and Mary, though American by birth, had grown up in England, contrary to the conventional idea of an American heiress fresh from New York. Her uncle, Pierpont Morgan, was an important figure in her life, and when he died in 1913 she wrote:

> I loved him dearly and his loss leaves a blank in my life which nothing can fill. Ever since Papa's death he had been the person to whom I turned in times of difficulty and he was ever ready to share one's joys as well as help one with his invaluable advice.[48]

Mary had a very close and affectionate relationship with the Harcourt family as well as with her own. The Harcourts were a close-knit circle: Lewis, the only surviving son of Sir William's first marriage, was devoted to his father and delayed his own political career in order to be his father's private secretary. Very much aware of his son's sacrifice, on the occasion of Lewis's engagement to Mary, Sir William had written to Joseph Chamberlain:

> You know what Loulou has been to me and I have often felt that I engrossed too much of his life. When I say that I am happy you may be quite sure that I feel convinced that his future happiness – which has ever been my first and last object – is assured.[49]

Elizabeth Harcourt's devotion as a daughter had been described in much the same terms by John Lothrop Motley to a close friend.[50] This may explain the close affinity between Lady Harcourt and her stepson, Loulou. Mary Burns was well aware that her marriage to Loulou might dislocate these close relationships, and she reassured Lady Harcourt: 'We must neither of us think of the word separation for Loulou and I hope that it will only mean the addition of two homes for each of us!'[51]

Loulou's parliamentary career provided the central concern of the family from 1904 onwards when he stood as the Liberal candidate for the Rossendale division of Lancashire. His father had been anxious that he pursue his own career, but it was not until March 1904 that Loulou and Mary travelled up to Bacup, Lancashire, to be interviewed by the local Liberal organization. Bacup was in the Rossendale Fells region, an area of cotton manufacture and small industrial towns. There was a by-election soon after Harcourt's adoption, but no Conservative-Unionist candidate came forward to

```
                           George Vernon
                           1st Baron Vernon
                            [1707–80]
                                |
                           Edward Harcourt
                           Archbishop of York
                                |
Juliet    = Junius         Rev. William        John      = Mary
Pierpont    Spencer        Harcourt,           Lothrop     Benjamin
            Morgan         Canon of York       Motley
            [1813–90]      [1789–1871]         [1814–77]

John          Mary = Walter   Mary (1) = Sir William = (2) Elizabeth
Pierpont             Hayes     Lister     Harcourt        Cabot
Morgan               Burns     d. 1863    [1827–1904]     Ives
[1837–1913]                                               (widow)
                                                          d. 1928

        Walter              Mary   = Lewis
                            d. 1961  Harcourt
                                     1st Viscount
                                     Harcourt
                                     [1863–1922]
```

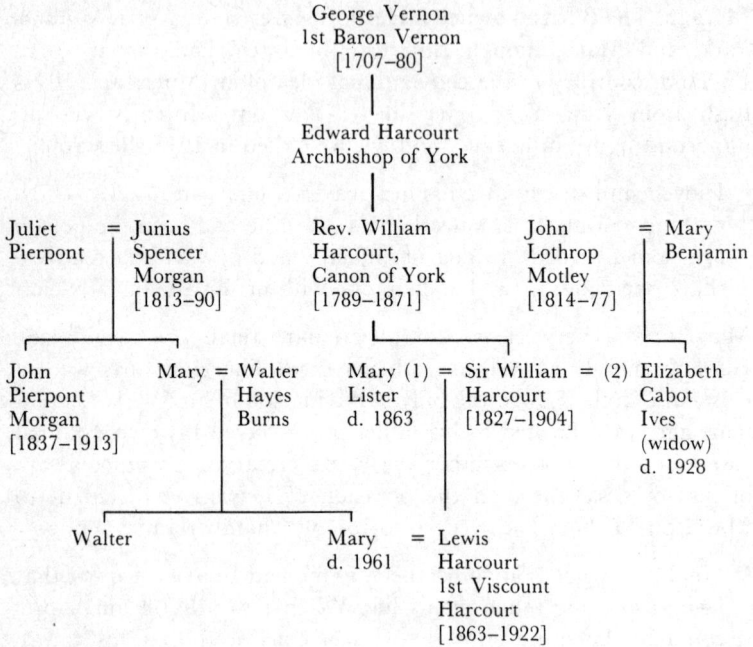

Select family tree of the Harcourt family

contest it, and he thus joined the Liberal benches in the Commons.
It was an auspicious time to enter the political fray: the Conservative and Unionist Party, which had been in power since 1895, was
losing heavily in by-elections. Tory measures on education and
licensing as well as their tariff policy had aroused much opposition;
free trade had once more become a burning issue; and the woman's
suffrage movement was stepping up its campaign.

At the outset of Lewis's parliamentary career, Mary had not been
very enthusiastic about her new duties. She tried to choose days
when there were social affairs for visiting the Rossendale constituency.[52] In January 1905 she wrote: 'it is only a stern sense of duty
which is dragging me to the constituency as it is a case of "now or
never", for me'.[53] What she hated most was being asked to make
short speeches to Liberal supporters, and she frequently complained

to Loulou's stepmother of the agony this caused her. It does not appear that Mary ever overcame her loathing of public speaking, even with more experience. In one letter she said how much she detested 'the role of a Public Woman standing on Platforms "saying a few words" ',[54] and in another she wrote:

> It is simply awful but there is nothing for it but just set one's teeth & go through with it. They are very lenient but I am much ashamed at my efforts. I cannot imagine why they want a person who can't speak to address them.[55]

As time went by, Mary Harcourt became more engrossed in Liberal politics. It is possible to trace an awakening of her political consciousness through her correspondence with Lady Harcourt. During the 1906 general election, a momentous occasion in the history of the Liberal Party, Mary and Lewis were staying at the Midland Hotel in Manchester with Winston Churchill and his mother. Mary became very excited by the atmosphere at election time and rejoiced at the Liberal victories in the South, scorned the effect on the Liberal votes of the Labour candidacy, and was almost gleeful when Balfour lost Manchester East, a seat he had held for twenty years – 'it seemed too good to be true', she wrote.[56] She entered into the spirit of it all and brimmed with enthusiasm at the Liberal sweep of the Manchester and Salford seats. Winston Churchill had run for North-West Manchester, which had been held by the Unionists; he won with a majority of 1,241.[57] Overall, the election was a landslide victory for the Liberals, who won 377 seats to the Unionists' 157.

Mary Harcourt's view of politics was much influenced by her background. She came from a family of prominent bankers. During the financial panic in New York in 1907 she applauded the efforts of a 'few big financiers' in saving the United States from a crash.[58] A few years later, fearing the influence of Lloyd George as Chancellor of the Exchequer, she wrote:

> I cannot refrain from a shudder when I think of the finance of the country in the hands of Lloyd George with Masterman as his lieutenant. Both of whom had splendid impulses of Social Reform untinged I fear by any sound business instinct. But then as Venetia James says, 'You are a banker's daughter.'[59]

Her class bias is discernible in a remark she made concerning the

225

Miners' Federation strike of 1912: 'There is no doubt the miners *meant* to have a week at least of holiday on strike & enjoy themselves.'[60] During the First World War she worked indefatigably for the American Women's Relief Fund, and Consuelo Marlborough made reference to Mary's background when describing her charitable work: 'Lady Harcourt, as honorary secretary, proved that she had inherited her uncle Pierpont Morgan's business acumen. She carried the brunt of the work and, when decorations were forthcoming, was made a Dame of the Order of the British Empire.'[61]

Lewis Harcourt also shared his wife's dislike of public speaking. He was always depressed when he had to make a speech and suffered for days with nerves.[62] At the Great Demonstration Against Woman Suffrage, a rally of anti-suffragists held at the Albert Hall in February 1913, Lewis was one of the major speakers. In a suffrage paper, the *Common Cause*, he was described thus:

> all the speeches, except Mr Harcourt's (which he appeared to be reading), were delivered with considerable oratorical accomplishment . . . . Mr Lewis Harcourt was not quite at his ease in his sneer at the fact that women were in a numerical majority in the country: it must be hard for a so-called Liberal to reconcile this fact with Anti-Suffragism.[63]

It was evident, in the *Anti-Suffrage Review* report of the meeting, that Harcourt had been singled out by the suffragists for attack: stewards had been posted throughout the Hall to forestall any counter-demonstration. After a few initial scuffles,

> Succeeding speakers were free from interruption, until it came to the turn of Mr Lewis Harcourt. Then the obligation of suffragette vows proved too strong; three female forms momentarily acquired undue prominence, and then three more seats were vacant.[64]

Harcourt and Winston Churchill were prominent Liberal anti-suffragists, and, since the militant Women's Social and Political Union, founded by Mrs Pankhurst in 1903, believed its chances of getting a Suffrage Bill introduced lay with the Liberals, its members harassed Liberal candidates in elections.[65] After 1909, however, the tactics of the suffragettes became more extreme, with attacks on property and hunger-strikes in prison. In December 1909 the house in which Lewis Harcourt was staying whilst visiting his constituency was plastered with notices about forced-feeding.[66] At the peak of suffragette action, in 1912, when Christabel Pankhurst was urging women on to more criminal acts of violence, Nuneham Park, the Harcourt residence in Oxfordshire, became the target for two militants. Thereafter, Lewis played a less overt part in trying to thwart women's suffrage: he refrained from public speeches on the subject and, behind the scenes, engineered the defeat of the Conciliation Bills in the Commons.[67]

Mary Harcourt might qualify for inclusion in Brian Harrison's category of 'self-effacing wives', since much of what she did in politics was not on her own initiative.[68] Her letters strongly suggest that her involvement in politics was reluctant and arose from her sense of commitment to her husband and his career, and from her concern for his health. At one stage during the second election in 1910 Lewis was so weak that he could not campaign and seemed on the point of a breakdown.[69] In the January election, Lewis had achieved a great personal triumph with a record majority of 2,490, but Mary looked to the aftermath with much apprehension: 'I cannot look forward to the next few months without being sick at heart of how he will stand the anxiety & responsibility which must of necessity attach to those in authority.'[70] Mrs Harcourt loathed electioneering – she called it 'hateful work' – but in December of that year she stepped into the breach and covered for her husband when he could not campaign. She described herself as a 'hostage to the constituency'.[71] Whatever her personal feelings about her political obligations as wife of a Cabinet minister, Mary Harcourt played a significant part in her husband's career. It was nevertheless a supportive role, and it is quite clear that she agreed with the arguments against women's suffrage. These, as stated in 'An Appeal Against Female Suffrage', claimed that women already possessed sufficient influence on politics, that their moral influence depended upon their natural position and duties within the family, and that women's emancipation had already reached the limit determined by their physical constitution.[72]

Women suffragists were quick to notice the apparent discrepancy between Mr Harcourt's publicly held views on women's suffrage and his dependence on his wife's efforts to conduct his election campaign. In February 1912 a deputation of women from the WSPU in his constituency was charged with asking him a series of questions about the Cabinet's division over the suffrage issue. Mrs Kay, a member of the party, asked Harcourt 'if he objected to Votes for Women how it was Mrs Harcourt was good enough to visit the Valley at the last election and run his political campaign so successfully for him. Would he not give her a vote?' His reply was: 'If I thought all women were like Mrs Harcourt and as intelligent I am not sure I might not be converted.' He went on to state, however, his reasons for opposing women's suffrage, and these had nothing whatsoever to do with female intelligence. On the other hand, they were consistent with the anti-suffragist view of women:

> Mr Harcourt: I believe that for women to become part of the political machine is bad for themselves and bad for the country. (Calls of 'Rot!') I think that it draws them from the spheres in which they shine, from duties which can adequately be performed by none but themselves. Women, of course, possess emotion and charm. ('So do men.') These are great assets, but I do not think they are conducive to sober political judgment. Then there are physical and physiological circumstances in their lives . . . which unfit them at times for public duty or judgment.[73]

Lewis Harcourt clearly subscribed to the view that the sphere of women was purely domestic and regarded his wife's political efforts on his behalf as supportive and not at all in conflict with his opposition to women's suffrage. Mary concurred with this view: she agreed with her husband's stand on the suffrage question and was a member of the National League for Opposing Women's Suffrage.

MARY VICTORIA LEITER, LADY CURZON (1870–1906)

George Curzon, a leading Conservative Party anti-suffragist, was also married to an American woman. Mary Leiter was the daughter of Levi Zeigler Leiter, a retired businessman and former partner of the famous Chicago wholesaler and retailer Marshall Field. Unlike most families who had rapidly risen to great wealth and sought to consolidate their financial gains in the social circles of New York, the Leiters chose to embark upon their social career in Washington, reinforced with trips to Europe. A letter of introduction to Sir Lyon Playfair, whose wife was Edith Russell of Boston, secured the Leiter's entry into London society, and it was after her success at the Duchess of Westminster's ball in 1890, where she danced with the Prince of Wales, that Mary Leiter met George Nathaniel Curzon, heir to Baron Scarsdale and an MP for Southport.[74] As a debutante, Mary had a successful career fêted by Washington's political and diplomatic community. Her friendship with Mrs Grover Cleveland brought her into the public eye and into contact with Henry Adam's circle. Michael Herbert, who was chargé d'affaires at the British Embassy at this time, wrote to his brother of his opinion of Mary:

> Mary Victoria is a very good sort of girl if you get her alone – but apt to be affected before numbers. However I imagine she is much more natural in Europe than she would be over here where she has to shine all the time to eradicate the painful impression caused by her baboon-like male parent on Society in general, and also try and conceal her Chicago origins for the porcine atmosphere of that western city stinks in the nostrils of the aristocratic mushrooms of the East.
>
> In London she partly feels that nobody cares whether she hails from Chicago or New York and is accordingly much more at her ease and more independent.[75]

However, when Mary married Curzon in 1895 she found it difficult to make the transition from a popular debutante in Washington society to a young matron in London. Although, as Nicolson, her biographer, suggests, she was hampered by an ambitious mother and a father more at ease amongst investors and stockbrokers than amongst the statesmen and men of letters who visited his Dupont Circle mansion, Mary looked forward to her parents' visits to her in London for relief from the boredom and homesickness that she felt in her first years of marriage. In her letters home, Mary complained of the obligation to make polite conversation to, and ingratiate herself with, her husband's constituents in Southport:

> I think I must pour out my heart to you, and tell you how I *loathe* this place. . . . This miserable 3rd-class seaside resort, a 4th-rate Brighton, is full of idle loafers. My only regret if he is elected here is that we shall have to spend part of every year among these people, frowsy women and horrid men.[76]

The adjustment to life in England was perhaps particularly hard for Mary Curzon: she had married a man who constantly undermined her role within the home, overriding her supervision of servants and checking her household accounts, and whose devotion to work at the Foreign Office prevented them from participating in the social life of the capital. She thus found it difficult to find fulfilment, either as a mother and wife or as a hostess.

Curzon's appointment as Viceroy of India in 1898 enabled Mary to play a more positive role in her husband's career. Not only did she assist him in his social duties as Viceroy, but she was also able to act in her own capacity as Vicereine, sponsoring charitable and medical causes. In 1902, for example, she founded the Victoria Scholarships for the medical training of Indian women and organized an appeal to finance them.[77] As wife of an under-secretary she had felt eclipsed in London society, but as Vicereine of India she was once more in the limelight, in the centre of Society and government.

Mary's devotion to her husband was remarked upon by her friends. Consuelo Marlborough, who visited India in 1903 for the Durbar in honour of Edward VII's accession to the throne, was surprised at the submissiveness of her compatriot:

I thought that she had shed her American characteristics more completely than I was to find myself able to do. Wholly absorbed in her husband's career, she had subordinated her personality to his to a degree I would have considered beyond an American woman's power of self-abnegation.[78]

But she was also 'moved' by the intensity of the Curzons' feelings for each other and Mary's staunch support of her husband in his work. Involving herself in Curzon's career and taking a large share of the social duties he had to perform as Viceroy provided Mary's life with a sense of purpose it had hitherto lacked. At the same time, there was also a very strong element of dependence in her devotion to her husband which is highlighted in a letter written by Mary to Belle Herbert in 1904, following a serious illness.

In January of that year Lady Curzon had returned to England for the birth of her third daughter, Alexandra Naldera, in March. She remained in England, and Curzon joined her for the summer. Soon after moving to Walmer Castle in August, Mary miscarried her fourth child and a few days before their planned return to India she nearly died from peritonitis. Curzon sat by her bedside writing down what he thought would be her last words. When she recovered, however, he left for India, anticipating a prolonged separation. The letter to Belle Herbert was written in pencil soon after Curzon's departure:

Belle darling,

How you understand I am utterly broken hearted and the world has begun to go round the other way. My dear Belle it is against nature to separate two people who worship one another as he and I do. I was braver than he was when he went because I fought to keep him up – but when he had gone the flood gates opened and I believe I nearly went mad. The dread of his going had weighed on me so many months – & when it came nearly killed me – he was so tender and was my nurse and lifted me and slept always on the sofa in my room on all the many nights that I was dying – oh the tenderness & the love! and *now* all gone. But Belle in my Braver heart I am *glad* he has gone[;] he is destined for higher things than comforting my aching back (I have been *over 3 months* in bed because of the cursed drain under my room at Walmer) but he *hated* me to say this & poor angel *sobbed* to go. Belle did you ever know that all my troubles began my miscarrying *a boy*? – is there *anything* left for me to bear? The three doctors who lived in the house a month say I should be *dead* by every law human divine surgical & medical, and that I am a law unto myself! I think the prayers & wonderful pity that thousands of people feel helped me. I am still very ill with 4 viruses – but as soon as the doctor will let me see a visitor will dear Belle come and see Broken winged Mary?[79]

Less than six months after her almost fatal illness, Mary Curzon returned to India, against all medical advice. Curzon did not complete his second term as Viceroy; he resigned after an acrimonious dispute with Kitchener, then Commander-in-Chief of the Indian Army, and after losing the support of the government. He and Mary returned to England at the end of 1905 just as the political tide was beginning to turn against the Conservative and Unionist Party. No member of Balfour's Cabinet welcomed them home, and the customary earldom for service in India was denied Curzon for several years. Mary died of a heart attack a few months later.[80] The obituary notices praised her for her charm and graciousness. The following was written by Lady Henry Somerset:

The untimely death of Lady Curzon was universally mourned. While she was not so much in the public eye personally as some others of the American peeresses, none of her countrywomen had made a more solid place for herself in the very best of British society.

She had in a marked degree the attributes which should be held by the wife of a public man. Beauty, dignity and tact were hers to a marked degree. She aided her husband not alone by the fortune she brought him, but in a great degree by the sympathy and remarkable aptitude for affairs of state.[81]

It was almost inevitable that Lady Henry Somerset should have mentioned that Mary Curzon had brought her husband a fortune. In the stereotypical terms already analysed, she subscribed to the conventional view of American peeresses. Not only did she mention the fact of Mary's dowry but, within the same sentence, she also referred to the personal and individual contribution Mary had made to Curzon's career. The two are unequal and cannot be compared, but the implication of the sentence is that both things were of equal, or related, value. The dowry was not Mary Leiter's personal contribution: she was an heiress, and the marriage settlement was part of the conventional procedure. Biographical evidence supports the conjecture that George Curzon made a calculated decision to marry a wealthy woman.[82] The heiress stereotype obviously denigrated whatever personal achievement titled Americans (and their husbands) attained. Even though the Leiter marriage settlement paved the way for Curzon to realize his ambitions, money alone did not guarantee his success. The selective nature of the stereotype tended to hide or depreciate personal achievement.

BELLE WILSON, LADY MICHAEL HERBERT (186?–1923)

Belle Herbert was another American heiress whose wealth was given undue prominence in the assessment of her contribution to her husband's career. She came from a family renowned for its marriage alliances with famous New York families. Her parents, Richard Thornton Wilson and Melissa Johnston, originally from Georgia, moved to New York after the Civil War and combined their talents for capital accumulation and social climbing with the aim of establishing their position amidst that city's elite. As the wife of Sir Michael Herbert, Belle became one of the wealthiest titled Americans in Britain, and this fact did not pass unnoticed by the

American press. The *New York Times* obituary of her husband, like that of Mary Curzon, linked wealth to ability:

> Lady Herbert's wealth and Sir Michael's unquestioned standing had made a distinct place for them, which, as time passed, would have approached in some degree the substantial and aristocratic position which Lord Pauncefote and his household maintained for so many years.[83]

Wealth and money, however, were subjects rarely discussed in the personal correspondence between Sir Michael and Lady Herbert and her parents which survives in the Wilton House archives. There is a hint that the marriage plans did not go altogether smoothly in the letters from the Earl of Pembroke, Herbert's eldest brother, to Belle Wilson before her wedding in November 1888. George Herbert wrote of Belle's 'long and unhappy uncertainty' and Richard Wilson's misgivings.[84] He was at pains to assure Belle of his brother's devotion:

> My dear Miss Wilson
> I must write you one line of most hearty welcome and thanks. I feel very fond of you already for making dear old Bungo [*sic*] so happy. I know how constantly and tenderly he has loved you though these long years of trial and that all his chances of real happiness were bound up in you – so that it is impossible that I and his other brothers and sisters should not feel full of welcome and gratitude towards you. I must congratulate you too, for you have won as tender and affectionate a heart as I have ever known, and one utterly and long devoted to you. It has been a very severe probation for him – perhaps for both of you. I hope and believe your happiness will be all the greater for it.[85]

The uncertainty was apparently on the Wilson side, but there are no definite clues as to its causes. One possibility is that they were concerned about Michael Herbert's health. He was a consumptive, and during this period his family was very concerned about him. George had told Belle in no uncertain terms that his brother's health was 'in a very critical state' and that it was 'very important that one should never forget it'.[86] There was some doubt as to whether Michael Herbert could remain in the diplomatic service. It is also possible that the Wilsons were hoping for a grander (or wealthier) title for their daughter: Michael Herbert was the son of a baron, third in line to an earldom and with a small younger son's pension. His prospects of either inheriting the Pembroke title or receiving one in his own right were uncertain at this stage in his life, to say the least.

Some light is thrown on the possible objections of the Wilsons by a letter written several years later by Belle to her parents, after the news of Michael's appointment as Ambassador to the United States:

> I am sure you must feel a great pride in the son-in-law I have chosen for you! He has arrived at the pinnacle of his profession the top-most point of interest and responsibility at an earlier age by two years than any other English Ambassador has ever done![87]

Could it be that Belle saw this promotion as the confirmation of her faith in his potential in contrast to parental cynicism? On the other hand, Belle's parents may have wanted her to marry within her own circle in New York. Her eldest sister, May, had married a real-estate millionaire, Ogden Goelet, in 1878; and her brother, Orme, had married an Astor. The lengths to which George Herbert went to assure Belle of a sincere welcome to his family may suggest that she had misgivings about marrying into the British aristocracy.[88] Whatever the reasons for the 'trial' or 'probation', the marriage appears to have been a particularly happy one.

Although Herbert's career in the diplomatic service was at times uncertain owing to his poor health, his advancement was swift. At the time of his marriage he was chargé d'affaires in Washington during Lord Sackville's embassy. Just prior to the wedding, Sackville was forced to resign over the Murchison affair, and Herbert temporarily took his place. Three years later his new chief, Sir Julian Pauncefote, recommended his promotion to First Secretary. Herbert asked his brother to write to Lord Salisbury and do all he could to secure this appointment. He regarded it as the making of his career and told his brother: 'I feel confident of my being able to undertake the post and I think, without wishing to appear too conceited, that I might really be of use here both to Sir Julian and to the public service.'[89] Herbert was promoted over the heads of nine Second Secretaries. He was posted to The Hague shortly after and then to Constantinople in 1894.

After fairly pleasant tours of duty in the United States and western Europe, the Turkish posting caused doubts in Belle's mind about the desirability of life in the diplomatic corps. She wanted to remain within easy reach of her family, but now she faced a three-day train journey on the Orient Express, all the way from Calais to Constantinople. Looking on the bright side, Belle considered the healthy climate, the promotion it entailed for her husband, and the exciting politics of the Near East in contrast to 'dull and dead' Holland. But she was forced to admit her anxiety to her mother:

> I foresee that you and papa will be distressed over this and I confess to being so myself. I don't think it an enviable career the diplomacy, and if I were making one for myself I shouldn't choose it – but on the other hand – I don't see how I can ask Mungo to give up what he is doing so well in for nothing at all. He is very decided in his decision to continue now that he is so near the top, but of course if I were quite unhappy in it I could persuade him to give it up. I am sure it would be a serious responsibility. I might cause him to be discontented all the rest of his life.[90]

She was not at all sanguine, however, about the alternatives. With no landed estate or 'literary tastes, or commercial interests', they would probably have joined the ranks of fashionable society and led 'a drone's life'. But Belle was too resourceful a woman to have found fulfilment in domesticity alone, or in self-amusement amidst the social butterflies. Her resolution to support her husband in his decision to accept the appointment may have been strengthened by her father's response to the news. He agreed with her that they had no right to ask 'Mungo' to give up his career, especially at such a promising stage, and believed that everyone had to follow the line of his career, or not have one worth living for.[91] Two years later, Belle wrote to her mother: 'I should never be so happy as I am if Mungo had no profession or any ambition to push us on in life.'[92] She had reconciled herself to the view that ambition was a worthwhile cause, a view which prevailed both within her own family and within the diplomatic corps. Although he was aware of the difficulties his wife faced in Constantinople,[93] Michael Herbert told his father-in-law how proud he was of Belle with her efforts to make him popular amongst the English colony.[94]

The trials and tribulations of life in Turkey were soon rewarded. In June 1902 Michael Herbert was posted back to Washington as Ambassador, to succeed Lord Pauncefote. It was difficult for the Foreign Office to find someone to replace a man of such great stature in Anglo-American relations. Herbert was only 45 years of age and a career diplomat. However, the American correspondent of the London *Times* suggested that the Americans were anxious to have a man who knew Washington and was familiar with the customs and the people, and Herbert fitted the bill because of his previous experience at the Embassy.[95] The *Daily Messenger* gave another reason for Herbert's selection: it mentioned that most of the other candidates in the running had American wives. These included Sir Francis Plunkett, Alan Johnstone, Sir Henry Howard, Austin Lee, and Lord Curzon.[96] The Foreign Office appears to have attached much significance to this and was possibly influenced by the fact that the representatives of France and Germany in Washington also had American wives. Herbert was delighted at the news and wrote to Mrs Wilson: 'there is one feature connected with the appointment which gives me unallayed satisfaction and that is the position which Belle will now have in her own country'.[97] Belle was naturally elated by her husband's success, but also a little anxious about the responsibility they now bore: 'at some minutes the feeling of the seriousness and duties which the post entails saddens me and I feel youth gone far behind me'.[98]

Greater demands were to be made on Belle's courage. Less than eighteen months later her husband died from tuberculosis in Switzerland. The American and British newspapers paid tribute not only to his ability and success, but also to Belle's 'brilliant personality', her devotion to her husband, and her popularity as Ambassadress. Of the many letters written to her and her parents, one in particular stands out. It is addressed to Richard Wilson and written by Belle's sister-in-law:

> My dear Mr Wilson
> You will care to hear about our poor Belle who is bearing it all so simply & courageously & unselfishly. I can't tell you with what admiration I sit & listen to her. . . . Belle was such a mutual support to Mungo; that he recently told Gladys he never could have got on in his profession without her. She made all his ambitions hers besides loving him so, & she did make him so happy.[99]

Very little is known about Belle after 1902. She went to live in London after her husband's death to bring up her two sons in Britain.

ALYS PEARSALL SMITH, THE HON. MRS BERTRAND
RUSSELL (1867–1951)

Of all American women who married peers or younger sons in the late Victorian and Edwardian years, Alys Pearsall Smith was at the furthest remove from the conventional stereotype of the rich, young American seeking social distinction amidst the world of London's smart society. A Quaker and a feminist by upbringing, with no interest in the hierarchical ramifications of British society, and with grave doubts about the state of matrimony and the inequalities it gave rise to in the relationship between husband and wife, Alys nevertheless came up against all the horrors and injustice of cultural stereotyping in the person of Lady John Russell, her husband's grandmother. With a cunning and venom which made James's Duchess of Bayswater pale into insignificance when compared with this embodiment of an aristocratic matriarch, Lady John Russell schemed to prevent the marriage of her grandson to Alys Smith.

Alys's family were Philadelphian Quakers, turned Evangelicals, of modest fortune who went to live in England in 1888. After completing her studies at Bryn Mawr,[100] Alys joined her parents in Surrey and took up philanthropic work. She became involved in the running of a working girls' club in London and the youth section of the British Women's Temperance Association.[101] She met Bertrand Russell, five years her junior, in the summer of 1889 when he was still an undergraduate at Cambridge. He was impressed by her degree of emancipation from the usual constraints upon the lives of women,[102] but did not follow up the acquaintance fully until four years later when he invited Alys and a cousin to visit him at Cambridge. Within a year they had decided to marry, but without reckoning on the staunch opposition of Bertrand's grandmother to the match.

Although Lady Russell and Alys's mother were agreed that the marriage should be postponed for at least six months, the two women had very different reasons for imposing this restriction on the couple. Hannah Whitall Smith had always counselled her daughters to postpone marriage till as late as possible because she felt that the cares and responsibilities of married life were best faced later in life – if, indeed, they had to be faced at all.[103] Lady Russell, on the other hand, hoped that by postponing the marriage the couple would reconsider their commitment to each other. She tried to frighten off Alys in a variety of ways. In March 1894, for example, Lady Russell invited Alys to Pembridge Lodge after hearing that Bertrand had arranged to meet Alys in Paris. An account of the interview appears in Alys's diary:

> Reached Pembridge Lodge at 4 o'clock, and saw Lady Russell alone for half an hour, then Lady Agatha came in. . . . I left at 5, as the conversation was painful and very fruitless. They think I am behaving in a very dishonourable and indelicate manner in seeing so much of Bertie and writing twice a week. And they do not understand how I can 'pursue' him to Paris. I saw it was hopeless to argue with Lady R, so I only repeated that I could not see the thing as she did.[104]

Bertrand's grandmother and maiden aunt accused Alys of being 'no lady, a baby-snatcher, a low-class adventuress, a person incapable of all finer feelings'.[105] The following month, notwithstanding this opposition, Alys and Russell became engaged.

Lady Russell's next ploy was to insinuate that the marriage was unsuitable on medical grounds – because of the history of insanity in both families. The couple then suggested that they would refrain from having children if the risks were so great. Doctors were consulted, including Lady Russell's own physician who advised that 'such a course [i.e. the use of artificial contraceptives] would have a disastrous effect' upon Russell's health. Alys and Bertrand, however, found a doctor who had more experience in methods of birth control and were able to quash the 'medical' objections to their marriage. Lady Russell's final attempt to prevent the marriage was to arrange for her grandson to spend three months at the British Embassy in Paris and to insist that he should not see Alys. When plans for the wedding finally went ahead in the winter of 1894, she made the experience as unpleasant as possible. Much unhappiness was caused by her objection to the inclusion of Bertrand's title 'the Honourable', on the wedding invitations. This was calculated to cause maximum resentment within the Smith family by hitting a sensitive American nerve about titles. When the Smiths went ahead and included it, after taking advice on the matter, Lady Russell commented acidly:

> Of course where different people give different advice, you were obliged to reject that of the persons whom you might think least

competent to give it, or least concerned in the matter, which *last* you could hardly think of us. You need not have feared, as Americans, that you would be thought to pay too little deference to titles – the invariable charge is the other way.[106]

In addition to all these difficulties she created for the couple, Lady Russell also absented herself from the ceremony at the Quaker Meeting House, Westminster.[107]

Unlike the examples of titled Americans already outlined, Alys Russell maintained her own independent interests after her marriage. She travelled throughout the country lecturing on temperance and promoting the BWTA. In the 1890s she began to turn more towards the woman's movement and the suffrage issue and, when visiting Bryn Mawr with her husband in 1895, she lectured on temperance and suffrage, and spoke to the students about 'paid motherhood' and 'free love'.[108] After her separation from Russell in 1911 (the marriage broke down owing to his adultery), Alys continued her philanthropic and suffrage work and became associated with the Labour Party.[109]

With the exception of the Hon. Mrs Russell, the careers of titled Americans were essentially identified with those of their husbands. Within the contemporary context of the sphere of women, they undertook a secondary and supportive role. Even so, it can be argued that this was an improvement on the purely ornamental function women performed in American high society. The young Belle Wilson, for example, who at one time was fascinated by the intricacies of royal etiquette and who might have married into the smart set in either Britain or America and spent the rest of her life competing with other London hostesses for the attention of the Prince of Wales, married an aspiring diplomat and came to despise the emptiness of fashionable society.

There is one set of women, however, who had careers in their own right and deserve brief mention here. Between 1879 and 1914 seven American actresses married into the British peerage. Strictly speaking, their marriages belong to the phenomenon of 'peers and players' – there were fourteen other marriages between peers and actresses in the same period[110] – but, at the same time, they prove the difficulty of making generalizations about American alliances with members of the British peerage. These particular marriages occurred at a time when the status of the acting profession was improving, when actors, and especially actresses, were being taken up by fashionable society, and when it was not unknown for peers to hover around the stage door of the Gaiety Theatre.[111] In an article on 'The Actress and Society', Christopher Kent puts forward the interesting argument that 'The legendary Gaiety Girls were the quintessence of all that was daring and exciting about actresses, and a godsend to the popular press, which breathlessly followed their saucy exploits and traced their fortunes.'[112] All seven of the American actresses who married British peers or younger sons were 'Gaiety Girls', that is to say, musical comediennes.

Their fortunes as wives of aristocrats were mixed. Five marriages ended in divorce, at least two of which were granted on the grounds of the wife's adultery. Mary Yohé, who married Lord Francis Hope (later Duke of Newcastle), continued her career after marriage. It was during an engagement in New York while her husband was in England that she had an affair which ended the marriage in 1902.[113] Anna Robinson's ill-fated marriage to Lord Rosslyn ended in divorce on her petition after less than two years. At the time Rosslyn was also making a living as an actor. He looked back upon the episode as 'an act of rash folly' when he had been 'madly attracted by her beauty and insanely in love'.[114] Lord Sholto Douglas, son of the Marquess of Queensberry, had also thought of making the stage his career. According to a New York paper, he had met Loretta Addis in Bakersfield, California, where he owned a ranch.[115] The news of his engagement prompted drastic action on the part of his family, who had him committed to gaol pending a medical examination. This did not deter Lord Sholto, who married Loretta in 1895. He also managed to alienate his mother-in-law by telling her that he was going to manage his wife's career and that he did not want to see her, or any of his wife's relatives, again. Mrs Addis publicly announced that she was going to Los Angeles to whip him.[116] A less publicized match took place between Lord Ashburton and Frances Donnelly in 1906. Miss Donnelly had been on the stage only four years when she became Lady Ashburton, and she did not pursue her career afterwards. The Bruce family was particularly upset at the engagement of the eldest son to Camille Clifford: Lord Aberdare withdrew his son's allowance. The Hon. Henry Bruce, however, retaliated by buying a car business to supplement his income and went ahead with his marriage.[117] The Boston *Globe* reported the rift in the Bruce family along with details of Miss Clifford's background, pointing out that her deceased father had been a ship's cook, that she had been brought up by relatives in Sweden working as 'a common scrub girl', and that she had run away in America.[118] Lord Aberdare was reconciled with his new daughter-in-law despite the fact that she continued to appear on the stage. Clare Taylor was another actress who married a titled Englishman. She had been divorced by her first husband, a subaltern in the Scots Guards, on the grounds of adultery, before marrying Lord George Cholmondeley in 1911. This marriage also ended in the divorce courts. The last of the seven was Mae Pickard of Memphis, Tennessee, who married the eldest son of Lord Cowley in 1914. They had four children, but the marriage was dissolved in 1933.

The high incidence of divorce amongst peerage marriages to actresses suggests that the glamour and attraction of actresses on stage did not carry over into domestic life. It is interesting to note that four of the five American actresses whose marriage ended in divorce continued performing on stage. Acting gave women independence and fame in their own right, and this may have been incompatible with aristocratic notions of the role of women.

The conclusion to be drawn from the foregoing examples of the activities of titled Americans outside the domestic sphere is that they played, by and large, a supportive role in their husbands' careers. Given the prevailing ideas about the role of women in the aristocracy and their virtual exclusion from paid labour, it is hardly surprising to find in these examples a reinforcement of the status quo. Even so, the participation of titled American women in their husbands' careers, particularly in the field of politics, signifies a departure from the more ornamental role of women in the American leisured elite. As we saw in Chapter 3, the social segregation of the sexes within American high society had reduced the function of women in the new business elite to an almost purely decorative one. Women in the American leisure class had neither the opportunity for paid work available to women in the classes below, nor the opportunity to participate in their husbands' sphere of high finance and business management. In view of these restrictions, it is possible that women from this business elite sought a more active role within marriage and perceived marriage with a member of the peerage as offering more opportunities of reaching beyond the ornamental to a more significant role as a public figure. The acknowledgement of titled Americans of their own power and influence is demonstrated by the action of Lady Randolph Churchill in conjunction with Consuelo, Duchess of Marlborough, Lady William Beresford, Lady Essex, Lady Arthur Paget, and fourteen other American women resident in Britain. These ladies organized, on their own initiative, an American hospital-ship to be sent to South Africa during the Boer War.[119]

In choosing a wife, some peers and younger sons, particularly those in politics or the public service, may well have given consideration to their partners' social skills, personality, and flair for entertaining and organizing public events. Lord Randolph Churchill, for example, in writing to his parents to inform them of his intention to marry Jennie Jerome, said of her:

> In the last year or so I feel I have lost a great deal of what energy and ambition I possessed . . . but if I were married to her whom I have told you about, if I had a companion, such as she would be, I feel sure, to take an interest in one's prospects and career, and to encourage me to exertions and to doing something towards making a name for myself, I think that I might become . . . all and perhaps more than you have ever wished and hoped for me.[120]

It was part of Lord Randolph's ploy to persuade his parents that Jennie Jerome was in every way a suitable partner for a duke's son. The idea of Jennie encouraging Randolph to exertions was clearly meant to deny any frivolous motivation on her part and to demonstrate that her interests were compatible with those of his parents. Behind this appraisal of her character and education, however, was the assumption that a wife of a man with political aspirations should identify with his ambitions and contribute towards a realization of them. This shows that not all members of the peerage considered American women in terms of the dowry they were likely to bring, but that the decision to marry involved questions of compatibility and companionship.

Conclusion:
stereotypes and their function

It is only when we begin to consider the individual lives of the American women who married into the British peerage that the superficiality of the stereotype is exposed. It is, by its very nature, a generalization. By examining contemporary attitudes towards transatlantic marriages, as opposed to approaching the subject from a purely biographical angle, I have attempted to show that the relationship between the American heiress stereotype and the women who married peers or younger sons is a problematic one. Like the cliché of title for money, the heiress stereotype is more important in indicating the concerns and preoccupations of those who held the stereotype than in giving us any accurate representation of the women to whom it refers. The fact that transatlantic marriages were often a topic for discussion in newspapers, journals, private letters, memoirs, and social commentary or the subject-matter of serious and popular fiction would seem to suggest that they had a significance which went beyond the usual kind of inter-elite marriages. The most noticeable concern was, as we have seen, about money. American newspapers boasted or complained about the amount of money spent on dowries and other 'extras', while British commentators attributed the social success of Americans in London predominantly to their superior financial resources. The obsessive nature of this interest in the financial aspect is seen in the frequent description of the husbands as impoverished, the wives as heiresses, and the marriages as bartering dollars for titles. Thus, transatlantic marriages, by being represented as convenient financial arrangements involving a rich American and a peer heavily in debt, came to signify a clash not only between aristocratic and plutocratic values but between aristocratic and democratic ones too.

Like the ennoblement of industrialists, they were, for the traditional landed elite in Britain, a highly visible and publicized way in which the social exclusiveness of the nobility was being undermined. Whereas, for the American public, they rubbed a sore nerve by seeming to acknowledge the prestige of hereditary titles in a nation which had renounced such things. On the other hand, they were also seen as an acceptance of Americans on equal terms in the highest social circles of European capitals.

How stereotypes are formulated and how they function have, of course, been the subject of extensive research by social psychologists, especially over the past twenty years. A variety of words, such as 'belief', 'impression', 'image', 'picture', 'category', and 'mode of perception', have been used by psychologists to define the term 'stereotype'. This poses problems for obtaining a clear conceptualization of the term, because there is considerable difference in meaning between 'belief' and 'picture', to take two of the words used in the definition of stereotypes. However, the consensus today, judging from specialist dictionary definitions, would appear to be behind 'belief'.[1] 'Stereotype', as used in everyday language, refers to the way that certain characteristics can be attributed to groups of people whether they are defined primarily by their age, gender, occupation, race, or nationality, and there is considerable agreement amongst people in the identification of these characteristics. For a psychologist, the stereotype is this and much more. The task of understanding the process by which one group of people (or an individual) stereotypes another involves assessing, amongst other things, the degree of consensus amongst the subject group being tested in identifying and attributing certain traits to a target group; the degree to which the stereotype is favourable or unfavourable; and the degree of accuracy between the attributed traits and the actual traits (which in themselves have to be established by acceptable criteria). There are, of course, innumerable factors to be taken account of in evaluating the stereotyping process, such as the relationship between the subject(s) and the target groups, prior knowledge or contact with the target groups, and whether the content of the stereotype changes. Whilst what we refer to as stereotyping may be a universal characteristic of human beings, it is certainly not one which lends itself to analysis easily, and, with the development of research, psychologists have changed assertions previously made about such aspects of stereotypes as their rigidity, their negative content, and their accuracy.

In utilizing such a concept when dealing with evidence of a very different nature, then, it has been important to establish a definition which concurs with the way in which the term is used in disciplines which have appropriated it as part of their object of study. As I understand it, stereotyping can involve two processes: (1) a reduction of information about a target person (group) to a limited number of traits which may be behavioural and/or physical; and (2) a constructive process with the attribution of other, associated traits which are not immediately perceivable. Both of these would occur in a face-to-face situation. Stereotyping, however, often takes place when only linguistic information is available (e.g. from newspapers or conversation), whereby a word identifying a category, such as 'student', 'German', or 'old-age pensioner', evokes the attribution of traits. The result is a stereotype, the linking of a label or key characteristic to a set of traits. The stereotype may be intensified through further contact or information or, on the other hand, may even be totally undermined. It would appear that stereotyping is, in the initial phase at least, a quick assessment of what a target person or group is like. This initial response, in turn, affects the subject's initial behaviour towards the target person(s). It may even be an intuitive form of reaction, involving minimal reflection. The strength of a subject's response, especially when negative, can be a barrier to interpersonal relations, and it may take considerable time before a subject is encouraged to revise her/his earlier responses, and even then the extent of the revision may be selective. An individual may be distinguished from the rest of a group without any modification to the group stereotype. This is suggested by rejoinders like 'I should never have thought *you* were an American'.[2]

In consideration of the research undertaken by psychologists in this field, then, I have incorporated some of the characteristics of stereotypes which have gained wide acceptance. In view of the fact that stereotypes vary in content, for example, I have not expected all newspaper accounts of titled marriages to contain a 'positive' description of the bride's physical appearance and information concerning her dowry or a set list of other factors. I have not proceeded along the lines that different types of sources, regardless of when they were written, should match each other in detail. One source may emphasize the expensiveness of a woman's attire, while another spends more time in describing the father's financial status or where the family has been living. There is, in any case, considerable variation in the range of response, and I have been able to identify a favourable stereotype of the American woman – the 'Isabel Archer type' – which was more prevalent in works of fiction and amongst those who welcomed the entry of Americans into London society. More common, however, is the pejorative stereotype which, as we have seen, increased in intensity in the Edwardian era with the upturn in transatlantic marriages and with the growing alarm about the impact of American peeresses on the health of the nobility. This touches upon a second aspect of the nature of stereotypes, whether they are necessarily unfavourable. Much depends, of course, on the receptiveness of the subject group, and in the case of London society there was considerable difference in opinion as to whether Americans were welcomed or not. The Marlborough House Set, as we have noted, was accessible to Americans, whereas the more conservative families of the aristocracy who tended not to keep up with 'fashionable society' were more likely to be much more cautious in issuing invitations to Americans. Much of the present study has dwelt upon the more negative stereotyping of American heiresses, as this became persistent in the newspapers and social commentary of the 1900s, despite the growth in contact between citizens of the two countries and growing diplomatic friendship between the two governments. But the American heiress stereotype is not simply a national stereotype – it involves the categorization of a certain social class of women. As regards the accuracy of stereotypes, I have taken the position that they do not necessarily have to be inaccurate – as was once thought. As a gross generalization about the physical and personality traits of American women, the American heiress stereotype does involve a large degree of distortion and speculation. Assessing to what extent it was inaccurate is exceedingly difficult, especially with regard to evaluations of physical appearance and behaviour. The only quantifiable trait is wealth, but, although there is evidence to show that titled Americans were generally wealthier than their British counterparts, there are difficulties in interpreting to what extent the size of their personal fortune was a factor in their marriages. As for the controversy over fertility, we were able to test the accuracy of the representation of Americans as degenerate and likely to be responsible for the extinction of titled families. We found that American women did have, in fact, smaller families, but as regards the higher incidence of childlessness important qualifications had to be made. Like the title-for-money cliché, there was a 'grain of truth' in the stereotype, and some women approximated more closely to the American heiress stereotype than others. But whatever the accuracy of the stereotype, the important question to raise has been, why were American women viewed in this way?

With regard to the way stereotypes function, one conclusion which might be drawn from the historical evidence of the aristocracy's attitude towards the business classes in general is that there was an attempt by aristocrats to distance themselves from commercial activities and to subscribe to a code of conduct which placed a high value on men who did not conduct their business affairs in the market-place. The stereotype of the businessman held by aristocratic landowners emphasized this difference. It was, in effect, a way of upholding social barriers and requiring men of wealth to make long-term plans if they wished to enter the ranks of the aristocracy (up until the late nineteenth century, that is). It can be seen from this that one function of stereotypes is the regulation of behaviour. Moreover, psychologists have argued that stereotypes are 'concomitantly projections of the motives and concerns of the stereotype holder'.[3] In this particular case of the assimilation of businessmen, we can see that one of the major concerns of aristocrats was the challenge to their predominant position in the elite. Likewise with the so-called American invasion of the British aristocracy: American women were negatively categorized as being socially ambitious or 'social climbers' because of their non-landed, non-aristocratic background. The force of such censure was explored by Henry James in his short story 'An International Episode', in which Bessie Alden's behaviour was affected by her discovery that she was being labelled as an 'adventuress'. Her response was to end her friendship with Lord Lambeth and leave England: a clear indication to her critics that she found their attitudes towards her inappropriate. The disapproval of exogamous marriages and liaisons with members of the business classes, as reflected in the American heiress stereotype, can be seen as a way of making both outsiders and insiders conform to the established pattern of the subject group's behaviour. As such, the negative stereotyping of Americans tells us more about the values and concerns of British society than about the American women who married into the peerage.

Essentially, this study of international marriages is one of the social interaction between men of a society with a longer tradition of hierarchical divisions and women of another society which professed an antipathy for privileges related to birth rather than talent. It was an interaction of two cultures and two genders and it fascinated Henry James as well as a number of his contemporaries. Stereotyping usually involves people of a different nationality, social class, or gender, but the American heiress stereotype embraces all three. Moreover, by approaching transatlantic marriages in this way I have been able to contextualize them in terms of (1) Anglo-American relations and anti-American feeling in Britain; (2) social change and the displacement of the landed elite; and (3) attitudes towards women and the perceived threat to the patriarchal order from women who were challenging the narrowly prescribed roles of wife and mother. As such, all three contexts are still issues in the late twentieth century: anti-American feeling in Britain entered a new phase with the deployment of US nuclear missiles at Greenham Common; the peerage is still a part of the British political process, and, even though long-established families may have become more entrepreneurial in seeking ways to consolidate their financial position, the debate continues as to whether or not the House of Lords is anachronistic and should be abolished; and third, gender relations have once again become a major source of friction as more and more women seek additional or alternative forms of self-fulfilment to motherhood and marriage but still face criticism about neglecting their maternal duties. Some or all of these may also explain why the cliché of title-for-money and the related stereotypes have persisted for so long.

Appendix A

Peers who married Americans 1870–1914

Title of peer (date of birth and death)	Marital details (giving year of marriage and divorce, name of spouse(s), date of her death, previous husband's name, father's name, and number of sons and daughters from the marriage)
1 2nd Earl of Ancaster (1867–1951)	m. 1905 Eloise (d. 1953), da. of William L. Breese of New York, 2s, 2d.
2 4th Marquess of Anglesey (1835–98)	m. (1) 1858 Elizabeth Norman (d. 1873); m. (2) 1874 Blanche Boyd (d. 1877), 1s; m. (3) 1880 Mary Livingston (d. 1931), widow of Hon. Henry Wodehouse, da. of Hon. John King of Georgia, no issue.
3 5th Baron Ashburton (1866–1938)	m. (1) 1889 Mabel Hood (d. 1904); m (2) Frances (d. 1959), da. J. C. Donnelly of New York (actress known as Frances Belmont), no issue.
4 4th Baron Bagot (1857–1932)	m. 1903 Lilian, da. of Henry May of Maryland, 1d.
5 3rd Baron Bateman (1856–1931)	m. 1904 Marion, widow of Henry Cabot Knapp, da. of James J. Graham of New York, no issue.
6 Hon. Henry Bruce[a] (1881–1914)	m. 1906 Camilla, da. of Richard Clifford (actress), 1d.
7 8th Baron Calthorpe (1862–1940)	m. 1891 Mary (d. 1940), da. of Ogden H. Burrows of Newport, RI, 1s.
8 5th Baron Camoys (1884–1968)	m. 1911 Mildred, da. of William W. Sherman of New York, 1s. 2d.
9 4th Earl Camperdown (1845–1933)	m. 1888 Laura (d. 1910), widow of John Adams, da. of John Dove of Andover, Mass., no issue.
10 3rd Baron Cheylesmore (1848–1925)	m. 1892 Elizabeth Richardson (d. 1945), da. of Francis O. French of New York, 2s.

11 11th Earl Cork
    (1864–1934)
m. 1890 Josephine (d. 1953), only child of Joseph P. Hale of San Francisco, no issue.

12 4th Earl Cowley
    (1890–1962)
m. (1) 1914 (div. 1933) Mae (d. 1946), da. of Mr Pickard of Memphis, Tenn. (actress), 2s, 2d; m. (2) 1933 Mrs Mary Himes of Phoenix, Arizona, 2s.

13 4th Earl of Craven
    (1868–1921)
m. 1893 Cornelia (d. 1961), only da. of Bradley Martin of New York, 1s.

14 Marquess of Curzon[b]
    (1859–1926)
m. (1) Mary (d. 1906), da. of Levi Z. Leiter of Chicago and Washington, DC, 3d; m. (2) Grace, widow of Alfred Duggan, da. of Alfred M. Hinds of Alabama, no issue.

15 5th Baron Decies
    (1866–1944)
m. (1) 1911 Vivien (d. 1931), da. of George J. Gould of New York, 1s, 2d; m. (2) 1936 Elizabeth Wharton (d. 1944), widow of Henry Lehr, da. of Joseph W. Drexel of Philadelphia, no issue.

16 Viscount Deerhurst[c]
    (1865–1944)
m. 1894 Virginia Lee (d. 1948), only da. of William Daniel of New Mexico and stepda. of Charles W. Bonynge of California, 2s, 2d.

17 6th Earl of Donoughmore
    (1875–1948)
m. 1901 Elena (d. 1944), da. of Michael P. Grace of New York, 2s, 1d.

18 2nd Marquess of Dufferin of Ava
    (1866–1918)
m. 1893 Florence (d. 1925), da. of John H. Davis of New York, 3d. (She m. (2) 1919 4th Earl Howe.)

19 3rd Baron Ebury
    (1868–1921)
m. 1908 Florence (d. 1927), da. of Edward M. Padelford of Savannah, Georgia, no issue.

20 8th Earl of Egmont
    (1856–1910)
m. 1881 Kate (d. 1926), da. of Warwick Howell of South Carolina, no issue.

21 5th Baron Ellenborough
    (1841–1915)
m. 1906 Hermione (d. 1942), da. of E. W. H. Schenley of Pittsburgh and ward of Andrew Carnegie, no issue.

22 3rd Viscount Esher
    (1881–1963)
m. 1912 Antoinette (d. 1965), only da. of August Heckscher of New York, 1s, 3d.

23 7th Earl of Essex
    (1857–1916)
m. (1) Elenor Harford (d. 1885), 1s; m (2) 1893 Adela (d. 1922), da. of Beech Grant of New York, 2d.

24 6th Viscount Exmouth
    (1828–1923)
m. (1) 1858 Eliza (d. 1869), da. of Judge William Jay of New York, 3s; m. (2) 1873 Augusta (d. 1917), da. of Judge William Jay of New York, 1d.

25 7th Viscount Exmouth
    (1863–1945)
m. (1) 1886 Margaret (d. 1922), da. Professor C. F. Chandler of New York, 1d; m. (2) 1923 Mabel (d. 1949), da. of

Richard Gray of Ireland and San Francisco.

26 12th Viscount Falkland (1845–1922)
m. 1879 Mary (d. 1920), da. of Robert Reade of New York, 3s, 1d.

27 3rd Baron Fermoy (1851–1920)
m. 1880 (div. 1891) Frances, da. of Francis Work of New York, 2s, 2d.

28 2nd Baron Fisher (1868–1955)
m. 1910 Jane Buck (d. 1955), da. of Randal Morgan of Philadelphia, 1s, 3d.

29 5th Earl of Gosford (1877–1954)
m. (1) 1910 (div. 1928) Mildred, only da. of John R. Carter of USA, 2s, 3d; m. (2) 1928 Beatrice, formerly wife of Robert P. Breese, da. of Arthur Claflin of New York.

30 8th Earl of Granard (1874–1948)
m. 1909 Beatrice, da. of Ogden Mills of New York, 2s, 2d.

31 5th Baron Grantley (1855–1943)
m. (1) 1879 Katharine (d. 1897), formerly wife of Charles Norton, da. of Commodore William H. McVickar of New York, 2s, 4d; m. (2) 1899 Alice, natural da. of Viscount Ranelagh.

32 3rd Baron Greville (1871–1952)
m. 1909 Olive (d. 1959), widow of Henry S. Kerr, da. of John Grace of New York, 1s.

33 7th Marquess of Hertford (1871–1940)
m. 1903 (ann. 1908) Alice, da. of William Thaw of Pittsburgh, no issue.

34 5th Baron Huntingfield (1883–1969)
m. (1) 1912 Margaret (d. 1943), only daughter of Judge Ernest Crosby of New York, 2s, 2d; m. (2) Muriel Duke.

35 3rd Baron Leigh (1855–1938)
m. (1) 1890 Frances Forbes (d. 1909), da. of Hon. N. M. Beckwith of New York, no issue; m. (2) 1923 Marie, da. of Alexander Campbell of New York, no issue.

36 13th Earl of Lindsay (1872–1943)
m. 1900 Ethel (d. 1942), da. of William A. Tucker of Boston, 1s.

37 Baron Malcolm[d] (1833–1902)
m. (1) 1861 Alice Ives (d. 1896), no issue; m. (2) 1897 Marie (d. 1927), widow of H. Gardner Lister of USA, no issue.

38 8th Duke of Manchester (1853–92)
m. 1876 Consuelo (d. 1909), da. of Antonio Yznaga of New York and Louisiana, 1s, 2d.

39 9th Duke of Manchester (1877–1947)
m. (1) 1900 (div. 1930) Helena, da. of Eugene Zimmerman of Cincinnati, 2s, 2d; m. (2) 1931 Kathleen Dawes (American actress), no issue.

40 8th Duke of Marlborough (1844–92)
m. (1) 1869 (div. 1883) Albertha, da. of Duke of Abercorn; m. (2) Lilian (d. 1909), widow of Louis Hammersley, da.

of Cicero Price of New York, no issue.
(She m. (3) 1895 Lord William Beresford, 1s.)

41 9th Duke of Marlborough (1871–1934)
m. (1) 1895 (div. 1921) Consuelo, da. of William K. Vanderbilt of New York, 2s; m. (2) 1921 Gladys (d. 1977), da. Edward P. Deacon of Boston, no issue.

42 9th Baron Monson (1868–1948)
m. 1903 Romaine (d. 1943), widow of Lawrence Turnure, da. of General Roy Stone of New Jersey, 1s.

43 4th Baron Newborough (1873–1916)
m. 1900 Grace (d. 1939), da. of Col Henry M. Carr of Kentucky, no issue.

44 8th Duke of Newcastle (1866–1961)
m. (1) 1894 (div. 1902), Mary (d. 1938), da. of William Yohe of USA (actress), no issue; m. (2) 1904 Olive Thompson, 1s, 1d.

45 5th Earl of Orford (1854–1931)
m. (1) 1888 Louise (d. 1909), da. of D. C. Corbin of New York, 1s, 1d; m. (2) 1917 Emily Oakes, 2d.

46 4th Marquess of Ormonde (1848–1943)
m. 1887 Ellen Sprague (d. 1951), da. of Gen. Anson Stager, 2s, 2d.

47 8th Earl of Portsmouth (1861–1943)
m. 1897 Marguerite (d. 1938), da. of S. J. Walker of Kentucky, 2s.

48 3rd Baron Revelstoke (1864–1934)
m. 1892 Maude (d. 1922), da. of Pierre Lorillard of New Jersey, 1s, 2d.

49 5th Earl Rosslyn (1869–1939)
m. (1) 1890 (div. 1902) Violet Vyner, 1s, 1d; m. (2) 1905 (div. 1907) Anna, da. of George Robinson of Minnesota, no issue; m. (3) 1908 Vera Bayley, 2s, 1d.

50 8th Duke of Roxburghe (1876–1932)
m. 1903 May (d. 1937), only daughter of Ogden Goelet of New York, 1s.

51 3rd Earl Russell (1872–1970)
m. (1) 1894 (div. 1921) Alys Pearsall (d. 1951), da. of Robert P. Smith, no issue; m. (2) 1921 (div. 1935) Dora Black, 1s, 1d; m. (3) 1936 (div. 1952) Patricia Spence, 1s, 1d; m. (4) 1952 Edith Finch of New York.

52 8th Earl of St Germans (1870–1960)
m. 1910 Helen, da. of Arthur Post of New York, 2s, 1d.

53 9th Earl of Sandwich (1874–1962)
m. (1) 1905 Alberta (d. 1951), da. of William Sturges of New York, 2s, 2d; m. (2) 1952 Ella Corbin.

54 7th Baron Somers (1864–1953)
m. 1896 Benita, da. of Major Luther Sabin of USA, 1s, 2d.

55 9th Baron Strabolgi (1853–1934)
m. 1884 Elizabeth, da. of George B. Cooper of Sacramento, Cal., 2s.

56 4th Earl of Strafford (1831–99)
m. (1) 1863 Countess Henrietta Samsoe (d. 1880); m. (2) 1898 Cora (d. 1932),

widow of Samuel Colgate, da. of Justice
H. Smith of USA, no issue.

57 19th Earl of Suffolk
(1877–1917)
m. 1904 Marguerite, da. of Levi Z. Leiter
of Chicago and Washington, DC, 3s.

58 7th Earl of Tankerville
(1852–1931)
m. 1895 Leonora (d. 1949), da. of James
Van Marter of New York, 2s, 2d.

59 7th Baron Vernon
(1854–98)
m. 1885 Frances (d. 1940), da. of Francis
C. Lawrence of New York, 2s, 1d.

60 14th Earl of Winchilsea
(1885–1939)
m. 1910 Margaretta (d. 1952), only da.
of Anthony J. Drexel of Philadelphia, 1s,
2d.

---

a Pre-deceased father, 2nd Baron Aberdare.
b Cr. Baron 1898, Earl 1911, and Marquess 1921; succeeded father in 1916 as
Baron Scarsdale.
c Pre-deceased father, 9th Earl of Coventry.
d Cr. Baron in 1896.

Appendix B

Younger sons who married Americans 1870–1914

Name of younger son (date of birth and death)	*Name of father; marital details (giving year of marriage and divorce, name of spouse(s), date of her death, previous husband's name, father's name, and number of sons and daughters from the marriage)*
1 Hon. Alfred Anson (1876–1944)	2nd Earl of Lichfield; m. 1912 Lela, widow of John Emery, da. of Gen. C. T. Alexander of Washington, DC, no issue.
2 Hon. Francis Anson (1867–1928)	2nd Earl of Lichfield; m. 1892 Caroline (d. 1951), da. of George Cleveland of Texas, 4s, 1d.
3 Lord Sir William Beresford (1878–1900)	4th Marquess of Waterford; m. 1895 Lilian (d. 1909), widow of (1) Louis Hammersley and (2) 8th Duke of Marlborough, da. of Cicero Price of New York, 1s.
4 Hon. William Beresford (1878–1949)	3rd Baron Decies; m. (1) 1901 (div. 1919) Florence, da. of Gardner Miller of Rhode Island, 3s, 2d; m. (2) 1919 (div. 1928) Laura Coventry, 1s, 1d; m. (3) 1933 (div. 1940) Georgina Mosselman, 1s, 1d.
5 Hon. Sir Cecil Bingham (1861–1934)	4th Earl of Lucan; m. (1) 1884 Rose Forfar (d. 1908), 2s, 1d; m. (2) 1911 Alys, widow of Samuel S. Chauncey, da. of Col Henry M. Carr of Kentucky, no issue.
6 Hon. Walter Buller (1859–1935)	1st Baron Churston;[a] m. (1) 1886 Leilah (d. 1904), widow of D. B. Blair, da. of Gen. R. Kirkham of California, no issue; m. (2) 1913 Alianor Chandos-Pole.
7 Hon. Sir William Carington (1845–1914)	2nd Baron Carrington; m. 1871 Juliet (d. 1913), only da. of Francis Warden of USA, no issue.

8 Lord George Cholmondeley (1887–1958) — 4th Marquess of Cholmondeley; m. (1) 1911 (div. 1921) Clara (d. 1925), formerly wife of Major Stirling, da of Charles H. Taylor of Washington, DC (actress), 1d; m. (2) 1921 (div. 1948) Ina Pelly; m. (3) 1948 Diana Beckett, 1d.

9 Lord Randolph Churchill (1849–95) — 7th Duke of Marlborough; m. 1874 Jennie (d. 1921), da. of Leonard Jerome of New York, 2s.

10 Hon. Charles Coventry (1867–1929) — 9th Earl of Coventry; m. 1900 Lily, da. of William F. Whitehouse of Newport, RI, 2s, 2d.

11 Hon. Henry Coventry (1868–1934) — 9th Earl of Coventry; m. 1907 Edith (d. 1949), formerly wife of Mr McCreevy, da. of Col Lawrence Kip of New York, 2s.

12 Lord Sholto Douglas (1872–1942) — 9th Marquess of Queensberry; m. (1) 1895 (div. 1920) Loretta Mooney (actress), 2s; m. (2) 1921 (div. 1925) Georgina Mosselman; m. (3) Lily Edmunds.

13 Hon. Alexander Erskine (1870–1914) — 4th Earl Rosslyn; m. 1905 Winifrede, da. of Henry W. Baker of California, no issue.

14 Hon. Edmund Fitzmaurice (cr. Baron in 1906) (1846–1935) — 4th Marquess of Lansdowne; m. 1889 (ann. 1894) Caroline, da. W. J. Fitzgerald of Lichfield, Conn., no issue.

15 Hon. Moreton Gage (1873–1931) — 4th Viscount Gage; m. (1) 1902 Anne (d. 1915), da. of William E. Strong of New York, 2s; m. (2) 1916 Frances, da. of Senator Henry F. Lippitt of Rhode Island, 1s, 1d.

16 Hon. Ernest Gibson (1875–1922) — 1st Baron Ashbourne; m (1) 1905 Mary (d. 1905), da. of Joseph L. R. Wood of New York, no issue; m. (2) 1909 Caroline, da. of Frederic de Billier of New York, 1s, 1d.

17 Hon. Thomas Grosvenor (1842–86) — 1st Baron Ebury; m. 1877 Sophie (d. 1938), only da. of S. Wells Williams of USA, no issue.

18 Hon. Frederick Guest (1875–1937) — 1st Baron Wimborne; m. 1905 Amy, da. of Henry Phipps of Pittsburgh, 2s, 1d.

19 Hon. Lionel Guest (1880–1935) — 1st Baron Wimborne; m. 1905 Flora, formerly wife of Charles S. Dodge, da. Hon. John Bigelow of New York, no issue.

255

20 Hon. Harold Hawke (1867–1913) — 6th Baron Hawke; m. 1906 Anne (d. 1912), widow of Arthur Bamford, da. John Nash of Chicago, no issue.

21 Hon. Sir Michael Herbert (1857–1903) — 1st Baron Herbert; m. 1888 Belle (d. 1923), da. of Richard T. Wilson of New York, 2s.

22 Hon. Edmund Hill (1860–1914) — 3rd Baron Sandys; m. 1884 Ida (d. 1926), da. of Maxwell Jones of New York, no issue.

23 Hon. Sir Horace Hood (1870–1916) — 4th Viscount Hood; m. 1910 Ellen, widow of George Nickerson, da. of A. E. Touzalin, 2s.

24 Hon. Melville Howard (1883–1919) — 6th Earl of Wicklow; m. 1908 May (d. 1941), only child of Benjamin Sands of New York, 1s, 1d.

25 Lord Alastair Innes-Kerr (1880–1936) — 7th Duke of Roxburghe; m. 1907 Anne (d. 1959), da. William L. Breese of New York, 2s.

26 Hon. Sir Alan Johnstone (1858–1932) — 1st Baron Derwent; m. 1892 Antoinette (d. 1934), only da. J. W. Pinchot of New York, 1s.

27 Hon. Lionel Lambert (1873–1940) — 9th Earl of Cavan; m. 1906 Adelaide, da. of Capt. Randolph and stepda. of William C. Whitney of New York, 1d.

28 Hon. Charles Lawrence (cr. Baron 1923) (1855–1929) — 1st Baron Lawrence; m. 1881 Catherine (d. 1934), da. of Frederick W. Sumner of New York, no issue.

29 Hon. James Leigh (1838–1923) — 1st Baron Leigh; m. 1871 Frances (d. 1910), da. of Pierce Butler of Philadelphia, 1s, 2d.

30 Hon. Rowland Leigh (1859–1943) — 2nd Baron Leigh; m. 1898 Mabel, da. of Gen. W. W. Gordon of Savannah, Georgia, 1s, 1d.

31 Hon. Sir Ronald Lindsay (1877–1945) — 26th Earl Crawford; m. (1) Martha (d. 1918), da. of Senator James D. Cameron of Pennsylvania, no issue; m. (2) 1924 Elizabeth, da. of Colgate Hoyt of New York, no issue.

32 Hon. Archibald Majoribanks (1861–1900) — 1st Baron Tweedmouth; m. 1897 Elizabeth (d. 1925), da. of Judge J. T. Brown of Tennessee, no issue. (She m. (2) 1905 Douglas Hogg, later 1st Viscount Hailsham.)

33 Hon. Amyas Northcote (1864–1923) — 1st Earl Iddlesleigh; m. 1890 Helen (d. 1936), da. James Dudley of Kentucky, 1s, 1d.

34 Hon. Murrough O'Brien (1866–1934) — 14th Baron Inchiquin; m. 1906 Marguerite, da. of William Lewis of New York, 2s, 1d.

256

35	Hon. Lyulph Ogilvy (1861–1947)	5th Earl Airlie; m. 1902 Edith (d. 1908), da. of Philip H. Boothroyd of Colorado, 1s, 1d.
36	Hon. Sir Francis Plunkett (1835–1907)	9th Earl of Fingall; m. 1870 May (d. 1924), da. Charles W. Morgan of Philadelphia, 2d.
37	Hon. Charles Ramsay (1859–1936)	12th Earl Dalhousie; m. 1885 Martha (d. 1964), da. of William R. Garrison of New York, no issue.
38	Hon. William Vernon (1856–1913)	6th Baron Vernon; m. 1884 Louisa, da. of Brig.-Gen. D. M. Frost of St Louis, Missouri, 2d.
39	Hon. Sir John Ward (1870–1938)	1st Earl Dudley; m. 1908 Jean (d. 1962), da. of Whitelaw Reid of Ohio, 2s.
40	Hon. Henry Wodehouse (1834–73)	2nd Baron Wodehouse;[a] m. 1872 Mary Livingston (d. 1931), da. of J. P. King of Georgia, no issue.

[a] Both given precedence of children of a baron by patent although their fathers as heirs pre-deceased the holder of the title.

Appendix C

Control groups: peers who married 1880–9 and 1900–9

CONTROL GROUP I: PEERS WHO MARRIED 1880–9

Title of peer (date of birth)	Details of marriage(s) in the 1880s: name of spouse(s), number of sons and daughters from marriage
1 3rd Marquess of Abergavenny (1854)	m. (2) Maud Beckett, 1d.
2 7th Earl of Abingdon (1836)	m. (2) Mary Dormer, 4s, 5d.
3 8th Earl of Abingdon (1860)	m. Hon. Rose Glynn, 1s, 1d.
4 4th Marquess of Ailesbury (1863)	m. Dorothy Haseley (actress), no issue.
5 8th Earl of Albemarle (1858)	m. Lady Gertrude Egerton, 2s, 1d.
6 2nd Baron Alington (1859)	m. Lady Feodorowna Yorke, 3s, 4d.
7 4th Earl of Amherst (1836)	m. (2) Alice Probyn, widow, no issue.
8 3rd Baron Annaly (1857)	m. Hon. Lilah Agar-Ellis, 1s, 2d.
9 5th Earl of Arran (1839)	m. (2) Winifred Reilley, widow, 1d.
10 5th Earl of Ashburnham (1840)	m. Emily Chaplin, 1s, 1d.
11 4th Earl of Bantry (1854)	m. Rosamund Petre, no issue.
12 9th Baron Barnard (1854)	m. Lady Catherine Cecil, 3s.
13 2nd Baron Basing (1860)	m. Mary Hargreaves, 1s, 2d.
14 9th Baron Beaumont (1848)	m. Violet Isaacson, no issue.

15 11th Duke of Bedford   m. Mary Tribe, 1s.
    (1840)
16 10th Baron Belhaven   m. Georgiana Richmond, 1s.
    (1840)
17 3rd Baron Bellew   m. Mildred de Trafford, no issue.
    (1855)
18 2nd Baron Brabourne   m. Hon. Amy Allendale, 2s, 2d.
    (1857)
19 2nd Earl Brassey   Lady Idina Nevill, no issue.
    (1863)
20 3rd Baron Brougham   m. Adora Wells, widow, 1s.
    (1836)
21 3rd Duke of Buckingham m. Alice Graham-Montgomery, 2d.
    (1823)
22 7th Earl of   m. Georgiana Henderson, 1s, 2d.
    Buckinghamshire (1860)
23 2nd Earl Cairns   m. Olivia Berens, 1d.
    (1861)
24 4th Earl of Caledon   m. Lady Elizabeth Graham Toler, 4s, 1d.
    (1846)
25 3rd Baron Carew   m. Julia Lethbridge, no issue.
    (1860)
26 4th Baron Carew   m. Maud Ramsay, no issue.
    (1863)
27 3rd Earl Charlemont   m. (2) Anna Lambart, no issue.
    (1820)
28 8th Earl of Chesterfield m. (2) Agnes Payne, no issue.
    (1822)
29 1st Viscount Churchill m. (div. 1927) Lady Verena Lowther, 2s,
    (1864)   2d.
30 5th Earl of Clancarty   m. Isabel Bilton (actress), 4s, 1d.
    (1868)
31 5th Baron Clarina   m. (2) Sophia Butler, no issue.
    (1837)
32 4th Baron Cloncurry   m. Laura Winn, no issue.
    (1840)
33 2nd Viscount Colville   m. Ruby Streatfield, 2s, 2d.
    (1854)
34 3rd Viscount   m. (2) Marian Chetwynd, 1s.
    Combermere
    (1845)
35 4th Baron Congleton   m. Elizabeth Dove, 3s, 1d.
    (1839)
36 4th Marquess of   m. Hon. Frances de Loleyns, 2s, 5d.
    Conyngham
    (1857)
37 1st Marquess of Crewe   m. Sibyl Graham, 2s, 3d.
    (1858)

38 8th Earl of Darnley (1856) m. Florence Morphy, 2s, 1d.

39 2nd Earl of Dartrey (1842) m. Julia Wombwell, 1s, 2d.

40 6th Baron De Blaquiere (1856) m. Lucianne Desbarats, 2s, 1d.

41 17th Earl of Derby (1865) m. Lady Alice Montagu, 2s, 1d.

42 4th Baron de Saumarez (1843) m. Jane Vere Broke, 1s, 3d.

43 5th Earl of Dunraven (1857) m. Lady Eva Bourke, 4s, 4d.

44 3rd Earl of Durham (1855) m. Ethel Milner, no issue.

45 9th Earl of Dysart (1859) m. Cecilia Newton, no issue.

46 6th Marquess of Ely (1854) m. Emily Vandeleur, 2s.

47 2nd Baron Emly (1858) m. Frances De la Poer, 1s, 1d.

48 7th Viscount Falmouth (1847) m. Hon. Kathleen Douglas-Pennant, 4s, 1d.

49 10th Earl Ferrers (1847) m. Lady Ina White, no issue.

50 1st Duke of Fife (1849) m. HRH Princess Louise, 2d.

51 4th Earl Fortescue (1854) m. Hon. Emily Ormsby-Gore, 3s.

52 3rd Earl of Gainsborough (1850) m. (2) Mary Dease, 3s, 2d.

53 3rd Baron Gifford (1849) m. Sophie Street, no issue.

54 5th Viscount Gort (1849) m. Eleanor Surtees, 2s.

55 3rd Viscount Gough (1849) m. Lady Georgiana Pakenham, 1s, 2d.

56 5th Earl of Harewood (1846) m. Lady Florence Bridgeman, 2s, 1d.

57 3rd Baron Harlech (1855) m. Lady Margaret Gordon, 1s.

58 9th Earl of Harrington (1859) m. Kathleen Wood, 2s, 1d.

59 5th Earl of Harrowby (1864) m. Hon. Mabel Smith, 1s, 3d.

60 20th Baron Hastings (1857) m. Hon. Elizabeth Harbord, 2s, 3d.

61 5th Viscount Hawarden (1842) m. Caroline Ogle, 1s.

62	5th Baron Henley (1858)	m. (1) Georgiana William, no issue; m. (2) Emmeline Maitland, 1d.
63	3rd Baron Heytesbury (1862)	m. Margaret Harman, 1s, 1d.
64	2nd Baron Hillingdon (1855)	m. Hon. Alice Harbord, 3s.
65	2nd Baron Howard of Glossop (1859)	m. Clara Greenwood, 1s, 1d.
66	14th Earl of Huntingdon (1868)	m. Maud Wilson, 1s, 3d.
67	5th Earl of Kenmare (1860)	m. Hon. Elizabeth Baring, 3s, 2d.
68	3rd Earl of Kilmorey (1842)	m. Ellen Baldock, 2s, 1d.
69	33rd Baron Kingsale (1855)	m. Emily de Courcy, 1s, 4d.
70	4th Baron Langford (1848)	m. Georgina Sutton, 2s, 1d.
71	6th Baron Langford (1849)	m. Hon. Mabel Legh, 1s, 2d.
72	2nd Earl Lathom (1864)	m. Lady Wilma Pleydell-Bouverie, 1s, 2d.
73	13th Earl of Lauderdale (1840)	m. (2) Ada Simpson, 1d.
74	10th Duke of Leeds (1862)	m. Lady Katherine Lambton, 1s, 4d.
75	5th Duke of Leinster (1851)	m. Lady Hermione Duncombe, 3s, 1d.
76	11th Earl of Leven (1835)	m. Hon. Emma Portman, 4s, 1d.
77	1st Marquess of Linlithgow (1860)	m. Hon. Hersey Alice De Moleyns, 2s, 2d.
78	6th Earl of Lisburne (1862)	m. Evelyn Probyn, 1s, 1d.
79	2nd Earl of Londesborough (1864)	m. Lady Grace Fane, 2s, 1d.
80	6th Earl of Lonsdale (1867)	m. Sophia Sheffield, 2s, 2d.
81	11th Earl of Loudoun (1855)	m. Hon. Alice Howard, no issue.
82	2nd Earl of Lovelace (1839)	m. (2) Mary Wortley, no issue.
83	3rd Baron Manners (1852)	m. Constance Fane, 2s, 2d.
84	7th Baron Massy (1864)	m. Ellen Wise, 2s, 4d.

85	7th Earl of Mayo (1851)	m. Geraldine Ponsonby, no issue
86	8th Earl of Mayo (1859)	m. Ethel Freeman, 4s, 2d.
87	3rd Baron Methuen (1845)	m. (2) Mary Sanford, 3s, 2d.
88	10th Baron Middleton (1847)	m. Ida Ross, 4s, 4d.
89	1st Earl Midleton (1856)	m. Lady Hilda Charteris, 1s, 4d.
90	4th Earl of Minto (1845)	m. Mary Grey, 2s, 3d.
91	8th Viscount Molesworth (1829)	m. (2) Agnes Dove, no issue
92	2nd Baron Montagu (1866)	m. Lady Cecil Victoria Kerr, 2d.
93	4th Baron Monteagle (1852)	m. Elizabeth Fitzgerald, 2s.
94	Lord Moreton[a] (1857)	m. Ada Smith, no issue.
95	5th Earl Nelson (1860)	m. Geraldine Cave, 5s, 3d.
96	9th Earl of Newburgh (1862)	m. Donna Maria Lanza di Trabia, 3s, 1d.
97	12th Baron North (1860)	m. Arabella Keppel, 1s.
98	5th Marquess of Northampton (1851)	m. Hon. Mary Baring, 2s, 1d.
99	5th Baron Norton (1854)	m. Grace Sackville, 1s, 5d.
100	3rd Baron Penrhyn (1864)	m. Hon. Blanche Fitzroy, 2s, 3d.
101	15th Baron Petre (1864)	m. Julia Cavendish-Taylor, 1s, 1d.
102	1st Earl of Plymouth (1857)	m. Alberta Paget, 3s, 1d.
103	3rd Baron Poltimore (1859)	m. Hon. Margaret Beaumont, 3s, 1d.
104	9th Baron Polwarth (1864)	m. Edith Buxton, 3s, 4d.
105	5th Earl of Portarlington (1858)	m. Emma Kennedy, 2s, 3d.
106	6th Duke of Portland (1857)	m. Winifred Dallas-Yorke, 2s, 1d.
107	4th Viscount Portman (1864)	m. (div. 1897) May Gordon-Cumming, 2d.

108	3rd Baron Raglan (1857)	m. Lady Ethel Ponsonby, 3s, 3d.
109	5th Earl of Ranfurly (1856)	m. Hon. Constance Caulfield, 1s, 3d.
110	7th Duke of Richmond (1845)	m. (2) Isabel Craven, 2d.
111	2nd Marquess of Ripon (1852)	m. Constance Herbert, widow, no issue.
112	11th Lord Rollo (1860)	m. Mary Hotham, 1d.
113	5th Baron Rossmore (1853)	m. Mittie Naylor, 2s, 1d.
114	8th Duke of Rutland (1852)	m. Marion Lindsay, 2s, 3d.
115	5th Viscount St Vincent (1855)	m. (div. 1896) Rebecca Baston, no issue.
116	4th Marquess of Salisbury (1861)	m. Lady Cicely Gore, 2s, 2d.
117	18th Lord Saltoun (1851)	m. Mary Bellew, 4s, 1d.
118	1st Viscount Sandhurst (1855)	m. Lady Victoria Spencer, 1s, 1d.
119	3rd Baron Sandhurst (1857)	m. Edith Higson, 1s, 3d.
120	18th Baron Saye and Sele (1858)	m. Marion Lawes, 5s, 2d.
121	3rd Baron Seaton (1854)	m. Elizabeth Fuller-Eliot-Drake, no issue.
122	2nd Earl of Selborne (1859)	m. Lady Beatrix Cecil, 3s, 1d
123	20th Earl of Shrewsbury (1860)	m. Ellen Morewood, widow, 1s.
124	4th Viscount Sidmouth (1854)	m. Ethel Tonge, 2s, 2d.
125	6th Marquess of Sligo (1856)	m. Agatha Hodgson, 1s, 3d.
126	16th Duke of Somerset (1860)	m. Rowena Wall, 1s.
127	6th Earl Spencer (1857)	m. Hon. Margaret Baring, 3s, 3d.
128	14th Earl of Strathmore (1855)	m. Nina Cavendish-Bentinck, 6s, 4d.
129	3rd Duke of Sutherland (1828)	m. (2) Mary Michell, widow, no issue.
130	4th Duke of Sutherland (1851)	m. Lady Millicent Erskine, 2s, 2d.
131	3rd Baron Teignmouth (1840)	m. Alice Bigge, no issue.

132 5th Baron Teignmouth (1847)	m. Mary Porteus, 3s.
133 3rd Baron Templemore (1854)	m. (2) Alice Dawkins, 2s.
134 4th Viscount Templetown (1853)	m. Lady Evelyn Heneage, 2s, 1d.
135 2nd Baron Tennyson (1852)	m. Audrey Boyle, 1s.
136 12th Baron Torphichen (1846)	m. (div. 1890) Frances Gordon, 3s, 1d.
137 8th Viscount Torrington (1841)	m. (1) Alice Jameson, 1d; m. (2) Emmeline Symour, 1s.
138 18th Baron Trimlestown (1861)	m. Margaret Stephens, 2s, 4d.
139 7th Baron Vaux (1860)	m. Eleanor Matheson, 3d.
140 7th Baron Walsingham (1849)	m. Elizabeth Grant, 2s, 3d.
141 5th Earl of Warwick (1853)	m. Frances Maynard, 3s, 1d.
142 11th Earl of Wemyss (1857)	m. Mary Wyndham, 1s, 1d.
143 3rd Baron Westbury (1852)	m. Lady Agatha Manners, 1s.
144 1st Duke of Westminster (1825)	m. (2) Hon. Katherine Cavendish, 2s, 2d.
145 2nd Earl of Wharncliffe (1856)	m. Ellen Gallwey, 2s, 4d
146 5th Earl of Winterton (1837)	m. Lady Georgiana Hamilton, 1s.
147 4th Earl of Yarborough (1859)	Marcia, Baroness Fauconberg, 4s.

ᵃ Pre-deceased his father, 3rd Earl of Ducie.

CONTROL GROUP II: PEERS WHO MARRIED 1900–9

Title of peer (date of birth)	Details of marriage(s) in the 1900s: name of spouse(s), number of sons and daughters from marriage
1 2nd Marquess of Aberdeen (1879)	m. Mary Clixby, widow, no issue.
2 2nd Baron Acton (1870)	m. Dorothy Lyon, 2s, 7d.

3 6th Marquess of
   Ailesbury (1873)   m. Caroline Madden, 1s, 2d.

4 4th Marquess of Ailsa
   (1872)   m. Frances Stewart, no issue.

5 9th Earl of Albemarle
   (1881)   m. Lady Judith Wynn Carrington, 3s, 2d.

6 3rd Baron Aldenham
   (1879)   m. Lillie Houldsworth, no issue.

7 6th Earl Annesley
   (1884)   m. Evelyn Mundy, divorcée, no issue.

8 7th Earl of Antrim
   (1878)   m. Margaret Talbot, 2s, 2d.

9 6th Earl of Arran
   (1868)   m. Maud Huyssen, 2s.

10 15th Baron Arundell
   (1861)   m. Ivy Seagrave, 1s, 2d.

11 6th Earl of Ashburnham
   (1855)   m. Maria Anderson, no issue.

12 1st Baron Ashton
   (1842)   m. (2) Florence Daniel, widow, no issue.

13 6th Viscount Bangor
   (1868)   m. Agnes Hamilton, no issue.

14 9th Viscount
   Barrington (1848)   m. (2) Charlotte Stopford, widow, no issue.

15 7th Earl Beauchamp
   (1872)   m. Lady Lettice Grosvenor, 3s, 4d.

16 6th Baron Borthwick
   (1867)   m. Susanna Stewart, 1d.

17 9th Viscount Bayne
   (1864)   m. Lady Margaret Lascelles, 5s, 1d.

18 5th Earl of Bradford
   (1873)   m. Hon. Margaret Bruce, 1s, 4d.

19 6th Baron Braye
   (1874)   m. Ethel Pusey, 2s, 1d.

20 5th Lord Burgh
   (1866)   m. (2) Phyllis Goldie, 2s, 1d.

21 4th Marquess of Bute
   (1881)   m. Augusta Bellingham, 5s, 2d.

22 Hon. Eyre Massey[a]   m. Alice Allhusen, no issue.

23 9th Baron Byron
   (1855)   m. Fanny Radmall, divorcée, no issue.

24 5th Baron Carew
   (1860   Catherine Conolly, 2s, 1d.

25 10th Earl of Chesterfield
   (1854)   m. Enid Wilson, no issue.

26 8th Viscount Chetwynd
   (1863)   m. (2) Hon. Mary Eden, 2s, 1d.

27 5th Earl of Clancarty
   (1868)   m. (2) Mary Ellis, 2s, 1d.

28 6th Baron Clanmorris (1879) — m. Leila Cloete, 1s.

29 5th Earl of Clanwilliam (1873) — m. Muriel Stephenson, widow, 1s, 2d.

30 5th Earl of Clarendon (1846) — m. (2) Emma Harch, widow, no issue.

31 6th Earl of Clarendon (1877) — m. Hon. Adeline Cocks, 2s, 1d.

32 7th Earl of Clonmell (1877) — m. Rachel Berridge, 2d.

33 9th Viscount Cobham (1881) — m. Violet Leonard, 1s, 4d.

34 3rd Baron Coleridge (1877) — m. Jessie Mackarness, 3s.

35 7th Earl of Courtown (1877) — m. Cicely Birch, 3s, 4d.

36 2nd Baron Cranworth (1877) — m. Vera Ridley, 2s, 2d.

37 Viscount Crichton (1872) — m. Lady Mary Grosvenor, 2s, 1d.

38 2nd Earl of Cromer (1877) — m. Lady Ruby Elliott, 1s, 2d.

39 7th Earl of Dartmouth (1881) — m. Lady Ruperta Wynn Carrington, 1s, 5d.

40 25th Baron de Clifford (1884) — Evelyn Chandler, 1s.

41 5th Baron De Freyne (1879) — m. Annabel Angus, no issue.

42 8th Earl De La Warr (1869) — m. (2) Hilda Tredcroft, no issue.

43 3rd Baron De L'Isle (1853) — m. Hon. Elizabeth Prendergast, widow, no issue.

44 5th Baron De L'Isle (1874) — m. Winifred Bevan, 1s, 1d.

45 3rd Baron Denman (1874) — m. Hon. Gertrude Pearson, 1s, 1d.

46 3rd Baron Deramore (1865) — m. (2) Violet Saltmarshe, no issue.

47 4th Baron Deramore (1870) — m. Muriel Grey, 2s, 1d.

48 5th Viscount De Vesci (1881) — m. (div. 1919) Georgiana Wellesley, no issue.

49 16th Earl of Devon (1875) — m. Marguerite Silva, 2s, 5d.

50 18th Viscount Dillon (1875) — m. Hilda Brunner, widow, no issue.

51 19th Viscount Dillon (1881) — m. Nora Beckett, 1s, 1d.

52	5th Marquess of Donegall (1822)	(2) Violet Twining, 1s.
53	14th Baron Dormer (1864)	m. Caroline Clifford, 2s, 3d.
54	6th Marquess of Downshire (1871)	(2) Evelyn Foster, no issue.
55	10th Earl of Drogheda (1884)	m. (div. 1922) Kathleen Burn, 1s, 1d.
56	5th Earl of Ducie (1875)	m. Maria Bryant, no issue.
57	12th Baron Dudley (1872)	m. Sybil Coventry, 1s, 1d.
58	10th Earl of Dundee (1872)	m. Edith Moffat, 2s, 1d.
59	8th Earl Dunmore (1871)	m. Lucinda Kemble, 1s, 2d.
60	18th Baron Dunsany (1878)	m. Lady Beatrice Villiers, 1s.
61	16th Earl of Eglinton (1880)	m. (div. 1902) Lady Beatrice Dalrymple, 2s, 3d.
62	2nd Viscount Elibank (1877)	m. Ermine Madocks, widow, no issue.
63	4th Earl of Ellesmere (1872)	m. Violet Lambton, 1s, 6d.
64	5th Earl of Enniskillen (1876)	m. (div. 1931) Irene Mundy, 1s, 3d.
65	21st Earl of Erroll (1876)	m. Mary Mackenzie, 2s.
66	5th Marquess of Exeter (1876)	m. Hon. Myra Powlett, 2s, 2d.
67	11th Baron Farnham (1879)	m. Aileen Coote, 3s, 2d.
68	2nd Baron Farrer (1859)	m. (2) Evangeline Knos, 1s, 1d.
69	Hon. Coulson Fellowes[b] (1883)	m. (div. 1912) Dorothy Jefferson, 1s.
70	2nd Earl of Feversham (1879)	m. Lady Marjorie Brooke, 2s, 1d.
71	4th Baron Garvagh (1878)	m. (ann. 909) Caroline Rube, no issue.
72	3rd Baron Gerard (1883)	m. Mary Gosseline, 1s, 4d.
73	8th Earl of Glasgow (1874)	m. Hyacinthe Bell, 2s, 3d.
74	3rd Baron Granville (1872)	m. Nina Baring, no issue.
75	6th Baron Graves (1871)	m. Mary Parker, 2d.

76	7th Baron Graves (1877)	m. (div. 1922) Vera Snepp, 1s.
77	1st Baron Grenfell (1841)	m. (2) Hon. Margaret Majendie, 2s, 1d.
78	5th Earl Grey (1879)	m. Lady Mabel Palmer, 2d.
79	Lord Guernsey^c (1883)	m. Hon. Gladys Fellows, 1s.
80	8th Earl of Guilford (1876)	m. Violet Pawson, 2s, 1d.
81	5th Baron Gwydr (1841)	m. (2) Anne Ord, no issue.
82	1st Earl of Halifax (1881)	m. Lady Dorothy Onslow, 3s, 2d.
83	2nd Earl of Halsbury (1880)	m. Esme Wallace, 1s.
84	13th Duke of Hamilton (1862)	m. Nina Poore, 4s, 3d.
85	8th Viscount Harberton (1869)	m. Mary Leatham, 2s, 3d.
86	21st Baron Hastings (1882)	m. Lady Marguerite Nevill, 2s, 3d.
87	4th Marquess of Headfort (1878)	m. Rose Boote, 2s, 1d.
88	4th Baron Henley (1848)	m. Augusta Langham, no issue.
89	Hon. Michael Hicks-Beach^d (1877)	Marjorie Brocklehurst, 1s, 1d.
90	5th Viscount Hill (1866)	m. Caroline Corbett, no issue.
91	6th Viscount Hill (1876)	m. Mildred Bulteel, 2s.
92	3rd Baron Hindlipp (1877)	m. Agatha Thynne, 2s, 2d.
93	13th Earl of Home (1873)	m. Lady Lilian Lambton, 5s, 2d.
94	Hon. Maurice Hood^c (1881)	m. Eileen Kendall, 1s.
95	6th Baron Hotham (1863)	m. Eliza Sanders, 2d.
96	6th Earl of Ilchester (1874)	m. Lady Helen Stewart, 2s, 2d.
97	2nd Earl of Iveagh (1874)	m. Lady Gwendolen Onslow, 2s, 3d.
98	8th Earl of Jersey (1873)	m. Lady Cynthia Needham, 2s, 1d.
99	6th Baron Kensington (1873)	m. Mabel Pilkington, 4s.

100	5th Baron Kilmaine (1878)	m. Lady Aline Kennedy, 2s, 1d.
101	34th Baron Kingsale (1882)	m. Constance Woodhouse, 2s, 4d.
102	12th Baron Kinnaird (1880)	m. Frances Clifton, 2s, 3d.
103	13th Baron Kinnoull (1855)	m. (2) Florence Darell, 2s, 2d.
104	2nd Baron Kinross (1870)	m. Caroline Douglas, 2s, 3d.
105	8th Baron Langford (1870)	m. Margarita Jamison, no issue.
106	6th Baron Latymer (1876)	m. Hester Russell, 3s, 1d.
107	4th Baron Leconfield (1877)	m. Hon. Maud Lyttleton, no issue.
108	4th Earl of Leicester (1880)	m. Marion Trefusis, 2s, 3d.
109	5th Earl of Leitrim (1879)	m. Violet Henderson, no issue.
110	5th Baron Lichfield (1883)	m. Gladys Farquhar, 3s, 1d.
111	4th Earl of Listowel (1866)	m. Hon. Freda Johnstone, 4s, 2d.
112	3rd Earl of Liverpool (1878)	m. Constance Holden, no issue.
113	2nd Baron Loch (1873)	m. Lady Margaret Compton, 2s, 3d.
114	6th Baron Londesborough (1876)	m. Sybil Anley, no issue.
115	2nd Baron Ludlow (1865)	m. Blanche Holden, widow, no issue.
116	2nd Earl of Lytton (1876)	m. Pamela Plowden, 2s, 2d.
117	7th Earl of Macclesfield (1888)	m. Lilian Boyle, 3s.
118	5th Earl of Malmesbury (1872)	m. Hon. Dorothy Calthorpe, 1s, 1d.
119	28th Earl of Mar (1868)	m. Sibyl Heathcote, no issue
120	12th Viscount Massereene (1873)	m. Jean Ainsworth, 2s, 1d.
121	13th Earl of Meath (1869)	m. Lady Aileen Wyndham-Quin, 1s, 2d.
122	5th Earl of Mexborough (1843)	m. (2) Sylvia Carlo, no issue.

123 6th Earl of Mexborough   m. Hon. Margaret Hugessen, 1s, 4d.
(1868)

124 1st Earl Midleton   m. (2) Madeleine Stanley, 2s.
(1856)

125 19th Viscount   m. Elizabeth Langworthy, 2s, 1d.
Molesworth
(1869)

126 Hon. Charles Monck[f]   m. Mary Portal, 1s.
(1876)

127 4th Baron Moncreiff   m. Lucy Anderson, 3s, 4d.
(1872)

128 3rd Baron Monkswell   m. Ursula Barclay, 1d.
(1875)

129 6th Duke of Montrose   m. Lady Mary Hamilton, 2s, 2d.
(1878)

130 4th Earl of Mount   m. (2) Caroline Edgcumbe, widow, no
Edcumbe (1833)   issue.

131 14th Viscount   m. (2) Robinia Hanning-Lee, 1s.
Mountgarret (1844)

132 5th Baron Muskerry   m. Charlotte Irvine, no issue.
(1874)

133 4th Baron Napier   m. Florence Perceval, 1s, 2d.
(1861)

134 4th Earl of Norbury   m. Lucy Ellis, no issue.
(1862)

135 3rd Marquess of   m. Gertrude Foster, 1s, 1d.
Normanby
(1846)

136 5th Earl of Onslow   m. Hon. Violet Bampfylde, 1s, 1d.
(1876)

137 3rd Baron Oranmore   m. Lady Olwen Ponsonby, 2s, 2d.
(1861)

138 5th Baron Ormathwaite   m. Lady Margaret Douglas-Home, 1s,
(1868)   2d.

139 5th Baron Penrhyn   m. (2) Alice Cooper, 2s, 1d.
(1865)

140 16th Earl of Perth   m. Hon. Angela Maxwell, 1s, 3d.
(1876)

141 6th Earl of Portarlington   m. Winnafreda Yuill, 1s.
(1883)

142 3rd Viscount Portman   m. Emma Kennedy, widow, 1d.
(1860)

143 7th Viscount Portman   m. Dorothy Sheffield, 2s, 1d.
(1875)

144 7th Earl Poulett   m. Sylvia Storey (actress), 1s, 1d.
(1883)

145 8th Viscount Powerscourt   m. Sybil Bouverie, 2s, 1d.
(1880)

146 4th Baron Rayleigh   m. Lady Mary Clements, 3s, 2d.
(1875)

147 12th Baron Reay   m. Baroness Maria Van Dedem, 2s, 1d.
(1870)

148 2nd Baron Redesdale   m. Sydney Bowles, 1s, 6d.
(1878)

149 8th Earl of Roden   m. Elinor Parr, 2s, 2d.
(1883)

150 6th Earl of Rosebery   m. (div. 1909) Lady Dorothy Grosvenor,
(1882)   1s, 1d.

151 5th Earl of Rosse   m. Lois Lister-Kaye, 2s, 1d.
(1873)

152 19th Earl of Rothes   m. Noel Edwardes, 2s.
(1877)

153 18th Baron St John   m. Evelyn Russell, 1s, 5d.
(1877)

154 1st Viscount   m. (2) Eleanor Arnold, widow, no issue.
Sandhurst (1855)

155 4th Baron Seaton   m. Caroline Vivian, no issue.
(1863)

156 2nd Viscount Selby   m. (2) Dorothy Grey, 1s, 3d.
(1867)

157 5th Baron Sheffield   m. Margaret Gordon, 2s, 3d.
(1875)

158 6th Baron Sherborne   m. Ethel Baird, 2s, 2d.
(1873)

159 16th Lord Sinclair   m. Violet Kennedy, 1s, 1d.
(1875)

160 17th Duke of Somerset   m. Edith Parker, 3s, 1d.
(1882)

161 12th Baron Stafford   m. Dorothy Worthington, no issue.
(1859)

162 2nd Baron Stalbridge   m. Gladys Nixon, 1s.
(1886)

163 12th Earl of Stair   m. Violet Harford, 1s, 2d.
(1879)

164 15th Earl of Strathmore   m. Lady Dorothy Osborne, 2s, 2d.
(1884)

165 4th Baron Stratspey   m. Alice Johnstone, 1s, 1d.
(1879)

166 5th Baron Sudeley   m. (div. 1922) Edith Cecil, no issue.
(1870)

167 3rd Baron Swansea   m. Hon Winifred Hamilton, 1s, 3d.
(1875)

168 5th Baron Talbot   m. (2) Isabel Humfrey, no issue.
(1883)

169 4th Baron Tenterden   m. Elfrida Turner, 1s, 1d.
(1865)

170 6th Baron Thurlow (1869)   m. Grace Trotter, 4s.

171 3rd Baron Tollemache (1883)   m. Wynford Kemball, 2d.

172 10th Viscount Torrington (1876)   m. (div. 1936) Louise Rawline, 1s, 3d.

173 6th Marquess Townshend (1866)   m. Gwlays Sutherst, 1s, 1d.

174 18th Baron Trimlestown (1861)   m. (2) Mabel Shuff, no issue.

175 7th Baron Vaux (1860)   m. (2) Margaret Plowden, no issue.

176 4th Earl of Verulam (1880)   m. Lady Violet Brabazon, 4s.

177 4th Baron Vivian (1878)   m. (div. 1907) Barbara Fanning, 1s, 1d.

178 6th Baron Walsingham (1843)   m. (2) Marion Withers, no issue.

179 6th Earl of Warwick (1882)   m. Elfrida Eden, 3s.

180 6th Baron Waterpark (1876)   m. (1) (div. 1906) Isabel Jay, 1d; m. (2) (div. 1913) May Burbidge, 2d.

181 5th Duke of Wellington (1876)   m. Hon. Lilian Coats, 1s, 1d.

182 10th Earl of Wemyss (1818)   m. (2) Grace Blackburn, no issue.

183 4th Baron Wenlock (1856)   m. Rhoda Know-Little, no issue.

184 2nd Duke of Westminster (1879)   m. (div. 1919) Constance Cornwallis-West, 1s, 1d.

185 6th Baron Wynford (1871)   m. Hon. Eva Napier, 3d.

186 2nd Marquess of Zetland (1876)   m. Cicely Archdale, 2s, 3d.

---

[a] Pre-deceased his father, 5th Baron Clarina.
[b] Pre-deceased his father, 2nd Baron De Ramsay.
[c] Pre-deceased his father, 8th Earl of Aylesford.
[d] Pre-deceased his father, 1st Viscount Aldwyn.
[e] Pre-deceased his father, 2nd Viscount Bridport.
[f] Pre-deceased his father, 5th Viscount Monck.

Appendix D

Control Groups: younger sons who married 1880–9 and 1900–9

CONTROL GROUP I: YOUNGER SONS WHO MARRIED
1880–9

Name of younger son	*Family title*
1 George Nevill	Marquess of Abergavenny
2 William Nevill	Marquess of Abergavenny
3 Alberic Bertie	Earl of Abingdon
4 George Bertie	Earl of Abingdon
5 Alexander Kennedy	Marquess of Ailsa
6 George Eden	Baron Auckland
7 Henry Somerset	Duke of Beaufort
8 Richard Bellew	Baron Bellew
9 Clement Tyrwhitt	Baron Berners
10 Hugh Tyrwhitt	Baron Berners
11 Cecil Irby	Baron Boston
12 Francis Bridgman	Earl of Bradford
13 Grey Neville	Baron Braybrooke
14 Ivan Campbell	Earl of Breadalbane
15 Reginal Brougham	Baron Brougham
16 Charles Scott	Duke of Buccleuch
17 Horace Hampden	Earl of Buckinghamshire
18 Arthur Cadogan	Earl of Cadogan
19 Walter Alexander	Earl of Caledon
20 Charles Alexander	Earl of Caledon
21 Charles Pratt	Marquess of Camden
22 Alexander Vaughn	Earl of Cawdor
23 William Cavendish	Baron Chesham
24 Evelyn Stanhope	Earl of Chesterfield
25 Thomas Pelham	Earl of Chichester
26 Frederick Trench	Earl of Clancarty
27 Albert Bingham	Baron Clanmorris
28 Sir Robert Meade	Earl of Clanwilliam

29	George Villiers	Earl of Clarendon
30	John Trefusis	Baron Clinton
31	Gilbert Coleridge	Baron Coleridge
32	Edward Stopford	Earl of Courtown
33	George Stopford	Earl of Courtown
34	John Cross	Viscount Cross
35	Sir Henry Legge	Earl of Dartmouth
36	Robert French	Baron De Freyne
37	Arthur Saumarez	Baron De Saumarez
38	Hugh Courtenay	Earl of Devon
39	Everard Digby	Baron Digby
40	Thomas Cochrane	Earl of Dundonald
41	D'Arcy Lambton	Earl of Durham
42	William Rice	Baron Dynevor
43	William Cecil	Marquess of Exeter
44	Sir William Fitzwilliam	Earl Fitzwilliam
45	Walter Forbes	Baron Forbes
46	Arthur Fortescue	Earl Fortescue
47	Edward Noel	Earl of Gainsborough
48	Fitzroy Stewart	Earl of Galloway
49	Horace Monckton	Viscount Galway
50	Robert Gerard	Baron Gerard
51	George Gough	Viscount Gough
52	Charles Fitzroy	Duke of Grafton
53	Edward Palk	Baron Haldon
54	Lincoln Stanhope	Earl of Harrington
55	Fitzroy Stanhope	Earl of Harrington
56	Cecil Littleton	Baron Hatherton
57	Arthur Henniker	Baron Henniker
58	George Devereux	Viscount Hereford
59	Geoffrey Hill	Viscount Hill
60	Cuthbert Edwardes	Baron Kensington
61	Robert Trollope	Baron Kesteven
62	Arthur Browne	Baron Kilmaine
63	Randolfe Conwy	Baron Langford
64	Maurice Fitzgerald	Duke of Leinster
65	Charles Fitzgerald	Duke of Leinster
66	Cornwallis Hewitt	Viscount Lifford
67	William Hewitt	Viscount Lifford
68	Francis Parker	Earl of Macclesfield
69	Edmund Parker	Earl of Macclesfield
70	Algernon Bourke	Earl of Mayo
71	Alexander Willoughby	Earl of Midleton
72	Arthur Elliott	Earl of Minto
73	William Elliott	Earl of Minto
74	Frederick Moncreiff	Baron Moncreiff
75	John Collier	Baron Monkswell
76	Edward Douglas	Earl of Morton

77	George Napier	Baron Napier
78	Charles Nelson	Earl Nelson
79	Alwyne Compton	Marquess of Northampton
80	Algernon Percy	Duke of Northumberland
81	Henry Scott	Baron Polwarth
82	Edward Strutt	Baron Rayleigh
83	Hedley Strutt	Baron Rayleigh
84	Henry Lennox	Duke of Richmond
85	Algernon Lennox	Duke of Richmond
86	Walter Lennox	Duke of Richmond
87	Robert Rodney	Baron Rodney
88	Eric Rollo	Baron Rollo
89	Sir Charles Parsons	Earl of Rosse
90	Lyston Leslie	Earl of Rothes
91	Cecil Jervis	Viscount St Vincent
92	Rupert Cecil	Marquess of Salisbury
93	Henry Mansfield	Baron Sandhurst
94	Frederick Twisleton	Baron Saye and Sele
95	Walter Talbot	Earl of Shrewsbury
96	Alfred Talbot	Earl of Shrewsbury
97	Harold Addington	Viscount Sidmouth
98	Lockhard St Clair	Baron Sinclair
99	North Dalrymple	Earl of Stair
100	Francis Bowes-Lyon	Earl of Strathmore
101	Ernest Bowes-Lyon	Earl of Strathmore
102	William Hammond	Baron Suffield
103	Edward Talbot	Baron Talbot
104	Reginald Talbot	Baron Talbot
105	John Tollemache	Baron Tollemache
106	Douglas Tollemache	Baron Tollemache
107	Ranulph Tollemache	Baron Tollemache
108	Arnold de Grey	Baron Walsingham
109	Alwyn Greville	Earl of Warwick
110	Louis Greville	Earl of Warwick
111	Slingsby Bethell	Baron Westbury
112	Lord Henry Grosvenor	Duke of Westminster
113	Edward Glyn	Baron Wolverton
114	George Wrottesley	Baron Wrottesley
115	Robert Best	Baron Wynford

CONTROL GROUP II: YOUNGER SONS WHO MARRIED
1900–9

Name of younger son	Family title
1 Victor Russell	Baron Ampthill

2	Alexander Russell	Baron Ampthill
3	Charles White	Baron Annaly
4	Reginald Flower	Viscount Ashbrook
5	Bernard Barrington	Viscount Barrington
6	Rupert Barrington	Viscount Barrington
7	Percy Barrington	Viscount Barrington
8	Benjamin Bathurst	Earl Bathurst
9	Robert Lygon	Earl of Beauchamp
10	Rupert Tyrwhitt	Baron Berners
11	Philip Tyrwhitt	Baron Berners
12	Arthur Russell	Viscount Boyne
13	Eustace Russell	Viscount Boyne
14	Maurice Nelson	Viscount Bridport
15	Wilfrid Brougham	Baron Brougham
16	Reginald Brougham	Baron Brougham
17	George Scott	Duke of Buccleuch
18	Herbert Scott	Duke of Buccleuch
19	Albany Erskine	Earl of Buchan
20	Ninion Stuart	Marquess of Bute
21	Oliver Howard	Earl of Carlisle
22	Arthur Dalzell	Earl of Carnwarth
23	Nigel Vaughan	Earl of Cawdor
24	Ralph Vaughan	Earl of Cawdor
25	Percy Thesiger	Baron Chelmsford
26	Wilfred Thesiger	Baron Chelmsford
27	Eric Theisger	Baron Chelmsford
28	Charles Stanhope	Duke of Chesterfield
29	Henry Pelman	Earl of Chichester
30	Anthony Pelman	Earl of Chichester
31	Edward Meade	Earl of Clanwilliam
32	Henry Trefusis	Baron Clinton
33	Sir Stanley Colville	Viscount Colville
34	George Colville	Viscount Colville
35	Reginald Fremantle	Baron Cottesloe
36	William Fremantle	Baron Cottesloe
37	Arthur Stopford	Earl of Courtown
38	Edwin Ponsonby	Baron de Mauley
39	Ferdinand Stanley	Earl of Derby
40	George Stanley	Earl of Derby
42	Gerald Digby	Baron Digby
43	Matthew Moreton	Earl of Ducie
44	Leslie Butler	Baron Dunboyne
45	George Lambton	Earl of Durham
46	Claud Lambton	Earl of Durham
47	Osmund Scott	Earl of Eldon
48	Denys Scott	Earl of Eldon
49	Michael Scott	Earl of Eldon
50	Thomas Egerton	Earl of Ellesmere

51	Arthur Crichton	Earl of Erne
52	Ruaraidh Erskine	Baron Erskine
53	Ralph Shirley	Earl of Ferrers
54	George Plumptre	Baron Fitzwalter
55	William Fitzwilliam	Earl Fitzwilliam
56	Francis Forester	Baron Forester
57	Charles Fortescue	Earl of Fortescue
58	Herbert Bailey	Baron Glanusk
59	John Bailey	Baron Glanusk
60	James Boyle	Earl of Glasgow
61	Richard Preston	Viscount Gormanston
62	Jeffrey Vereker	Viscount Gort
63	Leslie Hamilton	Baron Hamilton
64	Alfred Yorke	Earl of Hardwicke
65	George Lascelles	Earl of Harewood
66	Francis Lascelles	Earl of Harewood
67	Robert Ryder	Earl of Harrowby
68	Charles Littleton	Baron Hatherton
69	Henry Heneage	Baron Heneage
70	Arthur Hill	Viscount Hill
71	Gerald Hill	Viscount Hill
72	Geoffrey Mills	Baron Hillingdon
73	Charles Tufton	Baron Hothfield
74	Aubrey Hastings	Earl of Huntingdon
75	Granville Gordon	Marquess of Huntly
76	Arthur Guinness	Earl of Iveagh
77	Cecil Edwardes	Baron Kensington
79	Francis Butler	Earl of Lanesborough
80	Reginald Wilbraham	Earl of Lathom
81	Villiers Wilbraham	Earl of Lathom
82	Alfred Maitland	Earl of Lauderdale
83	Richard Coke	Earl of Leicester
84	Sir John Coke	Earl of Leicester
85	Arthur Coke	Earl of Leicester
86	Francis Brownlow	Baron Lurgan
87	Godfrey Macdonald	Baron Macdonald
88	Alexander Murray	Earl of Mansfield
89	Sir William Erskine	Earl of Mar
90	John Lister	Baron Masham
91	Claude Willoughby	Baron Midleton
92	Robert Montagu	Baron Montagu
93	Nigel Stourton	Baron Mowbray
94	Harold Fitzclarence	Earl of Munster
95	Charles Napier	Baron Napier
96	Cuthbert James	Baron Northbourne
97	Robert James	Baron Northbourne
98	Wilfrid James	Baron Northbourne
99	Ian Carnegie	Earl of Northesk

100	Arthur O'Neill	Baron O'Neill
101	Arthur Peel	Viscount Peel
102	Maurice Peel	Viscount Peel
103	Charles Pennant	Baron Penrhyn
104	Benjamin Plunkett	Baron Plunkett
105	Charles Scott	Baron Polwarth
106	Maurice Wingfield	Viscount Powerscourt
107	Kenelm Bouverie	Earl of Radnor
108	Esme Lennox	Duke of Richmond
109	Bernard Lennox	Duke of Richmond
110	Gilbert Rollo	Baron Rollo
111	Reginald Marsham	Earl of Romney
112	Nathaniel Rothschild	Baron Rothschild
113	Alexander Ruthven	Baron Ruthven
114	Robert Manners	Duke of Rutland
115	St Leger Jervis	Viscount St Vincent
116	Ivor Twisleton	Baron Saye and Sele
117	Francis Colborne	Baron Seaton
118	Walter Boyle	Earl of Shannon
119	Edward Boyle	Earl of Shannon
120	Alfred Browne	Marquess of Sligo
121	Ernest Seymour	Duke of Somerset
122	Kenneth Campbell	Baron Stratheden
123	Malcoln Bowes-Lyon	Earl of Strathmore
124	Algernon Tracy	Baron Sudeley
125	Felix Tracy	Baron Sudeley
126	Walter Hammond	Baron Suffield
127	Assheton Hammond	Baron Suffield
128	Reginald Talbot	Baron Talbot
129	Chandos Langton	Earl of Temple
130	Wyndham Curzon	Baron Teynham
131	Stanhope Tollemache	Baron Tollemache
132	Richard Wellesley	Duke of Wellington
133	Walter Bethell	Baron Westbury
134	Hugh Grosvenor	Duke of Westminster
135	Sir Matthew Best	Baron Wynford
136	Dudley Pelham	Earl of Yarborough
137	George Dundas	Marquess of Zetland

Appendix E

Probate calendar valuations (peers and their spouses)

CASE GROUP

Name	Peer Date of death	Amount £	Wife Date of death	Amount £
2nd Earl of Ancaster	1951	232,346		
4th Marquess of Anglesey	1898	22,978		
5th Baron Ashburton	1938	100,020	1959	118,835
8th Baron Calthorpe	1940	20,848	1940	817
3rd Baron Cheylesmore	1925	113,034	1945	20,537
11th Earl Cork	1934	3,510	1953	11,956
4th Earl of Craven	1921	318,709	1961	819,630
Marquess of Curzon			1906	12,187
5th Baron Decies	1944	25,948	1931	83,926
Viscount Deerhurst	1927	125,927	1948	11,302
6th Earl of Donoughmore	1948	17,400	1944	66,915
2nd Marquess of Dufferin	1918	25,501		
3rd Baron Ebury			1927	71,660
8th Earl of Egmont	1910	14,750	1926	12,165
5th Baron Ellenborough	1915	10,624	1942	31,112
3rd Viscount Esher	1963	434		
7th Earl of Essex	1916	190,562	1922	18,529
6th Viscount Exmouth	1923	453		
7th Viscount Exmouth	1945	46,891	1922	62,492
12th Viscount Falkland	1922	56,396	1920	998
3rd Baron Fermoy	1920	73		
2nd Baron Fisher	1955	28,545	1955	16,410
5th Earl of Gosford	1954	79		
7th Marquess of Hertford	1940	618		
5th Baron Huntingfield	1969	45,367	1943	1,896
3rd Baron Leigh	1938	55,386	1909	137,876
Baron Malcolm	1902	360,172	1927	54,502
8th Duke of Manchester	1892	25,190	1909	324,860
9th Duke of Manchester	1947	257		
8th Duke of Marlborough	1892	345,675		
9th Duke of Marlborough	1934	118,223		

9th Baron Monson			1943	41,730
4th Baron Newborough	1916	86,630	1939	13,004
8th Duke of Newcastle	1941	8,252		
5th Earl of Orford	1931	82,553	1909	6,296
4th Marquess of Ormonde	1943	104,258	1951	61,704
8th Earl of Portsmouth	1943	7,867		
3rd Baron Revelstoke	1934	406,773		
3rd Earl Russell	1970	69,243		
9th Earl of Sandwich	1962	222,209	1951	17,411
7th Baron Somers	1953	988		
4th Earl of Strafford	1899	23,507	1932	38,306
19th Earl of Suffolk	1917	114,159		
7th Baron Vernon	1898	81,700	1940	48,305
14th Earl of Winchilsea	1939	162,807	1952	68,481

CONTROL GROUP I

Name	Peer		Wife	
	Date of death	Amount £	Date of death	Amount £
7th Earl of Abingdon	1928	167,595		
8th Earl of Albemarle	1942	17,807	1943	35,000
4th Earl of Amherst	1910	137,657		
3rd Baron Annaly	1922	4,181	1944	983,451
5th Earl of Arran	1901	44,608	1922	22,085
9th Baron Barnard	1919	280,804	1918	12,392
9th Baron Beaumont	1892	9,835	1949	461,520
3rd Baron Bellew	1911	45,116		
2nd Baron Brabourne	1909	5,661	1949	89,623
3rd Baron Brougham	1927	68,344	1925	368
7th Earl of Buckinghamshire	1930	19,145	1937	125,000
2nd Earl Cairns	1890	5,135		
4th Earl of Caledon	1898	20,805	1939	109,645
3rd Baron Carew	1923	62,083		
4th Baron Carew	1926	27,613	1955	6,840
2nd Viscount Colville	1928	29,905	1944	39,283
3rd Viscount Combermere	1898	113,131	1930	2,071
4th Baron Congleton	1906	10,715	1931	61,175
4th Marquess of Conyngham	1897	59,146		
Earl of Darnley	1927	237,030	1944	3,340
17th Earl of Derby	1948	2,217,838	1957	104,594
9th Earl of Dysart	1935	2,374,712	1918	12,676
6th Marquess of Ely	1935	19,895		
7th Viscount Falmouth	1918	327,033	1953	3,760
10th Earl Ferrers	1912	38,078	1907	27,712
1st Duke of Fife	1912	1,000,000	1931	463,383
4th Earl Fortescue	1932	76,760	1929	3,931
3rd Earl of Gainsborough	1926	185,816	1938	2,745
3rd Baron Gifford	1911	34,122	1947	1,063
5th Viscount Gort	1902	79,216		

3rd Viscount Gough	1919	38,734		
3rd Baron Harlech	1938	74,931	1950	11,672
9th Earl of Harrington	1928	487,082		
5th Earl of Harrowby	1956	214,294		
20th Baron Hastings	1904	465,953	1957	4,737
5th Viscount Hawarden	1908	17,206	1930	43,115
3rd Baron Heytesbury	1903	213,226	1920	174,905
2nd Baron Hillingdon	1919	1,000,000	1940	6,087
2nd Baron Howard	1924	21,956		
14th Earl of Huntingdon	1939	9,153		
6th Baron Langford	1931	10,715		
2nd Earl Lathom	1910	111,921		
5th Duke of Leinster	1894	13,224	1895	4,242
11th Earl of Leven	1906	1,300,013	1941	105,399
6th Earl of Lisburne	1899	21,860	1931	2,268
6th Earl of Lonsdale	1953	1,067,488		
11th Earl of Loudoun	1920	220,864		
2nd Earl of Lovelace	1906	380,000	1941	149,773
3rd Baron Manners	1927	347,288	1920	9,685
7th Earl of Mayo	1928	56,288	1944	59,486
8th Earl of Mayo	1939	27,305		
3rd Baron Methuen	1932	165,911	1941	2,905
1st Earl Midleton	1942	124,213	1901	1,200
8th Viscount Molesworth	1906	12,310	1905	8,617
2nd Baron Montagu	1929	86,000	1919	5,076
5th Earl Nelson	1950	2,705	1936	40
5th Marquess of Northampton	1913	189,796	1902	23,486
5th Baron Norton	1945	45,925		
3rd Baron Penrhyn	1927	712,134	1944	43,110
1st Earl of Plymouth	1923	860,102	1944	1,204,428
3rd Baron Poltimore	1918	50,487	1931	55,224
5th Earl of Portarlington	1900	90,976		
4th Viscount Portman	1929	404,457		
3rd Baron Raglan	1921	43,237		
5th Earl of Ranfurly	1933	3,270	1932	2,829
7th Duke of Richmond	1928	310,830		
8th Duke of Rutland	1925	930,737	1937	14,752
4th Marquess of Salisbury	1947	317,457		
18th Lord Saltoun	1933	111,207	1940	13,602
1st Viscount Sandhurst	1921	38,573		
3rd Baron Sandhurst	1933	24,706	1939	4,483
18th Baron Saye and Sele	1937	57,983	1946	7,137
2nd Earl of Selborne	1942	18,649	1950	7,261
20th Earl of Shrewsbury	1921	600,655	1940	10,172
4th Viscount Sidmouth	1915	14,898		
6th Marquess of Sligo	1935	25,574		
16th Duke of Somerset	1931	20,362	1950	1,064
6th Earl Spencer	1922	1,205,710		
3rd Duke of Sutherland	1892	324,880		
4th Duke of Sutherland	1913	1,220,905		
3rd Baron Teignmouth	1915	46,259	1938	51,232
5th Baron Teignmouth	1926	17,155	1934	1,535
3rd Baron Templemore	1924	30,943		

7th Baron Vaux	1935	136,729	1896	2,902
5th Earl of Warwick	1924	10,749	1938	108,207
1st Duke of Westminster	1899	974,891	1941	221,611
2nd Earl of Wharncliffe	1926	17,118	1922	300
4th Earl of Yarborough	1936	150,000		

CONTROL GROUP II

Name	Peer		Wife	
	Date of death	Amount £	Date of death	Amount £
3rd Baron Aldenham	1939	433,783	1950	91,407
6th Earl of Arran	1958	44,941	1927	4,312
1st Baron Ashton	1933	208,926		
9th Viscount Barrington	1933	75,841	1935	62,465
7th Earl Beauchamp	1938	173,668	1936	96,359
9th Viscount Boyne	1942	416,796		
5th Earl of Bradford	1957	382,819	1949	13,060
5th Lord Burgh	1926	73,139		
5th Baron Carew	1927	19,918		
8th Viscount Chetwynd	1936	2,383	1925	7,006
5th Earl of Clarendon	1914	26,409	1935	11,485
6th Earl of Clarendon	1955	168,120		
9th Viscount Cobham	1949	194,889		
3rd Baron Coleridge	1955	95,189	1957	1,991
7th Earl of Courtown	1957	3,659		
2nd Baron Cranworth	1964	195,885		
2nd Earl of Cromer	1953	52,988	1908	48,057
7th Earl of Dartmouth	1958	467,397		
25th Baron de Clifford	1909	21,976		
8th Earl De La Warr	1915	153,893		
3rd Baron De L'Isle	1922	66,008	1958	3,669
5th Baron De L'Isle	1945	321,296	1959	13,919
3rd Baron Denman	1954	133,695	1954	156,481
3rd Baron Deramore	1936	110,635		
4th Baron Deramore	1943	25,285	1960	24,017
5th Viscount De Vesci	1958	66,210		
16th Earl of Devon	1935	309,956	1950	11,783
18th Viscount Dillon	1934	28,482	1966	20,735
19th Viscount Dillon	1946	110,868	1962	370
5th Marquess of Donegall	1904	27	1952	6,365
14th Baron Dormer	1922	4,066	1951	71,482
6th Marquess of Downshire	1918	135,540	1942	35,014
10th Earl of Drogheda	1957	78,412		
5th Earl of Ducie	1952	83,757		
12th Baron Dudley	1936	14,596	1958	8,139
5th Marquess of Exeter	1956	734,277		
11th Baron Farnham	1957	22,810	1964	5,178
4th Baron Garvagh	1956	47,187		
3rd Baron Gerard	1953	80,164	1954	147,456

3rd Baron Granville	1939	191,369	1955	43,982
6th Baron Graves	1937	1,592	1962	382
1st Baron Grenfell	1925	46,778	1911	10,551
1st Earl of Halifax	1959	351,281		
13th Duke of Hamilton	1940	187,352	1951	115,018
8th Viscount Harberton	1956	8,463		
21st Baron Hastings	1956	314,552		
4th Marquess of Headfort	1943	28,957	1958	164,733
4th Baron Henley	1926	8,285	1905	26,761
5th Viscount Hill	1924	578		
6th Viscount Hill	1957	31,389		
3rd Baron Hindlipp	1931	290		
6th Baron Hotham	1923	98,730	1954	1,704
6th Earl of Ilchester	1959	195,239	1956	129,266
2nd Earl of Iveagh	1967	262,149	1966	337,318
6th Baron Kensington	1938	11,401	1934	12,854
5th Baron Kilmaine	1946	23,037	1957	7,691
34th Baron Kingsale	1969	8,247		
8th Baron Langford	1953	18,446		
6th Baron Latymer	1949	357,180	1961	26,409
4th Baron Leconfield	1963	41,983	1953	7,984
4th Earl of Listowel	1931	480,605	1968	25,946
2nd Baron Loch	1942	80,386		
6th Baron Londesborough	1963	35,910	1963	4,470
7th Earl of Macclesfield	1950	119,661		
28th Earl of Mar	1932	21,766	1958	62,721
13th Earl of Meath	1949	29,199	1961	33,344
5th Earl of Mexborough	1916	71,923	1915	23,332
1st Earl Midleton	1942	124,213	1966	186,440
3rd Baron Monkswell	1964	873	1915	954
4th Earl of Mount Edcumbe	1917	206,000	1909	21,843
14th Viscount Mountgarret	1912	373,460	1944	7,649
5th Baron Muskerry	1954	13,566	1960	24,920
4th Baron Napier	1948	9,237		
4th Earl of Norbury	1943	35,599	1966	30,596
3rd Marquess of Normanby	1932	114,703	1948	45,955
5th Earl of Onslow	1945	227,116	1954	21,973
3rd Baron Oranmore	1927	54,731	1927	7,298
5th Baron Ormathwaite	1944	160,015	1955	10,866
5th Baron Penrhyn	1967	40,082	1965	19,772
6th Earl of Portarlington	1959	43,222		
3rd Viscount Portman	1923	615,088	1929	217,386
7th Viscount Portman	1948	4,494,205	1964	207,811
7th Earl Poulett	1918	187,200	1947	26,898
8th Viscount Powerscourt	1947	31,572	1946	21,735
4th Baron Rayleigh	1947	262,038		
12th Baron Reay	1921	83,500		
2nd Baron Redesdale	1958	129,400		
8th Earl of Roden	1956	56,440	1962	65,130
19th Earl of Rothes	1927	20,061		
1st Viscount Sandhurst	1921	38,573	1934	54,054
6th Baron Sherborne	1949	255,149	1969	6,285
17th Duke of Somerset	1954	270,248	1962	7,418

12th Baron Stafford	1932	369,535	1958	182,434
15th Earl of Strathmore	1949	110,000		
5th Baron Sudeley	1932	27,063		
3rd Baron Swansea	1934	32,511	1944	11,454
3rd Baron Tollemache	1955	5,316	1926	21,656
6th Marquess Townshend	1921	20,768		
7th Baron Vaux	1935	136,729	1922	2,902
4th Earl of Verulam	1949	19,027	1936	424
4th Baron Vivian	1940	57,495		
6th Earl of Warwick	1928	117,843		
5th Duke of Wellington	1941	134,262		
2nd Duke of Westminster	1953	10,703,000		
6th Baron Wynford	1940	183,714		
2nd Marquess of Zetland	1961	892,805		

Appendix F

Peers who married Americans
1915–39

Title of peer	Marital details: year of marriage and divorce, name of spouse(s), previous husband's name, father's name, and number of sons and daughters from the marriage
1 6th Baron Auckland	m. (1) 1917 (div. 1925) Susan, da. of Augustus Hartridge of Florida, 2d; m. (2) 1939 Mrs Constance Hart-Faure, da. of Benno Hart of San Francisco, no issue.
2 4th Baron Basing	m. (1) 1938 (div. 1944) Jeanette, da. of Neil Mackelvie of New York, 1s; m. (2) 1951 Cynthia, widow, da. of Charles Hardy of Salt Lake City, no issue.
3 2nd Earl Beatty	m. (1) 1937 (div 1945) Dorothy, formerly wife of Harry Hall, da. of Thomas Power of Virginia; m. (2) 1946 (div. 1950) Dorothy, widow, da. of Michael Furey of New Orleans, 1s; m. (3) 1951 (div. 1950) Adele, formerly wife of William O'Connor, da. of M. Dillingham of Oklahoma, 1d; m. (4) 1959 Diane Blundell, 1s, 1d.
4 8th Earl Berkeley	m. (1) 1887 Kate Brand; m. (2) 1924 Mary, da. of John Lowell of Boston, no issue.
5 7th Baron Braye	m. 1934 Dorothea, da. of Daniel Donoghue of Philadelphia, 1d.
6 6th Earl of Carnarvon	m. (1) 1922 (div. 1936) Anne, da. of Jacob Wendell of New York, 1s, 1d; m. (2) 1939 (div. 1947) Ottlie Losch.
7 8th Earl Carrick	m. (1) 1930 (div. 1938) Mrs Marion Edwards, da. of Daniel Donoghue of Philadelphia, 1s; m. (2) 1938 Mrs

Margaret Drum, da. of Charles Power
of Montana, no issue; m. (3) 1954 Ruth,
da. of Francis McEnery of Chicago.

8 7th Earl Castlestewart   m. 1920 Eleanor, da. of Solomon
Guggenheim of New York, 4s.

9 4th Baron Chesham   m. (1) 1915 (div. 1937) Margot Mills, 1s;
m. (2) 1938 Marion, formerly Countess
Carrick, da. of Daniel Donoghue of
Philadelphia, no issue; m. (3) 1941 his
first wife.

10 16th Baron Cobham   m. (1) 1923 (div. 1934) Christina
Honeybone; m. (2) 1934 Evelyn, widow,
da. of John Turnure of New York, no
issue; m. (3) 1949 his first wife.

11 4th Earl of Cottenham   m. (1) 1899 Lady Rose Leigh, 3s; m. (2)
1916 Patricia, da. of John Burke of
California, no issue.

12 4th Earl of Cromartie   m. (1) 1933 (div. 1945) Dorothy, da. of
B. G. Downing of Kentucky; m. (2) 1947
(div. 1962) Olga Laurance, 1s; m. (3)
1962 Lilias Macleod.

13 9th Earl of Denbigh   m. (1) 1884 Hon. Cecilia Clifford, 3s, 7d;
m. (2) 1928 Kathleen, da. of Dr Thomas
A. Emmet of New York, no issue.

14 2nd Baron Doverdale   m. (1) 1902 (div. 1934) Hon. Clara
Oliphant, 1s, 1d; m. (2) 1934 Leslie,
widow, da. of George Cornell of New
York, no issue.

15 10th Viscount Downe   m. 1928 Margaret, da. of Christian
Bahnsen of New Jersey, 2s.

16 6th Earl of Dunraven   m. (1) 1915 (div. 1932) Helen Swire; m.
(2) 1934 Nancy, da. of Thomas Yuille of
New York, 1s, 2d.

17 5th Earl of Effingham   m. (1) 1904 (div. 1914) Rosamond
Hudson; m. (2) 1924 Madeleine, widow,
da. of William Foshay of San Francisco,
no issue.

18 2nd Baron Essendon   m. 1938 Mary, widow, da. G. W. Booker
of Los Angeles, no issue.

19 1st Viscount Furness   m. (1) 1904 Daisy Hogg, 1s, 1d; m. (2)
1926 (div. 1933) Thelma, formerly wife
of James Converse, da. of Harry Morgan
of USA, 1s; m. (3) 1933 Enid Lindeman,
no issue.

20 12th Earl of Galloway   m. 1924 Philippa, da. of Jacob Wendell
of New York, 1s, 1d.

21 6th Earl of Gosford   m. (1) 1935 (div. 1960) Francesca, da. of
Francesco Cagiati of Boston, 1s, 2d; m.
(2) 1960 Cynthia West.

22	4th Baron Hemphill	m. 1927 Emily, da. of F. Irving Sears of USA, 1s.
23	4th Earl Howe	m. (1) 1883 Lady Georgina Spencer-Churchill, 1s; m. (2) 1919 Florence, Marchioness of Dufferin, da. of J. H. Davis of New York, no issue; m. (3) 1927 Lorna Curzon.
24	11th Marquess of Huntly	m. (1) 1869 Amy Brooks; m. (2) 1922 Charlotte, widow, da. of John Fallon of USA, no issue.
25	9th Earl of Jersey	m. (1) 1932 (div. 1937) Pat Richards, 1d; m. (2) 1937 (div. 1946) Virginia, formerly wife of actor Cary Grant, da. of James Cherill of USA, no issue; m. (3) 1947 Bianca Mottironi, 2s, 1d.
26	10th Earl of Kintore	m. 1937 Helena, formerly Duchess of Manchester, da. of Eugene Zimmerman of Cincinnati, no issue.
27	8th Marquess of Lansdowne	m. (1) 1938 Barbara, da. of Harold Chase of San Francisco, 2s, 1d; m. (2) 1969 Hon. Selina Eccles.
28	3rd Baron Lawrence	m. (1) 1907 Dorothy Hobson, 1s, 1d; m. (2) 1935 Jesse, widow, da. of Col Byron Daniels, no issue; m. (3) 1938 Catherine Fernihough.
29	10th Baron Monson	m. 1931 Betty, da. of Col Alexander Powell of Maryland, 3s, 1d.
30	18th Earl of Moray	m. 1924 Barbara, da. of John Murray of New York, 3d.
31	9th Duke of Newcastle	m. (1) 1931 (div. 1940) Mrs Jean Gimbernat, da. of David Banks of New York, no issue; m. (2) 1946 (div. 1950) Lady Diana Wortley, 2d; m. (3) 1959 Mrs Sally Hope.
32	4th Baron Northbourne	m. 1925 Katherine, da. of George Nickerson of Boston, 1s, 4d.
33	11th Earl of Northesk	m. (1) 1923 (div. 1928) Jessica, da. of F. A. Brown of Buffalo (dancer), no issue; m. (2) Elizabeth Vlasto.
34	7th Marquess of Ormonde	m. 1935 Nan, da. of Garth Gilpin of USA, 2d.
35	17th Earl of Perth	m. 1934 Nancy, da, of Reginald Fincke of New York, 2s.
36	9th Earl of Portsmouth	m. (1) 1920 (div. 1936) Mary, da. of Waldron Post of New York, 1s, 1d; m. (2) 1936 Bridget Crohan, 1s, 2d.

37	Baron Queenborough	m. (1) Pauline (d. 1916), da. of William C. Whitney of New York, 2d; m. (2) Edith, da. of William Starr of New York, 1d.
38	4th Baron Ribblesdale	m. (1) Charlotte Tennant, 2s, 3d; m. (2) Ava, formerly wife of J. J. Astor, da. of Edward Willings of Philadelphia, no issue.
39	4th Baron Sackville	m. (1) 1897 Maude Bell, 1s, 1d; m. (2) 1924 Anne, formerly wife of Stephen Bigelow, da. of William Meredith of New York, no issue.
40	2nd Baron Sysonby	m. 1936 Sallie, formerly wife of George Monkland, da. of Dr Leonard C. Sandford of New York, 1s, 1d.
41	3rd Baron Tennyson	m. (1) 1918 (div. 1928) Hon. Clarissa Glenconner, 3s; m. (2) 1934 (div. 1943) Carroll, widow, da. of Howard Elting of Chicago, no issue.
42	13th Baron Torphichen	m. 1916 Grace, da. of Winslow Pierce of New York, 2s, 1d.
43	1st Baron Vestey	m. (1) 1882 Sarah Ellis, 4s; m. (2) 1924 Evelyn, da. of Hans Brodstone of Nebraska, no issue.
44	HRH Duke of Windsor	m. 1937 Wallis, formerly wife of (1) Lt Earl Winfield, (2) Ernest Simpson, da. of Teakle Warfield, no issue.

See also Appendices A and G for additional marriages between peers and Americans which occurred between 1914 and 1939.

Appendix G

Men who married Americans 1870–1914 and who were subsequently raised to the peerage

Albert Stanley, BARON ASHFIELD (cr. 1920)
b. 1874
General Manager, American Electric Railways, Metropolitan Railway
and Tube Railway; Director, Midland Bank, Imperial Chemical Industries; MP 1916–20.
m. 1904 Grace Lowrey, da. of Edward L. Woodruff of Detroit, 2d.

Arthur Hugh Smith Barry, BARON BARRYMORE (cr. 1902)
b. 1843
MP 1886; Chairman and founder, Cork Defence Union.
m. (1) 1868 Mary Wyndham-Quin, da. of 3rd Earl of Dunraven.
m. (2) 28 February 1889 Elizabeth, widow of Arthur Post, da. of General
James Wadsworth and Mary Wharton of Philadelphia, no issue.

David Beatty, EARL BEATTY (cr. 1919)
b. 1871
Admiral of the Fleet, 1919; First Sea Lord, 1919–27.
m. 1901 Ethel, formerly wife of Arthur Tree, da. of Marshall Field of
Chicago, 2s.

Sir William Conway, BARON CONWAY (cr. 1931)
b. 1856
Traveller, author; Director-General, Imperial War Museum; Slade
Professor of Fine Arts, 1901–4; MP 1918–31.
m. (1) 1884 Katrina, da. of Charles Lambard of Maine, 1d.
m. (2) 1934 Iva, widow.

Sir Frederick Greer, BARON FAIRFIELD (cr. 1939)
b. 1863
Barrister, Lord Justice of Appeal 1927–38.
m. (1) 1901 Katherine, da. of Emanuel Van Noorden of South Carolina,
1d.
m. (2) 1939 Mabel Fraser.

Rt Hon. Sir Auckland Geddes, BARON GEDDES (cr. 1942)
b. 1879
Doctor of Medicine; Assistant Professor of Anatomy, Edinburgh University, 1906–9; Professor of Anatomy, Royal College of Surgeons, Ireland,

1909–18; Professor of Anatomy, McGill University, 1913–14; MP 1917–20; Ambassador Extraordinary to USA, 1930–4; company director.
m. 1906 Isabella, da. of William A. Ross of New York, 4s, 1d.

Douglas McGarel Hogg, VISCOUNT HAILSHAM (cr. 1928)
b. 1872
Barrister; Attorney-General, 1922–8; Lord High Chancellor; MP 1922–8.
m. (1) 1905 Elizabeth, widow of Hon. Archibald Majoribanks, da. of Judge James T. Brown of Nashville, 2s.
m. (2) 1929 Mildred Lawrence.
Renounced peerage in 1963.

Lewis Vernon Harcourt, VISCOUNT HARCOURT (cr 1917)
b. 1863
Private secretary to father, Sir William Harcourt; MP 1904–16; First Commissioner of Works, 1905–10, 1915–16; Secretary of State for the Colonies, 1910–15.
m. 1899 Mary, only da. of Walter H. Burns of New York and Hatfield, 1s, 3d.

Thomas Fermor-Hesketh, BARON HESKETH (cr. 1935)
b. 17 November 1881
Succeeded father as 8th Baronet; MP 1922–3.
m. 1909 Florence, da. of John W. Breckinridge of San Francisco and stepda. of Frederick Sharon of San Francisco, 3s, 2d.

Arthur Lee, VISCOUNT LEE (cr. 1918)
b. 1868
Professor of Strategy and Tactics, Canada, 1895–8; Military Attaché, 1899; MP 1900–18.
m. 1899 Ruth, da. of John G. Moore of New York, no issue.

Alexander John Forbes-Leith, BARON LEITH (cr. 1905)
b. 1847
Entered RN 1960; Lieutenant, 1869; retired 1871; DL, Aberdeenshire; company director.
m. 1871 Mary Louise, da. of Derick A. January of St Louis, 1d.

Sir Lyon Playfair, BARON PLAYFAIR (cr. 1892)
b. 1818
Professor of Chemistry, Manchester 1843–5; Professor in New School of Mines; Professor of Chemistry, Edinburgh, 1858–69; MP 1868–92.
m. (1) 1846 Margaret Oakes, 1s, 1d.
m. (2) 1878 Edith, da. of Samuel H. Russell of Boston, no issue.

Sir Bertram Falle, BARON PORTSEA (cr. 934)
b. 1859
Barrister; MP 1910–34.
m. 1906 Mary, widow of Lt-Col Leopold Seymour, da. of Russell Sturgis of Boston and London, no issue.

Thomas Shaughnessy, BARON SHAUGHNESSY (cr. 1916)
b. 1853 (in Milwaukee)
Associated with Canadian Pacific Railway Company, 1882–1918.
m. 1880 Elizabeth, da. of M. Nagle of Milwaukee, 2s, 3d.

Appendix H

Transatlantic marriages and family connections

(1) Peers with two American wives:
Earl Cowley, Marquess of Curzon, Baron Decies, 6th Viscount Exmouth, 7th Viscount Exmouth, Earl of Gosford, Baron Leigh, Duke of Manchester, Duke of Marlborough, Earl Russell.

(2) Fathers and sons with Americans wives:
1st and 2nd Earls of Beatty, 6th and 7th Viscounts Exmouth, 5th and 6th Earls of Gosford, 8th and 9th Dukes of Manchester, 8th and 9th Dukes of Marlborough, 9th and 10th Barons Monson, 8th and 9th Dukes of Newcastle, 8th and 9th Earl of Portsmouth. Sir William and Viscount Harcourt, Alfred Shaughnessy and Baron Shaughnessy.

(3) Brothers with American wives:
Alfred and Francis Anson; Viscount Deerhurst, Charles and Henry Coventry; Baron Decies and William Beresford; Frederick and Lionel Guest; Duke of Marlborough and Lord Randolph Churchill; Amyas and Hugh Northcote; Baron Queensborough and Sir Arthur Paget; Earl Rosslyn and Alexander Erskine; Duke of Roxburghe and Lord Alastair Innes-Kerr; Rowland and Baron William and Baron Vernon.

(4) Sisters who married British peers and/or younger sons of peers:
Anne and Eloise Breese; Alys and Grace Carr; Dorothea and Marion Donoghue; Katherine and Martha Garrison; Mary and Daisy Leiter; Anne and Philippa Wendell; Pauline Whitney and Adelaide Randolph (stepsister).

(5) Women who married into the peerage twice:
Elizabeth Brown, Marion Donoghue, May King, Lilian Price, Helena Zimmerman.

Appendix I

Case group: total acreage and gross annual rental[a]

Name of peer	Total acreage	Gross annual rental (£)	Other details
1 2nd Earl of Ancaster	165,505	120,900	
3 5th Baron Ashburton	36,772	46,685	
4 4th Baron Bagot	30,543	22,212	
5 3rd Baron Bateman	7,253	12,101	
6 Hon. Henry Bruce[b]	3,950	12,113	
7 8th Baron Calthorpe	6,470	122,628	incl. Edgbaston
8 5th Baron Camoys	6,640	8,809	
9 4th Earl Camperdown	13,892	11,720	
10 3rd Baron Cheylesmore	2,000[c]	—	
11 11th Earl Cork	38,313	17,343	
12 4th Earl Cowley	5,900	23,172	
13 4th Earl of Craven	30,789	37,593	
14 Marquess of Curzon	9,299	17,859	
15 5th Baron Decies	7,393	7,833	
16 Viscount Deerhurst[b]	14,419	24,878	
17 6th Earl of Donoughmore	11,950	10,224	
18 2nd Marquess of Dufferin	18,238	21,043	
19 3rd Baron Ebury	2,723	5,803	
20 8th Earl of Egmont	34,972	35,510	sold Cowdray Park 1909
21 5th Baron Ellenborough	2,000[c]	—	
22 3rd Viscount Esher	—	—	
23 7th Earl of Essex	14,850	18,936	sold 3 properties in 1908
24 6th Viscount Exmouth	2,864	2,755	
25 7th Viscount Exmouth	2,864	2,755	
26 12th Viscount Falkland	3,011	4,461	sold estates in c. 1900
27 3rd Baron Fermoy	21,314	11,071	
28 2nd Baron Fisher	—	—	
29 5th Earl of Gosford	18,594	17,934	
30 8th Earl of Granard	21,244	9,840	
31 5th Baron Grantley	10,721	14,154	

Name of peer	Total acreage	Gross annual rental (£)	Other details
32 3rd Baron Greville	18,698	18,194	
33 7th Marquess of Hertford	12,289	18,392	
34 5th Baron Huntingfield	16,869	22,177	
35 3rd Baron Leigh	20,905	32,013	
36 13th Earl of Lindsay	2,205	5,548	
37 Baron Malcolm	85,611	24,989	
38 8th Duke of Manchester	27,312	40,360	
39 9th Duke of Manchester	27,312	40,360	
40 8th Duke of Marlborough	23,511	36,557	
41 9th Duke of Marlborough	23,511	36,557	
42 9th Baron Monson	10,134	21,800	sold 2 estates after 1883
43 4th Baron Newborough	28,800	22,726	
44 8th Duke of Newcastle	35,547	7,451	
45 5th Earl of Orford	12,341	15,313	
46 4th Marquess of Ormonde	27,725	15,431	
47 8th Earl of Portsmouth	46,984	36,271	
48 3rd Baron Revelstoke	3,000c	—	sold estate in 1900 for £100,000+
49 5th Earl Rosslyn	3,310	9,310	sold estate
50 8th Duke of Roxburghe	60,418	50,917	
51 3rd Earl Russell	4,184	4,527	
52 8th Earl of St Germans	12,791	17,191	
53 9th Earl of Sandwich	11,377	16,423	
54 7th Baron Somers	13,067	16,849	
55 9th Baron Strabolgi	14,994	16,349	
56 4th Earl of Stafford	—	—	
57 19th Earl of Suffolk	11,098	14,209	
58 7th Earl of Tankerville	31,423	33,650	
59 7th Baron Vernon	9,801	24,433	
60 14th Earl of Winchilsea	12,882	18,216	

a Details taken from Bateman, *The Great Landowners of Great Britain and Ireland.*
b Figures for their father's estates.
c = less than.

Appendix J

Data on offspring

(1) Number and proportion (expressed as a percentage) of childless marriages of peers who married Americans compared with the number and proportion of childless unions of peers in the control groups:

	Total no. of marriages	Childless marriages No.	Proportion
Case group	60	17	28.33%
Control group I	149	27	18.12%
Control group II	187	46	24.60%

(2) Comparison of the mean number of children per marriage of peers and younger sons in the case and control groups:

	Total number of offspring	Mean number of offpsring
Peers:		
Case group	121	2.02
Control group I	433	2.91
Control group II	482	2.58
Younger sons:		
Case group	56	1.37
Control group I	266	2.31
Control group II	255	1.85

294

(3) Frequency distribution of data for marriages of peers, showing the percentage of the total number of families:

Family size	Case Group No.	Proportion	Control groups (combined) No.	Proportion
0	17	28.33%	73	21.73%
1	10	16.67%	37	11.01%
2	6	10.00%	49	14.58%
3	12	20.00%	58	17.26%
4	13	21.67%	50	14.88%
5	1	1.67%	37	11.01%
6	1	1.67%	13	3.87%
7			13	3.87%
8			3	0.89%
9			2	0.60%
10			1	0.30%
Total	60	100.01%	336	100.00%

(4) A comparison of the number of families (1) with at least two sons and (2) with daughters only, with proportions expressed as a percentage of the total number of marriages in the group:

	Two sons or more Number	Proportion	Daughters only Number	Proportion
Case group	21	35.01%	7	11.67%
Control group I	67	44.97%	11	7.38%
Control group II	73	39.04%	10	5.26%

Notes

INTRODUCTION

1 See Corelli Barnett, *The Collapse of British Power*, London: Eyre Methuen, 1972, p. 261; Charles S. Campbell, *The Transformation of American Foreign Relations 1865–1900*, New York: Harper & Row, 1976, p. 332; and *Harper's New Monthly Magazine*, vol. 98, 1899, pp. 387–8.

2 C. N. Williamson and A. M. Williamson, *The Fortune Hunters*, London: Mills & Boon, 1923, p. 24.

3 Ibid., p. 27.

4 David Thomas, 'Marriage patterns in the British peerage in the eighteenth and nineteenth centuries', M.Phil. thesis, University of London, 1969, p. 133; the proportion of American marriages was probably much higher than one-half, as Thomas excluded peers who were raised to the peerage after 1800. More than half of the peers in the present study were ennobled after 1800.

5 See Anton C. Zijderveld, *On Clichés: The Supersedure of Meaning by Function in Modernity*, London: Routledge & Kegan Paul, 1979.

6 Ruth Brandon's book, the most recent addition to the popular literature on the subject, is perhaps the most deliberate attempt to sensationalize titled marriages. She treats, for example, the more colourful reports in American newspapers about the finances of European nobles as though they were the only source of reliable information: 'Cynical such listings and comments might be, but there is no reason to suppose that their authors' tongues reached very far into their cheeks. They merely exhibit that curious and almost endearing lack of reticence with which the American press commented on social life. . . . If an American father was to sink his daughter and a large slice of his capital into some scion of the nobility, he wished to know what he was getting in return' (Ruth Brandon, *The Dollar Princesses: The American Invasion of the European Aristocracy 1870–1914*, London: Weidenfeld & Nicolson, 1980, p. 4). But lists of eligible peers and their landed incomes were not meant to be taken as serious advertisements, and to suggest that they were is to underestimate the shrewdness of American businessmen and to misunderstand the nature of these fanciful lists. The exaggeration of the

financial aspects of titled marriages was intended to highlight a more serious aspect of these marriages: the alleged waste of American capital on dowries used for the upkeep of aristocratic households and the fascination of the wealthy upper classes in the United States for hereditary titles in contradiction to democratic principles and, more especially, to the American way of life. In popular culture the self-made millionaire represented a figure of inspiration in a country where success was measured by the size of fortune accumulated in a lifetime. But if these same millionaires who had become cult figures were entrenching themselves at the top of the social ladder, they were preventing others from enjoying the fruits of their endeavours, and this upset the fluidity of the socio-economic structure and threatened time-honoured values of social equality and self-improvement. Brandon, however, ignores these other levels of meaning in her attempt to provoke disapproval of marriages which were based on an exchange of material benefits rather than on personal feelings.

7 Robert A. Stewart, Graham Powell, and S. Jane Chetwynd, *Personal Perception and Stereotyping*, with a foreword by Hans J. Eysenck, Farnborough, Hants.: Saxon House, 1979, p. 4.
8 *The Record*, Chicago, 10 September 1905, in Whitelaw Reid Papers, Library of Congress, Washington, DC.
9 See T. H. Hollingsworth, 'The demography of the British peerage', *Population Studies*, vol. 18, 1964, supplement; Patricia C. Otto, 'Daughters of the British aristocracy: their marriages in the eighteenth and nineteenth centuries with particular reference to the Scottish peerage', Ph.D dissertation, Stanford University, 1974; and Thomas, 'Marriage patterns in the British peerage'.
10 For example, Sir Almeric Paget, grandson of the first Marquess of Anglesey, twice married American women, but was not raised to the peerage in his own right until 1918 (i.e. after the death of his first wife, Pauline Whitney). He came from a family which boasted several American marital connections. Likewise, Viscount Harcourt's family had close American connections before his marriage to the wealthy Mary Burns. His stepmother was the daughter of a former American Secretary of the Legation in London, John Lothrop Motley. His father, Sir William Harcourt, had refused to be honoured with a peerage, but in 1917 Lewis accepted a viscounty from Lloyd George. Whilst reference will occasionally be made to such marriages, they have been excluded from the data because this study is primarily concerned with the clichéd representation of transatlantic marriages as exchanges of titles for money.
11 See William D. Howells, *Heroines of Fiction*, New York: Harper, 1901; William Wasserstrom, *Heiress of All the Ages: Sex and Sentiment in the Genteel Tradition*, Minneapolis; University of Minnesota Press, 1959; Ernest Earnest, *The America Eve in Fact and Fiction 1775–1914*, Urbana: University of Illinois Press, 1974; Mary Doyle Springer, *A Rhetoric of Literary Character: Some Women of Henry James*, Chicago: Chicago University Press, 1978; Virginia C. Fowler, *Henry James's American Girl: The*

Embroidery on the Canvas, Madison: University of Wisconsin Press, 1984; Elizabeth Allen, *A Woman's Place in the Novels of Henry James*, London: Macmillan, 1984; and Carol Wershoven, *The Female Intruder in the Novels of Edith Wharton*, London and Toronto: Associated University Presses, 1982.

12 Paul J. Eakin, *The New England Girl: Cultural Ideals in Hawthorne, Stowe, Howells and James*, Athens: University of Georgia Press, 1976, p. 5.
13 William T. Stead, *The Americanization of the World*, first published 1902; reprint edn New York: Garland, 1972, p. 123.
14 Ibid., pp. 121–2.
15 See, for example, the memoirs of Lord Rosslyn, the Duke of Manchester, and the Hon. James Leigh.

1 TRANSATLANTIC TRAVELLERS: 'DISCOVERERS OF A KIND OF HYMENEAL NORTH-WEST PASSAGE'

1 Henry James to the James family, 1 November 1875, in Leon Edel (ed.), *Henry James' Letters*, 4 vols, London: Macmillan, 1974–84, vol. 1, p. 486; and Henry James, *The Art of Fiction and Other Essays*, with an introduction by Morris Roberts, New York: Oxford University Press, 1948, p. 49.
2 Henry James to his parents, 9 September 1872, in Edel (ed.), *Letters*, vol. 1, p. 297; and Henry James to William James, Paris, 1 December 1872, ibid., vol. 1, p. 313.
3 See Henry James to Charles Eliot Norton, 16 January 1871, ibid., vol. 1, pp. 271–4, 252.
4 Van Wyck Brooks, *The Flowering of New England, 1815–1865*, London: Dent, 1936, p. 453.
5 Edith Wharton, *A Backward Glance*, London: Appleton-Century, 1934, p. 44.
6 See Richard McLanathan, *Art in America: A Brief History* London: Thames & Hudson, 1973, pp. 148–52.
7 Wharton, *A Backward Glance*, p. 62.
8 Frances Hodgson Burnett, *The Shuttle*, London: Heinemann, 1907, p. 2.
9 Francis E. Hyde, *Cunard and the North Atlantic 1840–1973: A History of Shipping and Financial Management*, London: Macmillan, 1975, p. 64.
10 Henry James, *The American Scene*, London: Chapman and Hall, 1907, p. 8.
11 J. M. Chapman and Brian Chapman, *The Life and Times of Baron Haussmann: Paris in the Second Empire*, London: Weidenfeld & Nicolson, 1957.
12 Mrs George Cornwallis-West, *The Reminiscences of Lady Randolph Churchill*, London: Edward Arnold, 1908, p. 5.
13 Ralph G. Martin, *Lady Randolph Churchill: A Biography*, 2 vols, London: Cardinal, 1974, vol. 1, pp. 24, 32.
14 Mrs Cornwallis-West, *Reminiscences*, p. 5.
15 Martin, *Lady Randolph Churchill*, vol. 1, p. 49.

16 Edith Saunders, *The Age of Worth: Couturier to the Empress Eugénie* London: Longmans, 1954, pp. 183, 96–9.
17 'There remained among the younger friends of this couple a legend, almost too venerable for historical criticism, that the marriage itself, the happiest of its class, dated from the far twilight of the age, a primitive period when such things – such things as American girls accepted as 'good enough' – had not begun to be; so that the pleasant pair had been, as to the risk taken on either side, bold and original, honourably marked, for the evening of life, as discoverers of a kind of hymeneal North-West Passage' (Henry James, *The Golden Bowl*, Harmondsworth: Penguin, 1966; reprint edn 1976, p. 51.)
18 A Foreign Resident, *Society in London*, London: Chatto & Windus, 1885, pp. 98–9.
19 Elizabeth Eliot, *Heiresses and Coronets*, New York: McDowell, Obolensky, 1959, p. 94.
20 Consuelo Vanderbilt Balsan, *The Glitter and the Gold*, London: Heinemann, 1953, p. 30.
21 Belle Wilson to Mrs Wilson, 14 August 1886, Sir Michael Herbert Papers, Wilton House Archives, Wilton.
22 Ibid.
23 See Leonore Davidoff, *The Best Circles: Society, Etiquette and The Season*, London: Croom Helm, 1973.
24 Mrs Paran Stevens and Mrs W. K. Vanderbilt were not alone in their escorting of their daughters in European society. The parents of Beatrice Mills (Lady Granard), Cornelia Martin (Lady Craven), and Margaretta Drexel (Lady Winchilsea) are among the very wealthy Americans who mixed in London society following the daughter's debut. Some American families had taken up permanent residence in England, such as the Walter Burnes and the Leonard Jeromes, while other families, for example the James Carters and the Whitelaw Reids, were in London on diplomatic tours of duty when their daughters were presented to society.

INTRODUCTION TO PART TWO

1 Henry James, *The American Scene*, London: Chapman and Hall, 1907, p. 8.
2 Ernest Samuels (ed.), *The Education of Henry Adams*, Boston: Houghton Mifflin, 1918; reprint edn by the same publisher, Riverside Edition, 1973, pp. 237–8, 499.
3 Frederic Cople Jaher, 'The gilded elite: American multimillionaires, 1865 to the present', in W. D. Rubinstein (ed.), *Wealth and the Wealthy in the Modern World*, London: Croom Helm, 1980, p. 222.

2 'PECUNIARY COMPETITION' AND THE SEARCH FOR STATUS: NEW YORK'S HIGH SOCIETY

1 Mrs John King Van Rensselaer, *The Social Ladder*, London: Nash & Grayson, 1925, pp. 53–9.

2 James W. Leigh, *Other Days*, London: Fisher Unwin, 1921, pp. 126–7.
3 Barbara Strachey, *Remarkable Relations: The Story of the Pearsall Smith Family*, London: Gollancz, 1980, pp. 106, 95–96, 40.
4 Sigmund Diamond, *The Reputation of the American Businessman*, New York: Harper & Row, 1955; reprint edn New York, Harper Colophon Books, 1966, p. 178.
5 Ibid., p. 53.
6 Frederic Cople Jaher, *The Urban Establishment: Upper Strata in Boston, New York, Charleston, Chicago and Los Angeles*, Urbana: University of Illinois Press, 1982, pp. 245–9.
7 Frederic Lundberg, *America's 60 Families*, New York: Vanguard Press, 1937, p. 3.
8 Ibid., p. 7.
9 Ibid., p. 15.
10 Frederic Cople Jaher, 'The gilded elite: American multimillionaires, 1865 to the present', in W. D. Rubinstein (ed.), *Wealth and the Wealthy in the Modern World*, London: Croom Helm, 1980, pp. 192–4.
11 C. Wright Mills, *The Power Elite*, New York: Oxford University Press, 1956, p. 49.
12 Van Rensselaer, *The Social Ladder*, pp. 53–5.
13 Ibid., pp. 22, 31, 36–7.
14 Ibid., p. 53.
15 Mills, *The Power Elite*, p. 49.
16 Baltzell, in fact, uses the terms 'aristocracy' and 'plutocracy' to denote the difference in character between the two elites, but then confuses the issue by calling the plutocracy 'an American business aristocracy' (E. Digby Baltzell, *An American Business Aristocracy*, New York: Collier, 1962, p. 34). In a field of study where the term 'aristocracy' is already overloaded by the specific political and social connotations it acquired in nineteenth-century America, the loose application of it can only further obscure the meaning it had in that particular period.
17 Mills, *The Power Elite*, p. 50.
18 Francis J. Grund, *Aristocracy in America: From the Sketchbook of a German Nobleman*, with an introduction by George E. Probst, first published in 1839; reprint edn New York: Harper Torchbooks, 1959, p. 10.
19 Jaher, *The Urban Establishment*, p. 280.
20 Ward McAllister, *Society As I Have Found It*, New York: Cassell, 1890, pp. 222–3.
21 Ibid., p. 215.
22 See Frederic Cople Jaher, 'Style and status: high society in late-nineteenth-century New York', in Jaher (ed.), *The Rich, the Wellborn and the Powerful: Elites and Upper Classes in History*, Chicago: University of Illinois Press, 1973, pp. 270–2, 277.
23 See Leonore Davidoff, *The Best Circles: Society, Etiquette and The Season*, London: Croom Helm, 1973, pp. 27, 37–49.
24 See Elizabeth Duer, 'New York society a generation ago', *Harper's New Monthly Magazine*, vol. 105, 1908, pp. 109–14.

25 Lloyd Morris, *Incredible New York: High Life and Low Life of the Last Hundred Years*, New York: Random House, 1951, pp. 145–6.
26 Dixon Wecter, *The Saga of American Society: A Record of Social Aspiration 1607–1937*, London: Scribner's, 1937, p. 338.
27 McAllister, *Society*, pp. 119–20.
28 Jaher, 'Style and status', p. 268.
29 Wecter, *Saga of American Society*, pp. 216–23; the list Jaher analysed consisted of 273 people of whom 138 were women.
30 Jaher, *The Urban Establishment*, p. 280.
31 Nigel Nicolson, *Mary Curzon*, London: Weidenfeld & Nicolson, 1977, p. 31.
32 Arthur E. Hartzell, *Titled Americans*, n.p., 1915. This list includes marriages with members of the continental nobility and aristocrats without titles. Jaher has used Hartzell's list in his article, 'The gilded elite', and in his more recent work, *The Urban Establishment*. In the latter, the information about the numbers of women marrying titled foreigners is briefly given in a section on Chicago society. This relegation of his analysis of the Four Hundred and argument about the 'status anxieties' of the New York *nouveaux riches* may indicate that Jaher had no more to add to his previous work or that he now considers it less important to a study of the New York business elite of the late nineteenth century.
33 Jaher, 'The gilded elite', p. 200.
34 Mills, *The Power Elite*, pp. 54–5.
35 Henry James, *The American Scene*, London: Chapman and Hall, 1907, p. 161.
36 See Mills, *The Power Elite*, pp. 64–5.
37 *Vanity Fair*, 14 April 1900, p. 452.
38 Wecter, *Saga of American Society*, p. 3.
39 Thorstein Veblen, *The Theory of the Leisure Class: An Economic Study of Institutions*, with an introduction by C. Wright Mills, London: Allen & Unwin, 1925; reprint edn Unwin Books, 1970, ch. 5.
40 Elizabeth Drexel Lehr, *King Lehr and the Gilded Age*, London: Constable, 1935, p. 6.
41 James, *The American Scene*, p. 77.
42 Ibid., p. 111.
43 Edith Wharton, *The Age of Innocence*, London: Constable, 1966; reprint edn Harmondsworth: Penguin, 1974, pp. 19–20.
44 Consuelo Vanderbilt Balsan, *The Glitter and the Gold*, London: Heinemann, 1953, p. 8.
45 Wecter, *Saga of American Society*, pp. 368–9; Margaret Blunden, *The Countess of Warwick: A Biography*, London: Cassell, 1967, pp. 95–9. Following a hard winter in Britain, Daisy Warwick held a costume ball for 400 guests with a view to creating employment for local tradesmen.

NOTES

3 'FOR THEM HE SLAVES': AMERICAN WOMEN OF THE LEISURE CLASS

1 Edith Wharton, *The House of Mirth*, London: Constable, 1966; reprint edn Harmondsworth, Penguin, 1979, p. 27.
2 Charlotte Perkins Gilman, *Women and Economics: A Study of the Economic Relation between Men and Women as a Factor in Social Evolution*, London: G. P. Putnam's Sons, 1920, p. 12.
3 Christopher Sykes, *Nancy, The Life of Lady Astor*, London: Collins, 1972, p. 50.
4 Consuelo Vanderbilt Balsan, *The Glitter and the Gold*, London: Heinemann, 1953, p. 16.
5 Carl N. Degler, *At Odds: Women and the Family in America from the Revolution to the Present*, Oxford: Oxford University Press, 1980, pp. 311–81; see also Adele Simmons, 'Education and ideology in nineteenth-century America: the response of educational institutions to the changing roles of women', in Berenice A. Carroll (ed.), *Liberating Women's History: Theoretical and Critical Essays*, Urbana: University of Illinois Press, 1976, pp. 115–26.
6 See Pierre Bourdieu, *Outline of a Theory of Practice*, trans. Richard Nice, Cambridge: Cambridge University Press, 1977, pp. 171–83.
7 Degler, *At Odds*, pp. 380–1.
8 See Patricia Jalland, *Women in British Political Families 1870–1914*, London: Oxford University Press, 1985.
9 Edith Wharton, *The Buccaneers*, New York: Appleton-Century, 1938, p. 262.
10 See Louisa May Alcott, *Work: A Story of Experience*, New York: Schocken Books, 1977; Sarah Orne Jewett, *A Country Doctor*, Upper Saddler River, New Jersey: Literature House/Gregg Press, 1970; and Charlotte Perkins Gilman, *The Yellow Wallpaper*, first published 1892; reprint edn London: Virago, 1981. There has been a recent revival of interest in the fictional works of nineteenth-century women novelists which have been out of print and are now published by feminist presses.
11 R. W. B. Lewis, *Edith Wharton: A Biography*, London: Constable, 1975, p. 33.
12 Ibid., pp. 44–6.
13 Ibid., pp. 48–9.
14 Ibid., p. 52.
15 Edith Wharton, *A Backward Glance*, London: Appleton-Century, 1934, p. 90.
16 Ibid., p. 112.
17 Ibid., p. 82.
18 See Olive Banks, *Faces of Feminism*, Oxford; Martin Robertson, 1981, pp. 86–7; Patricia Branca, *Women in Europe since 1750*, London: Croom Helm, 1978, pp. 96–9; Degler, *At Odds*, pp. 26–9, 52–60; Linda Gordon, *Woman's Body, Woman's Right: A Social History of Birth Control in America*, Harmondsworth: Penguin, 1977, pp. 17–21; Barbara Welter, 'The cult

302

of true womanhood, 1820–1860', *American Quarterly*, vol. 18, 1966, pp. 151–74.

19 Figures taken from table 11 in C. F. Westcott and Robert Parker Jr (eds), *Demographic and Social Aspects of Population Growth*, US Commission on Population Growth and the American Future, Washington, DC: Government Printing Office, 1972, vol. 1, p. 40; quoted in Daniel S. Smith, 'Family limitation, sexual control and domestic feminism in Victorian America', in Mary S. Hartman and Lois Banner (eds), *Clio's Consciousness Raised: New Perspectives on the History of Women*, New York: Harper, 1974, p. 121.

20 See Thorstein Veblen, *The Theory of the Leisure Class: An Economic Study of Institutions*, with an introduction by C. Wright Mills, London: Allen & Unwin, 1925; reprint edn Unwin Books, 1970, pp. 228–30, 232–3.

21 Clipping from the *New York World*, 8 June 1902, Sir Michael Herbert Papers, Wilton House Archives, Wilton.

22 *The Nation*, London, 9 March 1907, p. 68.

23 Veblen, *Theory of the Leisure Class*, p. 232.

24 Ibid., p. 64.

25 Entry under 26 November 1892 in F. O. Matthiesson and K. B. Murdock (eds), *The Notebooks of Henry James*, New York: Oxford University Press, 1961, p. 129.

26 See Henry James, 'An international episode', in Leon Edel (ed.), *The Complete Tales of Henry James*, 14 vols, London: Hart-Davis, 1962–4, vol. 4, pp. 243–327.

27 Captain Basil Hall, *Travels in North America in the Years 1827 and 1828*, 3 vols, Edinburgh: Cadell, 1829, vol. 2, p. 152; and Frances Trollope, *The Domestic Manners of the Americans*, ed. Donald Smalley, New York: Vintage Books, 1949, pp. 155–7.

28 Trollope, *Domestic Manners of the Americans*, pp. 155–7.

29 Elizabeth Drexel Lehr, *King Lehr and the Gilded Age*, London: Constable, 1935, p. 45.

30 Price Collier, *England and the English from an American Point of View*, London: Duckworth, 1909, p. 374.

31 Harriet Martineau, *Society in America*, ed., abridged, and with an introductory essay by Seymour M. Lipset, Gloucester, Mass.: Peter Smith, 1968, p. 268.

32 Daniel T. Rodgers, *The Work Ethic in Industrial America 1850–1920*, Chicago: Chicago University Press, Phoenix Edition, 1979, pp. 185–6.

33 Quoted in H. B. Marriott-Watson, 'The deleterious effect of Americanization upon women', *The Nineteenth Century and After*, vol. 54, 1903, p. 789. *The Nineteenth Century* changed its name to *The Nineteenth Century and After* after 1900.

34 Edith Wharton, *The Custom of the Country*, London: Constable, 1965; reprint edn Harmondsworth: Penguin, 1984, p. 28.

35 Ibid., p. 119.

36 Ibid.

37 See Sondra R. Herman, 'Loving courtship or the marriage market?

The ideal and its critics, 1871–1911', *American Quarterly*, vol. 25, 1973, pp. 235–52.

38 Carroll Smith-Rosenberg and Charles Rosenberg, 'The female animal: medical and biological views of woman and her role in nineteenth-century America', *Journal of American History*, vol. 60, 1973, pp. 332–56, esp. 340.

39 Alice Kessler-Harris, *Out to Work: A History of Wage-Earning Women in the United States*, New York: Oxford University Press, 1982, p. 113.

40 But in trying to find reasons for suggesting that women in the leisure class found any dignity in their role, one is daunted by the evidence that their lives were stultifying. For Charlotte Perkins Gilman, the marital relation was fundamentally a 'sexuo-economic' one by which women rendered their husbands a sexual and domestic service in return for financial support (see Gilman, *Women and Economics*, p. 37). Though she does not say it, she implies that marriage is a form of prostitution; the writer Olive Schreiner called it 'female parasitism'.

41 See Degler, *At Odds*, pp. 315–27.

42 *New York Times*, 3 February 1931, p. 1.

43 Lucas Cleeve, *Anglo-Americans*, London: Fisher Unwin, 1903, p. 85.

44 Ibid., pp. 39–40.

45 Ibid., p. 291.

46 Ibid., p. 296.

47 Gertrude Atherton, *American Wives and English Husbands*, London: Service & Paton, 1898, p. 247.

INTRODUCTION TO PART THREE

1 John L. Motley to Charles Sumner, 24 May 1870, Charles Sumner Papers, Houghton Library, Cambridge, Mass.

2 John L. Motley was the father of Lady Elizabeth Harcourt, who married the Liberal statesman Sir William Harcourt in 1876.

3 Ernest Samuels (ed.), *The Education of Henry Adams*, Boston: Houghton Mifflin, 1918; reprint edn by the same publisher, Riverside Edition, 1973, p. 284.

4 Ibid., p. 285.

5 Walter L. Arnstein, 'The survival of the Victorian aristocracy', in F. C. Jaher (ed.), *The Rich, the Wellborn and the Powerful: Elites and Upper Classes in History*, Chicago: University of Illinois Press, 1973, pp. 203–57.

6 See, for example, F. M. L. Thompson, *English Landed Society in the Nineteenth Century*, London: Routledge & Kegan Paul, 1963; reprint edn Routledge Paperbacks, 1971, ch. 11; and Ralph E. Pumphrey, 'The introduction of industrialists into the British peerage: a study in adaptation of a social institution', *American Historical Review*, vol. 65, 1959, pp. 1–16.

7 John Bateman, *The Great Landowners of Great Britain and Ireland*, New York: Leicester University Press, 1971, p. 515.

8 Pumphrey, 'The introduction of industrialists', table IV, p. 9.

9 Leonore Davidoff, *The Best Circles: Society, Etiquette and The Season*, London: Croom Helm, 1973, p. 59.
10 Walter Bagehot, *The English Constitution*, with an introduction by R. H. S. Crossman, London: Collins, 1963, esp. p. 124.
11 Esme Wingfield-Stratford, *The Victorian Aftermath 1901-14*, London: George Routledge, 1933, p. 52.

4 AMERICAN INVASION OR ARISTOCRATIC EMBRACE? THE ENTRY OF AMERICANS INTO LONDON'S HIGH SOCIETY AFTER 1870

1 Published in *The Man Upstairs and Other Stories*, London: Methuen, 1914; reprint edn London: Barrie & Jenkins, 1980, pp. 240–51.
2 See W. L. Guttsman, *The British Political Elite*, London: MacGibbon & Kee, 1965, chs 4 and 5.
3 See W. D. Rubinstein, *Men of Property: The Very Wealthy in Britain since the Industrial Revolution*, London: Croom Helm, 1981, ch. 7.
4 F. M. L. Thompson, 'Britain', in David Spring (ed.), *European Landed Elites in the Nineteenth Century*, Baltimore: Johns Hopkins University Press, 1977, pp. 29–30.
5 Louis T. Stanley, *The London Season*, London: Hutchinson, 1955; Leonore Davidoff, *The Best Circles: Society, Etiquette and The Season*, London: Croom Helm, 1973, pp. 27–8; and Hilary Evans and Mary Evans, *The Party That Lasted 100 Days: The Late Victorian Season, a Social Study*, London: Macdonald & Jane's, 1976, pp. 19–27.
6 'The London season', *Harper's*, May 1886, vol. 72, pp. 821–37.
7 Evans and Evans, *The Party*, pp. 43–4.
8 Leonore Davidoff indicates a tenfold increase over a period of at least 100 years. See *The Best Circles*, pp. 20, 61.
9 Ralph Nevill (ed.), *The Reminiscences of Lady Dorothy Nevill*, London: Thomas Nelson, 1908, p. 127. See also idem, *Leaves from the Notebooks of Lady Dorothy Nevill*, London: Macmillan, 1910, pp. 21–2: 'Society in the old days cannot in any way be compared with the motley crowd which calls itself Society today. . . . Today it would be difficult to discover accurately who is in or who out of Society, or, for the matter of that, whether Society itself exists. . . .'
10 Thompson, 'Britain', p. 33. This new wealth was more likely to be commercial or financial than industrial in origin. See Martin J. Wiener, *English Culture and the Decline of the Industrial Spirit 1850–1980*, Cambridge: Cambridge University Press, 1981, p. 128; or W. D. Rubinstein, 'Wealth, elites and class structure in modern Britain', *Past and Present*, vol. 76, 1977, pp. 99–126.
11 See Rubinstein, *Men of Property*, pp. 213–19, 136–7.
12 T. H. S. Escott, *England: Its People, Polity and Pursuits*, 2 vols, London: Cassell, 1880, vol. 2, p. 23.
13 William C. D. Whetham and Catherine D. Whetham, *The Family and the Nation: A Study in Natural Inheritance and Social Responsibility*, London: Longmans, Green, 1909, p. 184.

14 Nevill (ed.), *Leaves*, p. 30.
15 Thompson, 'Britain', pp. 22–44.
16 Rubinstein, *Men of Property*.
17 Thompson, 'Britain', p. 34.
18 Davidoff, *The Best Circles*, p. 17.
19 Quoted in Evans and Evans, *The Party*, p. 11.
20 Clipping from the *New York American*, 1 October 1909, Whitelaw Reid Papers, Library of Congress, Washington, DC.
21 *New York World*, 22 April 1906.
22 'The American woman', *The Nation*, London, 9 March 1907, p. 68.
23 E. F. Benson, *As We Were: A Victorian Peep-Show*, London: Longmans, 1934, pp. 98–101.
24 See Virginia Cowles, *Edward VII and his Circle*, London: Hamish Hamilton, 1956, see also Jamie Camplin, *The Rise of the Plutocrats: Wealth and Power in Edwardian England*, London: Constable, 1978, pp. 101–10.
25 Nevill (ed.), *Leaves*, p. 28.
26 Susan Tweedsmuir, *The Lilac and the Rose*, London: Duckworth, 1952, p. 82. Susan was related to two Americans: Sophia Williams, daughter of an American diplomat, and Florence Padelford of Georgia. Sophia used to fascinate her niece with stories about her life in China; Florence married Susan's cousin, the third Baron Ebury, and no mention is made of her in the autobiography.
27 Marie Corelli, *Free Opinions Freely Expressed on Certin Phases of Modern Social Life and Conduct*, London: Constable, 1905, p. 102.
28 F. M. L. Thompson, *English Landed Society in the Nineteenth Century*, London: Routledge & Kegan Paul, 1963; reprint ed Routledge Paperbacks, 1971, p. 302.
29 See ibid., ch. 11, esp. p. 303; and idem, 'Britain', p. 23.
30 T. H. Hollingsworth, 'The demography of the British peerage', *Population Studies*, vol. 18, 1964, supplement.
31 Thompson, 'Britain', p. 44, n. 26.
32 W. A. Swanberg, *Whitney Father, Whitney Heiress*, New York: Scribner's, 1980, p. 158.

5 THE LONDON MARRIAGE MARKET

1 See David N. Thomas, 'The social origins of marriage partners of the British peerage in the eighteenth and nineteenth centuries', *Population Studies*, vol. 26, 1972, pp. 99–111; also Patricia C. Otto, 'Daughters of the British aristocracy: their marriages in the eighteenth and nineteenth centuries with particular reference to the Scottish peerage', Ph.D dissertation, Stanford University, 1974, esp. pp. 1–46.
2 See below, Chapter 6, p. 131.
3 Otto, 'Daughters of the British aristocracy', p. 9.
4 Ibid., pp. 2, 37.
5 See below, pp. 93–4.
6 Thomas, 'The social origins of marriage partners', p. 104.
7 The following table is an extract from Thomas's table of in-marriages

and out-marriages in 'Marriage patterns in the British peerage in the eighteenth and nineteenth centuries', M.Phil. thesis, University of London, 1969, p. 104:

Cohort born	In-marriages		Cohort born	In-marriages	
	No.	%		No.	%
1800–9	26	44.1	1850–9	18	31.7
1810–19	24	42.9	1860–9	14	26.4
1820–9	16	35.7	1870–9	14	26.9
1830–9	26	44.9	1880–9	12	28.6
1840–9	25	42.3	1890–9	10	28.6

8 Ibid., p. 143; see also Thomas, 'The social origins of marriage partners'.
9 It should be noted that some of the men listed as nobles or gentry or as the relatives of peers and baronets were also businessmen, but in these cases the social rank is taken to be more significant. There may also be a number of businessmen in the category of men shown as unlisted.
10 See Lawrence Stone, *The Family, Sex and Marriage in England 1500–1800*, London: Weidenfeld & Nicolson, 1977.
11 See Leonore Davidoff, *The Best Circles: Society, Etiquette and The Season*, London: Croom Helm, 1973.
12 Marie Corelli, Lady Jeune, Flora Annie Steel, Susan, Countess of Malmesbury, *The Modern Marriage Market*, London: Hutchinson, 1898, pp. 160–9.
13 Otto, 'Daughters of the British aristocracy', p. 199.
14 E. M. Palmegiano, 'Women and British periodicals 1832–67: a bibliography', *Victorian Periodicals Newsletter*, vol. 9, 1976, pp. 1–36.
15 Census of England and Wales: *Preliminary Report with Tables of the Population Enumerated in England and Wales*, 3 April 1911, London: HMSO, 1911, table A, p. iv, and table 29.
16 See Carroll Smith-Rosenberg and Charles Rosenberg, 'The female animal: medical and biological views of woman and her role in nineteenth-century America', *Journal of American History*, vol. 60, 1973, pp. 332–56.
17 *The Times*, 27 June 1861, quoted in Constance Rover, *Love, Morals and the Feminists*, London: Routledge & Kegan Paul, 1970, pp. 61–2.
18 Edward Downes, who succeeded his cousin in 1902 as the fifth Baron Ellenborough, delayed marrying until 1905 when he was 65. The *New York World* reported: 'Lord Ellenborough is . . . many years older than his bride, but has done fine service in the Royal Navy and is hearty, bluff, popular. His family is not wealthy, so that the future Lady Ellenborough's share of the Schenley millions will not be unwelcome to him. Lord Ellenborough was regarded as a confirmed bachelor; the greatest compliment he could pay Miss Schrenley was lose his well-seasoned heart to her.'
19 Ralph G. Martin, *Lady Randolph Churchill: A Biography*, 2 vols, London: Cardinal, 1974, vol. 2, p. 90.

NOTES

20 Stone, *The Family*, pp. 42, 214.
21 Thomas, 'Marriage patterns', p. 98.
22 Otto, 'Daughters of the British aristocracy', pp. 268–76.
23 See George W. Smalley, *London Letters and Some Others*, 2 vols, London: Macmillan, 1890, vol. 2, pp. 118–19, 123.
24 F. M. L. Thompson, *English Landed Society in the Nineteenth Century*, London: Routledge & Kegan Paul, 1963; reprint edn Routledge Paperbacks, 1971, p. 74.
25 See R. H. Graveson and F. R. Crane (eds), *A Century of Family Law 1857–1957*, London: Sweet & Maxwell, 1957, pp. 15, 192.
26 See below, pp. 130–1.
27 Quoted in Martin, *Lady Randolph Churchill*, vol. 1, p. 77.
28 Ibid., pp. 92–3.
29 Ibid., p. 330, n. 23.
30 *New York Evening Journal*, 23 July 1901.
31 See Christopher Clay, 'Marriage, inheritance, and the rise of landed estates in England, 1660–1815', *Economic History Review*, 2nd series, vol. 21, 1968, pp. 503–18, esp. 505, 507.
32 Anthony Trollope *The Way We Live Now*, London: Oxford University Press, 1941, part 2, p. 59.
33 *Sixpenny Magazine*, London, vol. 1, 1861, p. 364.
34 Corelli *et al.*, *The Modern Marriage Market*, pp. 19–20.
35 George Smalley also compares the coming out of young women in Society to the auctioning of white slaves in the east (*London Letters*, vol. 2, p. 121).
36 George Moore, *A Drama in Muslin: A Realistic Novel*, with an introduction by A. Norman Jeffares, Gerards Cross, Bucks.: Colin Smythe, 1981, pp. 193–4.
37 Quoted in Joseph Hone, *The Life of George Moore*, London: Gollancz, 1936, p. 109.
38 Marie Corelli, *Free Opinions Freely Expressed on Certain Phases of Modern Social Life and Conduct*, London: Constable, 1905, pp. 82–4.
39 Corelli *et al.* *The Modern Marriage Market*, p. 78.
40 Moore was a close friend of the Californian, Lady Cunard, and her daughter, Nancy; see Corelli, *Free Opinions*, pp. 117–27, for views of American women.
41 Smalley, *London Letters*, vol. 2, p. 118.
42 Ibid., vol. 2, p. 131.
43 See John Carlos Rowe, *Henry Adams and Henry James: The Emergence of a Modern Consciousness*, Ithaca, NY: Cornell University Press, 1976, p. 41.
44 Mary Harcourt to Lady Elizabeth Harcourt, 30 October 1901, Harcourt Papers, dep. 647; fols 78–78v, Bodleian Library, Oxford.
45 Mildred Chelsea was, in fact, married to the heir of Lord Cadogan, a prominent Conservative peer. The '5 fools' turned out to be: the Rt Hon. Lord Stanley, PC, MC, MP, son of the seventeenth Earl of Derby; the third Baron Hillingdon; Capt. Sir Humphry Edmund de Trafford, fourth baronet; the tenth Duke of Marlborough; and John Gilmour

(later Sir John Gilmour, second baronet), only son of Brig.-Gen. Sir Richard Gilmour, first baronet.

46 Smalley, *London Letters*, vol. 2, p. 121.
47 Mrs George Cornwallis-West, *The Reminiscences of Lady Randolph Churchill*, London: Edward Arnold, 1908, p. 44.
48 Diana Cooper, *The Rainbow Comes and Goes*, London: Hart-Davis, 1958, p. 94.
49 Smalley, *London Letters*, vol. 2, p. 121.
50 Ibid., vol. 1, p. 123.
51 Consuelo Vanderbilt Balsan, *The Glitter and the Gold*, London: Heinemann, 1953, p. 25.
52 Smalley, *London Letters*, vol. 2, p. 124.
53 *New York Journal*, 13 October 1895.
54 Hannah Whitall Smith to friends, 13 August 1886, quoted in Barbara Strachey, *Remarkable Relations: The Story of the Pearsall Smith Family*, London: Gollancz, 1980, p. 40.
55 Smalley, *London Letters*, vol. 2, p. 122.
56 Henry James, 'An international episode', in Leon Edel (ed.), *The Complete Tales of Henry James*, 14 vols, London: Hart-Davis, 1962–4, vol. 4, p. 258.
57 Ibid., p. 276.
58 Ibid., p. 325.
59 See Davidoff, *The Best Circles*, pp. 41–9, esp. p. 42.
60 James, 'An international episode', p. 292.
61 Ibid., pp. 244–5.
62 Ibid., p. 327.
63 Quoted in Leon Edel, *The Life of Henry James*, 2 vols, Harmondsworth: Penguin, 1977, vol. 1, p. 526.
64 See the description in *Queen*, 1 December 1900, vol. 108, p. 878.
65 Martin J. Wiener, *English Culture and the Decline of the Industrial Spirit 1850–1980*, Cambridge: Cambridge University Press, 1981, p. 88; 'English writers began to identify the way of life associated with industrialism with the new American nation. Just those characteristics anxiously perceived in the rising new element in English society – the northern industrial middle class – were in this way projected across the Atlantic, where they could be more safely disparaged and repulsed.'

6 TITLE FOR MONEY: THE PERSISTENCE OF A CLICHÉ

1 From *Operette* (1938) in *The Collected Plays of Noel Coward*, 3 vols, London: Heinemann, 1939; reprint edn 1961, vol. 2, pp. 189–317.
2 'Heiress hunters', *Sixpenny Magazine*, vol. 1, 1861, pp. 363–4.
3 *Truth*, 14 November 1895, vol. 38, p. 1182. H. B. Marriott-Watson wrote in similar terms: 'these ladies were confessedly wealthy, and it would be absurd to ignore the obvious bargain upon which many such matches are based – on the one side money, on the other influence or position' ('The deleterious effect of Americanization upon women', *The Nineteenth Century and After*, vol. 54, 1903, p. 789).

4 Marie Corelli, *Free Opinions Freely Expressed on Certain Phases of Modern Social Life and Conduct*, London: Constable, 1905, p. 119.

5 John Bateman, *The Great Landowners of Great Britain and Ireland*, 1883, 4th edn, introd. by David Spring, Leicester: Leicester University Press, 1971.

6 See W. D. Rubinstein, *Men of Property: The Very Wealthy in Britain since the Industrial Revolution*, London: Croom Helm, 1981, pp. 12–19.

7 Idem, 'British millionaires, 1809–1949', *Bulletin of the Institute of Historical Research*, vol. 47, 1974, pp. 204–5.

8 Idem, *Men of Property*, p. 196.

9 See Appendix I.

10 All three men left personalty in excess of £50,000.

11 P. J. Perry, 'Where was the "great agricultural depression"?', in P. J. Perry (ed.), *British Agriculture 1875–1914*, London: Methuen, 1973, map III, p. 137.

12 The classes correspond to counties as follows: *Class I:* Cumberland, Westmoreland, Lancashire, Anglesey, Caernarvon, Merioneth, Montgomery, Cardigan, Radnor, Pembroke, Camarthen, Brecon, Monmouthshire, Cornwall. *Class II:* Northumberland, Durham, Derby, Staffordshire, Salop, Denbigh, Flint, Hereford, Gloucestershire, Glamorgan, Somerset, Dorset, Devon. *Class III:* Yorkshire, Cheshire, Northamptonshire, Surrey. *Class IV:* Lincolnshire, Rutland, Nottinghamshire, Leicestershire, Norfolk, Warwickshire, Worcestershire, Hertfordshire, Buckinghamshire, Oxfordshire, Berkshire, Wiltshire, Hampshire, Sussex, Kent. *Class V:* Bedfordshire and Suffolk. *Class VI:* Essex and Cambridgeshire. *Class VII:* Huntingdonshire.

13 Perry, 'Where was the "great agricultural depression"?', map III, p. 137.

14 Initially, the information was broken down to take account of the different methods of evaluating property since 1898. As Rubinstein has pointed out, before 1898 the valuation figure which appeared in the probate calendars referred to gross unsettled personalty, i.e. property other than land. Between 1898 and 1925, the date of the Settled Land Act, unsettled realty was taken into account, and after 1925 the gross valuation figure included personalty together with unsettled and settled realty. There is sufficient approximation in proportion between the case and control groups when data is broken down to take account of the different methods of calculating the valuation figure to concentrate on the total figures for the purpose of comparison.

   To calculate the value of settled realty, Rubinstein refers to the formula of multiplying the gross annual income from land by 33 which gives the sales' value of the land. There is the obvious danger of inflating the size of individual fortunes in using this method, and no alteration has been made in Table 6.3 to give the additional value of settled realty for peers who died before 1926 (See Rubinstein, 'British millionaires', p. 204).

15 Viscount Astor, excluded from this list as his marriage to Nancy Langhorne occurred before his father was ennobled, left over £974,000.

Lord Hesketh, also excluded for the same reason, left nearly £700,000 while his wife left nearly 2 million pounds.

16 The majority of the newspaper clippings amongst Whitelaw Reid's papers refer to Mildred Carter as a 'belle'. The *New York City Club Fellow*, however, referred to her as an heiress and mentioned both her mother's ambition for a titled son-in-law and her grandfather's disapproval of 'foreign marriages' (2 March 1910). Reid himself wrote to Mrs Taft after the weddings of Mildred Carter to Gosford (then Lord Acheson) and Helen Post to Montague Eliot (later Earl St Germans) that 'There is not much money on either side in either of them, so that they may fairly be considered love matches' (Reid to Mrs W. H. Taft, 24 June 1910, William Howard Taft Papers, Library of Congress, Washington, DC).

17 *New York Times*, 2 September 1920, p. 9.
18 Ibid.
19 See Appendix E.
20 Some women held personalty in the USA, and this would not have appeared in the British probate calendars. Consuelo Manchester, for example, was said to have property worth over £400,000 in the USA. A second factor depressing the average is the absence of those women who had divorced their husbands, especially as some of them (Helena Zimmerman, Alice Thaw, Consuelo Vanderbilt, and Frances Work) were wealthy women.
21 Clipping from the *Danville Press*, Pennsylvania, 16 December 1906, Whitelaw Reid Papers, Library of Congress, Washington, DC.
22 Clipping from the *New York Evening Journal*, 10 June 1901, ibid.
23 See *New York Times*, 26 September 1916, p. 11.
24 Clipping from *The Tribune*, Minneapolis, 6 September 1905, Reid Papers.
25 Clippings from the *Manchester Despatch*, 24 July 1906, and *The Star*, Kansas City, 8 August 1906, ibid.
26 Clipping from the *New York World*, 27 February 1019, ibid.
27 5th Earl of Rosslyn, *My Gamble with Life*, London: Cassell, 1928, pp. 64, 115, 143–56.
28 9th Duke of Manchester, *My Candid Recollections*, London: Grayson, 1932, pp. 47–8.
29 *New York Times*, 4 January 1908, p. 2.
30 *New York Evening Journal*, 27 April 1903.
31 *New York Times*, 5 January 1908, p. 8.
32 Ibid., 6 February 1908, p. 4.
33 *New York Evening Journal*, 10 November 1903; *World Magazine*, 23 August 1908, Reid Papers; *World Magazine*, January 1909, and *Globe and Commercial Adventurer*, 14 January 1909, ibid.
34 Florence Breckinridge, Lady Hesketh, left £1,790,141, and Mary Burns, Lady Harcourt, left £846,214.
35 At least twenty-five Americans married baronets between 1870 and 1914. Among the best known were: Florence Garner, Lady Gordon Cumming; Maude Burke, Lady Cunard; Florence Breckinridge, Lady Hesketh; Leonie Jerome, Lady Leslie; Marjorie Ide, Lady Leslie; and

Natica Yznaga, Lady Lister-Kaye. Amongst those who married men who received baronetcies after their marriage were Utica Welles, wife of the conductor Sir Thomas Beecham; Tennesee Claflin, wife of Sir Francis Cook; and Jeannie Chamberlain, a political hostess who married the MP Sir Herbert Naylor-Leyland. In addition to the baronets, there were nineteen alliances between Americans and men who were subsequently raised to the peerage.

36 Mayo Williamson Hazeltine, 'Studies of New York society', *The Nineteenth Century*, vol. 31, 1892, pp. 771–2.
37 Clippings from Richmond (Virginia) *News Leader*, 7 August 1906, and *New York City Club Fellow*, 6 May 1908, Reid Papers.
38 Whitelaw Reid to his wife, 9 January 1909, ibid.
39 Frances Hodgson Burnett suggests the opposite in a fictional text: 'At first younger sons, who "gave trouble" to their families were sent out. their names, their backgrounds of castles or manors, relatives of distinction, London seasons, fox hunting, Buckingham Palace and Goodwood Races, formed a picturesque allurement. That the castles and manors would belong to their elder brothers, that the relatives of distinction did not encourage intimacy with swarms of the younger branches of their families, that London seasons, hunting, and racing were for their elders and betters, were facts not realized in all their importance by the republican mind' (*The Shuttle*, London; Heinemann, 1907, p. 7).
40 Elizabeth Eliot, *Heiresses and Coronets*, New York: McDowell, Obolensky, 1959, pp. 86–91.
41 George W. Smalley, *London Letters and Some Others*, 2 vols, London: Macmillan, 1890, vol. 2, p. 136.
42 Ralph G. Martin, *Lady Randolph Churchill: A Biography*, 2 vols, London: Cardinal, 1974, vol. 1, pp. 77, 90; Anita Leslie, *Jennie: The Life of Lady Randolph Churchill*, London, Arrow Books, 1975, p. 35.
43 Ibid., vol. 2, pp. 17–18.
44 Ibid., vol. 1, p. 75.
45 See T. H. S. Escott's distinction between mercantile wealth and stockbroker wealth in *England: Its People, Polity and Pursuits*, 2 vols, 2nd edn London: Cassell, 1880, vol. 2, p. 41.
46 Martin, *Lady Randolph Churchill*, vol. 1, pp. 76–7.
47 Lindsay married Martha Cameron, daughter of Senator James Cameron of Pennsylvania, in 1909, and Elizabeth Sherman, daughter of Colgate Hoyt of New York, in 1924.
48 Beresford, a colonel in the 9th Lancers, had been Military Secretary to the Governor-General of India for more than ten years prior to his marriage; Bingham had reached the rank of Major-General in the army and served in the Boer War and First World War; Hood, a naval captain when he married Ellen Touzalin Nickerson, was promoted to Rear Admiral three years later and was killed in action off Jutland in 1916; Fitzmaurice had been a Liberal MP and served as an Under-Secretary of State for Foreign Affairs before his marriage.
49 *New York Times*, 1 and 4 December 1907, and *New York World*, 1 December 1907, Reid Papers.

50 *Boston Sunday Globe*, 5 February 1911.
51 Clipping from the *New York World*, 29 September 1907, Reid Papers.
52 *New York Times*, 11 November 1903.
53 See Ralph Nevill (ed.), *The Reminiscences of Lady Dorothy Nevill*, London: Thomas Nelson, 1908, p. 125.

7 THE AMERICAN HEIRESS: THE FORMATION OF A STEREOTYPE

1 Mrs George Cornwallis-West, *The Reminiscences of Lady Randolph Churchill*, London: Edward Arnold, 1908, p. 47.
2 Consuelo Vanderbilt Balsan, *The Glitter and the Gold*, London: Heinemann, 1953, p. 55.
3 Belle Wilson to her parents, 14 August 1886, Sir Michael Herbert Papers, Wilton House Archives, Wilton.
4 See Chapter 5, pp. 99–100.
5 H. B. Marriott-Watson, 'The American woman: an analysis', *The Nineteenth Century and After*, vol. 56, 1904, pp. 433–42.
6 R. H. Heindel, *The American Impact on Great Britain 1898–1914: A Study of the United States in World History*, New York: Octagon, 1968.
7 The framework for this discussion of the content of the American heiress stereotype is based on Gustav Ichheiser's *Appearances and Realities: Misunderstanding in Human Relations*, San Francisco: Jossey-Bass, 1970.
8 *Daily Mail*, London, 20 November 1900, p. 5.
9 Ibid.
10 *Vanity Fair*, London, 11 April 1895, p. 228.
11 Extracts from the *New York World*, 1 December 1907, 23 August 1908, and 29 September 1907.
12 See Frederic T. Martin, *Things I Remember*, London: Eveleigh Nash, 1913, pp. 171–81; R. B. Mowat, *Americans in England*, London: Harrap, 1935, p. 202.
13 The Duke of Portland, *Men, Women and Things*, London: Faber, 1937, p. 68.
14 *New York American*, 30 October 1898.
15 Balsan, *The Glitter*, p. 137.
16 See Marie Corelli, *Free Opinions Freely Expressed on Certain Phases of Modern Social Life and Conduct*, London: Constable, 1905, pp. 185–8, where she suggests that beauty is mistaken for adornment, i.e. that women who can afford to dress well are mistakenly regarded as beauties.
17 Martin, *Things I Remember*, p. 175.
18 *Queen*, 27 April 1895.
19 Belle Wilson to her parents, 14 August 1886, Herbert Papers.
20 Balsan, *The Glitter*, pp. 119–20.
21 *Illustrated London News*, 16 March 1895, p. 319; see also Edith Saunders, *The Age of Worth: Couturier to the Empress Eugénie*, London: Longmans, 1954.
22 'American women and the French fashions', *Harper's New Monthly Magazine*, vol. 35, 1867, pp. 118–20.

23 Thorstein Veblen, *The Theory of the Leisure Class: An Economic Study of Institutions*, with an introduction by C. Wright Mills, London: Allen & Unwin, 1925; reprint edn Unwin Books, 1970, p. 119.
24 Cornwallis-West, *Reminiscences*, p. 48.
25 Henry James, *The Art of Fiction and Other Essays*, New York: Oxford University Press, 1948, p. 49.
26 See Bernard DeVoto (ed.), *Mark Twain in Eruption: Unpublished Pages*, New York: Capricorn, 1968, p. 68; Edith Wharton, *A Backward Glance*, London; Appleton-Century, 1934, p. 62; Albert B. Paine (ed.), *Mark Twain's Notebook*, New York: Harper & Bros, 1935, p. 336; *Truth*, 5 February 1908, pp. 319–20; H. B. Marriott-Watson, 'The deleterious effect of Americanization upon women', *The Nineteenth Century and After*, vol. 54, 1903, p. 789.
27 Corelli, *Free Opinions*, pp. 138–9.
28 Ibid.
29 *Vanity Fair*, 6 July 1905, pp. 16–17.
30 A clipping from the *New York American*, 20 August 1905, Whitelaw Reid Papers, Library of Congress, Washington, DC.
31 Unidentified clipping, 16 July 1907, ibid.
32 T. H. S. Escott, *King Edward and his Court*, London: Fisher Unwin, 1903, pp. 169–70.
33 *Vanity Fair*, 6 July 1905, p. 16.
34 *The King*, London, 15 June 1902, p. 604.
35 Cornwallis-West, *Reminiscences*, p. 48.
36 *Vanity Fair*, 6 July 1905, p. 16.
37 Wharton, *A Backward Glance*, p. 62.
38 Chicago *Record*, 10 September 1905, Reid Papers.
39 Ibid.
40 Henry James, 'The siege of London' in Leon Edel (ed.), *The Complete Tales of Henry James*, 14 vols, London: Hart-Davis, 1962–4, vol. 5, p. 46.
41 Ibid., p. 61.
42 Ibid., p. 62.
43 Ibid., p. 49.
44 Ibid., p. 96.
45 Ibid., p. 97.
46 Ibid., p. 98.
47 Ibid., p. 99.
48 Ibid., pp. 98–9.
49 Edith Wharton, *The Buccaneers*, New York: Appleton-Century, 1938, p. 62.
50 R. W. B. Lewis, *Edith Wharton: A Biography*, London: Constable, 1975, p. 22.
51 Veblen, *Theory of the Leisure Class*, p. 88.
52 See Appendix H.
53 Ralph G. Martin, *Lady Randolph Churchill: A Biography*, 2 vols, London: Cardinal, 1974, vol. 1, p. 73. According to Martin, Jerome and August Belmont had founded The Coaching Club 'in an attempt to revive four-in-hand driving as a fashionable sport' (ibid., p. 30).

54 Reid to Mrs Taft, 8 December 1909, William Howard Taft Papers, Library of Congress, Washington, DC.
55 William C. D. Whetham and C. D. Whetham, *The Family and the Nation: A Study in Natural Inheritance and Social Responsibility*, London: Longmans, Green, 1909, pp. 195–6; G. R. Searle, 'The Edwardian Liberal Party and business', *English Historical Review*, vol. 98, 1983, pp. 51–2.
56 Marriott-Watson, 'The deleterious effect', pp. 782–93.
57 Ibid., pp. 791–2. This echoes a remark uttered by Theodore Roosevelt in a larger, national debate in America, prompted by the increasing birth rate of the immigrant population over the older Anglo-Saxon groups. See below, Chapter 9.
58 'Colonial', 'Titled colonials v. titled Americans', *Contemporary Review*, vol. 87, 1905, pp. 861–9.
59 Walter Lippmann, *Public Opinion*, New York, Harcourt, Brace, 1922, p. 53.
60 Ichheiser called this the 'mote-beam mechanism', *Appearances and Realities*, pp. 90–94.
61 Ralph Nevill (ed.), *Leaves from the Note-books of Lady Dorothy Nevill*, London; Macmillan, 1910, pp. 30–1.
62 George Cornwallis-West, *Edwardian Hey-Days*, London: Putnam, 1930, p. 128.
63 Corelli, *Free Opinions*, pp. 98–113.
64 Ibid., p. 122.
65 Elizabeth L. Banks, *Campaigns of Curiosity: Journalistic Adventures of an American Girl in London*, London: Cassell, 1894, p. 98.
66 See Leonore Davidoff, *The Best Circles: Society, Etiquette and The Season*, London: Croom Helm, 1973, p. 63, for other examples.
67 W. D. Rubinstein, *Men of Property: The Very Wealthy in Britain since the Industrial Revolution*, London: Croom Helm, 1981, p. 247.
68 Idem (ed.), *Wealth and the Wealthy in the Modern World*, London: Croom Helm, 1980, p. 41.
69 Balsan, *The Glitter*, p. 70.
70 This attack on materialism or commercialism also stemmed, I believe, from a rejection of the values of business classes which were beginning to invade many areas of life and directly clashed with those of the aristocracy (e.g. the bourgeois scorn of idleness).
71 Lippman, *Public Opinion*, pp. 95–6.
72 Frederic Harrison, 'Impressions of America', *The Nineteenth Century and After*, vol. 49, 1901, pp. 913–30.
73 A. S. Northcote, 'American life through English spectacles', *The Nineteenth Century*, vol. 34, 1893, pp. 476–88.
74 Ibid., p. 476.
75 See, for example, Harrison, 'Impressions of America', ibid., vol. 49, 1901, pp. 913–30; Lord Meath, 'A Britisher's impressions of America and Australia', ibid., vol. 33, 1893, pp. 493–514; Lord Brassey, 'A flying visit to the United States', ibid., vol. 20, 1886, pp. 901–12; Emily A. Acland, 'A lady's American notes', ibid., vol. 23, 1888, pp. 403–13; Hon. Maud Pauncefote, 'Washington, DC', ibid., vol. 53, 1903,

pp. 275–83; Sir Philip Burne-Jones, *Dollars and Democracy*, New York: Appleton, 1904.

76 Hippolyte Taine, *Notes on England*, trans. W. F. Rae, London: 1872, quoted in W. E. Houghton, *The Victorian Frame of Mind, 1830–1870*, New Haven: Yale University Press, 1957, p. 283.

77 Martin J. Wiener has arrived at a similar conclusion in his work on *English Culture and the decline of the Industrial Spirit 1850–1980*, London: Cambridge University Press, 1981, pp. 88–9.

78 See 'What is a gentleman?', *Truth*, 23 August 1877, pp. 246–7.

79 See Simone de Beauvoir, *The Second Sex*, trans. and ed. H. M. Parshley, Harmondsworth: Penguin, 1972, p. 283.

80 It is highly significant that in James's short stories – e.g. 'The siege of London' and 'An international episode' – it is the aristocratic mothers, Lady Desmesne and the Duchess of Bayswater, who are the greatest obtacles of American women marrying into the aristocracy.

8 SPECULATION, SENSATION, AND SCANDAL: THE AMERICAN RESPONSE TO TITLED MARRIAGES

1 Richard Harding Davis, 'Americans in Paris', *Harper's New Monthly Magazine*, vol. 91, July 1895, pp. 272–84.

2 *New York American*, 16 October 1898.

3 *New York Journal*, 15 December 1898.

4 Ibid., 9 October 1898.

5 Clipping from the *McKeesport Times*, 16 July 1907, Whitelaw Reid Papers, Library of Congress, Washington, DC.

6 *New York World Sunday Magazine*, 5 November 1905.

7 *New York World*, 22 September 1907.

8 *New York Evening Journal*, 10 November 1903.

9 See above, Chapter 5.

10 Clipping from the *New York World*, 17 November 1907, Reid Papers.

11 F. M. L. Thompson, *English Landed Society in the Nineteenth Century*, London: Routledge & Kegan Paul, 1963; reprint edn Routledge Paperbacks, 1971, pp. 100–3.

12 See Pierre Bourdieu, *Outline of a Theory of Practice*, Cambridge: Cambridge University Press, 1977, pp. 5–6.

13 Clipping from the *Omaha World Herald*(?), May 1909, Reid Papers; clipping from the *Danville Press*, Pennsylvania, 16 December 1906, ibid.; *New York Morning Journal*, 20 December 1895.

14 *New York Evening Journal*, 10 November 1903; *New York Times*, 8 November 1903.

15 *The Times*, London, 3 February 1908, p. 5.

16 Clipping from *Omaha World Herald*(?), May 1909, Reid Papers.

17 Ibid.

18 Gustavus Myers, *History of the Great American Fortunes*, 3 vols, Chicago: Charles Kerr, 1911, vol. 2, p. 273.

19 Congressional Record, House of Representatives, 62nd Congress, Session 1.3, 20 June 1911, p. 2362.

20 'Congressman anxious for "our dear peeresses" ', *New York World*, 21 June 1911, Reid Papers.
21 *New York Morning Journal*, 27 October 1895.
22 Indenture between Charles, Duke of Marlborough, and William Kissam Vanderbilt, 1895, quoted in Dixon Wecter, *The Saga of American Society: A Record of Social Aspiration 1607–1937*, London: Scribner's, 1937, p. 408.
23 Consuelo Vanderbilt Balsan, *The Glitter and the Gold*, London: Heinemann, 1953, p. 41.
24 Myers, *Great American Fortunes*, vol. 2, p. 274; also quoted by Wecter, *The Saga of American Society*, p. 411, and by Matthew Josephson, *The Robber Barons*, New York: Harcourt Brace Jovanovich, 1962, p. 340.
25 Gertrude Atherton, *His Fortunate Grace*, London: Bliss Sands, 1907, pp. 55–6.
26 Ibid., p. 139.
27 Frances Hodgson Burnett, *The Shuttle*, London: Heinemann, 1907, p. 5.
28 Ibid., pp. 63–4.
29 Ibid., pp. 252–3.
30 Ibid., p. 51.
31 Ibid., p. 2.
32 See Corelli Barnett, *The Collapse of British Power*, London: Eyre Methuen, 1972, p. 261; and Charles S. Campbell, *The Transformation of American Foreign Relations 1865–1900*, New York: Harper & Row, 1976, p. 332.
33 Jan W. Dietrichson, *The Image of Money in the American Novel of the Gilded Age*, New York: Humanities Press, 1969, pp. 107–17, 246–55.
34 Ibid., pp. 373–8.
35 Bourdieu, *Outline of a Theory*, p. 54.
36 Edith Wharton, 'The last asset', in *The Hermit and the Wild Woman*, London: Macmillan, 1908, p. 60.
37 Theodore Roosevelt to Whitelaw Reid, 27 November 1906, quoted in Henry F. Pringle, *Theodore Roosevelt: A Biography*, London: Cape, 1932, p. 117.
38 Clipping from the *New York City Club Fellow*, 2 March 1910, Reid Papers.
39 See Reid to Mrs Taft, 24 June 1910, William Howard Taft Papers, Library of Congress, Washington, DC; and J. H. Choate to J. R. Carter, 24 February 1910, Joseph Choate Papers, Library of Congress, Washington, DC.
40 *New York Times*, 11 September 1965.
41 See Elizabeth Eliot, *Heiresses and Coronets*, New York: McDowell, Obolensky, 1959, pp. 188–93; Hesketh Pearson, *The Pilgrim Daughters*, London: Heinemann, 1961, pp. 85–8; Ishbel Ross, *The Expatriates*, New York: Thomas Cromwell, 1970, pp. 185–9; Richard Kenin, *Return to Albion: Americans in England, 1760–1940*, with an introduction by Alistair Cooke, New York: Holt, Rinehart & Winston, 1979, pp. 152–4; Ralph G. Martin, *Lady Randolph Churchill: A Biography*, 2 vols, London: Cardinal, 1974, vol. 2, pp. 31–2; Frederick Cople Jaher, 'Style and status: high society in late-nineteenth-century New York', in Jaher (ed.), *The Rich, the Wellborn and the Powerful: Elites and Upper Classes in History*, Chicago: University of Illinois Press, 1973, p. 280; and Patricia Otto,

'Daughters of the British aristocracy: their marriages in the eighteenth and nineteenth centuries with particular reference to the Scottish peerage', Ph.D disseration, Stanford University, 1974, who writes: 'The marriage, which ended with divorce, was one of the clearest examples of the exchange of American wealth for the prestige of an English title' (p. 133).

42 Balsan, *The Glitter*, p. xi.
43 *New York Times*, 11 November 1926, p. 1; 15 November 1926, p. 1 and 21 November 1926, p. 1.
44 Ibid., 11 November 1926, p. 1; 15 November 1926, p. 1.
45 Balsan, *The Glitter*, p. 192.
46 Ibid., pp. 36–8.
47 *New York Morning Journal*, 13 October 1895.
48 Balsan, *The Glitter*, p. 40.
49 Ibid., p. 192.
50 *New York Times*, 21 November 1926, p. 1.
51 *New York World*, 18 November 1906.
52 Reid to Mrs Taft, 8 February 1910, Taft Papers; Ralph Martin puts it succinctly: 'Divorce meant scandal, and scandal damaged Society's image with the mass of people. . . . As soon as it seemed there might be an appeal to the Divorce Court, social pressure converged on the couple to avoid the final step. If the name were famous enough, such pressure often came from the highest quarters.' (*Lady Randolph Churchill*, vol. 1, p. 134).
53 *New York World*, 18 November 1906.
54 Reid to his wife, 14 February 1907, Reid Papers.
55 Reid to Mrs Taft, 8 February 1910, Taft Papers.
56 Roosevelt to Reid, 27 November 1906, quoted in Pringle, *Theodore Roosevelt*, p. 177.
57 Reid to Mrs Taft, 8 February 1910, Taft Papers.
58 Quoted in Frank L. Mott, *American Journalism: A History of Newspapers in the United States through 250 years 1690–1940*, New York: Macmillan, 1942, p. 434.
59 Balsan, *The Glitter*, p. 58.
60 Clipping from the *New Yorker*, 14 May 1905, Reid Papers.
61 Whitelaw Reid to his wife, 31 July 1906, ibid.
62 Ibid.
63 Reid to his wife, 1 August 1906, ibid.
64 Ernest Samuels (ed.), *The Education of Henry Adams*, Boston: Houghton Mifflin, Riverside Edition, 1973, p. 347.
65 Reid to his wife, 1 August 1906, Reid Papers.
66 See also Reid to his wife, 7 August 1906, ibid.
67 John Ridgely Carter to Joseph P. Choate, 9 July 1906, Joseph P. Choate Papers, Library of Congress, Washington, DC.
68 Clipping from the *New York Sun*, 16 December 1912, Reid Papers.
69 Reid was quoted as saying: 'I hope when the time comes for her to marry she will choose an honest young American for a husband.' See *The Gazette*, Altona, Pennsylvania, 14 December 1906, ibid.

70 Reid to his wife, 19 April 1908, ibid.
71 Clipping from the *New York World*, 21 June 1908, ibid.
72 Clipping from the Boston *Globe*, 7 July 1906, ibid.
73 *New York Journal*, 14 January 1900.
74 William Dean Howells, 'An opportunity for American fiction', *Literature*, 28 April 1899, in Clara M. Kirk and Rudolf Kirk (eds), *William Dean Howells: Criticism and Fiction and Other Essays*, New York: New York University Press, 1959, pp. 329–42.

9 WIVES AND MOTHERS: THE DOMESTIC ROLES OF TITLED AMERICANS

1 Marie Corelli, *Free Opinions Freely Expressed on Certain Phases of Modern Social Life and Conduct*, London: Constable, 1905, p. 119.
2 Thomas G. Dyer, *Theodore Roosevelt and the Idea of Race*, Baton Rouge: Louisiana State University Press, 1980, ch. 8.
3 Carroll Smith-Rosenberg and Charles Rosenberg, 'The female animal: medical and biological views of woman and her role in nineteenth-century America', *Journal of American History*, vol. 60, 1973, pp. 332–56, esp. 333–4, 339.
4 Ibid., p. 352.
5 Theodore Roosevelt to Hamlin Garland, 19 July 1903, in Elting E. Monson (ed.), *The Letters of Theodore Roosevelt*, 8 vols, Cambridge, Mass.: Harvard University Press, 1951–4, vol. 3, p. 521.
6 Dyer, *Theodore Roosevelt*, pp. 154–5.
7 Ibid., pp. 14–15.
8 *The Letters of Theodore Roosevelt*, vol. 5, p. 636.
9 Roosevelt to Albert Shaw, 3 April 1907, ibid., vol. 5, p. 637.
10 Francis Galton, *Hereditary Genius: An Inquiry into its Laws and Consequences*, London: 1869; reprint edn London: Macmillan, 1925, p. 130.
11 'Colonial', 'Titled colonials v. titled Americans', *Contemporary Review*, vol 87, 1905, pp. 861–9.
12 See Geoffrey R. Searle, *Eugenics and Politics in Britain 1900–1914*, Leyden: Noordhoof International, 1976, pp. 20–32.
13 The 'contention' probably refers to Marie Corelli's statement in *Free Opinions* (p. 119) quoted at the beginning of the chapter.
14 W. C. D. Whetham and Mrs Whetham, 'The extinction of the upper classes', *The Nineteenth Century and After*, vol. 66, 1909, p. 100.
15 Idem, *The Family and the Nation: A Study in Natural Inheritance and Social Responsibility*, London: Longmans, Green, 1909, pp. 195–6.
16 See Theodore Roosevelt, *An Autobiography*, London: Macmillan, 1913, p. 177; and Whetham and Whetham, 'The extinction of the upper classes', p. 97.
17 See Angus McLaren, *Birth Control in Nineteenth-Century England*, London: Croom Helm, 1978, p. 11; and Daniel S. Smith, 'Family limitation, sexual control, and domestic feminism in Victorian America', in M. Hartman and L. Banner (eds), *Clio's Consciousness Raised: New Perspectives on the History of Women*, New York: Harper, 1974, pp. 119–36. The

averages given by the latter are based on data from white women surviving to menopause.

18 Sidney Webb, *The Decline in the Birth Rate*, Fabian Tracts No. 131, 1907, p. 5; Whetham and Whetham, *The Family*, pp. 146–70; and Searle, *Eugenics and Politics*, p. 26.

19 Whetham and Whetham, *The Family*, p. 157.

20 John W. Taylor, 'The Bishop of London on the declining birth rate', *The Nineteenth Century and After*, vol. 59, 1906, p. 226. In the same piece, he defended Roosevelt's stand and asserted that the President's 'opinion and real knowledge of this subject are well recognized' (p. 225).

21 Smith-Rosenberg and Rosenberg, 'The female animal', p. 334. One of the earliest popularizers of birth control in America was, in fact, an Englishman, Robert Dale Owen, son of the famous philanthropist Robert Owen. One possible reason for the accusation is that the American birth rate in 1880 was lower than that of any country in western Europe save France (James Reed, *From Private Vice to Public Virtue: The Birth Control Movement and American Society since 1830*, New York: Basic Books, 1978, p. 17).

22 Taylor, 'The Bishop of London on the declining birth rate', and Webb, 'The decline in the birth rate'.

23 J. A. Banks and O. Banks, *Feminism and Family Planning in Victorian England*, Liverpool: Liverpool University Press, 1964, pp. 1–13.

24 Barbara Strachey is the great-niece of Alys Pearsall Smith.

25 Bertrand Russell, *The Autobiography*, 4 vols, London: Allen & Unwin, 1967, vol. 1, p. 124.

26 Constance Rover has treated this same passage in her book *Love, Morals and the Feminists*, London: Routledge & Kegan Paul, 1970, as a faithful representation of American women's attitude to sex, without reference to the circumstances of Russell's first marriage. It does not provide evidence that all American women were brought up in this way, and to give credence to a statement of such a high level of abstraction made in an autobiography reveals a lack of circumspection (p. 125).

27 Russell, *Autobiography*, vol. 1, p. 149.

28 Hannah Whitall Smith to Mary, 29 January 1882, quoted in Barbara Strachey, *Remarkable Relations: The Story of the Pearsall Smith Family*, London: Gollancz, 1980, p. 55.

29 Hannah W. Smith, 'On the authority of a husband', ibid., p. 80.

30 Hannah W. Smith, Diary, February 1854, ibid., p. 22.

31 Carl N. Degler, *At Odds: Women and the Family in America from the Revolution to the Present*, New York: Oxford University Press, 1980, pp. 269–72.

32 Ibid., pp. 279, 281.

33 Strachey, *Remarkable Relations*, p. 103.

34 Mary Costelloe to Hannah W. Smith, 18 January 1888, ibid.

35 Russell, *Autobiography*, vol. 1, p. 124.

36 Alys P. Smith to Bertrand Russell, 5 October 1893, quoted in Strachey, *Remarkable Relations*, p. 131.

37 Russell to Alys P. Smith, 4 October 1894, ibid., p. 140.

38 Hannah W. Smith to Lady Russell, 5 March 1895, ibid., p. 149.

39 The control of fertility could, of course, be achieved by a number of methods and did not necessarily involve the use of contraceptives. The most widely practiced is thought to have been *coitus interruptus*. Other non-artificial methods were: periodic or permanent abstention, the safe period, and prolonged lactation.

40 James W. Barclay, 'Malthusianism and the declining birth rate', *The Nineteenth Century and After*, vol. 59, 1906, pp. 80–9.

41 This still did not deal with the possibility of male impotency or even a mutual decision to limit the number of offspring.

42 Taylor, 'The Bishop of London on the declining birth rate', p. 225.

43 C. de Thierry, 'American women from a colonial point of view', *Contemporary Review*, vol. 70, 1896, pp. 516–28.

44 H. B. Marriott-Watson, 'The deleterious effect of Americanization upon women', *The Nineteenth Century and After*, vol. 54, 1903, pp. 782–93.

45 Barclay, 'Malthusianism and the declining birth rate', p. 86.

46 T. H. S. Escott, *England: Its People, Polity and Pursuits*, 2 vols, London: Cassell, 1880, vol. 2, pp. 13–14.

47 Ibid., pp. 15–17.

48 Whetham and Whetham, *The Family*, p. 198.

49 Ibid., pp. 195–6.

50 See W. E. Houghton, *The Victorian Frame of Mind, 1830–70*, New Haven: Yale University Press, 1957, pp. 4–6, for antecedents of this kind of conception of the new urban classes and the effects of industrialization on life-styles.

51 See Olive Banks, *Faces of Feminism*, Oxford, Martin Robertson, 1981, pp. 132, and Degler, *At Odds*, pp. 343–6.

52 Smith-Rosenberg and Rosenberg, 'The female animal', p. 335.

53 Linda Gordon, *Woman's Body, Woman's Right: A Social History of Birth Control in America*, Harmondsworth: Penguin, 1977, p. 18.

54 Consuelo Vanderbilt Balsan, *The Glitter and the Gold*, London: Heinemann, 1953, p. 57.

55 Escott, *England*, vol. 2, pp. 14–15.

56 Ibid., p. 15.

57 See Patricia Branca, *Silent Sisterhood: Middle-Class Women in the Victorian Home*, London: Croom Helm, 1975, pp. 108–12.

58 Degler, *At Odds*, p. 98.

59 Leonard Mosley, *Curzon: The End of an Epoch*, London: Longman, 1980, pp. 2–7.

60 Frances, Countess of Warwick, *Afterthoughts*, London: Longman, 1931, p. 81.

61 Rt Hon. Winston Spencer-Churchill, *My Early Life: A Roving Commission*, London: Reprint Society, 1944, p. 13.

62 Ralph G. Martin, *Lady Randolph Churchill: A Biography*, 2 vols. London: Cardinal, 1974, vol. 2., pp. 90–1.

63 Ibid., vol. 1, pp. 285–7.

64 Belle Herbert to R. T. Wilson, 1901, Sir Michael Herbert Papers, Wilton House Archives, Wilton.

65 Belle Herbert to Mr and Mrs Wilson, n.d., ibid.

NOTES

66 Sidney Herbert to Belle Herbert, 27 December 1903, ibid.
67 Belle Herbert to Sidney Herbert (son), 30 September 1916, ibid.
68 Michael Astor, *Tribal Feeling*, London: Murray, 1963, pp. 83–119.
69 Anne Chisholm, *Nancy Cunard*, London; Sidgwick & Jackson, 1979, pp. 12–18, 26–8.

10 HOSTESSES, POLITICAL CAMPAIGNERS, AND ACTRESSES: TITLED AMERICANS AND THEIR PUBLIC ROLES

1 The Duchess of Marlborough, 'The position of woman', *North American Review*, vol. 189, 1909, pp. 11–24, 180–93, 351–9.
2 Ibid., pp. 13–14.
3 Ibid., p. 356.
4 Consuelo Vanderbilt Balsan, *The Glitter and the Gold*, London: Heinemann, 1953, p. 168.
5 See Consuelo Marlborough, 'Hostels for women', *The Nineteenth Century and After*, vol. 69, 1911, pp. 858–66.
6 Balsan, *The Glitter*, pp. 168–9.
7 Ibid., pp. 170–2; see also *Notable American Women 1607–1950: A Biographical Dictionary*, Cambridge, Mass.: Belknap Press of the Harvard University Press, 1971, pp. 126–7.
8 Marlborough, 'The position of women', pp. 352–3.
9 See *The Nineteenth Century*, vol. 26, 1889, pp. 357–84, and *The Anti-Suffrage Review*, supplement, March 1912, p. 4.
10 Balsan, *The Glitter*, p. 156.
11 Ibid., pp. 178–81.
12 Christopher Sykes, *Nancy, The Life of Lady Astor*, London: Collins, 1972, pp. 16–50.
13 Parliamentary Debates (Commons), 5th series, 137 (1920).
14 See Chapter 3.
15 Michael Astor, *Tribal Feeling*, London, Murray, 1963, p. 52.
16 Ibid., p. 41.
17 Ibid., p. 45.
18 Ibid., p. 51.
19 Sykes, *Nancy*, pp. 172, 183.
20 On the question of titles, Lady Astor once asked the Prime Minister, in her indomitable style, if he would 'consider what a nuisance it is to people who want to sit in the House of Commons having to go to another house where there is nothing to do?' (Parliamentary Debates 222 [1929–30], p. 1085).
21 Parliamentary Debates 240 (1930), pp. 491–3.
22 Sykes, *Nancy*, pp. 58–61.
23 Duncan Crow, *The Edwardian Woman*, London: Allen & Unwin, 1978, p. 15.
24 Parliamentary Debates, 127 (1920), pp. 1792–4.
25 Sykes, *Nancy*, pp. 220–4.
26 Balsan, *The Glitter*, pp. 137, 161–2.

27 William T. Stead, *The Americanization of the World*, first published 1902; repr. New York: Garland, 1972, p. 124.
28 Lady Randolph Churchill to Leonie Leslie, 6 January 1906, quoted in Anita Leslie, *Jennie: The Life of Lady Randolph Churchill*, London: Arrow Books, 1975, p. 273.
29 Anthony Masters, *Nancy Astor: A Life*, London: Weidenfeld & Nicholson, 1981, p. 100.
30 Mrs George Cornwallis-West, *The Reminiscences of Lady Randolph Churchill*, London: Edward Arnold, 1908, p. 126.
31 Ralph G. Martin, *Lady Randolph Churchill: A Biography*, 2 vols, London: Cardinal, 1974, vol. 2, pp. 166–7.
32 Ibid., pp. 225–6.
33 Cornwallis-West, *Reminiscences*, p. 37.
34 Ibid., p. 54.
35 Ibid., p. 70.
36 Ibid., p. 87.
37 Ibid., pp. 90–1.
38 Ibid., p. 88.
39 Quoted in Anthony Masters, *Rosa Lewis: An Exceptional Edwardian*, London: Weidenfeld & Nicholson, 1977, p. 20.
40 George Smalley, *Anglo-American Memories*, London: Duckworth, 1911, p. 328.
41 Cornwallis-West, *Reminiscences*, p. 98.
42 Ibid., pp. 99–100.
43 Ibid., p. 143.
44 Reid to Mrs Taft, 25 February 1910, William Howard Taft Papers, Library of Congress, Washington, DC.
45 Cutting from the Boston *Globe*, 25 April 1909, Whitelaw Reid Papers, Library of Congress, Washington, DC.
46 Ibid.
47 Cutting from the *Columbia States*, 14 June 1908, ibid.,
48 Mary Harcourt to Lady Harcourt, 13 April 1913, Harcourt Papers, (hereafter HP), dep. 648; fol. 82, Bodleian Library, Oxford.
49 Sir William Harcourt to Joseph Chamberlain, 2 December 1898, quoted in A. G. Gardiner, *The Life of Sir William Harcourt*, 2 vols, London: Constable, 1923, vol. 2, p. 507.
50 Shortly after his daughter's wedding, Motley had written to the American writer Oliver Wendell Holmes: 'It was a great wrench parting with Lily who has been my constant and always interesting companion for so long. At the same time I always felt a kind of remorse (which however was unmeaning for I had always done my best to further this marriage) at the idea of her devoting her life to me and now I feel a happiness in her happiness' (30 January 1877, Oliver Wendell Holmes Papers, Houghton Library, Cambridge, Mass.).
51 Mary Burns to Lady Harcourt, 14 November 1898, North Mymms Park, HP, dep. 647; fol. 5v.
52 Mrs Harcourt to Lady Harcourt, January 1905, Rangemore, Burton-on-Trent, ibid., dep. 647; fol. 148.

53 Mrs Harcourt to Lady Harcourt, 27 January 1905, 14 Berkeley Square, London, ibid., dep. 647; fols. 150–150v.

54 Mrs Harcourt to Lady Harcourt, 26 November 1909, Nuneham, ibid., dep. 648; fol. 33.

55 Mrs Harcourt to Lady Harcourt, 3 December 1910, ibid., dep. 648; fol. 50v.

56 Mrs Harcourt to Lady Harcourt, January 1906, ibid., dep. 647; fol. 198v.

57 Randolph S. Churchill, *Winston Spencer Churchill*, 2 vols, London: Heinemann, 1967, vol. 2, pp. 114–15, 125.

58 Mrs Harcourt to Lady Harcourt, 28 October 1907, Manchester, HP, dep. 647; fols. 242–242v.

59 Mrs Harcourt to Lady Harcourt, 1912, London, ibid., dep. 648; fol. 71v.

60 Mrs Harcourt to Lady Harcourt, 1912, London, ibid., dep. 648; fols. 63v–64.

61 Balsan, *The Glitter*, p. 174.

62 Mrs Harcourt to Lady Harcourt, 15 October 1907, North Mymms Park, HP, dep. 648; fol. 239.

63 *Common Cause*, 7 March 1912, pp. 818–19.

64 *Anti-Suffrage Review*, supplement, March 1912, p. 3.

65 See Lady Randolph's comments above, p. 217.

66 *Votes for Women*, October 1909–September 1910, vol. 3, p. 170.

67 Brian Harrison, *Separate Spheres: The Opposition to Women's Suffrage in Britain*. New York: Holmes & Meier, 1978, pp. 165–7.

68 Ibid., p. 103.

69 Mrs Harcourt to Lady Harcourt, 3 December 1910, HP, dep. 648; fol. 50v.

70 Mrs Harcourt to Lady Harcourt, 25 January 1910, North Mymms Park, ibid., dep. 648; fol. 38v.

71 Mrs Harcourt to Lady Harcourt, 11 November 1910, Midland Hotel, Manchester, ibid., dep. 648; fol. 48v.

72 *The Nineteenth Century*, 1889, vol. 25, pp. 781–8.

73 *Votes for Women*, 2 February 1912, p. 276. The anti-suffrage argument that women were physically incapable of taking on the responsibilities of political franchise and extending their sphere of activity to the field of parliamentary politics was well grounded in contemporary opinion concerning women's health. The poor state of health amongst many middle- and upper-class women received much attention from medical practitioners, eugenicists, and psychologists. Much of their writings concentrated on women's reproductive organs, the malfunctioning of which was assumed to be the cause of headaches, nervous diseases, palpitations, and the like. (See Ann Douglas-Wood, ' "The fashionable diseases": women's complaints and their treatment in nineteenth-century America', in Mary Hartman and Lois Banner (eds), *Clio's Consciousness Raised: New Perspectives on the History of Women*, New York: Harper, 1974, p. 3.) In all probability anti-suffragists drew upon a mass of medical evidence for women's alleged frailty. Brian Harrison

has argued in his investigations of the anti-suffrage movement that many of the leaders were only too familiar with the risks of death or serious illness resulting from childbirth. Joseph Chamberlain's first two wives, for example, died in childbirth; Lewis Harcourt's mother died shortly after his birth; H. H. Asquith lost his first wife in childbirth; and the health of George Curzon's first wife was severely impaired by the miscarriage of their fourth child (see Harrison, *Separate Spheres*, p. 63). Barbara Kanner, in 'The women of England in a century of social change, 1815–1914: a select bibliography, part 2', in Martha Vicinus (ed.), *A Widening Sphere: Changing Roles of Victorian Women*, London; Methuen, 1980, pp. 199–270, has found a shortage of detailed studies of women's health in the Victorian and Edwardian periods. There are, however, a number of studies on American women, and she states: 'It is probably correct to interpret that studies for both England and the United States can demonstrate how questions of women's physical condition were related in the nineteenth and early twentieth centuries to questions of women's social position and to social attitudes and politics that guided opposition to their even limited opportunities in education, employment, and enfranchisement' (pp. 232–3).

74 Nigel Nicolson, *Mary Curzon*, London, Weidenfeld & Nicolson, 1977, pp. 37–9.
75 Michael Herbert to his brother, Lord Pembroke, 5 September 1890, Herbert Papers.
76 Nicolson, *Mary Curzon*, p. 85.
77 Ibid., p. 58.
78 Balsan, *The Glitter*, p. 137.
79 Lady Curzon to Belle, Lady Herbert, n.d., Herbert Papers (hereafter MHP).
80 Nicolson, *Mary Curzon*, pp. 206–9.
81 Clipping from *New York World*, 20 July 1906, Reid Papers.
82 Leonard Mosley, *Curzon: The End of an Epoch*, London: Longman, 1960, pp. 42–3, 57; Nicolson, *Mary Curzon*, pp. 58–9, 72; and Sir Oswald Mosley, *My Life*, London: Nelson, 1968, p. 116.
83 *New York Times*, 1 October 1903, p. 7.
84 Earl of Pembroke to Belle Wilson, 22 June 1888, MHP.
85 Earl of Pembroke to Belle Wilson, 31 May 1888, ibid.
86 Earl of Pembroke to Belle Wilson, 5 August 1888, ibid.
87 Belle Herbert to Mr and Mrs Wilson, 1902, ibid.
88 In one letter to Belle, George Herbert wrote: 'I wish we could have made friends at the time when I nearly stared you out of countenance at Dieppe – it would have made you feel so much more comfortable now about your new family – but I quite understand why you did not want it then' (31 May 1888, ibid.).
89 Michael Herbert to George, Earl of Pembroke, 14 December 1891, ibid.
90 Belle Herbert to Mrs Wilson, 14 August 1894, The Hague, ibid.
91 R. T. Wilson to Belle Wilson, 14 August 1894, ibid.

92 Belle Herbert to Mrs Wilson, 14 August 1896, Constantinople, ibid.
93 Michael Herbert to George, Earl of Pembroke, 27 November 1894, ibid.
94 Michael Herbert to R. T. Wilson, 6 September 1896, ibid.
95 *The Times*, London, 25 June 1902, p. 4.
96 Clipping from the *Daily Messenger*, 6 June 1902, MHP.
97 Michael Herbert to Mrs Wilson, Paris, 3 June 1902, ibid.
98 Belle Herbert to her parents, June 1902, ibid.
99 Mary von Hugel to R. T. Wilson, Wilton House, 1903, ibid.
100 Alys enrolled at Bryn Mawr, a women's college in Pennsylvania, in its first year of opening. Her cousin, Carrie Thomas, was Dean of Studies during Alys's time there. See Barbara Strachey, *Remarkable Relations: The Story of the Pearsall Smith Family*, London; Gollancz, 1980, p. 85.
101 Ibid., p. 127.
102 Bertrand Russell, *The Autobiography*, 3 vols, London: Allen & Unwin, 1967–9, vol. 1, p. 75.
103 Strachey, *Remarkable Relations*, pp. 22, 81, 134.
104 Ibid., p. 135.
105 Russell, *Autobiography*, vol. 1, p. 82.
106 Lady Russell to Hannah Whitall Smith, 22 November 1894, in Strachey, *Remarkable Relations*, p. 145.
107 Ibid., pp. 137–45.
108 Ibid., pp. 151–2.
109 Ibid., p. 278.
110 Cranstoun Metcalfe, *Peeresses of the Stage*, London: Andrew Melrose, 1913, pp. 174–5.
111 See Christopher Kent, 'Image and reality: the actress and society', in Vicinus (ed.), *A Widening Sphere*, pp. 94–116.
112 Ibid., p. 115.
113 Metcalfe, *Peeresses of the Stage*, pp. 163–7.
114 5th Earl of Rosslyn, *My Gamble with Life*, London: Cassell, 1928, p. 240.
115 *New York Journal*, 1 December 1895.
116 Ibid., 11 November 1895.
117 Metcalfe, *Peeresses of the Stage*, pp. 240–51.
118 Boston *Globe*, 8 July 1906.
119 Cornwallis-West, *Reminiscences*, pp. 308–22.
120 Martin, *Lady Randolph Churchill*, vol. 1, p. 68.

CONCLUSION: STEREOTYPES AND THEIR FUNCTION

1 See Rom Harré and Roger Lamb (eds), *The Encyclopedic Dictionary of Psychology*, Cambridge, Mass.: MIT Press, 1983, p. 614.
2 See, for example, Henry James, 'The siege of London', in Leon Edel (ed.), *The Complete Tales of Henry James*, 14 vols, London: Hart-Davis, 1962–4, vol. 5, p. 96; and Mrs George Cornwallis-West, *The Reminiscences of Lady Randolph Churchill*, London: Edward Arnold, 1908, p. 47.
3 Donald S. Campbell, 'Stereotypes and the perception of group differences', *American Psychologist*, vol. 22, 1967, pp. 812–29, esp. p. 827.

Bibliography

MANUSCRIPT COLLECTIONS

Joseph P. Choate Papers, Archive Division, Library of Congress, Washington, DC, USA.

Harcourt Papers, Bodleian Library, Oxford, England.

Sir Michael Herbert Papers, Wilton House, Wiltshire, England. By courtesy of the Earl of Pembroke and Montgomery.

Oliver Wendell Holmes Papers, Houghton Library, Harvard University, Cambridge, Massachusetts, USA.

Marlborough Papers, Blenheim Palace, Oxfordshire, England. By courtesy of the Duke of Marlborough.

Whitelaw Reid Papers, Archive Division, Library of Congress, Washington, DC, USA.

Charles Sumner Papers, Houghton Library, Harvard University, Cambridge, Mass., USA.

William Howard Taft Papers, Archive Division, Library of Congress, Washington, DC, USA.

NEWSPAPERS AND PERIODICALS

Anti-Suffrage Review, London.
Boston *Globe*.
The Common Cause, London.
Daily Mail, London.
Harper's New Monthly Magazine.
Illustrated London News.
The King, London.
The Nation, London.
New York American.
New York Journal (morning and evening editions).
New York Times.
New York World.

Queen, London.
The Sixpenny Magazine, London.
The Times, London.
Truth, London.
Vanity Fair, London.
Votes for Women, London.

WORKS OF REFERENCE

The Anglo-American Year Book: Directory and Guide to London, London: Unwin Brothers, 1913.
Burke's Peerage, Baronetage and Knightage, 1949, 1953, 1970.
Cockayne, G. E. *The Complete Peerage of England, Scotland, Ireland, Great Britain and the United Kingdom*, 13 vols, London: St Catherine's Press, 1910–59.
Debrett's Peerage and Baronetage, 1970, 1980.
Dictionary of American Biography, 11 vols, New York: Scribner's 1957.
Dictionary of National Biography, 22 vols, London: Smith, Elder, 1908–9.
Notable American Women 1607–1950: A Biographical Dictionary, 3 vols, Cambridge, Mass.: Belknap Press, 1971.
Whitaker's Peerage, Baronetage, Knightage and Companionage, 1914.
Who Was Who, 7 vols, London: A. & C. Black, 1935–81.

OTHER WORKS

Acland, E. A. 'A lady's American notes', *The Nineteenth Century*, vol. 23, 1888, pp. 403–13.
Alcott, L. M. *Work: A Story of Experience*, New York: Schocken Books, 1977.
Allen, E. *A Woman's Place in the Novels of Henry James*, London: Macmillan, 1984.
Arnstein, W. L. 'The survival of the Victorian aristocracy', in F. C. Jaher (ed.), *The Rich, the Wellborn and the Powerful: Elites and Upper Classes in History*, Chicago: University of Illinois Press, 1973.
Astor, M. *Tribal Feeling*, London: Murray, 1963.
Atherton, G. *American Wives and English Husbands*, London: Service & Paton, 1898.
Atherton, G. *His Fortunate Grace*, London: Bliss Sands, 1907.
Bagehot, W. *The English Constitution*, introduced by R. H. S. Crossman, London: Collins, 1963.
Balsan, C. V. *The Glitter and the Gold*, London: Heinemann, 1953.
Baltzell, E. D. *An American Business Aristocracy*, New York: Collier, 1962.
Banks, E. L. *Campaigns of Curiosity: Journalistic Adventures of an American Girl in London*, London: Cassell, 1894.
Banks, J. A. and Banks, O. *Feminism and Family Planning in Victorian England*, Liverpool: Liverpool University Press, 1964.
Banks, O. *Faces of Feminism*, Oxford: Martin Robertson, 1981.
Barclay, J. W. 'Malthusianism and the declining birth rate', *The Nineteenth Century and After*, vol. 59, 1906, pp. 80–9.

Barnett, C. *The Collapse of British Power*, London: Eyre Methuen, 1972.

Bateman, J. *The Great Landowners of Great Britain and Ireland*, 1883, 4th edn, introd. by David Spring, Leicester: Leicester University Press, 1971.

Beauvoir, S. de *The Second Sex*, trans. and ed. H. M. Parshley, Harmondsworth: Penguin, 1972.

Benson, E. F. *As We Were: A Victorian Peep-Show*, London: Longmans, 1934.

Blunden, M. *The Countess of Warwick: A Biography*, London: Cassell, 1967.

Bourdieu, P. *Outline of a Theory of Practice*, trans. Richard Nice, Cambridge: Cambridge University Press, 1977.

Branca, P. *Silent Sisterhood: Middle-Class Women in the Victorian Home*, London: Croom Helm, 1975.

Branca, P. *Women in Europe since 1750*, London: Croom Helm, 1978.

Brandon, R. *The Dollar Princesses: The American Invasion of the European Aristocracy, 1870–1914*, London: Weidenfeld & Nicolson, 1980.

Brassey, Lord 'A flying visit to the United States', *The Nineteenth Century*, vol. 20, 1886, pp. 901–12.

Brooks, V. W. *The Flowering of New England, 1815–1865*, London: Dent, 1936.

Burne-Jones, Sir P. *Dollars and Democracy*. New York: Appleton, 1904.

Burnett, F. H. *The Shuttle*, London: Heinemann, 1907.

Campbell, C. S. *The Transformation of American Foreign Relations 1865–1900*, New York: Harper & Row, 1976.

Campbell, D. S. 'Stereotypes and the perception of group differences', *American Psychologist*, vol. 22, 1967, pp. 812–29.

Camplin, J. *The Rise of the Plutocrats: Wealth and Power in Edwardian England*, London: Constable, 1978.

Carroll, B. A. (ed.) *Liberating Women's History: Theoretical and Critical Essays*, Urbana: University of Illinois Press, 1976.

Cauthen, N. R., Robinson, I. E., and Krauss, H. H. 'Stereotypes: a review of the Literature 1926–68', *Journal of Social Psychology*, vol. 84, 1971, pp. 103–25.

Census of England and Wales, *Preliminary Report with Tables of the Population Enumerated in England and Wales*, London: HMSO, 1911, table A, p. iv, and table 29.

Chapman, J. M. and Chapman, B. *The Life and Times of Baron Haussmann: Paris in the Second Empire*, London: Weidenfeld & Nicolson, 1957.

Chisholm, A. *Nancy Cunard*, London: Sidgwick & Jackson, 1979.

Churchill, R. S. *Winston Spencer Churchill*, 2 vols, London: Heinemann, 1967.

Clay, C. 'Marriage, inheritance, and the rise of landed estates in England, 1660–1815', *Economic History Review*, 2nd series, vol. 21, 1968, pp. 503–18.

Cleeve, L. *Anglo-Americans*, London: Fisher Unwin, 1903.

Collier, P. *England and the English from an American Point of View*, London: Duckworth, 1909.

'Colonial' 'Titled colonials v. titled Americans', *Contemporary Review*, vol. 87, 1905, pp. 861–9.

Cooper, D. *The Rainbow Comes and Goes*, London: Hart-Davis, 1958.

Corelli, M. *Free Opinions Freely Expressed on Certain Phases of Modern Social Life and Conduct*, London: Constable, 1905.

329

Corelli, M., Jeune, Lady, Steel, F. A., and Malmesbury, Susan, Countess of, *The Modern Marriage Market*, London: Hutchinson, 1898.

Cornwallis-West, G. *Edwardian Hey-Days*, London: Putnam, 1930.

Cornwallis-West, Mrs G. *The Reminiscences of Lady Randolph Churchill*, London: Edward Arnold, 1908.

Cotes, Mrs E. *Those Delightful Americans*, London; Methuen, 1902.

Coward, N. *The Collected Plays*, 3 vols, London; Heinemann, 1939; reprint edn 1961.

Cowles, V. *Edward VII and his Circle*, London: Hamish Hamilton, 1956.

Crow, D. *The Edwardian Woman*, London: Allen & Unwin, 1978.

Davidoff, L. *The Best Circles: Society, Etiquette and The Season*, London; Croom Helm, 1973.

Davis, J. H. *The Guggenheims*, New York; William Morrow, 1978.

Degler, C. N. *At Odds: Women and the Family in America from the Revolution to the Present*, Oxford: Oxford University Press, 1980.

DeVoto, B. (ed.) *Mark Twain in Eruption: Unpublished Pages*, New York: Capricorn, 1968.

Diamond, S. *The Reputation of the American Businessman*, New York: Harper & Row, 1955; reprint edn New York, Harper Colophon Books, 1966.

Dietrichson, J. W. *The Image of Money in the American Novel of the Gilded Age*, New York: Humanities Press, 1969.

Douglas-Wood, A. ' "The fashionable diseases": women's complaints and their treatment in nineteenth-century America', in M. Hartman and L. Banner (eds), *Clio's Consciousness Raised: New Perspectives on the History of Women*, New York: Harper, 1974.

Duer, E. 'New York society a generation ago', *Harper's New Monthly Magazine*, vol. 105, 1908, pp. 109–14.

Dyer, T. G. *Theodore Roosevelt and the Idea of Race*, Baton Rouge: Louisiana State University Press, 1980.

Eakin, P. J. *The New England Girl: Cultural Ideals in Hawthorne, Stowe, Howells and James*, Athens: University of Georgia Press, 1976.

Earnest, E. *The American Eve in Fact and Fiction 1775–1914*, Urbana; University of Illinois Press, 1974.

Edel, L. *The Life of Henry James*, 2 vols, Harmondsworth: Penguin, 1977.

Edel, L. (ed.) *The Complete Tales of Henry James*, 14 vols, London: Hart-Davis, 1962–4.

Edel, L. (ed.) *The Letters of Henry James*, 4 vols, London: Macmillan 1974–84.

Eliot, E. *Heiresses and Coronets*, New York: McDowell, Obolensky, 1959.

Escott, T. H. S. *England: Its People, Polity and Pursuits*, 2 vols, 2nd edn, London: Cassell, 1880.

Escott, T. H. S. *King Edward and his Court*, London: Fisher Unwin, 1903.

Evans, H. and Evans, M. *The Party That Lasted 100 Days: The Late Victorian Season, a Social Study*, London: Macdonald & Jane's, 1976.

Fowler, V. C. *Henry James's American Girl: The Embroidery on the Canvas*, Madison: University of Wisconsin Press, 1984.

Galton, F. *Hereditary Genius: An Inquiry into its Laws and Consequences*, London: 1869; reprint edn London: Macmillan, 1925.

Gardiner, A. G. *The Life of Sir William Harcourt*, 2 vols, London: Constable, 1923.

Gilman, C. P. *The Yellow Wallpaper*, first published 1892; reprint edn London: Virago, 1981.

Gilman, C. P. *Women and Economics: A Study of the Economic Relation between Men and Women as a Factor in Social Evolution*, London: G. P. Putnam's Sons, 1920.

Gordon, L. *Woman's Body, Woman's Right: A Social History of Birth Control in America*, Harmondsworth: Penguin, 1977.

Gordon, L. 'Voluntary motherhood: beginnings of feminist birth control ideas in the United States', in M. Hartman and L. Banner (eds), *Clio's Consciousness Raised: New Perspectives on the History of Women*, New York: Harper 1974.

Graveson, R. H. and Crane, F. R. (eds) *A Century of Family Law 1857–1957*, London: Sweet & Maxwell, 1957.

Grund, F. J. *Aristocracy in America: From the Sketchbook of a German Nobleman*, introduced by George E. Probst, first published 1839; reprint edn New York: Harper Torchbooks, 1959.

Guttsman, W. L. *The British Political Elite*, London: MacGibbon & Kee, 1965.

Guttsman, W. L. 'The changing social structure of the British political elite 1886–1915', *British Journal of Sociology*, 1951, vol. 2, pp. 122–34.

Hall, Captain B. *Travels in North America in the Years 1827 and 1828*, 3 vols, Edinburgh; Cadell, 1829.

Harré, R. and Lamb, R. (eds) *The Encyclopedic Dictionary of Psychology*, Cambridge, Mass.: MIT Press, 1983.

Harrison, B. *Separate Spheres: The Opposition to Women's Suffrage in Britain*, New York: Holmes & Meier, 1978.

Harrison, F. 'Impressions of America', *The Nineteenth Century and After*, vol. 49, 1901, pp. 913–30.

Hartman, M. and Banner, L. (eds) *Clio's Consciousness Raised: New Perspectives on the History of Women*, New York: Harper, 1974.

Hartzell, A. E. *Titled Americans*, n.p., 1915.

Hazeltine, M. W. 'Studies of New York society', *The Nineteenth Century*, vol. 31, 1892, pp. 762–77.

Heindel, R. H. *The American Impact on Great Britain 1898–1914: A Study of the United States in World History*, New York: Octagon, 1968.

Herman, Sondra R. 'Loving courtship or the marriage market? The ideal and its critics, 1871–1911', *American Quarterly*, vol. 25, 1973, pp. 235–52.

Hollingsworth, T. H. 'The demography of the British peerage', *Population Studies*, vol. 18, 1964, supplement.

Hone, J. *The Life of George Moore*, London: Gollancz, 1936.

Houghton, W. E. *The Victorian Frame of Mind, 1830–70*, New Haven: Yale University Press, 1957.

Howells, W. D. *Heroines of Fiction*, New York: Harper, 1901.

Hyde, F. E. *Cunard and the North Atlantic 1840–1973: A History of Shipping and Financial Management*, London: Macmillan, 1975.

Ichheiser, G. *Appearances and Realities: Misunderstanding in Human Relations*, San Francisco: Jossey-Bass, 1970.

Jaher, F. C. 'Style and status: high society in late-nineteenth-century New York', in F. C. Jaher (ed.), *The Rich, the Wellborn and the Powerful: Elites and Upper Classes in History*, Chicago: University of Illinois Press, 1973.

Jaher, F. C. 'The gilded elite: American multimillionaires, 1865 to the present', in W. D. Rubinstein (ed.), *Wealth and the Wealthy in the Modern World*, London: Croom Helm, 1980.

Jaher, F. C. (ed.) *The Rich, the Wellborn and the Powerful: Elites and Upper Classes in History*, Chicago: University of Illinois Press, 1973.

Jaher, F. C. *The Urban Establishment: Upper Strata in Boston, New York, Chicago, Charleston and Los Angeles*, Urbana: University of Illinois Press, 1982.

Jalland, P. *Women in British Political Families 1870–1914*, London: Oxford University Press, 1985.

James, H. 'An international episode', in L. Edel (ed.), *The Complete Tales of Henry James*, 14 vols, London: Hart-Davis, 1962–4, vol. 4.

James, H. 'The siege of London', in L. Edel (ed.), *The Complete Tales of Henry James*, 14 vols, London: Hart-Davis, 1962–4, vol. 5.

James, H., *The American Scene*, London: Chapman and Hall, 1907.

James, H. *The Art of Fiction and Other Essays*, introduced by Morris Roberts, New York: Oxford University Press, 1948.

James, H. *The Golden Bowl*, Harmondsworth: Penguin, 1966; reprint edn 1976.

James, H. *William Wetmore Story and his Friends from Letters, Diaries and Recollections*, London: Thames & Hudson, 1903.

Jewett, S. O. *A Country Doctor*, Upper Saddler River, New Jersey: Literature House/Gregg Press, 1970.

Josephson, M. *The Robber Barons*, New York: Harcourt Brace Jovanovich, 1962.

Kanner, S. B. 'The women of England in a century of social change, 1815–1914: a select bibliography', in M. Vicinus (ed.), *Suffer and Be Still: Women in the Victorian Age*, London: Methuen, 1980, pp. 173–206.

Kanner, S. B. 'The women of England in a century of social change, 1815–1914: a select bibliography part 2', in M. Vicinus (ed.), *A Widening Sphere: Changing Roles of Victorian Women*, London: Methuen, 1980.

Kenin, R. *Return to Albion: Americans in England, 1760–1940*, introduced by A. Cooke, New York: Holt, Rinehart & Winston, 1979.

Kent, C. 'Image and reality: the actress and society', in M. Vicinus (ed.), *A Widening Sphere: Changing Roles of Victorian Women*, London: Methuen, 1980, pp. 94–116.

Kessler-Harris, A. *Out to Work: A History of Wage-Earning Women in the United States*, New York: Oxford University Press, 1982.

Kirk, C. M. and Kirk, R. (eds) *William Dean Howells: Criticism and Fiction and Other Essays*, New York: New York University Press, 1959.

Lehr, E. D. *King Lehr and the Gilded Age*, London: Constable, 1935.

Leigh, J. W. *Other Days*, London: Fisher Unwin, 1921.

Leslie, A. *Jennie: The Life of Lady Randolph Churchill*, London: Arrow Books, 1975.

BIBLIOGRAPHY

Lewis, R. W. B. *Edith Wharton: A Biography*, London: Constable, 1975.
Lippmann, W. *Public Opinion*, New York: Harcourt, Brace, 1922.
Lundberg, F. *America's 60 Families*, New York: Vanguard Press, 1937.
McAllister, W. *Society As I Have Found It*, New York: Cassell, 1890.
McLanathan, R. *Art in America: A Brief History*, London: Thames & Hudson, 1973.
McLaren, A. *Birth Control in Nineteenth-Century England*, London: Croom Helm, 1978.
Manchester, Ninth Duke of *My Candid Recollections*, London: Grayson, 1932.
Marlborough, The Duchess of 'Hostels for women', *The Nineteenth Century and After*, vol. 69, 1911, pp 858–66.
Marlborough, the Duchess of 'The position of woman', *North American Review*, vol. 189, 1909, pp. 11–24.
Marriott-Watson, H. B. 'The American woman: an analysis', *The Nineteenth Century and After*, vol. 56, 1904, pp. 433–42.
Marriott-Watson, H. B. 'The deleterious effect of Americanization upon women', *The Nineteenth Century and After*, vol. 54, 1903, pp. 782–93.
Martin, F. T. *Things I Remember*, London: Eveleigh Nash, 1913.
Martin, R. G. *Lady Randolph Churchill: A Biography*, 2 vols, London: Cardinal, 1974.
Martineau, H. *Society in America*, ed., abridged, and introduced by S. M. Lipset, Gloucester, Mass.: Peter Smith, 1968.
Masters, A. *Nancy Astor: A Life*, London: Weidenfeld & Nicolson, 1981.
Masters, A. *Rosa Lewis: An Exceptional Edwardian*, London; Weidenfeld & Nicolson, 1981.
Matthiesson, F. O. and Murdock, K. B. (eds) *The Notebooks of Henry James*, New York: Oxford University Press, 1961.
Meath, Lord 'A Britisher's impressions of America and Australia', *The Nineteenth Century*, vol. 33, 1893, pp. 493–514.
Metcalfe, C. *Peeresses of the Stage*, London: Andrew Melrose, 1913.
Middlemas, K. *The Pursuit of Pleasure: High Society in the 1900s*, London: Gordon & Cremonesi, 1977.
Mills, C. W. *The Power Elite*, New York: Oxford University Press, 1956.
Monson, E. E. (ed.) *The Letters of Theodore Roosevelt*, 8 vols, Cambridge, Mass.: Harvard University Press, 1951–4.
Moore, G. *A Drama in Muslin: A Realistic Novel*, introduced by A. N. Jeffares, Gerards Cross, Bucks.: Colin Smythe, 1981.
Morris, L. *Incredible New York: High Life and Low Life of the Last Hundred Years*, New York: Random House, 1951.
Mosley, L. *Curzon: The End of an Epoch*, London: Longman, 1960.
Mosley, Sir O. *My Life*, London: Nelson, 1968.
Mott, F. L. *American Journalism: A History of Newspapers in the United States through 250 Years 1690–1940*, New York: Macmillan, 1942.
Mowat, R. B. *Americans in England*, London: Harrap, 1935.
Myers, G. *History of the Great American Fortunes*, 3 vols, Chicago: Charles Kerr, 1911.
Nevill, R. (ed.) *Leaves from the Note-books of Lady Dorothy Nevill*, London: Macmillan, 1910.

Nevill, R. (ed.) *The Reminiscences of Lady Dorothy Nevill*, London: Thomas Nelson, 1908.

Nicolson, N. *Mary Curzon*, London: Weidenfeld & Nicolson, 1977.

Northcote, A. S. 'American life through English spectacles', *The Nineteenth Century*, vol 34, 1893, pp. 476–88.

Otto, P. C. 'Daughters of the British aristocracy: their marriages in the eighteenth and nineteenth centuries with particular reference to the Scottish peerage', Ph.D dissertation, Stanford University, 1974.

Paine, A. E. (ed.) *Mark Twain's Notebook*, New York: Harper & Bros, 1935.

Palmegiano, E. M. 'Women and British periodicals 1832–67: a bibliography', *Victorian Periodicals Newsletter*, vol. 9, 1976, pp. 1–36.

Pauncefote, Hon. M. 'Washington DC', *The Nineteenth Century and After*, vol. 53, 1903, pp. 275–83.

Pearson, H. *The Pilgrim Daughters*, London: Heinemann, 1961.

Perry, P. J. (ed.) *British Agriculture 1875–1914*, London: Methuen, 1973.

Portland, The Duke of *Men, Women and Things*, London: Faber, 1937.

Pringle, H. F. *Theodore Roosevelt: A Biography*, London: Cape, 1932.

Pumphrey, R. E. 'The introduction of industrialists into the British peerage: a study in adaptation of a social institution', *American Historical Review*, vol. 65, 1959, pp. 1–16.

Reed, J. *From Private Vice to Public Virtue: The Birth Control Movement and American Society since 1830*, New York: Basic Books, 1978.

Resident, A Foreign. *Society in London*, London: Chatto & Windus, 1885.

Rodgers, D. T. *The Work Ethic in Industrial America 1850–1920*, Chicago: Chicago University Press, Phoenix Edition, 1979.

Roosevelt, T. *An Autobiography*, London: Macmillan, 1913.

Ross, I. *The Expatriates*, New York: Thomas Crowell, 1970.

Rosslyn, Fifth Earl of *My Gamble with Life*, London: Cassell, 1928.

Rover, C. *Love, Morals and the Feminists*, London: Routledge & Kegan Paul, 1970.

Rowe, J. C. *Henry Adams and Henry James: The Emergence of a Modern Consciousness*, Ithaca, NY: Cornell University Press, 1976.

Rubinstein, W. D. 'British millionaires, 1809–1949', *Bulletin of the Institute of Historical Research*, vol. 47, 1974, pp. 202–23.

Rubinstein, W. D. *Men of Property: The Very Wealthy in Britain since the Industrial Revolution*, London: Croom Helm, 1981.

Rubinstein, W. D. 'Wealth, elites and the class structure of modern Britain', *Past and Present*, vol. 76, 1977, pp. 99–126.

Rubinstein, W. D. (ed.) *Wealth and the Wealthy in the Modern World*, London: Croom Helm, 1980.

Rudorff, R. *The Belle Epoque: Paris in the Nineties*, London: Hamish Hamilton, 1972.

Russell, B. *The Autobiography*, 3 vols, London: Allen & Unwin, 1967–9.

Samuels, E. (ed.) *The Education of Henry Adams*, Boston: Houghton Mifflin, 1918; reprint edn by the same publisher, Riverside Edition, 1973.

Saunders, E. *The Age of Worth: Couturier to the Empress Eugénie*, London: Longmans, 1954.

Searle, G. R. 'The Edwardian Liberal Party and business', *English Historical Review*, vol. 98, 1983, pp. 51–2.

Searle, G. R. *Eugenics and Politics in Britain 1900–1914*, Leyden: Noordhoff International, 1976.

Simmons, A. 'Education and ideology in nineteenth-century America: the response of educational institutions to the changing roles of women', in B. A. Carroll (ed.), *Liberating Women's History: Theoretical and Critical Essays*, Urbana: University of Illinois Press, 1976.

Smalley, G. W. *Anglo-American Memories*, London: Duckworth, 1911.

Smalley, G. W. *London Letters and Some Others*, 2 vols, London: Macmillan, 1890.

Smith, A. P. 'A reply from the daughters', *The Nineteenth Century*, vol. 35, 1894, pp. 443–50.

Smith, D. S. 'Family limitation, sexual control, and domestic feminism in Victorian America', in M. Hartman and L. Banner (eds), *Clio's Consciousness Raised: New Perspectives on the History of Women*, New York: Harper, 1974.

Smith-Rosenberg, C. and Rosenberg, C. 'The female animal: medical and biological views of woman and her role in nineteenth-century America', *Journal of American History*, vol. 60, 1973, pp. 332–56.

Spencer-Churchill, Rt Hon. W. *My Early Life: A Roving Commission*, London: Reprint Society, 1944.

Spring, D. (ed.) *European Landed Elites in the Nineteenth Century*, Baltimore: Johns Hopkins University Press, 1977.

Springer, M. D. *A Rhetoric of Literary Character: Some Women of Henry James*, Chicago: Chicago University Press, 1978.

Stanley, L. T. *The London Season*, London: Hutchinson, 1955.

Stead, W. T. *The Americanization of the World*, first published 1902; reprint edn New York: Garland, 1972.

Stewart, R. A., Powell, G., and Chetwynd, S. J. *Person Perception and Stereotyping*, foreword by H. J. Eysenck, Farnborough, Hants.: Saxon House, 1979.

Stone, L. *The Family, Sex and Marriage in England 1500–1800*, London: Weidenfeld & Nicolson, 1977; reprint edn, rev., Harmondsworth: Penguin, 1979.

Strachey, B. *Remarkable Relations: The Story of the Pearsall Smith Family*, London: Gollancz, 1980.

Swanberg, W. A. *Whitney Father, Whitney Heiress*, New York: Scribner's, 1980.

Sykes, C. *Nancy, The Life of Lady Astor*, London: Collins, 1972.

Taylor, J. W. 'The Bishop of London on the declining birth rate', *The Nineteenth Century and After*, vol. 59, 1906, pp. 219–29.

Thierry, C. de 'American women from a colonial point of view', *Contemporary Review*, vol. 70, 1896, pp. 516–28.

Thomas, D. N. 'Marriage patterns in the British peerage in the eighteenth and nineteenth centuries', M.Phil. thesis, University of London, 1969.

Thomas, D. N. 'The social origins of marriage partners of the British peerage in the eighteenth and nineteenth centuries', *Population Studies*, vol. 26, 1972, pp. 99–111.

Thompson, F. M. L. 'Britain', in D. Spring (ed), *European Landed Elites in the Nineteenth Century*, Baltimore: Johns Hopkins University Press, 1977.

Thompson, F. M. L. *English Landed Society in the Nineteenth Century*, London, Routledge & Kegan Paul, 1963; reprint edn Routledge Paperbacks, 1971.

Trollope, A. *The Duke's Children*, London: Oxford University Press, 1974.

Trollope, A. *The Way We Live Now*, London: Oxford University Press, 1941.

Trollope, F. *The Domestic Manners of the Americans*, ed. Donald Smalley, New York: Vintage Books, 1949.

Tweedsmuir, S. *The Lilac and the Rose*, London: Duckworth, 1952.

Van Rensselaer, Mrs M. K. *The Social Ladder*, London: Nash & Grayson, 1925.

Veblen, T. *The Theory of the Leisure Class: An Economic Study of Institutions*, introduced by C. W. Mills, London: Allen & Unwin, 1925; reprint edn Unwin Books, 1970.

Vicinus, M. (ed.) *A Widening Sphere: Changing Roles of Victorian Women*, London: Methuen, 1980.

Vicinus, M. (ed.) *Suffer and Be Still: Women in the Victorian Age*, London: Methuen, 1980.

Vickers, H. *Gladys, The Duchess of Marlborough*, London: Weidenfeld & Nicolson, 1979.

Warr, P. B. and Knapper, C. *The Perception of People and Events*, London: Wiley, 1968.

Warwick, Frances, Countess of *Afterthoughts*, London: Cassell, 1931.

Wasserstrom, W. *Heiress of All the Ages: Sex and Sentiment in the Genteel Tradition*, Minneapolis: University of Minnesota Press, 1959.

Webb, S. *The Decline of the Birth Rate*, Fabian Tracts, No. 131, 1907.

Wecter, D. *The Saga of American Society: A Record of Social Aspiration 1607–1937*, London: Scribner's, 1937.

Wiener, M. J. *English Culture and the Decline of the Industrial Spirit 1850–1980*, London: Cambridge University Press, 1981.

Welter, B. 'The cult of true womanhood, 1820–1860', *American Quarterly*, vol. 18, 1966, pp. 151–74.

Wershoven, C. *The Female Intruder in the Novels of Edith Wharton*, London and Toronto: Associated University Presses, 1982.

Westcott, C. F., and Parker, R. (eds) *Demographic and Social Aspects of Population Growth*, Washington DC: Government Printing Office, 1972.

Wharton, E. *A Backward Glance*, London: Appleton-Century, 1934.

Wharton, E. *The Age of Innocence*, London: Constable, 1966; reprint edn Harmondsworth: Penguin, 1974.

Wharton, E. *The Buccaneers*, New York: Appleton-Century, 1938.

Wharton, E. *The Custom of the Country*, London: Constable, 1965.

Wharton, E. *The Hermit and the Wild Woman*, London: Macmillan, 1908.

Wharton, E. *The House of Mirth*, London: Constable, 1966, reprint ed Harmondsworth: Penguin, 1979.

Wharton, E. 'The last asset', in E. Wharton, *The Hermit and the Wild Woman*, London: Macmillan, 1908.

Whetham, W. C. D. and Whetham, C. D. 'The extinction of the upper classes', *The Nineteenth Century and After*, vol. 66, 1909, pp. 97–108.

Whetham, W. C. D. and Whetham, C. D. *The Family and the Nation: A Study in Natural Inheritance and Social Responsibility*, London: Longmans, Green, 1909.

Williamson, C. N. and Williamson, A. N. *Lady Betty across the Water*, London: Methuen, 1906.

Williamson, C. N. and Williamson, A. N. *Lord Loveland Discovers America*, London: Methuen, 1910.

Williamson, C. N. and Williamson, A. N. *The Fortune Hunters*, London: Mills & Boon, 1923.

Wingfield-Stratford, E. *The Victorian Aftermath 1901–14*, London: George Routledge, 1933.

Wodehouse, P. G. *The Man Upstairs and Other Stories*, London: Methuen, 1914; reprint edn London: Barrie & Jenkins, 1980.

Wyndham, H. *Chorus to Coronet*, London: British Technical & General Press, 1951.

Zijderveld, A. C. *On Clichés: The Supersedure of Meaning by Function in Modernity*, London: Routledge & Kegan Paul, 1979.

Index

actresses 239–41
Adams, Henry 29–30, 69, 181
Alcott, Louisa May 54
American artists 18–19
Americal girl in fiction 5, 9–10, 139, 168–72; *see also individual novels and stories*
American heiress stereotype 5–7, 32, 95, 135–6, 137–59, 200, 243, 246–7
American invasion 1, 32, 99
American Wives and English Husbands 64, 169
American woman 57–8; and appearance 140–3; and criticism of life-style 144–7, 152–3, 190, 198–201; and marriage 11–12, 32–3, 51–65
Ancaster, 2nd Earl of 119
Ancaster, Countess of (née Eloise Breese) 119, 140, 221
Anderson, Dr Elizabeth Garrett 196
Anglesey, Marchioness of (née Mary Livingston King) 42, 43, 119
Anglesey, 4th Marquess of 119
Anglo-American relations 2, 13
Anglo-Americans 63–4, 139
Anglo-American societies 138
anti-American sentiment 12, 71, 77–8, 85, 99, 106, 111–12, 136, 138, 152, 157, 190, 198
aristocratic embrace 75, 80
Arnstein, Walter 70
Ashburton, 5th Baron 240
Ashburton, Baroness (née Frances Donnelly) 240
Astor, Mrs William Backhouse (née Caroline Schermerhorn) 36, 38–40, 44–5, 59
Astor, John Jacob 30, 36
Astor, Michael 205–6, 214
Astor, Viscountess (née Nancy Langhorne) 8, 51, 205–6, 210, 212–16, 217
Astor, Pauline 97, 163

Astor, 2nd Viscount 8, 206, 212–13, 214
Astor, William Waldorf 97, 163

Bagot, 4th Baron 117
Baltzell, E. Digby 37
Balsan, Madame *see* Marlborough, Duchess of
Banks, Elizabeth 154
Barclay, James W. 197, 198
baronets, transatlantic marriages and 311–12 n. 35
Bateman's *Great Landowners* 8, 70, 114–15, 116
Belmont, August 36, 47, 48
Belmont, Mrs O. H. P. *see* Vanderbilt, Alva
Beresford, Lady William *see* Marlborough, Duchess of
Beresford, Lord Sir William 132–3, 193
Berry, Walter 55
Bingham, Hon. Lady Cecil (née Alice Carr) 134
Bingham, Sir Cecil 132, 133, 134
birth rate 61, 187–90, 193–4
Boston Globe 183
Bourdieu, Pierre 163, 171
Brandon, Ruth 5, 296–7 n. 6
British peerage: business peers 82–3; decline of landed income and 72, 81, 85, 115–19; marriage patterns 4, 7–8, 80–2, 86–91; membership of 70, 72, 86; younger sons 4, 74, 93–4, 128–35
Bruce, Hon. Henry, 240–1
Bruce, Hon. Mrs (née Camilla Clifford) 240–1
Burke Roche, Hon. Mrs (née Frances Work, wife of 3rd Baron Fermoy) 120, 121
Butler, Frances *see* Leigh, Hon. Mrs James

Calthorpe, 8th Baron 118, 119
Calthorpe, Baroness 119, 121

INDEX

Grantley, Baroness (née Katherine McVickar) 43
Grosvenor, Hon. Thomas 131–2
Grund, Francis 37
Guest, Hon. Frederick 132, 133
Guest, Hon. Mrs Frederick (née Amy Phipps) 132, 221, 222
Guttsman, William 70

Hall, Captain Basil 58
Hammersley, Mrs Lilian *see* Marlborough, Duchess of
Harcourt, 1st Viscount 223–8, 297 n. 10
Harcourt, Lady Elizabeth (née Elizabeth Motley, wife of Sir William) 221, 222, 223–5
Harcourt, Sir William 128, 223
Harcourt, Viscountess (née Mary Burns) 100, 128, 222–8, 297 n. 10
Harpers 160–1
Harrison, Frederic 156
Hazeltine, Mayo 128
Herbert, Lady Belle (née Belle Wilson) 4, 23–4, 43, 77, 135, 137, 141, 142–3, 204–5, 230–1, 232–6
Herbert, Sir Michael 4–5, 131–2, 133, 134, 229, 232–6
Hertford, 7th Marquess of 117, 120, 126–7
Hesketh, Lady (née Florence Breckinridge, wife of Sir Thomas Hesketh, later Baron) 128
His Fortunate Grace 139
Hollingsworth, T. H. 7, 81–2
Hope, Lady (née Mary Yohe, wife of 8th Duke of Newcastle) 240
Hood, Hon. Sir Horace 132, 133
hostesses, political 221–2
Howard, Sir Henry 236
Howe, Julia Ward 183
Howells, William Dean 171, 183
Hunt, Richard Morris 46–7
Huntingfield, Baroness (née Margaret Crosby, wife of 5th Baron) 42, 121

Ichheiser, Gustav 6
impoverished peer stereotype 5, 85, 123–6, 127, 157
Innes-Kerr, Lady (née Anne Breese) 134, 140
Innes-Kerr, Lord 134

Jaher, Frederic Cople, 38, 40–2, 43
James, Henry 9–10, 13, 17–18, 19, 21, 22, 29–30, 46, 58, 143–4, 171, 184, 248; *The American Scene* 29, 46; *The Golden Bowl* 22, 299 n. 17; 'An International Episode' 103–6, 247; 'The Siege of London' 147–9
Jay, Augusta *see* Pellew, Hon. Mrs Henry
Jerome, Clara 21

Jerome, Leonard 96, 130–1, 150
Jerome, Mrs Clarissa 21
Jewett, Sarah Orne 54
Jewish bankers 4, 69, 78
Johnstone, Alan 131–2, 133, 236

Kent, Christopher 240
Kip, Edith *see* Coventry, Hon. Mrs
King, Mary Livington *see* Anglesey, Countess of
The King 145

Lambert, Hon. Mrs Lionel (née Adelaide Randolph) 43
Lawrence, Hon. Charles (later Baron) 82
Lee, Austin 236
Lehr, Elizabeth Drexel *see* Decies, Lady
Leigh, Hon. James 32
Leigh, Hon. Mrs James (née Frances Butler) 32
Leigh, Hon. Rowland 132, 133
Leiter, Mary *see* Curzon, Lady
Lewis, R. W. B. 55
Lewis, Rosa 219–20
Lindsay, Hon. Ronald 131–2, 133
Lippmann, Walter 155
Lipton, Sir Thomas 74, 77
Livingston, Elizabeth *see* Cavendish-Bentinck, Mrs
Lloyd, Henry Demarest 33
London: the City 75; entry of Americans into society 4, 22, 72–84, 144–5; relaxation of social barriers 4, 85; the Season 72, 75, 76; society 4, 45, 72–84
Lundberg, Frederick 34–5, 44

McAllister, Ward 39–42, 44–5
McKeesport Times 161
McKim, Mead and White 47
Manchester, Duchess of (née Helena Zimmerman, wife of 9th Duke) 106, 120, 126, 161
Manchester, Duchess of (née Consuelo Yznaga, wife of 8th Duke) 77, 126, 130, 135, 140, 177
Manchester, 8th Duke of 117, 125
Manchester, 9th Duke of 106, 117, 120, 125
Marble House 47–8
Marlborough, Duchess of (née Gladys Deacon, second wife of 9th Duke) 175–6
Marlborough, Duchess of (née Lilian Price, second wife of 8th Duke) 99, 133, 138, 192, 242
Marlborough, Duchess of (née Consuelo Vanderbilt, first wife of 9th Duke) 23, 43, 47, 48, 51, 77, 101, 114, 126, 127, 137, 140, 141, 146, 155, 161, 167–8,